Montana
A Cultural Medley

Edited by Robert R. Swartout, Jr.

FARCOUNTRY
PRESS

Dedication

For my grandsons, Carter and Reed Swartout.

ISBN: 978-1-56037-612-5

For more information about our books, write Farcountry Press, P.O. Box 5630, Helena, MT 59604; call (800) 821-3874; or visit www.farcountrypress.com.

Library of Congress Cataloging-in-Publication Data

Swartout, Robert R., 1946-
  Montana : a cultural medley / ed., Robert R. Swartout, Jr.
    pages cm
  Includes bibliographical references and index.
    ISBN 978-1-56037-612-5 (softcover : alk. paper)
1. Minorities--Montana. 2. Immigrants--Montana--History. 3. Ethnicity--Montana. 4. Montana--History. I. Title.
  F740.A1S83 2015
  305.8009786--dc23
                              2015008975

 Produced and printed in the United States of America.

19   18   17   16   15   1   2   3   4   5

All essays used with permission.

"Creating a New Community in the North: Mexican Americans of the Yellowstone Valley," Laurie Mercier, originally published in *Stories from an Open Country: Essays on the Yellowstone River Valley*, edited by William L. Lang, Western Heritage Press, 1995.

"George 'Montana' Oiye: The Journey of a Japanese American from the Big Sky to the Battlefields of Europe," Casey J. Pallister, originally published in *Montana, The Magazine of Western History*, Autumn 2007.

"Love, Valor, and Endurance: World War II War Brides Making a Home in Montana," Seena B. Kohl, originally published in *Montana, The Magazine of Western History*, Autumn 2006.

"Breaking Racial Barriers: 'Everyone's Welcome' at the Ozark Club—Great Falls, Montana's African American Nightclub," Ken Robison, originally published in *Montana, The Magazine of Western History*, Summer 2012.

Acknowledgments

The publication of this book would not have been possible without the support and assistance of many people. I owe a special debt of thanks to Kathy Springmeyer, Director of Publications at Farcountry Press, who enthusiastically supported the belief that a volume focusing on the ethnic history of Montana was both timely and rewarding. Will Harmon, Senior Editor at Farcountry Press, contributed immeasurably to the preparation of this book. His conscientiousness and professionalism are second to none.

The staff of the Montana Historical Society has assisted me on various projects over several decades. For this project, I am especially indebted to Lory Morrow, Becca Kohl, Molly Kruckenberg, Zoe Ann Stoltz, Jeff Malcomson, Rich Aarstad, Barbara Pepper-Rotness, and Roberta Gebhardt. Brian Shovers and the late Dave Walter generously shared with me their expertise in Montana history. In a similar fashion, I have received crucial assistance from the staff of the Jack and Sallie Corette Library at Carroll College, my home institution, for longer than I care to mention. Christian Frazza, Heather Navratil, and Terence Kratz provided valuable support that made the completion of this project possible.

As has been true so many times before, my greatest debt is to my wife, Kyung-ok, and to our two children, James and Katherine. Their continuous support and encouragement have enabled me to pursue a career that has provided me with immense joy and satisfaction. Thank you all.

Table of Contents

Preface

The primary purpose of this anthology is a relatively simple one. The thirteen essays contained in this volume have been chosen to reflect the richness and diversity of ethnic history in Montana. For more than two centuries, an amazingly wide range of people have made Montana their home. In the process, they have helped to transform the state into what it is in the twenty-first century.

While detailing the diversity of Montana's historical population, these stories also allow us to gain a greater understanding of the everyday folk who helped to build Montana over the past 200 years. Almost without exception, there is no mention in these essays of governors, senators, or captains of industry—those figures who often dominate traditional narratives of state and nation. The people who do appear in these pages rarely rose to positions of prominence. Nonetheless, it would be a mistake to say that they were unimportant, for they were the people who provided the muscle that would fuel Montana's economic growth over several generations. Even more important, their efforts to maintain and foster distinctive cultural identities would often serve as the glue that would hold communities together.

Although this volume is meant to capture the rich flavor of ethnic history in Montana, it is not meant to be comprehensive. Crucial parts of Montana's ethnic history are yet missing from this story. For example, there are no essays on Swedes, Norwegians, Germans, Russians, Italians, or the Hmong, although they are all deserving of scholarly research. Systematic historical case studies have yet to be written on any of these groups in Montana. The same is true for the Hutterites, who have been the subject of sociological and journalistic studies, but not of detailed historical accounts set in Montana. Even the groups that are included in this anthology deserve additional examination, which could easily be done by shifting either the location or the time frame of the story. It is thus my hope that this volume will encourage readers to investigate other aspects of Montana's ethnic history that are yet to be discovered.

A quick glance through this volume will reveal one major omission. There are no essays that focus exclusively on Native Americans. (Indians are a crucial part of the first two essays in the book, but that is because they help to illustrate the importance of blended ethnic communities in Montana's past—a fact that is often overlooked in most historical accounts.) Detailed essays on Native American tribes were left out of this volume not because they lack importance; in fact, just the opposite is true. Had I included just two or three (or even four or five) essays on Indian history in the anthology, I would not have done justice to the richness and complexity of Native American communities and cultures. Indeed, I believe that the subject is so important that it deserves a book of its own. I hope that with the appearance of *Montana: A Cultural Medley,* one of our state's specialists in Native American studies will step forward to produce a volume similar to this one, but with the focus solely on Indian history in Montana. Such a volume would be a wonderful addition to the field of Montana history.

— *Robert R. Swartout, Jr.*

A Symphony of Cultures

There has been a tendency, both in Montana's history and in America's history as a whole, to view the experiences of ethnic peoples as being on the periphery of what might be labeled the mainstream historical narrative. This volume attempts to challenge that assumption. As the thirteen essays contained in this volume aptly illustrate, the ethnic history of Montana is not only rich in diversity, but is also of crucial importance in understanding the evolution of Montana's history over time.

Well before Montana was officially created as a territory in 1864, forces were at work—including the movement of native peoples westward to escape European penetration of the continent, the rise of the fur trade, and the expansion of international rivalries—that would draw an increasingly diverse population onto the Great Plains and into the Northern Rockies. The discovery of large deposits of placer gold in places like Grasshopper Creek, Alder Gulch, and Last Chance Gulch in the early 1860s attracted people from across the nation and around the globe. According to the 1870 U.S. census, the newly formed territory of Montana was home to substantial numbers of people from China, Denmark, France, Germany, England, Ireland, Scotland, Wales, Norway, Poland, Sweden, and Switzerland.[1]

These homesteaders setting out from Lewistown appear well provisioned.
COURTESY LEWISTOWN PUBLIC LIBRARY, CENTRAL MONTANA HISTORICAL PHOTOGRAPHS, 01647.

In addition to these groups, there would be smaller numbers of immigrants listed in the 1870 census coming from such countries as Belgium, Bohemia, Cuba, Greece, the Netherlands, Hungary, Luxemburg, Mexico, Portugal, Russia, and Spain.[2] One of the most significant sources of immigrants in Montana was Canada, although it was hard to categorize these people because many of them were simply passing through Canada on their way to the United States; moreover, they often represented a wide variety of different ethnic backgrounds that were not recorded in U.S. census records. In the decades to follow, substantial numbers of people coming from Japan, Italy, Finland, Croatia, and Slovenia—to name but a few countries— would be added to the mix. In one form or another, they were all drawn to Montana by the development of industrial mining for silver, copper, and coal; by the arrival of the railroads; and by the expansion of Montana agriculture.

The aggregate number of all these people streaming into Montana was astonishing. According to official census records, foreign-born residents in Montana made up 38.7 percent of the territory's total population in 1870 (which was probably a low figure, as Chinese immigrants were often significantly undercounted), 29.4 percent in 1880, 30.2 percent in 1890, and 27.6 percent in 1900.[3] These numbers were substantial, not just for Montana, but for any western state or territory within the nation. Indeed, among the seventeen states and territories that spanned from the Great Plains west to the Pacific Coast, Montana in 1900 ranked second, trailing only the state of North Dakota, in terms of the percentage of its residents who were foreign born.[4]

When the children of immigrants—that is, the second generation—are added to the total number, then the figure is even more astounding. According to the 1900 U.S. census, 29.2 percent of all residents in Montana had at least one parent who was foreign born. This meant that slightly more than 56.7 percent of Montana's population was composed of immigrants and their offspring. But these figures were for "whites" only; the total ethnic population in Montana was actually much greater when Asian immigrants, Native Americans, and African Americans are included. Collectively, all of these different groups represented more than sixty percent of Montana's total population. To state it somewhat differently, just thirty-eight percent of Montana's population in 1900 was composed of native-born Euro-Americans whose parents had also been born in the United States.[5]

Figures for the ethnic population in Montana changed over the next two decades, but not by much. The percentages for first- and second-generation ethnic groups declined a bit, but the number of individuals actually rose. For example, there were 94,713 foreign-born residents in Montana in 1910 (an increase of 27,646 over the 1900 figure), which represented 25.2 percent of the state's population. In that same year, second-generation ethnic Montanans totaled 106,809 (an increase of 35,836 over ten years earlier), and thus represented 28.4 percent of the state's total population. Another 10,745 Montanans were Indian (Native American), according to the 1910 census, while 1,834 were African American.[6]

It was not until 1920 that a majority of Montana's total population was made up of native-born Euro-Americans whose parents were born in the United States, and even then the figure was just 50.2 percent. According to the 1920 census, 95,566 Montanans, or 17.4 percent of the total population, were foreign born. Another 164,837, or thirty percent, had at least one parent who was foreign born, while 10,956 Native Americans, representing two percent of the total population, were counted in the census.[7] What these figures do not reveal is the fact that the disruptions of World War I, which would last from 1914 to 1918, dramatically cut the flow of emigrants leaving Europe. Those numbers might have rebounded in future years, but in 1924 the U.S. Congress severely resisted the arrival of new immigrants by passing the National Origins Act of 1924.

The controversy over the 1924 immigration act, which will be discussed in greater detail later in this essay, brings us to another important aspect of ethnic history in America. One of the more popular metaphors applied to the diverse make-up of American society is the notion of the "melting pot." While this metaphor certainly has some credence, a careful examination of America's—and Montana's—past suggests that another apt metaphor for the American experience might be that of the "pressure cooker." As tensions would build up in American society—often along ethnic, racial, and class lines— releases of steam, perhaps even explosions, could occur in the form of hateful rhetoric, discriminatory legislation, and violence. Social historians have argued for some time that such actions, while regrettable, were in some respects the natural consequence of America's embrace of slavery for more than 200 years. That institution, although clearly tied to special economic interests such as the cotton industry, rested on the belief that certain races were inherently inferior, and therefore did not deserve to receive the same protections and benefits as the superior race—sometimes simply known as "white," while at other times referred to as the "Anglo-Saxon" race.

These notions of race were first extensively applied to Native Americans and African slaves during the British colonial period, and would later appear on the American frontier. In Montana, such attitudes were not only directed against Indians and those of mixed-blood descent, but also toward the Chinese once they began arriving in Montana in significant numbers. Fortunately for Chinese pioneers in Montana, they were not subject to the kind of mass violence that was directed toward other Chinese in places such as Rock Springs, Wyoming, and Tacoma, Washington.⁸ Unfortunately for the Chinese, they were confronted with territorial and state laws that attempted to deny them the same rights that were enjoyed by their fellow Montanans. For example, the Montana territorial legislature passed laws that were aimed at restricting Chinese access to mining claims, a primary source of income for many Chinese from the 1860s through the 1880s. Although the territorial supreme court initially ruled in favor of protecting the rights of Chinese miners, by 1883 it had reversed itself. In a similar fashion, the state supreme court (Montana became a state in 1889) upheld a special laundry tax that was clearly aimed at Chinese-owned laundries, another important source of income for many Chinese immigrants.⁹

The public animosity directed toward the Chinese—found in so many Montana newspapers in the late nineteenth century—reflected national trends. In fact, by the early 1880s pressure was building, especially in the Western states and territories where most Chinese immigrants lived, to block further Chinese immigration into the United States. The so-called "threat" of the Chinese to domestic American interests, of course, was a complete fabrication. The total Chinese population in the United States in 1880 was slightly more than 105,000, which represented just one-fifth of one percent of the entire population in the United States. Nonetheless, in 1882 Congress passed legislation, known as the Chinese Exclusion Act, which barred further immigration of Chinese laborers into the United States. The law was renewed by Congress ten years later, and then made permanent in the early twentieth century. While all of this was occurring, the federal government had concluded that Chinese immigrants, due to their race, were ineligible from becoming naturalized American citizens—the first time that such a prohibition had been explicitly applied to any immigrant group coming to America.¹⁰

Since most Chinese who were inclined to come to the United States fell into the category of "laborers," as was true for most all immigrant groups coming to this country, the Chinese Exclusion Act severely affected the structure and make-up of Chinese communities in the American West. Few Chinese women had emigrated to the United States before the passage of various exclusionary laws. For example, in 1880, there was just one Chinese female in the United States for every twenty-one Chinese males. This gender imbalance made it very difficult for the first generation of Chinese immigrants to produce a second generation that might follow in its footsteps. By 1920, there were just 61,639 Chinese Americans living in the United States. Of these, only 18,532 were U.S. citizens—that is, second-generation Chinese Americans born in the United States. Even as late as 1920, a significant gender imbalance still existed, with just one female for every seven Chinese males.[11]

While legislation was being passed at the federal level that adversely affected Chinese Americans, a new law was taking shape in Montana that reflected the Progressive era's attitude toward race. In general, Americans are inclined to view the Progressive era—a period that covered the first two decades of the twentieth century—as a time of enlightenment. With regard to such issues as child labor, women's suffrage, the direct election of U.S. senators, landscape conservation, and food inspections, this perspective has considerable merit. On the issue of race, however, it was a different matter. In the American South, Jim Crow (racial segregation) laws had replaced the hopes of Reconstruction, and lynchings were a frequent occurrence. Throughout much of the country, anti-miscegenation laws—laws that prohibited interracial marriage—were increasingly common.

The issue came to the forefront in Montana in 1907 when Charles S. Muffly, a Democratic state senator from Winston who represented Broadwater County, proposed such a bill. The proposed legislation was defeated that year, but Muffly reintroduced his bill in 1909. Despite fierce opposition from an African-American newspaper in the capital, the Helena *Plaindealer*, the bill became law on March 3, 1909. The Senate vote was 15 to 11 in favor of the legislation, and the House vote was 42 to 18. Although much of the debate over Muffly's bill dealt with relations between blacks and whites, the actual title of the bill indicated that the focus was broader than that. It was put forward as "An Act Prohibiting Marriages between White Persons,

Negroes, Persons of Negro Blood, and between White Persons, Chinese and Japanese, and making such Marriage Void, and prescribing punishment for Solemnizing such Marriages."[12] To place this story within its proper context, it should be noted that in 1910, Montana was home to just 1,834 African Americans, 1,285 Chinese, and 1,585 Japanese.[13] The law would remain on the books until 1953.

Another important event that directly affected the well-being of certain ethnic groups in Montana was World War I. The war had begun in Europe in the summer of 1914; the United States officially joined the fight in April 1917 by declaring war against Germany and the other Central Powers. Calls to support the war effort erupted across the state.

In 1909, Montana Senator Charles S. Muffly, from Winston in Broadwater County, successfully sponsored a bill prohibiting mixed-race marriage. The law remained on the books for four decades. COURTESY MONTANA HISTORICAL SOCIETY, 944-030.

Drives to encourage the purchase of war bonds were common, and 12,500 Montanans volunteered for military service. Another 28,000 were drafted. With roughly 40,000 men in uniform—ten percent of the state's total population—Montana "had a rate of contribution that exceeded that of the next highest state by 25 percent."[14] Passions aroused by the war soon provided an opportunity for superpatriots and conservatives to attack those whom they saw as "enemies" of the state and nation. Organizations such as the Montana Council of Defense, created by Governor Sam Stewart in 1917 to promote support for the war effort at the state and local levels, often took the lead in going after supposed "troublemakers."[15]

Members of certain ethnic groups were reluctant to embrace the call for war. A good number of Irish Montanans resented American support of Great Britain at a time when the British continued to oppress the Irish and deny freedom to the nation of Ireland. Certain immigrants who had come from Germany and areas within the Austro-Hungarian

Laborers take a break at a brickyard in Lewistown, circa 1917.
COURTESY LEWISTOWN PUBLIC LIBRARY, CENTRAL MONTANA HISTORICAL PHOTOGRAPHS, 03524.

Empire found it difficult to support a war effort being directed against the countries of their birth, especially when those countries were often demonized by officials of the U.S. government and the American press. In addition to these war-related emotions, tensions were brewing in Montana's timber and mining industries between labor and management, tensions that often erupted in strikes.

Conservatives in Montana used the passions generated by the war to go after their longtime foes, the labor unions. They attacked the unions, especially those that might threaten to call for a strike in wartime, as being unpatriotic. The rhetoric turned violent when six men abducted labor organizer Frank Little from his Butte boarding house room on August 1, 1917, and lynched him on the outskirts of town. The murderers were never apprehended. Federal troops were dispatched to Butte to prevent further violence, but also to prevent the unions from challenging the authority of companies like the Anaconda Copper Mining Company. By the time World War I ended, the unions had been crushed and the Anaconda Company had instituted its infamous "rustling card" system, which in effect allowed the company to blackball any workers sympathetic to unionization. The workers of Butte, many of whom were of Irish, Italian, and Slavic descent, would not regain their rights to negotiate for higher pay and better working conditions until the passage of new federal legislation in the mid 1930s.

Industrial workers in Butte and elsewhere were not the only Montanans to feel the wrath of the superpatriots. A mob made up of local residents in Glendive almost lynched a German Mennonite minister due to his pacifist position. The Montana Council of Defense banned the use of the German language in the state, with the result that the *Staats-Zeitung,* the primary German-language newspaper in Montana, ceased publication. Certain residents in Lewistown went so far as to publicly burn German high school textbooks, as well as other books that had been written by German authors. Perhaps the most vivid, and controversial, example of this suppression of freedom of speech was the creation of the Montana Sedition Law, and the prosecution of dozens of Montanans charged with violating that law.

Under intense pressure from groups such as the Montana Council of Defense and newspaper editors like Will Campbell of the *Helena Independent,* Governor Stewart called a special session of the state legislature to deal with various war-related issues. As part of its task, the legislature in February 1918 enacted the Montana Sedition Law. (The law would serve as a model for the federal Sedition Law that was created just three months later.) The Montana law defined sedition in the broadest possible terms. The law declared:

> . . . any person or persons who shall utter, print, write or publish any disloyal, profane, violent, scurrilous, contemptuous, slurring or abusive language about the form of government of the United States, or the constitution of the United States, or the soldiers or sailors of the United States, or the flag of the United States, or the uniform of the army or navy . . . or shall utter, print, write or publish any language calculated to incite or inflame resistance to any duly constituted Federal or State authority in connection with the prosecution of the War . . . shall be guilty of the crime of sedition.[16]

In the midst of this statewide hysteria, seventy-nine Montanans would be found guilty of violating the Montana Sedition Law in 1918 and 1919. Of these, forty-seven would be sent to the state penitentiary, with sentences ranging from a few months to as much as twenty years. What is most revealing is the fact that more than half of those sent to prison were immigrants from Europe, primarily from Germany and regions within the Austro-Hungarian Empire. Their "crimes," often committed under the influence of alcohol, usually consisted of simply saying that wartime food regulations were a "joke," or that Americans "had no business being there."

Once the war ended, some measure of reasoned judgment returned to Montana's legal system. Seven of those sent to the prison in Deer Lodge would have their convictions reversed by the Montana Supreme Court, while several others would have their sentences shortened. But the damage had been done. Many of those convicted of breaking the law had been forced to pay extremely heavy fines, and those sent to the penitentiary would, collectively, spend more than sixty-five years in that depressing and dangerous institution. It was not until 2006, years after all of those involved had passed away, that the State of Montana admitted its mistake. On May 3, 2006, Governor Brian Schweitzer signed a Proclamation of Pardon exonerating those who had been convicted of sedition in Montana.[17]

The powerful passions unleashed by America's participation in the First World War, coupled with the unprecedented size of prewar immigration (between 1900 and 1914, one million new immigrants arrived in the United States each year), quickly spawned a national movement to limit future immigration numbers. In 1921, the U.S. Congress passed legislation that established a quota system for the very first time. The quotas restricted immigration from Europe to three percent of the number of nationals from each country living in the United States in 1910. Many native-born opponents of immigration, however, believed that the law did not go nearly far enough. Within the law's parameters, more than 500,000 Europeans would still be allowed to emigrate to the United States in 1923; moreover, many of those slots could be filled by people from southern and eastern Europe.

Prodded by organizations such as the Immigration Restriction League, the U.S. Congress passed new legislation in 1924 that was quickly and eagerly signed by President Calvin Coolidge. The chief author of the National Origins Act (also known as the Immigration Act of 1924) was Republican Congressman Albert Johnson, a staunch restrictionist who then chaired the House Committee on Immigration. The new law lowered the immigration quota from three percent to two percent. It also moved the baseline used to determine the number of immigrants for each country back to the 1890 census, which would sharply curtail the number of immigrants coming from southern and eastern Europe. For example, under the new formula, the annual Italian quota fell from 42,000 to just 4,000; the quota number for Poles went from 31,000 to 6,000. By the end of the decade, the overall numbers were restricted even further, in part to favor immigrants who might be coming from western Europe and the Scandinavian countries. Finally, the 1924 law made it almost impossible for anyone from Asia to immigrate to the United States, including Japanese who, like the Chinese before them, were designated as "aliens ineligible for citizenship."[18]

The immigration laws of the 1920s came about, in large measure, because of the racist and xenophobic attitudes prevalent in American society at that time. Such attitudes were not limited to organizations like the Immigration Restriction League or the Ku Klux Klan (the latter organization was vehemently anti-immigrant as well as anti-black). Calvin Coolidge, when he was vice president of the United States, wrote an article entitled "Whose Country is This?" in *Good Housekeeping*.[19] In answering his own question, Coolidge advanced the notion of "Nordic" racial supremacy. He also warned Nordic Americans to avoid marrying non-Nordics, as such marriages would produce "deterioration" in their offspring. Albert Johnson, the father of the 1924 law, justified that act by declaring that "our capacity to maintain our cherished institutions stands diluted by a stream of alien blood, with all its inherited misconceptions respecting the relationships of the governing power to the governed. . . . The United States is our land. . . . We intend to maintain it so. The day of unalloyed welcome to all peoples, the day of indiscriminate acceptance of all races, has definitely ended."[20] The quota system of the 1920s, created by such notions about race, would define America's immigration policy for the next four decades.

The severe restrictions placed on Japanese immigration in the National Origins Quota Act were a reminder of the many challenges facing Japanese Americans at that time, including those in Montana. Despite the animosity often directed their way, many Japanese immigrants had become successful farmers in the American West, producing various commodities, especially fruits and vegetables, that the public craved. Resentful of such success, racists in the West proposed legislation that would prevent Japanese immigrants from owning land. California, with a Japanese population of 71,952 (still just 2.1 percent of the state's total population), was the first state to take such action. The California legislature passed a series of acts known as Alien Land Laws. These laws prohibited any "alien ineligible for citizenship" from owning or leasing land in California. While the Japanese were not specifically named in the laws, it was understood that the laws were aimed primarily at them, as European immigrants, of course, were eligible for citizenship.[21]

Other western states soon followed California's lead, including Montana. In 1923, a Republican state senator from Carbon County by the name of J. C. F. Siegfriedt introduced a bill in the state legislature that would restrict Japanese land ownership. Section Two of the bill declared: "Aliens not eligible for citizenship shall not own land or take hold of title thereto. No person shall take or hold land or title to land for an alien. Land now held by or for aliens in violation of the constitution of the state is forfeited to and declared to be the property of the state."[22] On February 15, the Senate passed the bill by a vote of 48 to 2; two weeks later, the House gave its unanimous approval by a vote of 82 to 0. On March 1, 1923, Governor Joseph M. Dixon signed the measure into law.[23] The law was put on the books despite the fact that there were just 1,074 Japanese living in Montana in 1920. Collectively, they owned just 10,000 acres of farmland out of more than 30 million farmed acres in the state.[24]

In some instances, Japanese farmers were able to hold on to their lands by placing them in the names of their American-born children,

At the end of their shift, workers leave the grounds of the Anaconda smelter.
RUSSELL LEE, COURTESY LIBRARY OF CONGRESS. LC-DIG-FSA-8D22530.

who, by virtue of being born in the United States, were American citizens. In a few instances, families were forced to sell their property and go to work as agricultural workers for white landowners. Others moved into the city looking for new employment opportunities.

Despite such discrimination and racism, many Japanese Americans, especially those of the second generation, were able to establish deep roots in American society. As sociologists might say, they had become well acculturated. But as Casey Pallister's essay in this volume vividly demonstrates, the Japanese Navy's December 7, 1941, attack on Pearl Harbor, and the war that ensued, produced unprecedented challenges for Japanese Americans. More than 110,000 of them living in West Coast states were forced by the federal government into so-called relocation centers—a polite term for concentration camps. In the process they would lose more than $400,000,000 worth of property.

Because of Montana's location in the interior West, its Japanese-

American residents—just 508 people in 1940—were not ordered into one of the ten relocation centers spread across the country. They faced considerable hardship nonetheless. Some lost employment simply because of their ethnicity. Many were confronted with hostile stares and insulting language. There was strong public opposition to the suggestion that Japanese-American students enrolled in West Coast universities be allowed to transfer to Montana schools in 1942. Similar opposition arose to the idea of allowing Japanese Americans into the state to address an increasingly serious labor shortage. The opposition subsided a bit when Japanese Americans who had received furloughs from their relocation centers assisted in saving the sugar-beet harvest of 1942 by providing necessary labor in the fields. For the workers themselves, the experience was mixed at best.[25]

Although World War II would lead to considerable hardship and suffering for many Japanese Americans, the war years would also be the beginning of changing attitudes toward ethnicity and race in America. Military units were still segregated, but African Americans and Asian Americans who fought in the war were aware of what they had accomplished, and were increasingly determined to exercise their rights as Americans once they returned home. The same thing was true for other ethnic groups in the United States that had often been kept on the fringes of American society. One significant legal change that had long-term diplomatic and domestic implications was the termination of the Chinese Exclusion Act in 1943. (The quota system that largely determined immigration numbers remained in place.) China, of course, was an ally of the United States in the war against Japan. A pro-China sentiment arose in the United States during the war, often reflected in Hollywood films of the era, and the racially inspired exclusion acts no longer seemed appropriate.[26]

Changing social attitudes were even more apparent in the two decades following the war. In 1947, Jackie Robinson integrated the national pastime of baseball, and sports in America would never be the same.[27] The next year, President Harry Truman ordered the desegregation of the military. In 1952, the federal government finally changed the law that had identified certain "aliens" as being ineligible for U.S. citizenship. Now, finally, Asian immigrants could become naturalized American citizens if they fulfilled the same requirements as any other immigrant group. The following year, the State of Montana dropped the anti-miscegenation law that had been on the books since 1909.[28]

In 1954, the U.S. Supreme Court would issue its famous *Brown v. Board of Education* decision. The discriminatory laws that had marked much of the country since the late nineteenth century—and were clearly at odds with America's democratic and egalitarian values—were no longer in vogue. In 1964, Congress, with the urging of President Lyndon Johnson, passed the most sweeping civil rights legislation since the end of the Reconstruction era nine decades earlier. Johnson immediately signed the historic act into law.

Given all of these changes occurring at both the state and federal level, it was not surprising that the issue of immigration would come to the fore. Since the end of the Second World War, some piecemeal adjustments had been made, particularly for those people classified as refugees, but the system as a whole was still tied to the decisions made back in the 1920s. America's rise as a superpower, and the active role that it played on the international stage in economic as well as political matters, meant that the immigration policies of the past would have to change. Congress responded by passing a sweeping piece of legislation known as the Immigration Act of 1965. It did away with the old system based largely on racial attitudes that tended to favor certain countries and regions over others. This act, more than any federal legislation, would open the doors to a new era of immigration and a new wave of immigrants. The immigrants who have streamed into the United States, and into Montana as well, over the past five decades have begun to transform America, just as an earlier generation of immigrants did between roughly 1880 and 1914. The recent immigrants have come from every corner of the globe, but especially from the regions of Latin America and Asia. Collectively, they, their children, and now even their grandchildren, are changing the very face of American society.

It is crucial for students of history to understand that the past is never static. We tend to be aware of physical changes occurring around us, especially if some time has passed between visits to a particular location. But societies, and the traditions and values that bind them together, are also continually evolving. This is especially true of ethnic groups situated within a larger community. If a group of people happens to come from abroad through the process of immigration, then the generational changes are particularly important.

The first generation, being new to the community, is caught between two worlds. For people who emigrate to America as adults, their language skills, social institutions, and cultural values are largely determined by their country of origin. Settling in a place such as Montana, they are often confronted by sights, sounds, and behaviors that may make little sense to them. The war brides featured in Seena Kohl's essay in this book are a case in point. Although they arrived in Montana well after the frontier era had ended, and usually spoke English as their native language, several nonetheless experienced a severe case of what might be called culture shock.

To cope with this feeling of living in a "strange land," immigrants have often attempted to create a community of their own that would reinforce their sense of identity. Historian Roger Daniels has described the process in this fashion:

> The ethnic enclave, a place where the language and the customs of the old country were transplanted, however inexpertly, was a typical development of most American ethnic groups wherever their numbers reached a certain critical mass. Though today, ahistorically, they are called ghettos and are often viewed as a bad thing, in the past these enclaves provided an important transitory phase for millions [in the case of Montana, hundreds or thousands] of urban immigrants. If, in some instances, these enclaves survived long enough to serve as a brake on the pace of acculturation, they nevertheless provided an important way station for immigrants on the road to fuller integration into the larger streams of American life.[29]

When we think about the Chinatowns of Helena and Butte, the Italian community known as Meaderville, or the many other ethnic communities scattered across the state, it would be useful to keep Daniels's description in mind.

The next generations—children and grandchildren of immigrants—have faced a different set of challenges. Because of their schooling and their command of English, acculturation has been a natural process for most of them. But in part because they have been more fully integrated into the larger society, questions sometimes arise as to their own identity. For the most part, they think of themselves simply as Americans, but they cannot completely dismiss the stories and traditions handed down by their elders. Nor, in some cases, can they always ignore the labels that others are inclined to put on them.

As our society has become increasingly diverse during the late twentieth and early twenty-first centuries, another interesting development has occurred, and that is the blending of once distinct ethnic and racial categories. (It is critical to keep in mind that the concept of "race" is a social construction, not a biological one, as all human beings are members of the same species.) The sheer diversity of the population, coupled with high social mobility and an egalitarian spirit, have helped to blur some of the lines that traditionally divided Americans, and Montanans, for that matter. The colors and contours of ethnicity in Montana—and in the United States as a whole—are much like those found in a medley of musical themes in a symphony. Each melody has its own unique characteristics, but listening to the whole symphony reveals that the individual themes complement one another in such a way as to create an even greater design: a pattern that, at its best, produces an amazing level of harmony and balance.

NOTES

1   Census Office, *Ninth Census of the United States, 1870: Population* (Washington, D.C.: Government Printing Office, 1872), pp. 336-342.

2   Ibid.

3   Ibid., 315; Census Office, *Tenth Census of the United States, 1880: Population* (Washington, D.C.: Government Printing Office, 1883), p. 3; Census Office, *Eleventh Census of the United States, 1890: Population, Part 1* (Washington, D.C.: Government Printing Office, 1895), p. 399; Census Office, *Twelfth Census of the United States, 1900: Population, Part 1* (Washington, D.C.: Government Printing Office, 1901), p. 482.

4   Census Office, *Twelfth Census of the United States, 1900*, p. 482.

5   Ibid., pp. 482-483.

6   Bureau of the Census, *Thirteenth Census of the United States, Volume II: Population, 1910* (Washington, D.C.: Government Printing Office, 1913), p. 1147.

7   Bureau of the Census, *Fourteenth Census of the United States, Volume III: Population, 1920* (Washington, D.C.: Government Printing Office, 1922), p. 574.

8   Paul Crane and Alfred Larson, "The Chinese Massacre," *Annuals of Wyoming* 12 (January 1940): pp. 47-55, and (April 1940): pp. 153-160; Shih-shan Henry Tsai, *China and the Overseas Chinese in the United States, 1868-1911* (Fayetteville: University of Arkansas Press, 1983), pp. 72-78, 83-86; Robert R. Swartout, Jr., "In Defense of the West's Chinese, *Oregon Historical Quarterly* 83 (Spring 1982): pp. 25-36; Jules Alexander Karlin, "The Anti-Chinese Outbreak in Tacoma, 1885," *Pacific Historical Review* 23 (August 1954): pp. 271-283. For a similar tragedy along the Snake River, see R. Gregory Nokes, *Massacred for Gold: The Chinese in Hells Canyon* (Corvallis: Oregon State University Press), 2009.

9   John R. Wunder, "Law and Chinese in Frontier Montana," *Montana, The Magazine of Western History* 30 (Summer 1980): pp. 18-31.

10 Shih-shan Henry Tsai, *The Chinese Experience in America* (Bloomington: Indiana University Press, 1986), 64-66, 73-76,102-05; Roger Daniels, *Asian America: Chinese and Japanese in the United States since 1850* (Seattle: University of Washington Press, 1988), pp. 55-58, 91-92; Iris Chang, *The Chinese in America: A Narrative History* (New York: Viking, 2003), pp. 130-156.

11 Daniels, *Asian America*, 69.

12 Montana, *Laws, Resolutions and Memorials of the State of Montana Passed at the Eleventh Regular Session of the Legislative Assembly* (Helena, MT: Independent Publishing Co., 1909), pp. 57-58. For a discussion of these events, see William L. Lang, "The Nearly Forgotten Blacks of Last Chance Gulch, 1900-1912," *Pacific Northwest Quarterly* 70 (April 1979): pp. 56-57.

13 Bureau of the Census, *Thirteenth Census of the United States, Volume II*, p. 1147.

[14] Michael P. Malone, Richard B. Roeder, and William L. Lang, *Montana: A History of Two Centuries*, rev. ed. (Seattle: University of Washington Press, 1991), pp. 268, 270. See pp. 268-279 of the Malone, Roeder, and Lang text for an excellent summary of the impact that World War I had on Montana.

[15] On the Montana Council of Defense, see Chapter 10, entitled "Patriots Gone Berserk: The Montana Council of Defense, 1917-1918," in Dave Walter, *More Montana Campfire Tales: Fifteen Historical Narratives* (Helena: Farcountry Press, 2002), pp. 157-173; Arnon Gutfeld, *Montana's Agony: Years of War and Hysteria, 1917-1921* (Gainesville: University Presses of Florida, 1979), pp. 60-69.

[16] Quoted in Malone, Roeder, and Lang, *Montana*, pp. 276, 278. For the entire law, see Montana, *Laws, Resolutions and Memorials of the State of Montana Passed by the Extraordinary Session of the Fifteenth Legislative Assembly* (Helena, MT: State Publishing Co., 1918), pp. 28-29.

[17] Clemens P. Work, *Darkest Before Dawn: Sedition and Free Speech in the American West* (Albuquerque: University of New Mexico Press, 2005); University of Montana School of Journalism, "The Montana Sedition Project," http://www.sedition.net/ (accessed January 15, 2014). Regarding conditions in the state penitentiary, see Keith Edgerton, *Montana Justice: Power, Punishment, & the Penitentiary* (Seattle: University of Washington Press, 2004).

[18] For a solid summary of these events, see Roger Daniels, *Coming to America: A History of Immigration and Ethnicity in American Life*, 2nd ed. (New York: HarperPerennial, 2002), pp. 277-284.

[19] Calvin Coolidge, "Whose Country Is This?" in *Good Housekeeping*, February 1921, Volume 72, Number 2, 13-107.

[20] Quoted in Daniels, *Coming to America*, pp. 283-284.

[21] Roger Daniels, *The Politics of Prejudice: The Anti-Japanese Movement in California and the Struggle for Japanese Exclusion*, 2nd ed. (Berkeley: University of California Press, 1977), pp. 58-64, 87-91.

[22] Montana, *House Journal of the Eighteenth Legislative Assembly of the State of Montana* (Helena, MT: State Publishing Co., 1923), p. 238; Montana, *Laws, Resolutions and Memorials of the State of Montana Passed at the Eighteenth Regular Session of the Legislative Assembly* (Helena, MT: State Publishing Co., 1923), p. 124.

[23] Montana, *House Journal of the Eighteenth Legislative Assembly of the State of Montana*, p. 619; Montana, *Senate Journal of the Eighteenth Legislative Assembly of the State of Montana* (Helena, MT: State Publishing Co., 1923), pp. 335, 651.

24   Son B. Nguyen, "Testing the 'Melting Pot': The Anti-Japanese Movement in Montana, 1907-1924" (Research Seminar paper, Department of History, Carroll College, 1990), p. 13.

25   Kevin C. McCann, "Montana's Treatment of Japanese Americans during World War II," in *Montana Vistas: Selected Historical Essays*, ed. Robert R. Swartout, Jr. (Landam, MD: University Press of America, 1981), 237-253. For a somewhat more positive view of the Japanese American experience in Montana, see Chapter 13, entitled "Montana's Wartime Japanese," in Dave Walter, *Montana Campfire Tales: Fourteen Historical Narratives* (Helena, MT: Twodot, 1997), 185-203. A valuable source on the subject is the documentary film, *From the Far East to the Old West: Chinese & Japanese Settlers in Montana*, VHS, directed by Kathy Witkowsky, produced by Pat Murdo (Washington, D.C.: The Mansfield Center for Pacific Affairs, 1999). To understand what most West Coast Japanese Americans had to endure during the war, the best place to start is with Yoshiko Uchida's personal account, *Desert Exile: The Uprooting of a Japanese-American Family* (Seattle: University of Washington Press, 1982). See also K. Scott Wong, *Americans First: Chinese Americans and the Second World War* (Cambridge: Harvard University Press, 2001), pp. 109-124.

26   Daniels, *Asian America*, pp. 191-198.

27   The single best book on Jackie Robinson remains Jules Tygiel, *Baseball's Great Experiment: Jackie Robinson and His Legacy* (New York: Oxford University Press, 1983). See also Arnold Rampersad, *Jackie Robinson: A Biography* (New York: Alfred A. Knopf, 1997). Jackie Robinson joined the Brooklyn Dodgers in 1947. He entered professional baseball with Brooklyn's farm team, the Montreal Royals, in 1946.

28   Montana, *Laws, Resolutions and Memorials of the State of Montana Passed by the Thirty-third Legislative Assembly in Regular Session* (Helena, MT: State Publishing Co, 1953), pp. 4-5. The vote to repeal the 1909 law in the House was 81-0. In the Senate, the vote was 47-3. The three state senators who voted against repeal were Kenneth Cole of Winnett, Fred H. Padbury of Helena, and Fred L. Robinson of Malta. All three were Republicans. See Montana, *House Journal of Thirty-third Legislative Assembly of the State of Montana* (Helena, MT: State Publishing Co., 1953), pp. 60-61; Montana, *Senate Journal of the Thirty-third Legislative Assembly of the State of Montana* (Helena, MT: State Publishing Co., 1953), p. 86.

29   Daniels, *Coming to America*, p. 170.

Angus McDonald:
A Scottish Highlander among Indian Peoples

— *James Hunter*

The development of the fur trade as an international business, especially during the late eighteenth and early nineteenth centuries, brought the first significant wave of non-Indian people into the region that would become known in time as Montana. Two powerful British firms, the London-based Hudson's Bay Company and the Montreal-based North West Company, were at the center of this expanding fur empire. American firms, following quite literally in the footsteps of the historic Lewis and Clark expedition of 1804–1806, soon joined the race for economic opportunity. These included such important operations as the Missouri Fur Company, the Rocky Mountain Fur Company, and John Jacob Astor's American Fur Company.

The rapidly expanding fur trade, which increasingly focused on beaver pelts, attracted an especially wide variety of ethnic groups. French Canadians, drawing upon decades of experience in the Great Lakes region, played a crucial role in the trade, but so too did recent immigrants from such places as England, Wales, Ireland, and Scotland. Indeed, the Scots would provide some of the most important figures connected with the fur trade, including the famed explorer, Alexander Mackenzie, and Angus McDonald, the focus of the following essay.

The intense competition that accompanied the fur trade could

*sometimes boil over into conflict and violence, but it could also pro-
duce—at least temporarily—what some historians have referred to as
a "frontier of inclusion." To put it simply, the fur trade could not flour-
ish without the assistance and participation of large numbers of native peoples. As Scottish historian and author James Hunter vividly
illustrates by examining the life and career of Angus McDonald, the
interaction between Europeans (and Euro-Americans) and their Indian
counterparts could lead to a rich fusion of cultural traits that would reflect both the needs of the fur trade at a given time and the power of
kinship ties that spanned multiple generations.*

The Mission Valley, at the center of Montana's Flathead Reservation, is bisected by the highway that runs north from St. Ignatius
to Pablo, the reservation's administrative center. Eight miles along the
highway, and a little to the right, a log cabin stands in the middle
of a field. Despite being one of the oldest buildings in Montana, few
people visit this cabin, all that remains of Fort Connah, the fur trading post the Hudson's Bay Company constructed 150 years ago. Still
fewer people are probably aware even of the existence—in woodland
at the bottom of the slope on which the trading post's one surviving
cabin stands—of the family graveyard where is buried the man who
had the job of managing Fort Connah from the time he came to the
Mission valley in 1847.

This man was Angus McDonald. His tombstone is flanked by that
of his wife, Catherine, the Nez Percé woman Angus married at Fort
Hall in present-day southern Idaho in 1842 and with whom he spent
the greater part of his life. That Angus McDonald was once thought
to be of some local importance is suggested by the mountain that so
spectacularly overlooks his last resting place. This mountain, called
McDonald Peak, is one of several nearby geographical features to
bear the McDonald name. But it is not only to the map of Montana
that one should look for reasons why Angus McDonald is worth
commemorating. Much of the most valuable testimony to Angus's

Born in Scotland, Angus McDonald arrived in the Mission Valley in 1847 as a representative of the Hudson's Bay Company. COURTESY MONTANA HISTORICAL SOCIETY, HELENA, 943-622.

significance is the way he continues to be honored by his descendants on the Flathead Reservation more than a century after his death. By these Indian people, "the fur trader," as his great-grandchildren and his great-great grandchildren habitually call Angus, is regarded as a man of consequence.

Angus McDonald was born on October 15, 1816, at Craig in the Highlands of Scotland. Located beside Loch Torridon, one of many Atlantic inlets reaching deep into the Highland hills, the place today is both uninhabited and isolated. The nearest road—a narrow, twisting thoroughfare redeemed only by its constantly changing views of the Torridon mountains—gives out finally at Diabeg, some four miles short of Craig.

From Diabeg, a village consisting of a handful of stone-built and white-painted homes, a footpath leads westward across a series of steeply sloping hillsides. The terrain is the sort that it has recently become fashionable in Scotland to call wildland. Most such land is, by definition, scenically impressive. And despite the fact that Torridon's summits are only one-third as high as McDonald Peak, those Highland mountains are every bit as magnificent, in their way, as those of the Flathead country—partly because the Torridon hills rise directly from the Atlantic rather than from a valley floor that is itself some 4,000 feet above sea level.

The ocean's proximity, however, makes the Highlands far wetter than Montana. The path to Craig is boggy and broken as a result, its surface badly eroded by Scotland's storm-driven rains. To pick one's way along this path, especially on the sort of day when downpour after downpour comes hurtling inland on a southwesterly gale, is to appreciate why the people who once occupied this area automatically gravitated toward such little shelter as their surroundings provided.

By Torridon standards, Angus McDonald's birthplace is a sheltered spot. Craig is enclosed by hills. Those hills fence out the wind sufficiently to allow trees—of which none are to be seen along the entire length of the path from Diabeg—to grow in several lower-lying corners. The consequent sense of Craig being the Torridon equivalent of a desert oasis is heightened by the presence of a piece of land both flatter and more fertile than any other for miles around.

Clearly this piece of land was cultivated in former times, and equally clearly it contains the ruins of several buildings, any one of which could have been the home in which Angus McDonald was born. Angus, however, was in the habit of referring to this home as "Craig House." In a Scottish context, that suggests a building rather more substantial than the average, and the one such building to have existed at Craig, as it happens, is still standing. Formerly it was a farmhouse.

Now it is a hostel that offers basic, but welcome, accommodation to the growing number of trekkers and backpackers who come each summer to the Scottish Highlands from—as the Craig Hostel's visitor book demonstrates—practically every corner of the world.

In winter the hostel is normally deserted. But its front door is permanently—and trustingly—unlocked. It is irresistibly tempting, therefore, to enter by this door; to climb the wooden staircase leading to bunk-filled dormitories that must, in the building's earlier incarnation, have been family bedrooms; to wonder, while standing quietly there, if one of those bedrooms once resounded to the infant Angus McDonald's earliest cries.

From the former farmhouse's upstairs windows—which are just high enough to provide a clear line of sight across an intervening ridge—it is possible to see Loch Torridon, its waters scuffed and ruffled by the wind. Beyond is Applecross, the district where Angus McDonald's father, a farmer by profession, went in October 1816 to register his son's birth. Beyond Applecross, like Torridon a mainland locality, is the Isle of Skye. Beyond Skye is the more distant, and only intermittently visible, Isle of Lewis. Beyond Lewis is the open Atlantic. And beyond the Atlantic, some thousands of miles to the west, is North America.

That continent, at the time of Angus McDonald's birth, was one with which Highlanders—who had loomed large among transatlantic emigrants since the 1760s—were increasingly familiar. It is little surprise, then, that the Craig household had links with North America. What is surprising, and what made the Craig family almost unique among early nineteenth-century whites, is that their American relatives included a man who had lived for a period in what is now Montana. This man, Finan McDonald, was possibly the brother, but more probably the cousin, of Angus's father, Donald MacDonald.[1] In 1786, as a small boy accompanying emigrant parents, Finan had left Knoydart—another Highland area some forty miles south of Torridon—for what is now Glengarry County, Ontario. There the teenage Finan joined the formidable fur trading organization, the North West Company.

The North West Company was a creation of men whose background was similar to Finan's. Foremost among the company's founders was Simon MacTavish, who came originally from Stratherrick, a valley situated to the east or southeast of Knoydart and Torridon. MacTavish reached North America in the 1760s. Like many other Highland emigrants, he settled in New York's Mohawk valley. Like most Mohawk valley Highlanders, MacTavish chose the loyalist, as opposed to the patriot, side during the Revolutionary War. By the war's end, he had left the newly independent United States for Canada where, during the 1780s and 1790s, he masterminded the emergence of the North West Company and its fostering of fur trading talent, most of which consisted of Highlanders like himself.

Territorial expansionism was integral to North West Company strategy from the outset. The organization's great rivals, those Hudson's Bay Company men with whom MacTavish and his Nor'Westers were sometimes literally at war, had long relied on the Cree and other Indian peoples to bring furs from the North American interior to their base at York Factory on Hudson Bay. The Nor'Westers, in contrast, regarded their Montreal headquarters as the launching pad for trading expeditions that took them farther inland. Within a few years, thanks to a growing mastery of Indian technology in the shape of the birchbark canoe and to their skill in exploiting the Canadian river system, North West Company traders could be found everywhere from the Great Lakes to the Athabasca country. Nor was Athabasca, nearly 2,000 miles from Montreal, the limit of the Nor'Westers' reach. Well before the eighteenth century's end, one of the most enterprising of all Nor'Westers, Alexander Mackenzie, had made his way both to the Arctic Ocean and to the Pacific. More than a decade ahead of Lewis and Clark, therefore, and in only a fraction of the time taken by those explorers, Mackenzie, a Scottish Highlander, became the first white man to cross North America from coast to coast.

Following Mackenzie's pioneering venture in the nineteenth century's opening decade, the Nor'Westers moved in strength across the Rocky Mountains, and in 1807 a North West Company party made its way across the Continental Divide into the fragmented and fractured hill country that surrounds the upper reaches of the Columbia River.

This party was led by David Thompson. A pious and teetotal

Welshman, Thompson, at first sight, seems to have had little in common with the boozy and boisterous Highlanders who dominated the North West Company's upper echelons and who were more than capable—as Alexander Mackenzie and one of his fellow traders demonstrated on a famous occasion in Montreal—of drinking themselves senseless. But Thompson was an outstanding surveyor whose colleagues warmly appreciated his talents. What the Nor'Westers needed, if they were to exploit Columbia country furs, was to develop a worthwhile communications system both inside the Columbia country itself and between the Columbia country and the wider world. Thompson, as his North West Company associates evidently appreciated, was the man to undertake the necessary explorations. He spent years mapping the Columbia Basin's myriad streams, lakes, and watercourses. So meticulous were his charts and plans that they were consulted long after his death.

Thompson's trusted lieutenant and close confidant in the Columbia country was Angus McDonald's Knoydart-born kinsman, Finan McDonald—this "bough of the same tree as my own,"

The snowcapped Mission Range rises above the valley of the same name, where in 1847 Angus McDonald established Fort Connah, a fur trading post of the Hudson's Bay Company. W. C. ALDEN, COURTESY U.S. GEOLOGICAL SURVEY, AWC02390.

as Angus called him. "He belonged to a . . . family which emigrated
. . . to Canada while he was a lad," one of Finan's Columbia country
colleagues observed. Much the same was true of many other North
West Company Highlanders, but none was physically so memorable
as Finan McDonald. "His appearance was very striking," Finan's colleague wrote. "In height he was six feet four inches, with broad shoulders, large bushy whiskers and red hair which, for some years, had
not felt the scissors and which, sometimes falling over his face and
shoulders, gave to his countenance a wild and uncouth appearance."[2]

Because one of his more talked-about feats turned on his having wrestled to the ground a buffalo bull that had tried to gore him,
Finan's strength was clearly in proportion to his size. And his temper,
it seems, was as fiery as his hair—there being more than one report of
his having dueled with men who had allegedly insulted him. His fellow
Nor'Westers were inclined to make occasional mock of Finan, especially of the "ludicrous mélange of Gaelic, English, French, and half-
a-dozen Indian dialects" into which this originally Gaelic-speaking
Highlander tended to lapse when infuriated by some suspected slight.
Still, they were entirely appreciative of his undoubted ability—as
signaled by his fluency in "Indian dialects"—to get along with the
Columbia country's native peoples. Among these peoples Finan's particular favorites were apparently the Flathead, or Salish, bands among
whom Angus McDonald was later to live in the Mission valley.[3]

In fall 1807 Finan McDonald, on David Thompson's instructions,
pushed up the Kootenai River, one of the Columbia's many tributaries,
into present-day Montana. There, at a spot near the modern town of
Libby, Finan established the first fur trading post in Flathead country.
Along with another Highland-born Nor'Wester, James MacMillan,
whose boyhood home had been within twelve miles of McDonald's
own father's farm in Knoydart, Finan traded for several years in this
general area. His dealings with the Flathead people, or so one of Finan's
contemporaries commented, were by no means strictly commercial.
"McDonald frequently, for the mere love of fighting, accompanied the
Flatheads in their war excursions against the Blackfeet," this observer
noted. "His eminent bravery endeared him to the whole tribe, and in
all matters relating to warfare his word was law."[4]

Although worlds apart, Scotland's Highland hills possess remarkable similarities to the mountains and valleys of Montana's Flathead country. In a scene that would've been familiar to Angus McDonald, three tepees near St. Ignatius are framed by the Mission Range in the background. COURTESY MONTANA HISTORICAL SOCIETY, HELENA, 954-583.

When, in 1821, the Nor'Westers at last agreed to merge with the Hudson's Bay Company, Finan McDonald threw in his lot with the new, and increasingly powerful, consortium. Pushing into the Snake River country in what is now south Idaho, they encountered a number of the younger traders hired by George Simpson. These men were the revitalized Bay Company's driving force, and Simpson, like so many of his subordinates, was a Highlander.

Among Simpson's recruits was Archibald McDonald, younger brother of Angus McDonald's paternal grandmother. Archibald was born in 1790 in Glencoe, a part of the Scottish Highlands to the south both of Finan's Knoydart and Angus's Torridon. He arrived in North America in 1813, when he played a key role in establishing a Highland emigrant party in the Red River area of present-day Manitoba, a settlement that would develop into the modern city of Winnipeg. On being hired by George Simpson, following the Nor'Wester-Bay Company link-up, Archibald was promptly dispatched across the prairies to take charge of operations to the west of the Rockies. It was in the course of the many years he spent there that Archibald McDonald was to compile the notes that make it possible to trace his descent—and that of his Mission valley great-nephew, Angus McDonald—from one of the leading families of the Scottish Highlands.[5]

These notes date from December 1830. They were written at Fort Langley, a Hudson's Bay Company post on the Fraser River in present-day British Columbia. They start with Archibald's statement that he was "Gillespie, Moach Aonish, Ic Iain, Ic Alan Dhu, Glenocoan." This is a phonetic rendering of a genealogical formulation originally passed on to Archibald in the Gaelic that was, until fairly recently, the common speech both of Glencoe and the rest of the Scottish Highlands. Although relatively well schooled in English, Archibald, like many Highlanders of his and later generations, could neither read nor write his own first language. But he could, and did, reproduce the sound of his Gaelic *sloinneadh*, or lineage, as he would have heard that lineage voiced often by his father.[6]

Such lineages were—and, to an extent, still are—the common currency of the Gaelic-speaking Highlands. All that is unusual about Archibald McDonald's is that its possessor set it down in writing.

The "Gillespie" with whom the Fort Langley trader began his sloinneadh was himself—Gilleasbuig being a Gaelic name which is commonly rendered into English as Archibald. "Moach Aonish," properly Mac Aonghais, means simply "son of Angus." This Angus, the sloinneadh continues, was the son of Iain, or John, in turn the son of Ailean Dubh, or Black Allan. As for Allan, he was closely related, it can be inferred from that final "Glenocoan," to men who were among the chiefs of the MacDonald clan—itself a branch of the wider Clan Donald, as Scotland's various MacDonald groupings were collectively known—which had occupied Glencoe, or so it would have seemed to Archibald, for centuries without number.

Having thus outlined his descent, Archibald—who can readily be imagined as having taken up this task to give purpose to a Fraser valley winter's evening—goes on to relate what he had been told of the ancestors he has listed. Angus—Archibald's father and the later Angus of the Mission valley's great-grandfather—is described as the principal farming tenant of Inverigan, one of several small communities in Glencoe.

His father, Archibald adds, was born in 1730. While still "but a stripling," or so his son asserts, Angus served with the largely Highland army that was defeated by British government forces at the Battle of Culloden in 1746. Having escaped unscathed from that debacle, Angus MacDonald returned to Glencoe where, in due course, he married a local woman called Mary Rankin—a surname still to be encountered in the Glencoe area.

Archibald's grandfather, John MacDonald, is said by his grandson to have been born in 1680. This means that grandfather and grandson were separated by no fewer than 110 years—something which is rendered less implausible than might otherwise be the case by Archibald's father having been fairly elderly when his fur trader son was born and by Archibald's grandfather also having become a parent at a relatively advanced age. His grandfather, Archibald goes on, "with difficulty escaped with his mother and brother, Donald, from the slaughter committed by William's troops at Inverigan" in February 1692. Here Archibald refers to the notorious massacre of the Glencoe MacDonalds by a military detachment acting on the authority, as Archibald observes, of then recently enthroned King William. The youthful Archibald had heard, no doubt repeatedly, how his grandfather had been lucky to evade death at the hands of government soldiers and how his great-grandfather, the man whom Archibald calls "Alan Dhu," had played a vital part in ensuring that other government soldiers went down to defeat at the various seventeenth-century battles that Archibald so carefully enumerates.

Although Archibald's notes succeed in conveying the wholly accurate impression that the Glencoe MacDonalds were regularly embroiled in conflict with Scotland's rulers, the Fort Langley trader, it has to be said, went slightly astray in naming "Alan Dhu" as his great-grandfather.[7]

What the Fort Langley trader did not get wrong, however, was his family's claim to kinship with Glencoe's chiefs—men who were as important to the Glencoe clan as their Nez Percé counterparts were to the Indian tribe into which Archibald's great-nephew, Angus, was one day to marry. Ailean Dubh, who is known from quite in-dependent historical sources both to have existed and to have held lands at Laroch, a little to the south of Glencoe proper, was a son of Iain Dubh, which translates as Black John. And this Black John was a son of Iain Og, Young John, a sixteenth-century chief of the Glencoe MacDonalds.

Archibald McDonald's detailed knowledge of his family tree seems to have extended little further back than the time of Ailean Dubh. That is far enough, however, to enable Archibald's ancestry to be con-nected with the fairly well-known genealogy of Glencoe's MacDonald chiefs. And this connection, once established, has the effect of push-ing Archibald's lineage into a much more distant past than he himself could access.

The sixteenth-century chief of the Glencoe MacDonalds, Iain Og, whose second son was Archibald's great-great-great-grandfather, is generally thought to have been himself descended, through some eight generations, from the similarly named Iain Og an Fhraoich, Young John of the Heather. This John, the first MacDonald to occupy lands in the vicinity of Glencoe, was both the founder of a long line of MacDonald chiefs and the man through whom those chiefs were to claim kinship with still more remote figures. Young John's father was Angus of Islay who, by means of the military assistance which he rendered to King Robert Bruce in the course of Scotland's early fourteenth-century War of Independence, helped decisively to curtail the medieval English monarchy's attempts to bring the more north-erly kingdom under England's jurisdiction. Angus of Islay's forebears were also men of substance. His father—the first known holder of the name which Angus of the Mission valley also bore—was Angus MacDonald. This Angus's father was Donald, founder—in principle anyway—of Clan Donald and son of Ranald who, in turn, was son of Somerled.

Somerled, born some 400 years before Christopher Columbus sailed from Spain to America, was a warrior-aristocrat who made him-self overlord of an extensive realm, which for a time included much of the Highland mainland as well as most of Scotland's west coast islands. To anchor one's genealogy on so prestigious an individual might be thought to have been sufficient for even the most ancestor-obsessed member of what was certainly an ancestor-obsessed society. A man's standing in his clan depended on his having suitably high-ranking forebears. But Clan Donald poets and tradition-bearers, not content with tracing their people's beginnings to Somerled and his grandson, Donald, claimed customarily that Somerled, who died in 1164, was himself descended from an infinitely more shadowy figure—an Irish hero-king, called Conn of the Hundred Battles by Highland storytellers, who was said to have lived as much as 1,000 years earlier.

Here history admittedly becomes confused with legend. But this account of Angus of the Mission valley's remote origins need not, for all that, stop with Somerled. The early part of Somerled's own genealogy, as regularly recited in the Scottish Highlands of some centuries ago, is undoubtedly incomplete and possibly fictitious. The seven or eight names that precede Somerled's in that particular formulation are a very different matter—"the genealogy of Somerled's ancestors," according to authoritative researchers in this area, being "almost certainly authentic back to Gofraid, son of Fergus, who . . . came over to Scotland from Ireland" in 835.[8]

While it would be hazardous to insist on the absolute dependability of the extraordinarily long lines of descent that have been traced in preceding paragraphs, these lines, because of the comparatively detailed nature of the evidence on which they rest, are by no means implausible. There is clearly a possibility, perhaps even a probability, of Gofraid, son of Fergus, having been the ancestor—across more than 1,000 years and across some three dozen generations—of the present-day Flathead Reservation's McDonald family. But even if these Indian people's Scottish pedigree is not quite as here suggested, the McDonald family's roots clearly go deep into Clan Donald. These roots go equally deep into the Nez Percé and several other Indian tribes. Not the least fascinating aspect of the McDonald story, therefore, is the way in which the history of this single family encapsulates the destruction of two traditional, or tribal, societies—first that of the Scottish Highlands, then that of the American West.

"O children of Conn, remember hardihood," the men of Clan Donald were urged by one of their bards in a Gaelic war-incitement that contains repeated references to the long-dead soldier king from whom Glencoe's chiefs claimed descent.

> O children of Conn, remember hardihood. . . . Be watchful, be daring, be dexterous, winning renown; be vigorous, pre-eminent; be strong. . . . O children of Conn of the Hundred Battles, now is the time for you to win recognition, O raging whelps, O sturdy bears, O most sprightly lions, O battle-loving warriors, O brave, heroic firebrands, the children of Conn of the Hundred Battles.[9]

Whether in John of the Heather's time or later, sentiments of this sort would have been warmly appreciated in Gaelic-speaking Glencoe where the traditions of Clan Donald were always carefully nurtured. Such sentiments would have been appreciated, too, in much of the rest of the Gaelic-speaking Highlands. But from the perspective of more southern or Lowland parts of Scotland, where Gaelic ceased to be spoken during the middle ages, Highland clans and all they represented seemed increasingly alien, even threatening. Lowlanders, a Scottish churchman observed as early as the 1380s, were "domesticated and cultured." Highlanders, though, were "untamed people." And during the fifteenth century, as this type of distinction between a "civilized" south and a "wild" north began to be made routinely by Scotland's Lowland rulers, it was inevitable that these rulers should have begun to behave as if their more and more acrimonious dealings with the Highland clans had something of the character of a conflict between good and evil—with Lowlanders, needless to say, representing the forces of enlightenment and with Highlanders, just as predictably, cast in the role of agents of the devil.[10]

The eventual results of such thinking are plain to see in the opinions held about Highlanders by James VI, the Scottish monarch who, following the union of the two countries' crowns in 1603, became England's king as well as Scotland's. James was typical of Lowland Scots in thinking Highlanders "utterly barbarous"—not least in their conspicuous lack of enthusiasm for the Protestant faith that had been firmly established in southern Scotland in the course of the

sixteenth century. Because Highlanders lacked "religion and humanity," King James commented, they were "void of all fear . . . of God."
Some were "cannibals." Others were collectively responsible, or so it
was alleged by the king and his ministers, for the "most detestable,
damnable and odious murders, fires, ravishing of women, witchcraft
and depredations."[11]

These sentiments have a great deal in common with the views that
a number of King James's English subjects were just then beginning
to express about the Native Americans they had encountered in the
course of England's early colonizing ventures in places like Virginia
and Massachusetts. It is not at all surprising, therefore, that there
are striking similarities between what was done to Highlanders and
what was done to American Indians on the orders of the Scottish and
English politicians who, from this point forward, were looking to gain
more and more control over both these sets of "savages."

When King James commented that parts of the Highlands should
ideally be taken over by Lowlanders and that this should be accomplished "not by agreement with" Highlanders "but by extirpation of
them," he was advocating a course of action which—in the seventeenth century and later—would have been endorsed by the numerous whites to whom North America's indigenous peoples were simply
so many obstacles in the way of their own settler society's expansion.
And when James's Scottish ministers decreed in 1616 that the Gaelic
language, being "one of the principal causes of the continuance of
barbarity" in the Highlands, should be "abolished and removed," they
were espousing attitudes of a kind that would influence white thinking about Indian culture well into the twentieth century.[12]

Because Highlanders, like Indians, were not thought to be part of
civilized society, Highlanders, like Indians, could be treated in ways
that would otherwise not have been countenanced. That is why men
who answered ultimately to King William were able to give orders of
the type issued in February 1692 to Captain Robert Campbell, commander of a military unit then recently arrived in Glencoe. Campbell,
these orders ran, was "to fall upon the MacDonalds . . . and to put
all to the sword under seventy." Campbell was "to have a special
care that the old fox and his sons," meaning Glencoe's chiefs and his

immediate heirs, "do upon no account escape." Campbell was "to secure all the avenues" leading out of Glencoe with a view to ensuring
that the MacDonalds were utterly annihilated. And all of these things
Campbell was to do "by the king's special command," it being "for the
good and safety of the country that these miscreants be cut off root
and branch."[13]

The "slaughter committed by William's troops"—to borrow the
phrase the Fort Langley fur trader, Archibald McDonald, would long
afterwards apply to this government-sanctioned massacre of his people—began several hours before dawn on Saturday, February 13, 1692,
a day of snow and bitter cold. Because the Glencoe MacDonalds were
asleep when the killing started and because they had earlier hidden
away their weapons for fear they would be confiscated by troops they
had treated as their guests, Robert Campbell's soldiers encountered
practically no resistance. Alexander MacDonald, chief of Glencoe,
died as he struggled into his clothes. One bullet had entered his body.
Another had passed through his head, from the back to the front,
blowing his face apart in the process. And as the sound of musket
fire spread inexorably across Glencoe, from one township to the next,
plenty of other men, women, and children of the dead chief's clan suffered a similar fate.[14]

Not all the Glencoe people were to die, however. Among the
survivors was John MacDonald, Archibald of the Bay Company's
grandfather, then barely twelve years old. Precisely where John, his
brother, and his mother headed on fleeing their Inverigan home—
which Captain Robert Campbell had made his headquarters—
Archibald did not say. But the family had relatives among a neighboring clan, the Stewarts, in whose country, the district known as
Appin, a number of Glencoe folk are known to have found refuge. It is
probable, therefore, that the Inverigan MacDonalds—twelve-year-old
John among them—struck out across the hills to the south of Glencoe
and, by way of passes called Glen Duror and Glen Creran, came down
eventually into Appin. That is no mean journey to undertake in summer. On the February day in question, a day that had already brought
so much terror, it is little short of amazing that women and children
were physically able to walk so far across this rough terrain in the

most appalling weather. "The mountains," as was remarked by the author of one early account of what confronted the Glencoe massacre's survivors, "were covered with a deep snow, the rivers impassable, storm and tempest filled the air . . . and there were no houses to shelter them within many miles."[15]

The 1692 killings, for all their horror, failed to cow the Highlands. As late as 1745, Highlanders were able to mount a rebellion that momentarily threatened the existence of the British state, created in 1707, by the merging of Scotland with England. Despite its initial successes, however, that rebellion ended in total defeat at the Battle of Culloden in April 1746. And Culloden was followed by the virtual disintegration of the Highland clans.

This disintegration was as inevitable—and had many the same causes—as the collapse, 100 or so years later, of the American West's Indian societies. The civilization that was coming into existence in eighteenth-century Britain—and which, in the course of the next century, was to become dominant in most other parts of the world also—was utterly intolerant of older forms of social organization. This civilization, founded on trade and, increasingly, on industry, was predominantly urban in character, and consequently looked to land primarily as a source of the commodities—whether foodstuffs or other raw materials—that its burgeoning cities required in ever larger quantities. It followed, this new civilization being universal in its impact, that land had everywhere to be reorganized; that it was no longer sufficient for the Scottish Highlands to be given over to subsistence agriculture of the sort that had been practiced by the area's clans; that it was no longer sufficient either for the American West, a region that possessed many more natural resources than the Highlands, to remain the exclusive preserve of its indigenous peoples.

Thus, it came about that the Highlands, during the decades following Culloden, were made wholly subordinate to the economic and other needs of Britain's urban centers. The American West, for all its comparative remoteness from such centers, had begun, by the start of the nineteenth century, to be affected by forces of the kind that were transforming the Scottish Highlands. And it was indicative of the global nature of these events that Highlanders who were set adrift, so to speak, by what happened to their homeland—men like Finan McDonald, Archibald McDonald, and Angus McDonald—should have become the means, very often, by which the lives of the West's Indian peoples were, in turn, to be altered irrevocably.

One of the few aspects of clanship to survive Culloden and its aftermath was the huge importance that Highlanders had always attached to ties of kinship. Hence the extent to which organizations like the North West Company and the Hudson's Bay Company—organizations run largely by men of Highland extraction—became, in effect, commercialized clans in which sons followed fathers, nephews followed uncles, and cousins followed cousins into the fur trade. The McDonalds—Finan, Archibald, and Angus—constituted one such dynasty, its most junior member, the man who was born in Torridon in 1816 and who was to die in the Mission valley more than seventy years later, joining the Hudson's Bay Company in 1838.

In 1839, a year after arriving in North America, Angus McDonald made his way to Fort Colville (shown here in 1860) on the Columbia River, where his great-uncle Archibald McDonald was in charge. COURTESY LIBRARY OF CONGRESS, LC-USZC4-11422.

Having sailed from Scotland to Hudson Bay that summer, Angus McDonald wintered at York Factory prior to traveling, in the course of the following year, to Fort Colville, on the Columbia River, where his great-uncle, Archibald McDonald, was then in charge. From Fort Colville, in the spring of 1840, Angus went south into the Snake River country, which had been opened to the fur trade by one more of his kinsmen, Finan McDonald. That year's fall found Angus in Fort Hall, a Bay Company post located on the southern bank of the Snake River at a spot some seventy miles north of the present-day border between Idaho and Utah.

Fort Hall was one of those places where the Bay Company's trading activities overlapped with those of the company's deadliest rivals, the American mountain men who were pushing across the Rockies from the east and who regarded the British-owned Bay Company as emblematic of everything that the Revolutionary War had been waged

A historical marker locates the site of the original Fort Hall (1834-1856) near the Snake River in today's eastern Idaho. COURTESY NATIONAL PARK SERVICE.

Joe Meek (1810-1875), a Virginian who came west in 1828 with the Rocky Mountain Fur Company, later settled in the Tualatin Valley, Oregon. JOSEPH BUCKTEL, COURTESY MONTANA HISTORICAL SOCIETY, 943-836.

against. "Mr McDonald has perilled his life in support of the company's rights in squabbles with some of the Rocky Mountain men," one of Angus's superiors noted. But by no means were all of Angus's dealings with his American counterparts to be conducted in this climate of hostility.[16]

Fort Hall, in Angus's recollection, was "a four-sided establishment," built of adobe, or sun-dried mud, and with "a large, strong horse park on the north side of it." There were generally some 200 or 250 horses on hand at Fort Hall, Angus reckoned. It was a measure of the general lawlessness of the time that the horses, as Angus put it, "were always attended with a horse guard of one man, who sometimes had another with him, who stayed with them day and night."[17]

Fort Hall's horses were much needed by Angus and the other Bay men stationed at what was rapidly becoming, for all its apparent remoteness, a leading communications center. From Fort Hall, Angus remembered, trapping parties were sent for hundreds, even thousands, of miles north, east, and south: in the direction of the Flathead country; toward the upper reaches of the Missouri in present-day North and South Dakota; and down the Green and Colorado Rivers into present-day Utah and Arizona.

Fort Hall, then, was something of a rendezvous point for all kinds and varieties of people. It was while Angus McDonald was on the fort's staff, for instance, that emigrant parties in their covered wagons began to treat Fort Hall as a useful staging post on what would soon be known as the Oregon Trail. Mountain men like Joe Meek—still calling the Bay Company "the North West" in unconscious tribute to the Nor'Westers of twenty or more years before—came regularly to Fort Hall to buy the few pieces of equipment they could not make themselves. And Indians, as Angus commented in his occasionally old-fashioned English, "did often stay there"—the Snake country being one of the favored hunting grounds of the Nez Percé.[18]

Among those Indians was the woman Angus McDonald married in 1842 at a civil ceremony performed by the Bay Company's senior representative at Fort Hall, Richard Grant. This woman's name was Catherine. And her life, even more than Angus's own, was bound up with the fur trade—to which, in a sense, Catherine owed her very existence. In the United States census returns of 1860, Catherine McDonald's age is given as forty-five. Although no such information is ever wholly reliable, this suggests that Catherine was born about 1815 and that she was, therefore, of much the same age as the man she was to marry. What is certain is that Catherine's mother was Nez Percé and belonged to one of the leading families of this Indian people. Writing much later of his mother-in-law, Angus McDonald described her as "one of the last of the old royals of the Nez Percé." Rather like Angus's own Glencoe grandmother, then, Catherine's mother was descended from a long line of chiefs. And her appearance seems to have been in keeping with this ancestry. "She in her age was still fine of face and of a decidedly aristocratic style of speech and conduct," Angus commented.[19]

Through Catherine's mother the McDonald family was connected with a number of the most prominent men of the Nez Percé. Catherine's father, however, came from a very different background. Known only as Baptiste, he was one of many mixed-blood traders who had made their way into the Columbia country in the wake of the Nor'Westers. Part Mohawk in origin, Baptiste had taken part in the War of 1812—when, as also happened during the Revolutionary War, the Mohawk and other peoples making up the Iroquois Confederation tended to take the British side. "He was full of the story of the American War," Catherine McDonald was afterwards to recall of what her father had said about his part in the fighting that took place in the Great Lakes region,

> . . . and used to tell how the British ran this way and the
> Americans ran that way, how the British fought there and

Catherine McDonald (1815-1902), shown here circa 1880, was about the same age as her husband, Angus, and from a lineage of similarly high status.
COURTESY MONTANA HISTORICAL SOCIETY, HELENA, 943-628.

the Americans charged here, and sometimes how both ran away, leaving the Indians behind them. And he would then dance and sing Indian songs of the east, songs of chiefs long gone to join the dead.[20]

About a year before she married Angus McDonald at Fort Hall, Catherine accompanied her father—to whom she was very close—on a trapping and trading expedition made by 100 or more Indians and mountain men into the arid regions of the American Southwest. This was "a long trip," Angus McDonald wrote later to a friend, "the first from the Rocky Mountains . . . down by the deserts and ravines of the Colorado to the Gulf of California. My wife was there with her father and she it was and is who tells and told me these things."[21]

As was the custom with Indian mothers, Catherine entertained her children with long stories featuring events in which she herself had been involved. Because of this, as he indicated in the letter quoted in the preceding paragraph, Angus, too, became familiar with the frequently repeated tale of Catherine's Colorado River excursion—a tale that he duly took down in the ledger he kept for such purposes and which is partly preserved today in the University of Montana library in Missoula. In its surviving version, Catherine McDonald's story bears the imprint of Angus's literary style. But the story's narrative thrust and content—not least its wealth of detail—are indubitably Catherine's own.

In the month "when the antelope were fawning," as Catherine put it, she and Baptiste joined their traveling companions, who included women and children as well as men, at "the place of gathering"—a predetermined spot just to the west of the modern Idaho-Wyoming border in the vicinity of today's Yellowstone National Park. In charge of their party was Thomas L. Smith, a veteran mountain man, who was better known as Pegleg because one of the bone-shattering accidents to which all mountain men were prone had forced him personally to amputate the limb in question just below the knee.

Pegleg Smith's foray along the line of the Colorado River was to last for several months. Its fur-gathering results are unclear. But there is some evidence that Angus McDonald, in his Hudson's Bay Company capacity, had a hand both in organizing and financing Smith's expedition. If that were so, it would go some way to explain how Catherine met her future husband. But nobody now knows the exact circumstances of their meeting; just as nobody now knows what it was exactly that attracted Angus, who must have encountered many such young women both at Fort Hall and in the course of the extensive travels he had already made across the Pacific Northwest, to this young woman in particular. Catherine, it should be stressed in this context, ought not to be imagined as anything other than supremely self-assured. Her mother's elevated social origins—together with the life she had led in her father's company—would have seen to that.

Many later-nineteenth-century Americans were to regard all alliances of Catherine and Angus's type as automatically degrading to the whites involved in them. By such Americans, then, the "squawman" and his "squaw" were generally treated with much the same mixture of condescension and contempt as was also to be heaped on their "half-breed" children—children like Catherine's and Angus's eight sons and four daughters. Such condescension and contempt, however, can seldom have been more inappropriate than in the case of Angus McDonald and his Indian wife. Both of them, after all, were the products of societies that valued an individual largely by that individual's ancestry, pedigree, and connections. When viewed from this standpoint, rather than from the perspective of people who reckoned human worth by racial categories, the marriage of Angus and Catherine was very much a marriage of equals, and of comparatively high-born equals at that—the family from which Angus was descended having occupied a position among the Highland clans that was very similar to the position occupied among the Nez Percé by the family to which Catherine belonged.

Angus and Catherine McDonald eventually moved north from Fort Hall. Angus's career, which culminated in his taking charge of all Hudson's Bay Company operations in those western territories which, during the 1840s, became part of the United States, brought him into close contact with a whole series of the soldiers and administrators whose task it was to supervise the white settlement of the West. But for all that, much of this Highland-born fur trader's time continued to be spent in the company of Indians. A particular companion was Chief Kamiakin of the Yakima people. "He was . . . a fine, well-formed and powerful Indian, standing five feet eleven in his moccasins," Angus observed of Kamiakin, "his hair, twisted down over his shoulders, of auburn color at its points, but as usual darker near the roots. His weight was about two hundred pounds, muscular and sinewy."[22]

From the Yakima chief, with whom he was "enjoying a pipe" at the time, Angus heard how Kamiakin, when a youth of fifteen, spent "five days and nights" near the summit of Mount Rainier "without food [or] water." This most "sagacious" of Indians, Angus reported, maintained that his time on Mount Rainier had been "the severest feat of his life. . . . He said that he was glad when the number of his initiating suns and nights had passed and he came down to speak again with man."[23]

What Kamiakin thus described was the "vision quest," a common rite among the West's indigenous peoples. Usually involving fasting, isolation, and meditation, such a quest provided each Indian teenager with the opportunity to search out the guardian spirit—*wyakin* this spirit was called by the Nez Percé—that would henceforth watch over his or her life. Most nineteenth-century whites regarded beliefs and rituals of this type as the rankest superstition. But Angus McDonald took a different view. The "simple yet profound theology" of the Indian, he commented, compared favorably with "anything of that kind . . . from . . . Jerusalem." All "the volumes of Christendom could not bring a more splendid dispensation" than that which Indians "enjoyed" prior to Europeans arriving in America. "As to their moral principles," Angus noted of native peoples who were routinely characterized by whites as murderous, thieving, dishonest, lazy, and untrustworthy, "I think they are ahead of the Christian."[24]

Something of how the steadily maturing Angus McDonald was regarded by his Bay Company juniors is evident in the reaction of one of those juniors, Edward Huggins, to his meeting with Angus at Fort Nisqually on the Pacific Coast in July 1855. "I had heard a good deal about McDonald and was anxious to see him," Huggins wrote.

> He was rather a good-looking man, about six feet in height, straight and slim, but . . . said to be wiry and strong. He had a dark complexion and long, jet-black hair reaching to his shoulder, and a thick, long and very black beard and moustache. He wore a dressed deerskin shirt and pants . . . and had a blackish silk handkerchief tied loosely round his neck. He was fond of telling Indian stories and legends and would sometimes keep an audience entranced when . . . telling some Indian story. . . . He was fairly educated and well up in the politics of the day. He was a good French linguist, but his native language was the Gaelic of the Scotch Highlands, and he was very fond of singing . . . Gaelic songs or verses improvised by himself.[25]

Edward Huggins may have got wrong points of detail. McDonald family tradition, for example, insists that Angus's hair was "reddish" and that his eyes were blue. What emerges clearly from Huggins's account of Angus, however, is the extent to which the latter—from Huggins's viewpoint—was "excessively fond of living the life of an aborigine." McDonald, Huggins noted critically, "would much prefer to live in a tent, or lodge, than in a house built in accordance with civilized plans."

That Angus spent a lot of time in the company of Indians—not least, of course, his wife—is undoubted. "He could talk several Indian languages," Edward Huggins reported. What Huggins probably underestimated, however, was the sheer effort Angus must have put into acquiring such fluency. He had "set to in earnest to learn the Indian language," another fur trader once commented of his own linguistic studies, "and wrote vocabulary after vocabulary." In similarly disciplining himself through countless winter evenings, Angus McDonald would have been motivated partly by commercial considerations. He had to trade with Indians, after all. But Angus, as has been indicated already, was also interested in Native American languages and cultures for their own sake. There was much "that may be learned from the campfire stories of the . . . Indians," he once observed by way of preliminary to recounting just such a campfire tale that he had been told originally "by an old Flathead chief."[26]

This Flathead, or Salish, chief was almost certainly Victor, as he was known to whites. Such was Victor's feeling for Angus, an early Montana newspaper reported, that when the chief fell mortally ill in the course of a buffalo-hunting expedition to the Great Plains in summer 1870, "he requested those who surrounded his deathbed to give his old warhorse to Mr McDonald as a present from a dying friend."[27]

Victor, it seems likely, was present in 1850 when Angus—at a spot near the present-day town of Polson on what was five years later to become the Flathead Reservation—took part in the Indian ceremonial he called the San-ka-ha. This was "the red man's farewell," Angus explained, "before he leaves for battle." To have heard the *San-ka-ha* song "sung by five or six hundred voices in a calm, starry night," Angus went on, had been a "rare thing." What had been still rarer was to be given the chance to participate in such an event. "I stripped with the leading men," Angus recalled, "painted with vermilion the grooves and dimples of my upper body, mounted on my black buffalo charger with my full eagle-feather cap and cantered round and round . . . keeping time to the song."[28]

More than a century after Angus's death, one of his Indian grandsons, the late Charlie McDonald, a Salish tribal elder, said this about his grandfather: "In all his trading and everything else with Indians, he was always fair with them and, I guess, more or less leaning in their favor most of the time. That's why they all respected him and why he got along so good with the different tribes wherever he went."[29]

From Chief Victor, Charlie explained, Angus obtained permission, first, to construct in the Mission valley the Hudson's Bay Company

Named in honor of Angus McDonald, McDonald Peak (9,820 feet) is the tallest summit in the Mission Range. C. D. WALCOTT, COURTESY U.S. GEOLOGICAL SURVEY, WCD000675B.

post that became known as Fort Connah and, second, to establish, on a site immediately adjacent to the post, the house which—following Angus's retirement from the Bay Company in 1871—became the McDonald family home. There Angus developed a successful ranching operation. There he entertained the Indian friends who continued to be his most regular visitors. Among his favorite guests, Angus wrote, was Catherine McDonald's close kinsman, Eagle from the Light, a "most eloquent . . . old blood," as Angus described this aging chief. "From him I learned many an item about the Nez Percé," he added.[30]

His many bonds with the Nez Percé were to make the Nez Percé War of 1877 a peculiarly agonizing experience for Angus McDonald—the more so as a part of that war, which had begun in Idaho but had spilled over into Montana on the Nez Percé crossing the Bitterroot Mountains, was conducted within a day's ride of the McDonald home in the Mission valley.

The Hudson's Bay post established by Angus McDonald in the Mission valley became known as Fort Connah. MCKAY, COURTESY MONTANA HISTORICAL SOCIETY, HELENA, 947-203.

For most of its Indian participants, the Nez Percé War ended, some five months after the conflict had begun, with their surrender to the United States military in the Bear Paw Mountains of north-central Montana. One Nez Percé detachment, however, took advantage of the cover provided by night and a swirling snowstorm to escape the encircling soldiers. At this group's head was a veteran chief called White Bird. His aim, White Bird told the few dozen men, women, and children who accompanied him, was to reach the Canadian border, just forty miles to the north. Once across the border, White Bird went on, he hoped to make his way to the camp of Sitting Bull, the Sioux chief who had himself escaped into Canada in the aftermath of the crushing defeat that he had famously helped to inflict on General George A. Custer and his Seventh Cavalry in 1876.

"I felt that I was leaving all that I had," one of the women who followed White Bird said afterwards. "But I did not cry. You know how you feel when you lose kindred and friends through sickness. . . . You do not care if you die. With us it was worse. Strong men, well women and little children killed and buried. They had not done wrong. . . . We had only asked to be left in our homes, the homes of our ancestors. Our going was with heavy hearts, broken spirits. . . . All lost, we walked silently on into the wintry night."[31]

Duncan McDonald, Angus's son, dressed in full regalia for a portrait on his horse in 1895. Catherine McDonald is seated in the tent at far left.
COURTESY MONTANA HISTORICAL SOCIETY, HELENA, 954-538.

In much the same spirit, and in much the same cheerless state of mind, the survivors of the Glencoe massacre nearly 200 years earlier had slipped into the snow-covered hills above their devastated townships. And just as the MacDonalds who survived that night of killing were taken in by neighboring clans, so White Bird and his people were to be cared for by the Sioux.

It was well into their journey's "second sun," according to a further survivor of these events, when White Bird's party "crossed the border into Canada." There they bivouacked. "Next morning," this same survivor remembered, "we had not gone far when we saw Indians coming." These Indians were Sitting Bull's men. They warmly welcomed the Nez Percé refugees and led them into Sitting Bull's camp where the arrival of White Bird's people—who, as one of them later recalled, had gone "five suns without food"—was watched, not without compassion, by an officer of the Royal Canadian Mounted Police. Hunger and frostbite had added terribly to the sufferings of the many members of White Bird's group who had been more or less seriously wounded, this officer reported. "Some were badly shot through the body, legs and arms," he observed. One woman, the mountie added, had been "shot in the breast and the ball had turned upward, passing through the side of her head. Despite her condition, she valiantly rode a small pony with a child strapped on her back."[32]

The Sioux were by no means the natural allies of the Nez Percé, the two peoples having warred more than once. But Sitting Bull, it appears, was more than ready to forget all such enmities in the face of the white threat to the last vestiges of Indian independence. "We, too, have lost our country by falsehood and theft," the Lakota chief told White Bird. "If I had known you were surrounded by soldiers at [the] Bear's Paw Mountains," Sitting Bull continued, "I certainly would have helped you. What a pity that I was not there with my warriors. But now you are here and, as long as you are with me, I will not allow the Americans to take even a child from you without fighting for it."[33]

All this, and much more, White Bird told a young kinsman who joined him, as that young kinsman put it, by the "campfires in the Sioux camp." This close relative of Chief White Bird was afterwards to write the story of the Nez Percé War from the Nez Percé point of view. His name was Duncan McDonald. He was the son of Angus and Catherine McDonald. And it should surely be noted in this context that he was the great-great-great-grandson of John MacDonald who, as a little boy in February 1692, had fled from the soldiers whose mission it was to kill Glencoe's MacDonald chief and all his clan.

Neither this article nor the book on which it is based could have been written without the present-day McDonald family's support and encouragement. It was of no small importance to this article's author, therefore, that he was able, in June 1997, to offer hospitality in his home in Scotland to Dr. Joe McDonald, president of the Salish Kootenai College on the Flathead Reservation, and to Joe's wife Sherri. In the course of his stay in Scotland, Joe McDonald, Angus

McDonald's great-grandson, visited both Torridon and Glencoe. He also gave a well-received presentation on the work of his college to the staff and students of Sabhal Mor Ostaig, an educational institution that is attempting to do for Scotland's Gaelic language and culture what Salish Kootenai College and similar institutions aspire to do for the Indian languages, cultures, and traditions of the American West. To have been associated with Joe McDonald's visit to the Scottish Highlands, then, was to have had a very pleasing sense of a circle being completed.

This article originally appeared in *Montana, The Magazine of Western History,* Winter 1997.

James Hunter is Professor Emeritus of History at the University of the Highlands and Islands (UHI) in Scotland. Between 2005 and 2010, he was director of the UHI Center for History. The author of twelve books about the Highlands and about the region's worldwide diaspora, Hunter has also been active in the public life of the area. In the mid-1980s, he became the first executive director of the Scottish Crofters Union, which campaigns on behalf of the north of Scotland's smallholders. Later he served for six years as chairman of Highlands and Islands Enterprise, a regional development agency. In the course of a varied career, Hunter has also been an award-winning journalist. He regards the time he spent with the McDonald family on the Flathead Reservation as one of his most interesting and rewarding experiences.

NOTES

1   The spelling of Highland surnames has varied greatly over the centuries. This article employs the spellings favored by the individuals it names.

2   Angus McDonald, "A Few Items of the West," ed. F. W. Howay, William S. Lewis, and Jacob A. Meyers, *Washington Historical Quarterly,* 8 (July 1917), p. 194; Ross Cox, *Adventures on the Columbia River,* 2 vols. (London, 1831), 1, pp. 348-349.

3   Cox, *Adventures on the Columbia River,* 1, p. 349; J. A. Meyers, "Finan

McDonald: Explorer, Fur Trader and Legislator," *Washington Historical Quarterly*, 8 (July 1922), pp. 196-208.

4 Peter C. Newman, *Caesars of the Wilderness: The Story of the Hudson's Bay Company*, 2 vols. (London, 1988), 1, p. 278; John Fahey, *The Flathead Indians* (Norman, 1974), p. 28; *Dictionary of Canadian Biography*, 12 vols. (Toronto, 1991-1996), 8, pp. 583-584; Cox, *Adventures on the Columbia River*, 1, pp. 355-357; Dale Lowell Morgan, *Jedediah Smith and the Opening of the West* (Lincoln, 1953), p. 122.

5 On Archibald McDonald's involvement in the Red River settlement, see James Hunter, *A Dance Called America: The Scottish Highlands, the United States and Canada* (Edinburgh, 1994), pp. 172-197. Previous writers have stated that Angus McDonald was Archibald McDonald's nephew. This omits a generation. See, for example, Albert J. Partoll, "Angus McDonald: Frontier Fur Trader," *Pacific Northwest Quarterly*, 42 (April 1951), pp. 138-139.

6 Jean Murray Cole, *Exile in the Wilderness: The Biography of Chief Factor Archibald McDonald, 1790-1853* (Don Mills, Ontario, 1979), p. 6. For the main text of Archibald's family note, see William S. Lewis, "Archibald McDonald: Biography and Genealogy," *Washington Historical Quarterly*, 9 (April 1918), p. 94.

7 Lewis, "Archibald McDonald," p. 94. See also A. MacDonald and A. MacDonald, *The Clan Donald*, 3 vols. (Inverness, Scotland, 1896-1904), 3, pp. 216-226.

8 W. D. H. Sellar, "The Origins and Ancestry of Somerled," *Scottish Historical Review*, 45 (1966), pp. 123-142; J. W. M. Bannerman, "The Lordship of the Isles: Historical Background," in K. A. Steer and J. W. M. Bannerman, *Late Medieval Monumental Sculpture in the West Highlands* (Edinburgh, 1977), p. 201.

9 Derick S. Thomson, *An Introduction to Gaelic Poetry* (London, 1974), pp. 30-31.

10 Ranald Nicholson, *Scotland: The Later Middle Ages* (Edinburgh, 1974), pp. 205-206.

11 David Harris Willson, *King James VI and I* (London, 1956), p. 119; Paul Hopkins, *Glencoe and the End of the Highland War* (Edinburgh, 1986), p. 18; William C. MacKenzie, *History of the Outer Hebrides* (Edinburgh, 1974), pp. 174-196.

12 Hopkins, *Glencoe*, p. 19; A. I. Macinnes, "Scottish Gaeldom," in *New Perspectives on the Politics and Culture of Early Modern Scotland*, ed. John Dwyer, Roger A. Mason, and Alexander Murdoch (Edinburgh, 1982), p. 62.

[13] John Prebble, *Glencoe: The Story of the Massacre* (London, 1968), p. 203.

[14] Lewis, "Archibald McDonald," 9, p. 4; Prebble, *Glencoe: The Story of the Massacre*, pp. 211-220.

[15] Lewis, "Archibald McDonald," p. 94; Hopkins, *Glencoe*, p. 338; J. Drummond, ed., *Memoirs of Sir Ewen Cameron of Locheil* (Edinburgh, 1842), p. 321.

[16] Edwin E. Rich, ed., *The Letters of John McLoughlin from Fort Vancouver to the Governor and Committee*, Third Series, 1844-1846, 3 vols. (Toronto, 1941-1944), 3, p. 135.

[17] *Report of the British and American Joint Commission for the Settlement of the Claims of the Hudson's Bay Company*, 7 vols. (Washington, D.C., 1868), 1, pp. 151-152.

[18] *British and American Joint Commission*, 1, pp. 151-152; Frank C. Robertson, *Fort Hall: Gateway to the Oregon Country* (New York, 1963), p. 15; Louis S. Grant, "Fort Hall under the Hudson's Bay Company, 1837-1856," *Oregon Historical Quarterly*, 41 (March 1940), pp. 34-39.

[19] Partoll, "Angus McDonald: Frontier Fur Trader," p. 142; Note in Angus McDonald's hand, commencing "Died 3rd November," undated (hereafter Angus McDonald Note), SC 429, Duncan McDonald Papers, Montana Historical Society Archives, Helena (hereafter MHS Archives). Catherine McDonald's tombstone in the Mission valley gives her age in 1902 as seventy-five, making her fifteen years old at the time of her marriage.

[20] Winona Adams, ed., "An Indian Girl's Story of a Trapping Trip to the Southwest about 1841," *Frontier*, 10 (May 1930), pp. 338, 343. Adams used original text by Angus McDonald, SC 81, Angus McDonald Papers, University of Montana Library, Missoula.

[21] Angus McDonald to Hiram A. Knowles, May 1, 1878, MC 2, Hiram Knowles Papers, MHS Archives (hereafter Knowles Papers).

[22] McDonald, "Items of the West," p. 228.

[23] Ibid., pp. 228-229.

[24] Angus McDonald to Hiram A. Knowles, July 1, 1878, Knowles Papers; Angus McDonald Note.

[25] "The Story of the Coming of the Hudson's Bay Company Brigade," undated, pp. 4760-4761, Edward Huggins Papers, University of Washington Library, Seattle.

[26] Ibid.; Alexander Ross, *Adventures of the First Settlers on the Oregon or Columbia River* (Chicago, 1923), p. 159; Deerlodge, Montana, *New Northwest*, May 24, 1878.

27 Missoula, Montana, *Missoula and Cedar Creek Pioneer*, November 3, 1870.

28 McDonald, "Items of the West," pp. 191-192; J. F. McAkear, *The Fabulous Flatheads As Told to Sharon Bergman* (1962; Polson, Mont., 1988), p. 17.

29 Charlie McDonald, conversation with author, August 20, 1994.

30 Angus McDonald to Knowles, October 7, 1877, Knowles Papers.

31 Clifford E. Trafzer, *The Nez Percé* (New York, 1992), p. 88.

32 Lucullus Virgil McWhorter, *Yellow Wolf: His Own Story* (1940; reprint, London, 1977), p. 153; Bruce Hampton, *Children of Grace: The Nez Percé War of 1877* (New York, 1994), pp. 299-300; Robert M. Utley, *The Lance and the Shield: The Life and Times of Sitting Bull* (New York, 1993), p. 193; L. V. McWhorter, *Hear Me, My Chiefs! Nez Percé History and Legend*, ed. Ruth Bordin (Caldwell, Idaho, 1992), 509.

33 Duncan McDonald, "Through Nez Percé Eyes," in *In Pursuit of the Nez Percés: The Nez Percé War of 1877 as reported by Gen. O. O. Howard, Duncan McDonald, Chief Joseph*, ed. Linwood Loughy (Wrangell, Alaska, 1993), pp. 272-273.

"Just Following the Buffalo":
Origins of a Montana Métis Community

— Martha Harroun Foster

By the 1840s, the once flourishing beaver trade was clearly in decline, partly because of over-trapping of the animal in certain areas, but primarily because of changing styles of fashion. Silk, which was now available from sources in Asia, had replaced beaver as a sign of high fashion. As the market demand for beaver pelts began to fall off, the fur trade itself began to shift from the high mountain valleys and streams of the West out onto the grasslands of what would eventually be known as eastern and central Montana, where buffalo still roamed in considerable numbers.

The expansion of the buffalo robe trade by the 1840s drew hunters from many different backgrounds. Initially, most were Native American; after all, Plains Indians for generations had turned to the great buffalo herds as a primary source of food, clothing, and materials for shelter. One group that was especially connected to the buffalo robe trade were the Métis, the subject of the following essay. The Métis are a blended people who can trace their roots back to the Great Lakes region and the Red River Valley that straddles the U.S.-Canadian border. Over time, they developed a unique cultural mix that drew upon European, Euro-American, and Indian practices and traditions to create their own vibrant communities.

Historian Martha Harroun Foster focuses primarily on a Métis community known as Spring Creek that settled in the Judith Basin of central Montana to illustrate important themes in Métis history. Viewing the story through the lens of ethnicity, her essay captures the vitality and generosity that were markers of this community. Unfortunately, as time passed and more Euro-Americans began to settle in the Judith Basin and in central Montana as a whole, the Métis were confronted with challenges that were difficult to overcome. The richness of their cultural traditions and their long-standing ties to the land notwithstanding, they often became the victims of discrimination and prejudice. They were sometimes accused of being "foreigners"—that is, Canadians— even though many were born in the United States. They were often denigrated for being of Indian or mixed-blood descent. That they would be able to maintain their sense of identity over many generations in the face of such challenges serves as testimony to the strength of their cultural traditions.

By 1879, the vast buffalo herds were all but gone from the Great Plains. Many of the remaining animals had moved south from the Milk River of northern Montana and Alberta into the Judith Basin of central Montana. In these rich grasslands, for a few more years, life went on as it had for centuries. Following the buffalo came many Indian bands, as well as Métis who had been hunting on the Milk River for decades. A buffalo-based economy had brought prosperity to the Native people of the Plains. The animals provided essential food and materials in addition to products for trade.

For Métis people, buffalo had replaced beaver as the backbone of their fur trade economy. Their production of robes for the eastern markets and pemmican for the Hudson's Bay and American fur companies provided the economic base of a growing number of communities spreading westward from the Red River of Manitoba, Minnesota, and North Dakota. Among the people moving into central Montana was a group of Métis families who would settle where the old Carroll Trail crossed Spring Creek in the gentle hills watered and protected by the Judith, Moccasin, and Snowy Mountains. Here they would found a Métis community, the Spring Creek settlement (Lewistown), where their descendants still live today.[1]

The Spring Creek band's Métis roots go far back into the fur trade history of what is today Canada, the Great Lakes, and the upper Mississippi River drainage. Over the years, their ancestors, like other children of European and Indian unions, entered the fur trade. Their knowledge of both European and Indian languages and customs made them an asset to the fur trade companies. Gradually they began to develop a distinctive culture, neither Indian nor European. They maintained a characteristic village organization of long narrow lots fronting on streams and reaching back to commonly held grazing lands. They developed a language (Michif) that combined elements of Cree, French, and Chippewa, and they occupied an important economic niche centered on the buffalo trade. Their unique language, dress, music, and dance became characteristic and occupied a central position in an open, friendly, and generous social round in which Métis-style foods and holiday celebrations held a central place.[2]

Gradually, economic and environmental factors encouraged the fur trade's steady movement westward. By the early 1800s, beaver depletion decimated the traditional economic foundation of Métis communities in the Great Lakes region, upper Mississippi drainage, and eastern Canada. It was on the western Great Plains, with its plentiful supply of beaver, bison, and game, that the Métis established new communities. Here they created interconnected social and cultural centers on the rivers and streams that flow to the Red River of the North. Throughout the first half of the nineteenth century, the Red River Métis, as the mixed-descent peoples of the Red River trade area came to be known, flourished, all the while absorbing new peoples and extending their far-flung kinship networks.

The Red River trade region extended from Red Lake and Lake of the Woods in present-day Minnesota and Ontario to the Rocky Mountains on the west, and from northern Saskatchewan and Alberta south to Minnesota, the Dakotas, and Montana, including the upper Missouri River. Various unrecorded non-Indian trappers probably reached the heart of this region, the Red River drainage, in the early 1700s. By 1743, Pierre Gaultier de Varennes, Sieur de La Verendrye, had established two posts in the Red River basin, one at present-day Winnipeg and another, just to the west, near Portage la Prairie. Métis families, including many ancestors of those who would later settle near Spring Creek, steadily moved into the area as beaver and the market for their skins disappeared. More and more families turned to the buffalo trade, especially of pemmican and robes. But a buffalo-based economy has unique requirements, including the proximity of large herds. The Métis soon exhausted nearby game supplies, and individual, close-to-home hunting no longer yielded sufficient provisions for the communities. In response, by the 1830s, large-scale, organized buffalo hunts to distant areas became more prevalent. As before, meat, pemmican, and robes from these hunts supplied the Métis throughout the year, while surpluses (especially of pemmican) were sold to the Hudson's Bay Company, which provided a small but constant market.[3]

In addition to buffalo becoming scarce along the Red River, another development fundamentally changed the nature of the Red River fur trade after 1830. U.S. traders, eager for a supply of buffalo robes and other furs, opened posts on the upper (southern) Red and upper Missouri Rivers. Métis and Indian hunters found that they could make greater profits by dealing with American traders whose access to cheap water transportation on the Missouri and Mississippi Rivers made transport of bulky robes to eastern markets economical. Popular as bedding, wraps, boots, coats, and military clothing, the robes attracted American domestic and export markets eager to absorb all that the Métis produced. In response to this demand, U.S. trader Norman Kittson established a post at Pembina in 1844. Here on the upper Red River in U.S. territory, he actively courted the Canadian and U.S. Métis buffalo-robe trade. The forty-ninth parallel as yet made little difference to the hunters, who ignored it. No one enforced tariffs, nor could they in such a vast area still under Native control.[4]

With a good market established by the 1840s, the buffalo hunt took on grand proportions, becoming the principal support of many Red River Métis families. The success of the buffalo trade depended on an efficient means to move products overland to ports, especially St. Paul, Minnesota, where they could be shipped cheaply by boat or barge. Red River carts, organized into long trains, provided the Métis with a cost-effective mode of transport. Joseph Kinsey Howard, journalist and historian, wrote a classic description of this vehicle:

> The cart was built entirely of wood and the noise of its wheel hubs as they rubbed on the axle, which usually was an unpeeled poplar log, was a tooth-stabbing screech which was never forgotten by anyone who heard it; it was as if a thousand fingernails were drawn across a thousand panes of glass. . . . The Red River cart brigades never sneaked up on anybody. On a still day you could hear them coming for miles, and see the great cloud of yellow dust they raised; and if the buffalo of the plains did finally flee into holes in the ground as the Indians believed—well, it was no wonder.

Hundreds of these carts now rolled across the prairie, carrying provisions to the hunt and products to river ports.[5] But as the buffalo disappeared near the Red River, it was the western plains,

Red River carts line up on 5th Avenue in Lewistown, circa 1880.
COURTESY LEWISTOWN PUBLIC LIBRARY, CENTRAL MONTANA HISTORICAL PHOTOGRAPHS, 00273.

including the upper Missouri River drainage, that began to attract the robe trade. The Missouri, in addition to providing an inexpensive means of transportation, flowed through the heart of the Northern Plains herd. However, it was not until 1830 that Kenneth McKenzie, a former North West Company employee working for the American Fur Company at Fort Union (near the confluence of the Yellowstone and Missouri Rivers), was able to open trade along the entire length of the Missouri River. The stumbling block had always been the hostility to the United States of the Blackfeet on the northern tributaries, who traded with the Hudson's Bay Company (HBC). The Blackfeet had long resented and repelled American incursions into their trade area. To accomplish the dangerous task of meeting with the Blackfeet, McKenzie selected an experienced Métis employee, Jacque Berger, probably the father of Pierre Berger of the Spring Creek band. Berger proved an excellent choice, for he knew the Blackfeet, their customs, and their language, having traded with them while working for the HBC. With Berger, McKenzie sent a small group of French Canadian and Métis who, as French speakers, he hoped would be less offensive to the Blackfeet than English-speaking Americans. Barely surviving the dangerous mission, Berger succeeded in bringing a Blackfeet trading party to Fort Union, thereby opening that profitable trade and bringing what is today Montana into the heart of the Missouri River fur trade.[6]

By 1832, Missouri River traders shipped robes regularly out of Fort Union. After 1832, as more steamboats reached Fort Union, the transport of heavy robes became easier, cheaper, and more profitable. Estimates indicate that between 1841 and 1870, traders transported the products (robes, skins, meat, and tongues) of approximately 115,000 buffalo a year down the Missouri River, far surpassing the HBC's 17,000 a year. In 1858, Fort Benton (Montana) alone shipped close to 20,000 robes. The HBC, St. Paul markets, and the Missouri River trade allowed the Métis buffalo hunters to enjoy competitive markets and good prices.[7]

Even though the buffalo trade was moving west, Métis families continued, as they had for decades, to organize their buffalo hunts in and to set out from Pembina (North Dakota). Although they

Pierre and Judith Berger were among Métis families who settled Lewistown in 1879.
COURTESY LEWISTOWN PUBLIC LIBRARY, CENTRAL MONTANA HISTORICAL PHOTOGRAPHS, 01457.

increasingly participated in the Missouri River trade, Pembina (and later St. Joseph) remained the economic and social centers of Métis life south of the boundary. The 1850 Minnesota Territorial census (including, at that time, Pembina) shows that many of the families (or their parents) who later made up the central Montana Spring Creek band resided in Pembina. Representatives of each of the Spring Creek extended families (which included the relatives of married women and the in-laws of their sons and daughters) were in residence during September 1850. For example, Judith Wilkie Berger, daughter of respected elder and hunt chief Jean Baptiste Wilkie, her husband, Pierre Berger, and their children lived in the Pembina district. This large family later provided the core and leadership of the Spring Creek band. Also included in the census were Judith's father and her mother, Amable Azure. Their son and Judith's brother, Alexander Wilkie, also joined the Spring Creek band in the company of his daughters' families. Catherine Charette and her husband, Peter Laverdure, were members of the band as were their daughters Virginia (whose husband, Francis Janeaux, became the band's principal trader and community leader) and Eliza (whose daughter married Janeaux's employee, Paul Morase). Nearby lived Michel and Magdelaine Klyne, the parents of Ben Kline, another of the band's traders. Two houses away from the Klynes, Isabell McGillis and her husband, Edward Wells, resided. Their son, daughter-in-law, and grandchildren also joined the band. Joseph Fagnant, half-brother of Charlotte Adam Lafountain (mother and sister of several band members), and his wife, Marguerite, were neighbors of Judith and Jean Baptiste Wilkie.

The Fagnant's daughter, Madeline, married Joseph Larocque and accompanied cousins and other relatives in the band to Spring Creek in 1879. These extended families living in the Pembina district in 1850 included representatives of all the original Spring Creek band families and associated traders. They participated at the heart of Pembina community life, but as the buffalo grew scarce, many would be among those to move west.[8]

Moving West

By the mid-1860s, while the prices received for robes climbed and hunting increased, the buffalo disappeared from the Red River vicinity. Many observers had been commenting on the shrinking range of the herds for years. The failure of the animals to return to the immediate area of Red River Settlement underlay tensions that resulted in the Pemmican War of 1814-1816. By 1857, the Plains Cree of the Qu'Appelle River complained of the scarcity of buffalo, and again in 1858 the Cree reported the buffalo "very scarce."[9]

The Métis hunters had no choice but to move farther and farther west. At first, the wintering sites on the plains of Saskatchewan, Alberta, and Montana were temporary communities where families lived in lodges. Occasionally, they would build rough cabins, but as these camps lasted only as long as the herds remained nearby, they would abandon the sites after a winter or two. The camps varied in size, as did the hunting bands that occupied them. Sometimes just one extended family traveled together; other times several bands, as many as 200 individuals, would congregate.

Band membership constantly shifted as groups broke up and re-formed.

Gradually it became easier to remain near the herds year round, far west of the Red River. The Métis spent summers following the herds, making jerky and pemmican from the meat. In the fall, after the buffalo coats became prime, the families went out again for robes and fresh meat. In 1873, George Dawson, a member of the United States-Canadian boundary survey, noted Métis wintering camps at Wood Mountain and Cypress Hills, and along the Milk River and the Whitemud (Frenchman's) River. Dawson described a summer camp that resembled the hunting camps of the 1840s. The circle arrangement with the carts tightly side by side, trams outward, protected the band, their stock, and their supplies. Priests often accompanied the hunting parties to say Mass, perform marriages, and educate the children.

In the winter, the band that Dawson observed moved to Wood Mountain, where they had already erected cabins. He reported that rather than returning to Red River markets, these Métis sent their robes out on the Missouri River, fifty or sixty miles to the south.[10]

By the early 1870s, wintering sites included the older ones of Turtle Mountain, Wood Mountain, and Qu'Appelle River as well as more than a dozen others scattered throughout present-day Alberta, Saskatchewan, North Dakota, and Montana. Many of these camps grew into permanent communities, and ones such as St. Laurent (Batoche) played important roles in Métis history. Many remain Métis communities to this day. A favored wintering site, especially for the Pembina Métis and a number of their St. Francis Xavier (Red River) relatives, was along the Milk River and its tributaries. The Milk River winds across the Canadian-Montana border, through the vast semiarid grasslands of north-central Montana and southern Alberta, which was among the last refuges of the buffalo.[11]

The Milk River Years

As early as 1835, Métis were already making a living on the Milk River. Charles Larpenteur, a Fort Union employee, noted that "half-breeds" frequented the river valley, "which abounded with beaver." By 1853, the beaver were scarce, but Euro-American travelers wrote of Métis buffalo hunters pushing into the traditional territory of the Milk River peoples (Assiniboine and Gros Ventre). Large, organized bands of Métis buffalo hunters, including individuals who would later join together and move south to Spring Creek, were on the Milk River by at least 1866, when Ben Kline, a Pembina Métis (later a member of the Spring Creek band), found many Métis already living there.[12]

In 1868, Turtle Mountain Métis Baptiste Gardipee and his family left their game-depleted Dakota home and came to the Milk River accompanied by other Métis and their 400 carts. When the Gardipees reached the Milk River they found a "great camp of breeds . . . somewhere in the vicinity of where Dodson [Montana] is now." Before traveling on to Fort Benton, they spent a few weeks resting, visiting, and hunting. Eli Gardipee, the young son of Baptiste, later recorded his memories of the Milk River Métis camp.

> It was truly a happy life that these people were living. The camp was in the midst of the buffalo herds and they hunted and worked hard during the day but when night came they danced and sang the old French songs, until the late hours, arranged for many and divers horse races for the following day,—then slept the sleep of people who had no cares for the moment.[13]

Other accounts also stress the good life that the Métis led on the Milk River, recounting the fun that they had, the plentiful buffalo, and their relative prosperity. Clemence Gourneau Berger, later a member of the Spring Creek band, described her life as a winterer for the *Lewistown* (Montana) *Daily News*. Born in Pembina in 1842, she was the oldest of Red River Métis couple Joseph and Judith McMillan Gourneau's eleven children. Her parents had moved to Pembina from Red River Settlement before her birth. Clemence Gourneau married Isaie Berger, son of Pierre and Judith Wilkie Berger, at St. Joseph in 1870. After their marriage, the couple traveled extensively in Dakota, Montana, and Canada, as Clemence put it, "just camping here and there without thought of settling permanently in any place, just following the buffalo trails." Clemence's first two children were born at Wood Mountain (southern Saskatchewan) where her husband's family was hunting buffalo. They did not stay long in any one place. From Wood Mountain, they moved back to the Milk River and then to the

Cypress Hills (southern Saskatchewan and Alberta). As the herds became harder to find, they stayed longer in Montana, remaining in the Milk River area continuously for about six years before moving as part of the Spring Creek band to the Judith Basin.[14]

Clemence Berger remembered that "for . . . supplies we generally had some trader with us, like Francis Janeaux and others, who always had a supply of tea, sugar, tobacco and so forth." While the men did the hunting, "women did all the tanning of the buffalo hides, made jerky meat, pemmican and moccasins." Although her memories were pleasant, she noted:

> We endured many hardships, too. There were times when we could not find any buffalo or other game, and occasionally even water was hard to find. Yet, somehow, we were all happy and, with all our miseries, we never heard any complaints.[15]

Like many observers, she remembers Métis cheerfulness in the face of deprivation. While they "roamed the prairies," Berger noted that she and her husband were "always in the company of people of part Indian blood" who traveled in "many groups." Her portrayal is consistent with traditional Métis band structure as well as that of their Chippewa and Cree ancestors. But while band organization and lifestyle had many similarities to that of Indian relatives, Clemence Berger was careful to point out the differences between her people and the Indians:

> You might think that we lived the life of real Indians, but one thing we had always with us which they did not—[our] religion. Wherever we were we had some Jesuit missionaries with us. . . . Every night we had a prayer meeting. Just before a buffalo hunt, we would see our men on bended knee in prayer.[16]

Other accounts round out a picture of everyday life on the Milk River that underscores the separate and distinct nature of Métis community life from that of their Euro-American and Indian neighbors. The Métis had what amounted to their own organized government, much like that developed years earlier for the large buffalo hunts. Samuel O'Connell, bookkeeper for Francis Janeaux, noted that the Métis on the Milk River "had a code of laws and were governed by a council of Twelve, under their chosen [leader] Gabriel Ausur [Azure]."

The laws, he remembered, were "in some cases very severe." For example, punishment such as "flogging and confiscation of their horses, carts, buffalo, etc.," resulted if "one of their number use[d] disrespectful language towards any of the women, or girls or offer[ed] any insult." Although strict, O'Connell continued, "there [were] not many occasions to administer the law as the infractions . . . were very few."[17]

In addition to explaining camp government, O'Connell also described Métis women's dress during the period. He remembered that "their garb was quite picturesque always clean and neat." The older women "wore dark colored dresses and double width broadcloth cloaks with black handkerchiefs around their raven black hair," while the younger women and girls "wore head gear of brighter colors." The women "always wore the insignia of their faith, a german silver cross about 5 inches long."[18]

As well as noticing their distinctive dress, many visitors commented on the lively dances the Métis enjoyed. In his recollections of an 1860s Milk River camp, Métis traveler Louis Shambow, like so many commentators before him, noted what "a happy people" the Métis were and what good times they had. He reported that "one of the first things they would do when they got in a permanent camp was to build a dance house." They constructed the building from hewn cottonwood logs with hides stretched tightly over them to make a good floor for the dancing. He remembered that "the fun that we had was beyond telling." The dances were so important to the Métis community that, according to Shambow, "the Priest could do anything with them but stop [the] dancing."[19]

Recorded memories of the Milk River years are of a pleasant life, carefree and happy as long as buffalo were plentiful. Most accounts underplay the harassment by territorial officials that began almost upon arrival. Growing ill feeling toward the Métis on the part of Euro-American settlers and business people ostensibly centered on suspected illegal sales of liquor and arms to Indians. Increasingly, they saw the Métis in terms of their Indian connections and feared them as an auxiliary of the Indian community. These Montanans also questioned Métis national identity, viewing them as illegal Canadian immigrants.[20]

The problems faced by the Métis on the Milk River were compounded when, during the 1870s, greater numbers of Métis moved onto the plains of Saskatchewan, Alberta, and Montana. Several factors influenced this migration, including changing conditions in Red River Settlement after the 1869-1870 Manitoba Resistance and the scarcity of buffalo on the Red River. But the Métis presence in Montana became particularly visible because of the profitable markets located on the Missouri River. One of the trading posts, Fort Benton, became an important export point for the robes gathered in Montana, southwestern Saskatchewan, and southern Alberta. Gradually, though, as the increase in unregulated cross-border trade came to the attention of tariff collectors, the transport of robes across the boundary became both more expensive and more difficult. The Métis had traditionally avoided the ten percent duty on robes by moving them unnoticed across the unpatrolled border. By 1874, laws not only increased the duty to twenty percent but also provided more effective enforcement.[21]

Montana ranchers' and business people's fears of the Lakota also threatened the relative peace on the Milk River. The Lakota had been moving into Montana since early in the century as agricultural settlement and the disappearance of the buffalo forced them west. During the 1870s, like other peoples dependent upon the buffalo, they moved into Montana in greater numbers. Fearful and not knowing the source of the well-armed Lakotas' supplies, guns, and ammunition, U.S. government suspicion centered on Métis traders and the traffic in merchandise from Canada. The U.S. Army and reservation agents launched several investigations to uncover any Métis plot to sell provisions, guns, or ammunition to the Lakota. Though officials found no proof, by March of 1874, Brigadier General Alfred Terry had become concerned enough about supposed Métis provisioning of hostile bands that he ordered Colonel John Gibbon to "break up" the "halfbreed settlement[s]" found illegally camped within reservation boundaries. Matters only worsened for the Métis after the 1876 army defeat at the Battle of the Little Bighorn when fear of the Lakota reached epidemic proportions. Many Montanans called for the removal of all Métis in Montana regardless of their U.S. citizenship.[22]

Compounding the pressure to remove the Métis for military reasons were renewed complaints from reservation agents and U.S. trading company personnel (fearful of Métis competition in the Indian trade) demanding that the army expel all "Canadian" Métis. Tirades appeared in Montana newspapers, including the *Benton Record,* whose editor accused the Métis of carrying "on an illicit trade with hostile savages."

> These Canadian half-breeds pay no taxes; they produce nothing but discord, violence and bloodshed where ever they are permitted to locate. They are a worthless, brutal race of the lowest species of humanity, without one redeeming trait to commend them to the sympathy or protection of any Government.[23]

Accusations of illegal arms and liquor trading, of Canadian citizenship, and of sympathy for their Indian relatives created a hostile climate for Métis buffalo hunters. In response to these accusations against the Métis, the U.S. Army complained to the Canadian government about "British halfbreeds" and Indians on U.S. soil. But Canadian officials, in the person of British minister to the United States, Sir Edward Thornton, argued that since U.S. Indians and Métis were allowed to hunt in Canada, the reverse was only fair. In spite of Canadian objections, the army removed many Métis to Canada, where the Canadians disagreed as to their nationality. In 1879, for example, the Canadian Indian Commissioner complained that Americans had arrested "about 140 half-breeds" despite the fact that most of these Métis claimed U.S. citizenship. General Nelson Miles, in command of the area, defended his removal of "Red River half-breeds" and confiscation of their goods. Despite the lack of evidence, he accused them of selling arms and ammunition to the Lakota and of Canadian citizenship.[24]

At the same time, there was a great deal of confusion in both the United States and Canada not only as to the nationality of the Métis but also as to their rights as individuals. In general, those Métis who had not become enrolled members of tribes assigned to a reservation were not considered Indians or wards of either government. As non-Indians, if not already U.S. citizens, they should have been able to immigrate and register their intention to become citizens before a county judge—the same rights accorded other Canadian immigrants. But their association with Indians in the minds of both the Canadian and U.S. governments led officials to deny them basic liberties. Their civil rights were often violated in the United States during the 1870s by reservation agents and government officials such as Miles, who arbitrarily sentenced them to expulsion and destroyed their possessions without due process. Nor did they receive protection from or compensation for Indian depredations. When, for example, Lakota raiders stole the horses of several Milk River Métis bands, they faced starvation. Nevertheless, the Métis were neither compensated for their lost property, as Euro-American settlers would have been, nor did the army help them retrieve their stolen property. The Métis were on their own as far as protecting themselves from raiding Indians. On the other hand, since the Métis were not reservation Indians, they did not receive rations to get them through the winter.

Territorial and army officials had devised no fair, uniform policy that acknowledged the Métis as non-Indian citizens enjoying full rights, nor had they provided them with benefits similar to those of other Native peoples. Conservatively, there were more than 30,000 Métis in western Canada and the northwestern United States, but neither government had developed a consistent policy to deal with their rights and needs.[25]

The Spring Creek Band Moves to the Judith Basin

As the army stepped up its program to expel Canadian Métis (in their opinion any Métis who could not immediately prove their U.S. citizenship), many Métis were already leaving the Milk River region of their own accord. The number of buffalo in the area declined sharply in the late 1870s. In the summer of 1878, fires had destroyed much of the grass in the Milk River region on both sides of the boundary, causing the herds to move south toward the Judith Basin of central Montana. Consequently, Métis bands were starting to break up and move away. Some returned to Dakota Territory or Canada, while others traveled to new locations in Montana. Canada was a poor option because the buffalo had already disappeared there and many Canadian Métis and Indians were suffering from starvation. Things were not much better in the Dakotas. The Judith Basin seemed the best choice, but it was becoming crowded. Assiniboine, Cree, Blood, Gros Ventre, Piegan, Pend d'Oreille, Crow, Lakota, and Métis were already hunting in the region.[26]

It was in early May 1879 that a group of related Milk River families, under the leadership of Pierre Berger, formed what would later informally be known as the Spring Creek band and moved toward the Judith Basin. Like others, they had heard of the area's plentiful game and buffalo. The army encouraged, but apparently did not force, the families to make this decision. Nevertheless, to ensure that they reached the Judith Basin, Captain Williams of Fort Benton sent two soldiers and two civilians to accompany them. The band traveled from the Milk River to Fort Benton, where they crossed the Missouri River by ferry. They then continued on to Judith Basin accompanied as far as Cottonwood Creek by their military escort. From Cottonwood Creek the band traveled southeast to Spring Creek and camped at a site north of the Great Northern freight depot in present-day Lewistown.[27]

After the families arrived on Spring Creek, band member Ben Kline remembered that two hunters set out almost immediately to search for buffalo. From Black Butte (a prominence several miles to the east, commanding a view of the surrounding countryside) they sighted the herds. The band moved again toward the buffalo. Ben Kline noted that the hunting was good and that the men "killed lots of them." The families then continued in a southeasterly direction toward Flat Willow Creek and followed that stream west. They circled south of the Snowy Mountains to the "Gap in the West," probably what is now called Judith Gap, where the Judith River makes its way between the Snowy and Little Belt mountains. Here Ben Kline remembered that they killed so many buffalo that it took them a "whole week to dress and dry the meat." On returning to Spring Creek, they met trader Paul Morase (grandson-in-law of elder Pierre Laverdure and employee of

Janeaux) camped with his family on Spring Creek at Reed's Fort, near the present site of Lewistown. The traders had followed the hunting families to provide supplies and market their buffalo products.[28]

Ben Kline (1845-1930) was born near Devil's Lake, in today's North Dakota. COURTESY LEWISTOWN PUBLIC LIBRARY, CENTRAL MONTANA HISTORICAL PHOTOGRAPHS, 01349.

The Spring Creek band apparently left the Milk River just before public pressure to force all Métis from the area resulted in military action. In the midst of the confusion among officials and the non-Métis public as to who the Métis were racially and nationally, Colonel (soon to be General) Nelson A. Miles took matters into his own hands. In the fall of 1879, he broke up the remaining Milk River Métis camps, forcing many Métis across the border into Canada. He was concerned about raiding parties that had come down from Sitting Bull's camp north of the Canadian line during the winter. By summer, Sitting Bull's bands moved south of the boundary, where Lieutenant W. P. Clark of the Second Cavalry encountered them on Frenchman's Creek. The ensuing "sharp engagement" convinced Miles that something had to be done about the Lakota. He believed that the "location of such a large camp of hostile Sioux near the border was a menace to the peace and welfare of the citizens of the United States in that vicinity."[29]

His campaign against the Lakota involved depriving them of supplies, especially of weapons and ammunition. To this end, he informed Canadian officials that "in the future all property—horses, carts, and cargoes—of any Canadian halfbreed found trading ammunition with United States Indians will be confiscated." In spite of much evidence to the contrary, Miles assumed all the Métis on the Milk River to be "practically British subjects, living most of the time on Canadian territory." In treating the Métis as foreign arms suppliers to hostile Indians, Miles justified their expulsion and the confiscation of their goods without due process. Even later, as he faced the protests of U.S. Métis and the Canadian government, he insisted that the majority of Métis in the Milk River region were Canadian subjects.[30]

Army records are not specific on the point, but Miles did not send all of the Métis still hunting on the Milk River to Canada. He proposed to settle at least one band in the Judith Basin where game was still plentiful and the land somewhat more suitable for cultivation. The Judith Basin was also far enough from reservation land to prevent illegal trading with reservation Indians and competition over their game supplies. In this, Ben Kline's version of events differs somewhat from that of Miles. Kline maintained that Mile "rounded up the breeds along the Milk River for trading with the Sioux and gave them their choice either to go to Canada or the Judith Basin." In any case, about fifty families did travel to the Judith Basin. Kline remembers that Miles's soldiers "escorted" the families, who with their Red River carts and possessions crossed the Missouri by steamboat near the mouth of the Musselshell River. This party probably included the Wells and Ouellette families who settled with their already established relatives near Spring Creek.[31]

The army under General Miles continued its attempt to remove all Métis from the Milk River area. These efforts resulted in a dramatic but temporary disruption of the Milk River Métis communities. Soon, however, despite the army's efforts, the Métis returned across the difficult-to-patrol border, and the army grew tired of its expensive efforts to keep them north of the line. Even today, the Milk River of north-central Montana secures the northern base of an inverted triangle, reaching to Lewistown in the south, that is home to the many descendants of the Milk River bands.

The Métis experience on the Milk River illustrates how U.S. government interests used confusion over Métis ethnic and national identity to solve perceived problems without regard to rights that other citizens and immigrants took for granted. When the Métis presence became suspect or inconvenient, as it did in Montana during the Lakota troubles, Euro-American settlers and government representatives responding to their concerns emphasized the Métis' Canadian background. By ignoring their long history in U.S. territory,

Antoine Ouellette (with son) donated land for Lewistown's first cemetery.
COURTESY MONTANA HISTORICAL SOCIETY, HELENA, 944-233.

Angelique Bottineau Ouellette, wife of Antoine. COURTESY MONTANA HISTORICAL SOCIETY, HELENA, 944-234.

Montanans were able to rationalize Métis removal to Canada. Although this scheme ultimately failed, the perception of Métis as illegal immigrants lived on. Euro-Americans who settled in Montana and the Dakotas after the 1870s were celebrated as "pioneers." The Métis, who made the area home decades earlier, were labeled illegal Canadian aliens.

Spring Creek Settlement

As Métis continued to be harassed on the Milk River, the Spring Creek band settled along the tributaries of Big Spring Creek, using the area as a base from which to conduct their hunts. While they were the first Métis families to settle here permanently, they were not the first Métis to live in the area. Various other Métis had hunted and traded in the immediate vicinity decades before their arrival. Armell Creek, a few miles to the east of Spring Creek, was named for Augustin Hamell (Armell), a Métis trader and trapper who operated a trading post there around 1845.[32]

The attraction of the Spring Creek drainage for the Métis was its abundant game, protected valleys suitable for summer gardens, and the nearby buffalo herds. The area held potential for both the band's traders and the hunting families. As they settled in the fall of 1879 and spring of 1880, certain residential patterns reflecting occupational divisions became evident. The trader group built homes and a trading post on Spring Creek about three miles south of the crossing of the Carroll Trail, which ran from Carroll on the Missouri River to Helena. Francis Janeaux, leader of the traders, Paul Morase, Pierre Laverdure, and Antoine Ouellette immediately took advantage of the promising location by applying for homesteads near the post on land that is now within Lewistown city limits. By doing so they became the town's founders.[33]

The hunting families moved a few miles east, dispersing along the small tributaries of Spring Creek near hills rich in game. Much as they had done on the Milk River and in the Pembina region, these families settled in family clusters, far enough apart to ensure adequate pasture for their stock, sufficient garden or farm land, and plentiful small-game hunting territory, but not so far as to make frequent contact difficult. Relatively few of the hunting families applied for homesteads in the first years. The application process required cash for the filing fee (a rare commodity on the plains) and considerable inconvenience. Filing on homestead land entailed traveling over 100 miles to the southwest around the Little Belt Mountains and across the prairie to White Sulphur Springs, the Meagher County seat. Undertaking

Betsy Kiplin (1859-1952) married John Berger, Pierre and Judith Berger's son, in 1876 and moved to the Lewistown area three years later. COURTESY LEWISTOWN PUBLIC LIBRARY, CENTRAL MONTANA HISTORICAL PHOTOGRAPHS, 04058.

such a project required not only an appreciation of the importance of legal title, but also a need for such title. Of the hunting families, only the Bergers and Wilkies, who were experienced in Dakota Territory treaty allotments, applied for homestead land by 1883.[34]

Residence and homestead filings reflect the occupational priorities of the band. The trader families clustered closely together, surrounding the trading post and, as noted above, filed for title almost immediately after arriving. Those who farmed as well as hunted (like the Bergers and Wilkies) were more likely to file for homestead land than hunters and likely to live closer to Spring Creek. Families concentrating most exclusively on hunting lived farthest from Spring Creek and were the least likely, or the latest, to obtain land title. Residential patterns also reflect class differences within the community. The relatively prosperous traders, the band leaders, and the few skilled craftsmen filed on homesteads early and on better agricultural land closer to Spring Creek.[35]

The Berger family (that of band leader Pierre Berger) settled very soon after arrival, building cabins less than three miles east of the traders on and near Peter Berger's homestead on what was later called upper Breed Creek. Not until the following spring did the rest of the hunting families build homes, although during the winter they cut the necessary timber. Ben Kline located just to the south of Pierre and Judith Berger and their married and unmarried children, while Judith's brother, Alexander Wilkie, and his daughters' families (the LaFountains) settled to the northeast. Wilkie's two-room cabin was the largest in the area, having one room that measured twenty by thirty feet. This was quite a luxurious size for that place and time, but Wilkie planned ahead, knowing that the families would need a large room for visiting missionaries' services. Another cluster of families settled just beyond the "Berger place," closer to the Judith Mountains. These families established "a little village" near the head of Blind Breed Gulch. John B. LaFountain, husband of one of Alexander Wilkie's daughters, settled there soon after arrival. LaFountain was partially blind and his condition gave the creek its name.[36]

The band quickly established a trail around the foot of Black Butte on the east end of the Judith Mountains. Known simply as the "halfbreed trail," it led to the plains east of the Judith Mountains and to the buffalo, which were plentiful there. This trail passed the homes of the remaining band members. Joe Doney and his wife, Philomene LaFountain, and Joe Larocque and his wife, Madeline Fagnant, halfsister of Charlotte Adam LaFountain and therefore half-aunt of Philomene, located near this trail about twelve miles northeast of the Wilkies and LaFountains. Eli Gardipee and his wife, Mary Larocque (Joe Larocque's sister), made their home even farther to the northeast, at the head of Bear Creek on the northeast side of the Judith Mountains in the midst of buffalo country.[37]

Granville Stuart, an early Montana gold miner and cattleman, traveled through the area in the summer of 1880 and described both the new village and the hunters abroad in the Judith Basin. While searching for cattle-grazing land, Stuart met a large Métis hunting party with their fifty carts as they moved from McDonald to Flat Willow Creek (east of the Judith Mountains). The next day, on June 26,

Left to right, Joe Doney, Joe Fayant, and Eli Gardipee.
COURTESY LEWISTOWN PUBLIC LIBRARY, CENTRAL MONTANA HISTORICAL PHOTOGRAPHS, 01354.

he encountered forty more "carts and halfbreed families" traveling from Black Butte. Describing "carts with two very large wheels
in which the families ride," he remembered their "peculiar 'screechy'
noise that [could] be heard for miles." While visiting the Métis, Stuart
asked for information about good grazing land. One of the hunting
party, Sevire Hamlin, told him of fine pasturage in the Ford Creek area
east of Spring Creek. Stuart took advantage of this advice, and after
examining the land, established a large cattle ranch there.[38]

Earlier, in May 1880, when Stuart passed through the Spring Creek
settlement, he was favorably impressed with the village, noting that
it was "quite a settlement." He approved of the plowed fields and the
neatness of the post and homes. His only criticism was of the post's
defenses, which he found insubstantial. "The logs are small so that . . .
a bullet . . . would go right through them," he complained—an important consideration in an area where Lakota and Blackfeet horse-
stealing parties were very active, and where, just three nights before,
the Lakota had stolen thirty head of the settlement's horses. The community was far more to Stuart's liking than the rough Missouri River
trade towns, and he commented dryly that "the houses of the Red
River half breeds are in marked contrast to the posts of the whitemen
through here."[39]

That the Métis had built such a tidy and substantial settlement
so quickly is all the more remarkable since they arrived with so little. Presumably Janeaux, as a trader, was well supplied with tools,
but most families had only the axes that they always carried on their
carts. Just one of the hunting families owned a shovel. Pierre Berger,
who had experience in blacksmithing and tin working, had a few met-
alworking tools and a metal hoe, and Isaie Berger had a small number
of carpentry tools. None had furniture, few had more than one cart,
and all had only the few possessions that they were able to carry in
their carts.[40]

Cabins were especially difficult to construct with only an axe, and
the carts, being too small to haul logs, were no help in this chore. All
of the logs had to be dragged, a few at a time, out of the mountains
with a horse. Elizabeth Berger Swan described the building of the cabins and their furnishings:

Elizabeth (Berger) Swan, shown here circa 1920, was the eldest daughter of John and Betsy Berger. COURTESY LEWISTOWN PUBLIC LIBRARY, CENTRAL MONTANA HISTORICAL PHOTOGRAPHS, 07070.

Building the log cabins was quite a task . . . being they were skil-
ful with the use of an axe they made all their roofing, flooring,
framework and some furniture with smoothly hewn logs. No
one had a stove and they cooked in the fireplace builded on a
casing of small timbers and finished with a mortar, made with
a mixture of grass and dirt. When the roofing is all up in place
the cracks were filled with mortar and the top covered with
sod, for the doors and windows the framework was covered
with raw hide, was not altogether transparent, still gave plenty
light inside and was weatherproof.[41]

From such meager supplies, the Métis quickly built a community. Before long they were ready for their traditional celebrations, which had long been a part of Métis culture on the Red River. Already, by Christmas of 1880, they were celebrating in their accustomed manner. Christmas, as it had been earlier at Red River Settlement and Pembina, was a relatively quiet family day, but it began a round of visiting and dancing that lasted until New Year's. On New Year's Day, the traditional, large, community-wide parties and dances were held. The women worked for weeks cooking enough food for their guests. The entire community was welcome in each home, and groups of celebrants moved from house to house. When evening came and the meal was finished, they removed the furniture from one or two rooms to make space for dancing. Lively Métis fiddling and jigs would continue all night.[42]

Although the Spring Creek Métis maintained their traditional way of life, they also attempted to learn the customs of the trickle of Euro-American settlers making their way into the Judith Basin. They established schools almost immediately, hired English-speaking teachers, and welcomed non-Métis newcomers. Many of the Spring Creek band elders were educated and could speak and read French, as well as speak Cree, Chippewa, and Michif. Several of the younger members of the band had attended school in Pembina and could also read and speak these languages. Most could not speak English, but traders Francis Janeaux and Ben Kline could speak and read English as well as French and several Indian languages. These families valued education and made schools one of their community priorities. They organized the first school in 1880, and by the winter of 1881-1882 had hired Edward Brassey, later Lewistown mayor, to teach. Brassey lived in Janeaux's stockade and taught in a nearby cabin. The cabin had no plank flooring, and the children simply sat on the ground while Brassey managed as best he could with few books and no blackboards. Thirty children attended this early school: twenty-six Métis and four Euro-American siblings. The next year, in 1882, the community built a one-room schoolhouse with seating for thirty-six students. It was often crowded, with three students sometimes sharing the double seats.[43]

Non-Métis, including newly settled ranchers and a growing number of small-business owners, were also welcome to the Spring Creek band's religious services. The Métis families had made space and arrangements for these services from the very first. Francis Janeaux held services in his home, and Alexander Wilkie had built his log house large enough to accommodate Mass and religious instruction. A fiddler and singer, Wilkie had learned liturgical music in Pembina and St. Boniface. In his new home, he organized a church choir, which sang the old hymns in French or "Cree" (probably Michif). Visiting priests, discouraged by what they considered to be depraved behavior in such towns as Fort Benton and Carroll, were, as Joseph Kinsey Howard later described, "astonished and delighted to find this oasis of gracious worship in what they regarded as a desert of dissent and apostasy."[44]

The 1880 census provides a snapshot of Métis life in the Judith Basin while indicating some of the problems that the people faced. By the summer of 1880, the census taker (who prudently did not brave the open country—much of which was still under Indian control—to count the families temporarily away hunting) found thirty Métis families living in the Spring Creek settlement area. Some of these families supported themselves in the traditional manner, hunting buffalo and trading pemmican and robes for supplies. Many had also started farming. The relatively high proportion of farmers (as opposed to hunters) in residence on Spring Creek in mid-June is not surprising. This was still planting time in an area where the last snowstorm is very often during the first week of June. Families who were hunting that season had already left for the herds by the time that the enumerator arrived, leaving others, often older members of the community, to plant gardens and crops.[45]

Interestingly, in addition to occupation, the 1880 census provided space for the notation of race. In the Montana census, "color," as listed there, was a very subjective matter but indicated the growing tendency of Euro-Americans to view Métis as Indian and not as a distinct people with ties to both Euro-American and Indian relatives. The census taker in enumeration district 23, which included the Spring Creek area, recorded all the Métis families as Indian. Traders

Francis Janeaux and Paul Morris (Morase), who at least occasionally were identified by the community as white (or French-Canadian) but who were married to Métis women, were also described as Indian. Comparison to another community where many Métis lived suggests the subjectivity and socially constructed nature of ethnic designations in Montana. In enumeration district 3, Fort Benton, the enumerator handled the subject of "color" differently. He listed as "white" a Wells, an Ouellette (Willett), and a Laverdure family, all from Pembina and almost certainly related to the Spring Creek Métis families of the same name, while tabulating Antoine A. Janeaux and his children as white but his wife, Josephine, as Indian. On the other hand, this enumerator described the children of Robert S. Tingley as Indian even though Tingley himself was designated white (his wife, Louise, was listed as Indian). Class may have entered into designations of ethnicity in Fort Benton, where mixed-descent families had been living off and on since the 1830s. Prosperous farmers, traders, and skilled laborers were invariably listed as white, as were their children. Eli Gardipee, a teamster, therefore somewhat lower on the local social scale, was entered as "<1/2> br" and his wife as Indian. Unfortunately, they had no children to show us how the enumerator would have solved that ethnic puzzle. Enumerators in both districts listed hunters and trappers as Indian. The Wells family again illustrates the contradictions inherent in establishing racial and ethnic identity. John Wells, a sixty-four-year-old trapper found by an enumerator in the Musselshell Valley, east of the Spring Creek drainage, reported his parent's place of birth to be Ireland. Nevertheless, the enumerator entered him as Indian, as he did John's wife, Mary, and their children.[46]

Feelings about race ran high in Montana, and not everyone agreed with a family's own or the enumerator's designations. In enumerator district 4, Shonkin Creek, Chouteau County, the enumerator's original "w" (white) for Pierre (white) and Rose (Indian) Charboneau's children was heavily overwritten with a large "I."

At the side, in different writing, is a heavy black "HB" (half-breed). Obviously, three commentators had three separate opinions as to these individuals' "color."[47]

Confusion as to both their national and ethnic identity led to

A boy and girl dance in front of the Wells's family home near Lewistown. Note the man in the chair, right of center, playing fiddle. COURTESY MONTANA HISTORICAL SOCIETY, HELENA, 945-559.

constant difficulties for Métis people in Montana. While the Spring Creek Métis were in part protected from the worst abuses because of their relative prosperity, they too suffered discrimination as "breeds" and "Canadians." Continued close ties to Indian relatives and Chippewa treaty designations of some Spring Creek family members as "Pembina Chippewa Half-Breeds" only compounded confusion and led to further discrimination as Indians. This confusion exacerbated ethnic tensions when Cree and Métis from Canada sought refuge after the Northwest Rebellion in Saskatchewan; the Little Shell Chippewa (who included their Métis relatives as members) struggled to become enrolled members of the Turtle Mountain Chippewa tribe, and the Rocky Boy Chippewa and Little Bear Cree sought to avoid starvation by obtaining a reservation of their own. In the face of discrimination, the families maintained both their Métis identity and their close ties to Indian relatives. They overcame obstacles such as language and custom differences to participate in building a community and welcomed non-Métis newcomers as they arrived. They built schools and churches and taught their children English, while creating ties to central Montana. Their adaptability, as it had throughout their history, served them well and enabled them to establish a vibrant new community quickly. Despite, or perhaps even because of, the buffalo's disappearance, the Spring Creek Métis community continued to grow. With the addition of new families, the Spring Creek settlement had a population of about 150 Métis families before many Euro-Americans joined the community.[48]

By 1883, however, more Euro-American families moved to the area and gradually Métis economic and social domination ended in the newly named town of Lewistown. Recent non-Métis arrivals opened almost all the new businesses. Non-Métis began to take over the administration of the schools and even of the Catholic Church. In 1883, influential band trader and businessman Francis Janeaux, unable to meet rising debts, sold out to his creditor and supplier, T. C. Power. It is both significant to Janeaux's financial situation and symbolic of the Métis future that his business failure occurred in the same year that the last of the buffalo disappeared from central Montana.

Conclusion

From 1879 to 1883, the Métis of the Spring Creek drainage successfully established a Métis community, but the decimation of the buffalo herds and gradual control of the area by incoming non-Métis settlers precluded Métis economic, social, and political dominance in their new community. Socially, in the Euro-American mind, they were linked increasingly to their Indian relatives. While the Métis, when speaking English, respectfully referred to themselves as "half-breeds," their Euro-American neighbors came to use the word "breed" to mean something more akin to a degenerate Indian—one who is Indian but inferior to "pure bloods." In Montana, references to the Métis, as those in the 1880 census, emphasized their Indian connections more often than their Euro-American ones, ignoring their distinctive values and lifestyle. Many Euro-Americans confused the Métis and their Cree relatives, with whom they often camped and hunted.

Their ascribed legal and social identities in conflict, the Métis faced the greatest challenge of their long history, the end of the fur trade.

While the Spring Creek band welcomed and accommodated Euro-American newcomers to the most prosperous Métis community in Montana, their life in the Judith Basin had changed forever. By 1884, the Spring Creek Métis had not only lost economic control of their community, but also witnessed incoming Euro-American settlers reverse their numerical and, consequently, their political advantage. Above all, they watched in dismay as their economic base abruptly disappeared from the Plains.

That the Spring Creek Métis met the new challenges of the next century was apparent in 1979 when the Métis of Lewistown held a Centennial Celebration. The celebration honored the mixed-descent people of Montana, the Dakotas, and Canada with cultural demonstrations and a locally published history documenting their unique culture and common past. Hundreds of Métis, Indian, and non-Indian people attended events ranging from panel discussions to Métis dances, fiddling, and a powwow. Celebrations continue in Lewistown to the present in recognition of both the Métis past and their hopes for the future.

—∿∿∿—

This essay originally appeared in *Great Plains Quarterly,* Summer 2006.

Martha Harroun Foster, a longtime resident of Montana now living in Nashville, Tennessee, is Professor Emeritus of American History at Middle Tennessee State University. Her publications include We Know Who We Are: Métis Identity in a Montana Community *(2006), as well as articles examining issues of ethnic identity among people of mixed American Indian descent. These works address the nature of ethnic identity and how that identity plays out historically in the lives of individuals and kinship groups. Métis people in the United States have experienced a lack of official recognition and acknowledgment of their role in Montana and U.S. history. In addition to these studies, Foster has examined issues of gender and women's roles in traditionally matrilineal societies such as Crow, Hidatsa, and Iroquois.*

NOTES

1 The word "Indian" is preferred here rather than Native American, First Peoples, or other equally appropriate terms, especially when attempts are made to distinguish between Indian and Métis. Since the Métis are also "Native," the term Indian, even with all its colonial baggage, seems to generate less confusion. It is also the term employed historically and legally in the United States. A more troubling term is "half-breed." The word is offensive to many because of its historical and contemporary pejorative connotations. Originally, the term "half-breed" simply meant a person of mixed-Indian descent. Louis Riel, famed Métis leader, used it as the English equivalent of "métis" when speaking or writing in English. Even today, some Montana Métis use the term, respectfully, to distinguish themselves from whites or Indians. I use "half-breed" in this same sense unless exploring its historical usage. Additionally, my use of "Chippewa" (rather than Anishinaabe or other, perhaps more appropriate, self-identifiers in reference to the Ojibwa people) stems from current and historical use in Montana. Interestingly, many Montanans, both past and present, refer to all Métis, Chippewa, and Cree indistinguishably as "Cree." Finally, in any discussion of Métis people, it is necessary to distinguish between the terms "Métis" and "métis." Lowercase "métis," as employed here, refers to all people of mixed American Indian and European descent. The capitalized term "Métis" refers more specifically to an ethnic or social group that is, or is in the process of becoming, distinguishable from others.

These families, referred to here as the Spring Creek band, are also known as the Lewistown Métis. To avoid confusion with later arrivals, and since not all the families lived within Lewistown (many settled along the tributaries of Spring Creek well outside the present-day city limits), I will refer to the original related Métis families as the Spring Creek band rather than as the Lewistown Métis. It should also be noted that historically the Métis referred to their community as Spring Creek—it was Euro-American settlers who later named the town Lewistown. The term "band" is used here in the Anishinaabe sense of small groups of related families coming together for a specific purpose.

The Spring Creek families and their relatives who remained on the Milk River formed the kinship network that has come to be known as the Lewistown/Havre/Glasgow triangle or the Lewistown/Milk River triangle. Other of their relatives traveled southwest from the Milk River to settle at St. Peter's Mission and vicinity where Cree and Canadian Métis joined them. These families established settlements along the Front Range of the Rocky Mountains and became the second principal cluster of Métis in Montana. Members of the two networks, related before they settled in Montana, preserved and extended their common ties.

For early Métis on the Milk River, see Charles Larpenteur, *Forty Years a Fur Trader on the Upper Missouri: The Personal Narrative of Charles Larpenteur, 1833-1872* (1933; reprint, Lincoln: University of Nebraska Press, 1989), pp. 75-76.

For an extensive look at the Spring Creek (Lewistown) Métis community and Montana Métis identity, see Martha Harroun Foster, *We Know Who We Are: Métis Identity in a Montana Community* (Norman: University of Oklahoma Press, 2006) and Martha Harroun Foster, "'We Know Who We Are': Multiethnic Identity in a Montana Métis Community" (Ph.D. diss., University of California, Los Angeles, 2000).

2   There are several studies of the development of Métis culture and identity, including Jennifer S. H. Brown, *Strangers in Blood: Fur Trade Company Families in Indian Country* (Norman: University of Oklahoma Press, 1980); Lucy Eldersveld Murphy, *A Gathering of Rivers: Indian, Métis, and Mining in the Western Great Lakes, 1737-1832* (Lincoln: University of Nebraska Press, 2000); Jacqueline Peterson and Jennifer Brown, eds., *The New Peoples: Being and Becoming Métis in North America* (Winnipeg: University of Manitoba Press, 1985); Lawrence J. Barkwell, Leah Dorion, and Darren R. Prefontaine, *Métis Legacy: A Métis Historiography and Annotated Bibliography* (Winnipeg: Pemmican Publications Inc., 2001); Heather Devine, *The People Who Own Themselves: Aboriginal Ethnogenesis in a Canadian Family, 1660-1900* (Calgary: University of Calgary Press, 2004).

3   V. Havard, "The French Half-breeds of the Northwest," *Smithsonian Reports* (Washington, D.C.: Smithsonian Institution, 1879), p. 311; A. P. Nasatir, ed., *Before Lewis and Clark: Documents Illustrating the History of the Missouri, 1785-1804* (1952; reprint, Lincoln: University of Nebraska Press, 1990), pp. 32-33; Joseph Kinsey Howard, *Strange Empire: A Narrative of the Northwest* (1952; reprint, St. Paul: Minnesota Historical Society Press, 1994), pp. 25-26; Gerhard J. Ens, *Homeland to Hinterland: The Changing Worlds of the Red River Métis in the Nineteenth Century* (Toronto: University of Toronto Press, 1996), pp. 38-39; Frank Gilbert Roe, *The North American Buffalo: A Critical Study of the Species in its Wild State* (1951; reprint, Toronto: University of Toronto Press, 1970), p. 371.

4   William T. Hornaday, *The Extermination of the American Bison* (Washington, D.C.: U.S. Government Printing Office, 1889), pp. 443-444; Clarence Rife, "Norman W. Kittson, A Fur Trader at Pembina," *Minnesota History* 6, no. 3 (September 1925): pp. 232-234.

5   Rhoda R. Gilman, Carolyn Gilman, and Deborah M. Stultz, *The Red River Trails: Oxcart Routes between St. Paul and the Selkirk Settlement, 1820-1870* (St. Paul: Minnesota Historical Society, 1979). Gerhard J. Ens, in *Homeland to Hinterland*, pp. 28-92, discusses the growth of both the

Hudson's Bay Company and free-trader buffalo production during these years. Howard, *Strange Empire,* pp. 55-56 ("The cart was built").

6 Larpenteur, *Forty Years,* pp. 90-97.

7 Merrill G. Burlingame, "Buffalo in Trade and Commerce," *North Dakota Historical Quarterly* 3, no. 4 (July 1929): pp. 274-276; Larpenteur, *Forty Years,* pp. 63-64, 72-80, 90-97; Michael P. Malone, Richard B. Roeder, and William L. Lang, *Montana: A History of Two Centuries* (1976; reprint, Seattle: University of Washington Press, 1991), p. 55; Hiram Martin Chittenden, *The American Fur Trade* (1935; reprint, Lincoln: University of Nebraska Press, 1986), pp. 338-339; William A Dobak, "Killing the Canadian Buffalo, 1821-1881," *Western Historical Quarterly* 27, no. 1 (Spring 1996): pp. 42-46.

8 Nancy L. Woolworth, "Gingras, St. Joseph and the Métis in the Northern Red River Valley, 1843-1873," *North Dakota History: Journal of the Northern Plains* 42, no. 4 (Fall 1975): pp. 17, 20-21. After Pembina, St. Joseph (present-day Walhalla, ND) became the center of Red River Métis activity south of the boundary. Woolworth comments upon the isolated nature of these Métis communities; for example: "Between 1851 and 1858, the district elected Norman W. Kittson as Councilor and Joseph Rolette, Jr., and Antoine B. Gingras as its representatives to the Territorial Legislature. The sessions met in January in St. Paul, and the three men therefore had to walk almost 700 miles on snowshoes behind dog sleds to attend" (20).

U.S. Bureau of the Census, *1850 Minnesota Territorial Census,* Pembina District, no. 54, house visit no. 94 (father and mother of Judith Wilkie Berger), pp. 108, 75 (Klynes), 73 (Isabell and Edward Wells), 93; Foster, "'We Know Who We Are': Multiethnic Identity in a Montana Métis Community," pp. 130-131, 221-223; Foster, *We Know Who We Are: Métis Identity in a Montana Community,* pp. 41-42, 83-85.

9 D. Bruce Sealey and Antoine S. Lussier, *The Métis: Canada's Forgotten People* (Winnipeg: Manitoba Métis Federation Press, 1975), 37; John Hesketh, "History of the Turtle Mountain Chippewa," *Collections of the State Historical Society of North Dakota,* ed. O. G. Libby (Grand Forks, 1923), 5: pp. 107-109; William T. Hornaday, *The Extermination of the American Bison* (Washington, D.C.: U.S. Government Printing Office, 1889), p. 489 ("very scarce").

10 George M. Dawson, "Surveying the International Boundary: The Journal of George M. Dawson, 1873," *Saskatchewan History* 21, no. 1 (Winter 1968): p. 19; Ens, *Homeland to Hinterland,* pp. 78, 213-214.

11 Ens, *Homeland to Hinterland,* pp. 118, 213-214; Sealey and Lussier, *The Métis,* pp. 99-100. Examples of Métis community and family histories include Catherine E. Bell, *Alberta's Métis Settlements Legislation: An Overview of*

Ownership and Management of Settlement Lands (Regina: Canadian Plains Research Center, University of Regina, 1994); Heather Devine, *The People Who Own Themselves: Aboriginal Ethnogenesis in a Canadian Family, 1660-1900* (Calgary: University of Calgary Press, 2004); Nicole St. Onge, Saint Laurent, *Manitoba: Evolving Métis Identities, 1850-1914* (Regina: Canadian Plains Research Center, University of Regina, 2004).

12 Larpenteur, *Forty Years a Fur Trader*, pp. 75-76 ("which abounded"); I. I. Stevens, "Report of Explorations for a Route for the Pacific Railroad, I. I. Stevens, Governor of Washington Territory, 1853," 33rd Cong., 2nd sess., 1855, Senate Ex. Doc. Vol. 13 no. 78, Cong. Doc. Series no. 758, pp. 148-149; John C. Ewers, "Ethnological Report on the Chippewa Cree Tribe of the Rocky Boy Reservation and the Little Shell Band of Indians," in *American Indian Ethnohistory: North Central and Northeastern Indians*, ed. David Agee Horr (New York: Garland Publishing Inc., 1974), 6: pp. 52-56. Ben Kline, interview with Oscar Mueller, 1931, "Ben Kline Reminiscences," SC942, Montana Historical Society Archives, Helena, MT (hereafter cited as MHSA), p. 2; Victor Van Den Broeck, "Sketch of Ben Kline's Life, Gathered by Father Van Den Broeck during Many Private Conversations with His Friend Ben," "Ben Kline Reminiscences," SC942, MHSA, p. 1.

13 Eli Guardipee, interview by John B. Ritch, 27 August 1940, "Eli Guardipee Reminiscence," SC772, MHSA, pp. 2-3.

14 Clemence Gourneau Berger, "The Métis Come to Judith Basin," *Lewistown* (Montana) *Daily News,* 31 December 1943, reprinted in Alberta C. Sparlin, *The Trail Back* (Great Falls, MT: Blue Print and Letter Company, 1976), pp. 11-12.

15 Ibid., p. 11.

16 Ibid.

17 Marcel Giraud, *The Métis in the Canadian West,* trans. George Woodcock (1945; reprint, Edmonton: University of Alberta Press, 1986), 2: p. 405; Samuel O'Connell, "Juneaux's Trading Post on Milk River, Montana Territory: Story of Medicine Lodge Known as Juneaux's Post," Samuel O'Connell Papers, SC597, box 1, folder 1, MHSA, pp. 1-2.

18 O'Connell, "Juneaux's Trading Post," pp. 1-2.

19 Louis Shambow, interview by A J. Noyes. 17 December 1916, "Louis Shambow (Chambeau) Reminiscence," SC 792, box 1, folder 1, MHSA, p. 6.

20 For a look at the motives of some Euro-American business people, see Paul F. Sharp, *Whoop-Up Country: The Canadian-American West, 1865-1885* (Minneapolis: University of Minnesota Press, 1955).

21 Ens, *Homeland to Hinterland*, pp. 151-154.

22 William W. Alderson, Indian Agent, Office of the Milk River Agency, Fort Peck, Montana Territory, to Edwin P. Smith, Commissioner of Indian Affairs, 1 May 1874, National Archives (hereafter NA), RG75, M234, roll 498; Brig. Gen. Alfred H. Terry to Major W. B. Sweitzer, Fort Ellis, 23 March 1875, NA, RG75, M234, roll 503 ("break up"); Michael J. Koury, *Military Posts of Montana* (Bellevue, NE: Old Army Press, 1970), p. 5 (after 1876).

23 *Benton Record,* 17 October 1879, 2. For further discussion, see Foster, "'We Know Who We Are': Multiethnic Identity in a Montana Métis Community," chapter 3; Foster, *We Know Who We Are: Métis Identity in a Montana Community,* chapter 2.

24 Sir Edward Thornton to William Evarts, 15 November 1879, NA, RG75, M234, roll 517, 2: Department of Indian Affairs, Dominion of Canada, "Annual Report, 1879," Ottawa, 1880, p. 88 ("about 140 half-breeds"); Nelson A. Miles, *Personal Recollections and Observations of General Nelson A. Miles* (Chicago: Werner Co., 1897), pp. 309-310.

25 H. M. Black to Captain C. H. Potter, Helena, MT, 26 November 1879, NA, RG75, M234, roll 518, 2; Black to Assistant Adjutant General, 28 January 1880, NA, RG75, M234, roll 518, 6; Mueller, "Ben Kline," p. 4; Ewers, "Ethnological Report," p. 85 ("30,000").

26 John C. Ewers, *The Blackfeet: Raiders of the Northwestern Plains* (Norman: University of Oklahoma Press, 1958), p. 72; Giraud, *The Métis,* 2: pp. 413-414 (buffalo disappear in Canada). Frederick C. Jamieson reported that "[t]here were no more [buffalo hunting] expeditions after 1877, when the herds suddenly disappeared from the Great Plains of Rupert's Land." Jamieson, "The Edmonton Hunt," *Alberta Historical Review* 1, nos. 1, 2 (1953): p. 10. Andrew Garcia, *Tough Trip through Paradise, 1878-1879* (1967; reprint, San Francisco: Comstock Editions, 1981), pp. 184-185.

27 Elizabeth Swan, "A Brief History of the First Catholic Pioneers of Lewistown, Montana," file 541, Merrill G. Burlingame Special Collections, Montana State University Library, 1; copies also held by Carnegie Public Library, Lewistown, MT, and in the Joseph Kinsey Howard Papers, MC 27, MHSA, Helena, MT; Van Den Broeck, "Ben Kline," pp. 2-3. Band members included Pierre Berger, his wife, Judith Wilkie Berger, their four unmarried children, four married sons and their families, two married daughters and their families (Turcotte and Ouellette), and a married granddaughter (Wells). Judith Berger's brother, Alexander Wilkie, and his married daughters (LaFountain) and Judith's sister, Betsy Wilkie Fleury, and her married son and family also accompanied them. Two Doney families, the wife in each case a sister of the husbands of Alexander Wilkie's daughters (LaFountain), and the families of three Fagnant brothers and

a sister (Larocque), all half brothers or the half sister of Charlotte Adam LaFountain (mother-in-law of the married daughters of Alexander Wilkie) also joined the band. The John Ledoux family, which was probably related to the LaFountains and Fagnants, the Gayion family, and Ben Kline, employee of Francis Janeaux, and Kline's childhood friend, Mose LaTray, and family made up the body of the initial party. (Swan, "A Brief History," p. 1; Van Den Broeck, "Ben Kline," pp. 2-3). Other sources for information concerning these relationships and kinship diagrams may be found in Foster, "'We Know Who We Are': Multiethnic Identity in a Montana Métis Community," pp. 215-224, and *We Know Who We Are: Métis Identity in a Montana Community*, pp. 78-79.

[28] Swan, "'A Brief History," pp. 3-5; Van Den Broeck, "Ben Kline," p. 3 ("killed lots"; "whole week").

[29] Lieutenant Colonel H. M. Black, Eighteenth Infantry, to Assistant Adjutant General, Department of Dakota, St. Paul, Minnesota, 28 January 1879, NA, RG75, M234, roll 518 (Miles broke up the Métis camps). Miles, *Personal Recollections*, pp. 306, 309 ("sharp engagement"; "location of such").

[30] John P. Turner, *The North-West Mounted Police, 1873-1893* (Ottawa: Edmond Cloutier, 1950), 1: p. 466 ("future all property"); Miles, *Personal Recollections*, p. 309 ("practically British subjects"). Reference to this campaign is also found in the following: United States Secretary of War, Annual Report (Washington, D.C.: U.S. Government Printing Office, 1879) "Miles' Report" (September 1879), pp. 61-64; *Army and Navy Register* 16 (2 August 1879), p. 954; Virginia Johnson, *The Unregimented General: A Biography of Nelson A. Miles* (Boston: Houghton Mifflin Company, 1962), pp. 217-221.

[31] Mueller, "Ben Kline," p. 3 ("rounded up the breeds").

[32] Berger, "Métis Come to Judith Basin," p. 13; Swan, "A Brief History;" Joel Overholser, *Fort Benton: World's Innermost Port* (Helena: Falcon Publishing, 1987), p. 288.

[33] Swan, "'A Brief History," pp. 4, 6; Dorman Jackson, "Early History, Lewistown and Missions," 1974, Catholic History File, St. Leo's Catholic Church Library, Lewistown, Montana; Homestead Entry Applications, Bureau of Land Management (hereafter referred to as BLM), Billings, MT, Montana Tract Books, roll 36, T15/R18, T15/R19.

[34] Swan, "A Brief History," p. 6.

[35] Homestead Entry Applications, BLM, Billings, MT; Foster, "'We Know Who We Are': Multiethnic Identity in a Montana Métis Community," pp. 269-279, 318-328, and *We Know Who We Are: Métis Identity in a Montana Community*, pp. 101-118.

36 Breed Creek, which parallels Boyd Creek just to the south, is a tributary
of Spring Creek. Swan, "A Brief History," pp. 3, 6-7; Van Den Broeck, "Ben
Kline," p. 3; Homestead Entry Applications, BLM, Billings, MT; Marie
D. Elhert (granddaughter of Elizabeth Berger Swan), interview with author, Lewistown, MT, 16 July 1996; Foster, "'We Know Who We Are':
Multiethnic Identity in a Montana Métis Community," pp. 269-279, 318-
328, and *We Know Who We Are: Métis Identity in a Montana Community*,
pp. 101-118.

37 E. C. Abbott ("Teddy Blue") and Helena Huntington Smith, *We Pointed
Them North: Recollections of a Cowpuncher* (1939; reprint, Norman:
University of Oklahoma Press, 1954), p. 192; Isabelle Larocque, interview
with Conrad Anderson, in Conrad Anderson, "History of Roy, Montana"
(unpublished, undated), Fergus County, MC 978.6 AND, Carnegie Public
Library, Lewistown, MT, p. 22.

38 Granville Stuart, *Forty Years on the Frontier as Seen in the Journals and
Reminiscences of Granville Stuart*, ed. Paul C. Phillips (1925; reprint,
Glendale, CA: Arthur H. Clark Company, 1967), 2: pp. 142-144.

39 Ibid., 2: p. 134.

40 Swan, "A Brief History," pp. 4-5.

41 Ibid., p. 5.

42 Howard Paul, interview with Nicolas Vrooman, Great Falls, MT, excerpts
reproduced in Nicholas Vrooman, "When They Awake: Métis Culture in
Contemporary Context," video (Institute for Métis Studies, University of
Great Falls, Great Falls, MT, 1995); Marie D. Elhert, interview with au-
thor, Lewistown, MT, 16 July 1996; Francis Morgan Shoup (granddaugh-
ter of Ben Kline), interview with author, Lewistown, MT, 16 July 1996;
Sarah Larocque, interview with Nicholas Vrooman, Roy, MT, in "When
They Awake."

43 Most informants identified Métis speech as "Cree" or "Chippewa" when
actually it was Michif (John C. Crawford, "What Is Michif? Language in
the Métis Tradition," in *The New Peoples*, pp. 232, 238). For additional in-
formation see Peter Bakker, *A Language of Our Own: The Genesis of Michif,
the Mixed Cree-French Language of the Canadian Métis* (New York:
Oxford University Press, 1997). Howard, *Strange Empire*, p. 345; Swan,
"Mrs. Swan," 22 December 1968, *Lewistown News Argus;* Francis Morgan
Shoup, interview with author; Mercy Jackson, "Lewistown Schools," Mercy
Jackson Collection, SC544, Merrill G. Burlingame Special Collections,
Montana State University Library, 1; Margaret Jackson Seilstad, "George
R. Jackson Family History," in *The Heritage Book of Central Montana*,
ed. Babbie Deal and Loretta McDonald (Lewistown, MT: Fergus County
Bi-Centennial Committee, 1979), pp. 157-158.

44 Swan, "A Brief History," pp. 3, 7-8; Howard, *Strange Empire*, pp. 344-345; Marie D. Elhert, interview with author, Lewistown, MT, 16 July 1996.

45 U.S. Bureau of the Census, *1880 Montana Territorial Census*, Meagher County, Judith Basin, National Archives Microfilm (NAM), T9, roll 742.

46 *1880 Montana Territorial Census*, Meagher County, Judith Basin, NAM, T9, roll 742, Supervisor's District No. 78, Enumerator District No. 23; Choteau County, Fort Benton, Enumerator District 3; Meagher County, Musselshell Valley, Enumerator District 23.

47 *1880 Montana Territorial Census*, Choteau County, Shonkin Creek, NAM, T9, roll 742, Enumerator District 4.

48 Howard, *Strange Empire*, 344; Marie D. Elhert, interview with author, Lewistown, MT; Francis Morgan Shoup, interview with author, Lewistown, MT; Treena LaFountain, interview with author, 26 July 1996.

From Guangdong to the Big Sky:
The Chinese Experience in Frontier Montana, 1864-1900

— Robert R. Swartout, Jr.

The discovery of gold deposits in the Northern Rockies in the early 1860s dramatically altered the landscape that became known as Montana. It seemed as though almost overnight rough-hewed urban communities sprang up in the high mountain valleys—Bannack along Grasshopper Creek on the upper reaches of the Jefferson River in 1862, Virginia City in Alder Gulch in 1863, and Helena in a place called Last Chance Gulch in 1864. Almost as quickly, transportation routes such as the Mullan Road, the Bozeman Trail, and James Liberty Fisk's Northern Overland Route began linking the region to outside national and international forces. The dramatic growth of the non-Indian population also led directly to territorial status for Montana in 1864.

As mining activities and other related economic enterprises spread throughout the region, an amazingly broad mix of peoples appeared in Montana from across the country and, indeed, from around the world. Among these groups were Chinese pioneers, many of whom had come to Montana by way of California. The following essay, by Robert R. Swartout, Jr., suggests that these new arrivals—like many other immigrants from around the globe—were influenced by classic "push/pull" factors. That is, they were inclined to leave China for opportunities abroad because of internal forces that prompted emigration;

at the same time, the lure of jobs available in the American West drew them across the Pacific. Once they arrived in the Northern Rockies, they played a vital role in the development of nineteenth-century Montana. The first Chinese arrivals worked largely as placer miners, but they soon began to pursue other types of work, including railroad construction, household duties, gardening (Chinese-operated gardens supplied many of the vegetables consumed by Montana urbanites of the era), and independent business enterprises that catered to a wide variety of customers.

Like the Métis, these early Chinese pioneers in Montana were often confronted with prejudice and discrimination, which made their accomplishments all the more remarkable. Yet for much of this nation's history, their story was almost completely untold as part of the larger American narrative. Fortunately, historians in recent years have begun to focus much more of their attention on the richness and importance of the Asian experience in America.

Into the early twentieth century, Montana contained a remarkably heterogeneous society, with significant numbers of Native Americans, Irish, black Americans, Scandinavians, Jews, and Slavs— to name only a few of the many groups living and working in the region. Among the racial and ethnic minorities that contributed to this fascinating mix, the Chinese were certainly one of the most important. Yet, for far too long, many of the historical studies about Chinese immigration to the American West have tended to use these Chinese pioneers simply as a backdrop for analyzing the thinking and behavior of non-Chinese groups.[1] It is time that we begin to focus more of our attention on the Chinese themselves.[2]

By focusing more directly on the Chinese experience, we may better appreciate the valuable economic and cultural contributions that these Asian pioneers made to the development of early Montana society. To understand the extent of the Chinese involvement in Montana's history, we must move beyond the retelling of "colorful and humorous" accounts. The Chinese struggle—and it was a struggle—to achieve social and economic security in Montana was demanding, and it deserves serious historical attention.[3]

The Chinese immigrants arriving in America in the mid-nineteenth century overwhelmingly came from the delta region surrounding Canton in Guangdong Province. The general reasons behind the desire of certain Chinese to emigrate during the nineteenth century are not too difficult to identify. The great population explosion in China between roughly 1700 and 1850 had placed tremendous pressures on China's traditional agrarian production, and in many parts of China the population had outstripped the land's ability to produce adequate foodstuffs. Another factor contributing to emigration was the gradual decline of the Qing dynasty. The dynasty's inability to rule effectively had resulted in a series of rebellions, the largest and most famous of which was the Taiping Rebellion of 1850-1864. In a broader sense, the decline of the dynasty also led to a rise in both government corruption and banditry, problems that created special burdens for the peasantry.[4] Finally, there was the American factor itself. Between the 1840s and the 1890s, the resource-rich, labor-poor American West offered opportunities to foreign workers searching for financial and material security. In many important respects, Montana was a perfect microcosm of these forces at work within the developing American West.[5]

Why the Chinese immigrants would come almost exclusively from Guangdong Province—in fact, from just three major regions within the province—is more difficult to pinpoint.[6] One factor might have been the influence of the West on and around Canton during the first half of the nineteenth century. The penetration of imperialist powers during this era certainly led to considerable social and economic dislocation for the Chinese.[7] Another factor might have been the maritime traditions of the southeastern China coast. The story of Chinese migration to America during the nineteenth century is just part of a much larger movement. For decades, people of this area had traveled abroad in search of wealth and adventure. Between 1850 and 1900, roughly five million Chinese from the southern coastal area would leave the country, only a half million of whom would go to the United States.[8]

Wong See Q lived in Helena, circa 1925. COURTESY MONTANA HISTORICAL SOCIETY, HELENA, 940-897.

Perhaps one of the most critical local forces leading to emigration was that many of these people were "have-nots," with only limited ties to the traditional Chinese order. Some were members of an ethnic minority known as the Hakka, while many others were locally oriented rural poor who viewed emigration simply as a "means of survival" for themselves and their families.[9] Large-scale Chinese immigration to America began in the late 1840s and early 1850s. Spurred on initially by the great gold discoveries in California, first hundreds and then thousands of Chinese headed east across the Pacific Ocean.[10] With the gradual decline in the placer fields, Chinese workers entered other lines of employment and moved on to other regions of the western United States and Canada. By the 1860s and 1870s, important Chinese communities had been established all along the West Coast—in Oregon, Washington, British Columbia, and California—and within the interior West—in places like Nevada, Idaho, Colorado, Wyoming, and Montana.[11] Of all these Chinese, few have received less attention from historians than those found in the isolated Rocky Mountain state of Montana.[12] By 1870, census surveyors counted 1,949 Chinese in the first official census taken for the territory of Montana. This may not appear to be an impressive figure, but those 1,949 Chinese represented approximately ten percent of Montana's official population in 1870. Moreover, because census records were often notorious for underestimating the Chinese population in any given community, the actual Chinese population may have been much higher—by perhaps fifty percent or more. In 1880, the official figure for the Chinese population in Montana dipped to 1,765, but by 1890 it was back up to 2,532. From that point on, the number of Chinese in the state, and in the United States as a whole, steadily declined. This decline was due partly to local factors as well as to the passage of various Chinese exclusion acts passed by Congress during the 1880s and 1890s. By 1920, there were fewer than 900 Chinese residents left in Montana out of a total state population of 548,889.[13] It is clear, then, that the major period for Chinese influence in Montana was roughly the last third of the nineteenth century. This period not only represented the largest numbers of Chinese immigrants within the region, but it was also a time when those Chinese made up a large percentage of Montana's total population.

Chinese sluice miners work a gravel deposit in Madison County, circa 1871.
WILLIAM H. JACKSON, COURTESY U.S. GEOLOGICAL SURVEY, JWH00908.

As was true in so many other regions of the West, the discovery of major gold deposits during the 1860s had a profound effect on the history of Montana. The great gold-mining boom in the high mountain valleys of the Northern Rockies would attract thousands of American miners and would-be miners almost overnight and would lead directly to the creation of Montana Territory in 1864.[14] And as was the pattern in many other western states and territories, the development of the goldfields also resulted in the arrival of the first Chinese pioneers in Montana.

As placer camps like Bannack, Virginia City, and Last Chance Gulch built up across western Montana, word went out to the older mining districts of the new opportunities in Montana Territory. Chinese miners—many with extensive mining experience in California, Oregon, Idaho, or elsewhere—began moving into Montana. An 1870 federal government study on mining in the American West reported that "some 2,000 to 3,000 Chinese are domiciled in the Territory of Montana. . . . It is reasonable to expect their numbers will rapidly increase." The same report commented on the techniques of Chinese miners:

> The Chinese work their own placer claims, either taking up abandoned ground or purchasing claims too low in yield to be worked profitably by white labor. The ground thus obtained sometimes turns out to be very valuable, but usually they work or rework only what would otherwise remain untouched. . . . They are frugal, skillful, and extremely industrious. Frequently maltreated by evil-disposed whites, they rarely, if ever, retaliate.

The author of this valuable report had the insight to note that, contrary to much popular opinion, the Chinese miners working in Montana "are not coolies or living in a state of slavery. . . . They seem to be their own masters, only associating together for mutual assistance."[15]

By the early 1870s, there were dozens of Chinese mining operations in western Montana. The 1880 census listed 149 Chinese in Missoula County, 710 in Deer Lodge County (which included Butte), 265 in Madison County (Alder Gulch), and 359 in Lewis and Clark County (Helena). Many mining camps that are almost forgotten today, such as the small community of Pioneer located southwest of present-day Garrison, were the site of widespread Chinese activities. Unfortunately, the very success of these Chinese miners helped create a backlash among many members of Montana's white population. For example, in 1872, the territorial legislature passed a bill prohibiting aliens (that is, Chinese) from holding titles to any placer mine or claim. Even though this law was later struck down by the territorial supreme court, it was typical of much of the popular sentiment of the day.[16]

Because the passage of such laws was, at least in part, racially motivated, supporters of the legislation consistently overlooked the contributions that Chinese miners made to the development of Montana. As one outsider commented at the time, the law concerning Chinese mining titles

> . . . is certainly destructive of the interests of the community, as may be shown in numerous instances where the Chinese have purchased, for cash, claims which white men could no longer afford to work, and have proceeded to make them productive, at a smaller profit to themselves than to the Territory. Besides being bad policy, this course toward the Chinese is rank dishonesty.[17]

The notion that Chinese miners competed directly against white miners and thus "stole" badly needed work from them is largely untrue. In fact, Chinese miners generally complemented the work being done by white miners and played a vital role in helping to develop the mineral and commercial resources of the territory.[18]

As placer mining began to fade from the scene during the late 1870s and 1880s, the role of the Chinese immigrants in Montana also began to change.[19] Chinese railroad workers in America had first been used on a large scale in the construction of the Central Pacific Railroad during the 1860s. In fact, roughly four-fifths of all the grading done from Sacramento, California, to Ogden, Utah, was completed by Chinese laborers. Of the 13,500 workers on the Central Pacific payroll at the time of construction, 12,000 were Chinese.[20]

It is not too surprising, then, that Chinese railroad workers found their way to Montana. During the early 1880s, the first transcontinental railroad to pass through Montana—the Northern Pacific—was being constructed at a frantic pace under the leadership of Henry Villard. Because of the critical shortage of skilled labor at the western end of the project and the reputation of the Chinese as experienced and dependable workers, Villard and his associates hired 15,000 Chinese to work on the Northern Pacific line through Washington, Idaho, and Montana.[21]

The press often referred to these Chinese workers, especially those constructing the Northern Pacific along the Clark Fork River

The labor of Chinese workers, such as those in this section gang on a handcar, circa 1890, was essential to the completion of the Northern Pacific Railroad through Montana.
F. JAY HAYNES, COURTESY MONTANA HISTORICAL SOCIETY, HELENA, H-2191.

in northern Idaho and western Montana, as "Hallett's Army" after construction manager J. L. Hallett. This region of the Clark Fork contained some of the most rugged terrain found anywhere along the Northern Pacific line. One newspaper reported on October 28, 1882:

> One must ride over the completed track, or watch the thousands of men at work in these rock-ribbed hills, see the deep cuttings, the immense fillings, count the bridges and miles of trestle-work that carry the trains safely over streams and arms of lakes and inlets, to fairly realize the expenditure of muscle . . . necessary for such a work as building a great railway route through this mountainous country. At places, for instance, a point near Cabinet Landing, to the men who do the labor, and even to subordinate leaders, the passage seemed closed against

them. The mountain towers like a prop to the sky, and from the water's edge it rises like a wall, presenting no break or crevice for a foothold.[22]

The special skills, dedication, and perseverance of the Chinese workers were critical in overcoming these tremendous obstacles. The same reporter took note of this Chinese contribution, although in somewhat condescending terms. To conquer nature's

> . . . insurmountable barrier . . . cable ropes holding a plank staging go down the precipitous sides of the mountain. Down the rope ladders, to this staging clamber Chinamen armed with drills, and soon the rock sides are filled with Giant powder. Then they clamber up, the blast is fired, and the foothold made by the explosive soon swarms with Celestials; the "can't be done" has been done. . . .[23]

Chinese workmen not only had to overcome great physical obstructions, but they also had to contend with bitter winter weather: "It was terrible work last winter," one source noted, "with deep snow to clear away at every step, the thermometer registering on an average ten and twelve degrees below zero [Fahrenheit], abetted by razor-like winds.[24]

The Chinese also played a crucial role in constructing the Mullan Tunnel, which enabled the Northern Pacific to cross over the Continental Divide not far from Helena, Montana. Chinese workers built the critical stretch of line leading to Stampede Pass in Washington Territory's North Cascade Mountains, which allowed the Northern Pacific to reach Puget Sound. For all of these remarkable efforts, the average Chinese worker was paid about one dollar per day, approximately half of what white workers received.[25] This disparity was but another indication of the racial attitudes existing in nineteenth-century America, attitudes that permitted white employers to exploit Chinese laborers because of their "inferiority."

Once the Northern Pacific Railroad reached Puget Sound in 1887, the railroad dismissed most of its Chinese workers, retaining only a

Passengers watch Chinese rail workers take a lunch break, for which the train briefly stopped near Missoula. COURTESY MONTANA HISTORICAL SOCIETY, HELENA, 940-903.

few Chinese as section hands. The Great Northern Railroad, which also built a transcontinental line across Montana (it was completed in 1893), employed very few Chinese workers. Both railroads turned increasingly to an even cheaper source of labor, the Japanese workers.

The contributions of Chinese railroad workers to the development of Montana are of significant historical importance. Their expertise in grading, drilling, masonry, and demolition was vital to the construction of the Northern Pacific, which opened Montana to settlement, particularly during the homestead era of the early twentieth century. Thousands of pioneer homesteaders would move into the state and transport their bountiful farm products to markets outside the state along tracks laid by the forgotten pioneers of another sort—the Chinese.

The arrival of Chinese miners and railroad workers during the 1860s, 1870s, and 1880s helped to create other economic opportunities for Chinese pioneers. Local Chinese communities began to develop through much of western Montana. For example, the 1890 census listed 602 Chinese living in Lewis and Clark County (Helena) and another 584 living in Silver Bow County (Butte).[26] Throughout the late nineteenth and early twentieth centuries, the state's largest "Chinatowns" were in Helena and Butte.

These urban residents came from a variety of backgrounds. Some were former miners and railroad workers who had been in Montana for some time, while others were recent arrivals from the West Coast who brought with them particular skills and trades. A few came directly from China, enticed to Montana by relatives and friends already living in the state.

Once the Chinese settled in Montana communities, they pursued a variety of occupations. They owned and operated restaurants, grocery stores, tailor shops, mercantile stores, vegetable gardens, and laundries. In 1890, Helena alone had twenty-six Chinese-owned laundries.[27] Laundry businesses were common because some Chinese had experience in this area, but also because it took little capital to start up such a business and, at least for a while, Chinese laundries posed little threat to established white businesses.[28] In addition to commercial activities, many Chinese provided important social and professional services. In 1900, Butte had at least seven Chinese physicians, some of them serving white as well as Chinese patrons.[29] Chinese skills and diligence were such that their movement into new fields of work was limited only by the unwillingness of the larger white community to accept the Chinese as equal members of society.

Despite intermittent white hostility, Chinese entrepreneurs were valuable to the general community. For instance, they operated pharmacies, laundries, restaurants, mercantile stores, and vegetable gardens that might have otherwise been absent in Montana's early frontier towns. Less well known is the contribution that Chinese businessmen made to the community by paying local taxes, which helped to support community growth not commonly associated with the Chinese. The 1870 tax lists for Lewis and Clark County, for instance, reveal a total assessment of Chinese taxpayers of $38,900. By 1890, the figure had climbed to $80,905. Similar statistics can be found for other Montana communities that had significant Chinese populations.[30]

The Wah Chong Tai Company store in Butte carried specialty items from China, such as the porcelainware in the front cabinet. COURTESY MONTANA HISTORICAL SOCIETY, HELENA, 946-135.

At the pre-inflation prices of nineteenth-century America, these figures represented a sizable amount of taxable property.

These figures also indicate that many Chinese were not "day laborers" simply passing through the state. Nor were they all sojourners planning to return immediately to China. Although large numbers did return to their homeland, still others decided to remain in the United States to establish what they hoped would be permanent livelihoods for themselves and their families. Perhaps most impressive of all, these self-reliant entrepreneurs were often forced to struggle against significant odds in their efforts to create businesses that would become an integral part of their local communities.

The Chinese pioneers in Montana created a vibrant and complex social network. As was true for many other immigrant groups in nineteenth-century America, the recent arrivals from China organized themselves to perpetuate many of their traditional social and cultural practices. Such activities were important in helping the immigrants maintain a sense of identity, particularly when they were confronted by a rather hostile social climate in America.

American conditions alone, however, were not the only factors influencing the unique structure of Chinese immigrant society. Because the overwhelming majority of these people came from one part of China, Chinese immigrants were often able to maintain or to create new social organizations based along traditional clan or district lines. This was especially important because local districts in China, even at the village level, had their own distinct lineages and dialects. Place of origin thus played a critical role in the development of Chinese social relationships in America.[31]

Another important feature of Chinese society in America was the general absence of women. The 1870 Montana census listed only 123 females out of a total Chinese population of 1,949. In 1880, the figures were 80 women out of 1,765; in 1890, 59 out of 2,532; and in 1900, 39 out of 1,739. Chinese women made up no more than seven percent, and sometimes as little as two percent, of the total Chinese population in Montana during the nineteenth century.[32]

The absence of women in the Chinese community had a clear effect on the nature of Chinese society in America. To begin with, it helps explain the difficulty the Chinese had in producing future generations in America after the passage of the Chinese exclusion acts. Moreover, Chinese men could not depend on a traditional family dwelling to provide all their social and cultural needs. Consequently, Chinese communities in this country worked to establish institutions that would help to bind people together as they attempted to adjust to the difficulties of living in a new and sometimes hostile country.[33]

One of the most important institutions within Montana's Chinese communities was the local temple, or joss house. Sometimes this institution was contained within a store or private dwelling; other times, particularly in Butte, it was a separate structure entirely. The joss house was a focal point for both social and religious activities within the Chinese community. "The great Chinese Joss," a November 1882 Butte newspaper reported,

. . . arrived last night by express from California and is being feasted to-day with all the delicacies of the season. . . . The room in which he has taken up his quarters is gaily decorated with flags, roast hogs, chickens, drums, and a thousand and one articles which defy description. [The Chinese] will wind up with a grand free lunch to-night, at which at least three hundred . . . will be present.[34]

Butte's Chinatown had two separate temples, one of which was not torn down until 1945.[35]

Another institution that sometimes played an important role in the lives of early Montana settlers was the Chinese masonic temple. In addition to providing its members with an opportunity for relaxation and entertainment, this institution, with its emphasis on brotherhood, also reinforced Chinese social and cultural values.

In an effort to maintain a sense of order and group identification, members of the Chinese Masonic Temple in Virginia City compiled a list of twenty-one regulations. Some were designed to protect the group from outside interference and threats. For example, members were required to defend the secrecy of their lodge, and if a member were arrested, he "may not compromise any other brother" of the lodge.[36] Members were also prohibited from assisting Chinese who might belong to rival organizations.

Other regulations were guidelines for ethical social behavior. For instance, members were not to "covet the wife or sisters of brethren because of their beauty." They were warned: "do not occupy by force the property of your brethren" nor "deceive your brethren through fast talking." Members were prohibited from quarreling or feuding in public for fear of damaging the reputation of the brotherhood. More powerful members of the lodge were reminded to not "bully your brethren because of your might." Finally, the regulations established rules for the proper handling of such important social occasions as weddings and funerals.[37] To ensure obedience, specific punishments—such as 306 strokes with a cane—were enumerated.

Taken as a whole, these regulations indicate that Chinese pioneers were often concerned about maintaining order within their communities. Moreover, the masonic temple, like other Chinese institutions, provided its members with a sense of belonging and a feeling of camaraderie in an apparently harsh and frequently intimidating world.

In the case of Butte, a council of elders representing the four-clan associations eventually formed to provide valuable leadership for the Chinese community. The council, general made up of leading businessmen, also attempted to resolve conflicts that might flair up among the Chinese.[38] One early Chinese resident in Butte recalled:

When I first came to Butte about fifty years ago [1890s], there were about thirty-two laundries in the city. About twenty belonged to our clan cousins, while the others belonged to the members of the opposite four-clan association. There were then two large four-clan associations, but the members were not friendly toward each other. Many disputes arose between associations.

In case of a dispute within our own association, it would be settled here. The elders—businessmen and those men who have lived in Butte longest—would hear the facts from the parties in dispute. The council of elders would decide who was right and who was wrong.[39]

When a dispute could not be resolved locally, the case was sent to association headquarters in San Francisco for final settlement. The Chinese communities in Montana, although geographically isolated, were still able to maintain important social, economic, and cultural ties with the outside world.

The celebration of traditional festivals was also an important feature of Chinese social life. Celebrations included the Ching Ming, Dragon Boat, Moon, and Winter Solstice festivals, but most important of all was the New Year festival.[40] The February 15, 1872, *Helena Weekly Herald* began its story on the Chinese New Year by declaring: "One of the most interesting days we have ever spent in the Territory was on yesterday, during a visit which we made to Chinatown. When we went there, we put ourselves under the care of Tong Hing, and Tong, with his usual urbanity and courtesy, put us through the more prominent of the Celestials." The reporter described in detailed, if rather patronizing, terms the local arrangements made to celebrate this most famous of Chinese festivals.[41]

Ancestor worship, a product of China's strong Confucian heritage, was reinforced through funeral rites and special days of commemoration.[42] The *Herald* reported on April 8, 1869, that

> . . . to-day is the [Chinese] annual Josh Day, on which occasion their custom is to visit the burial places—as our China men and women have done, closing their ceremonies about 2 p.m.—burn incense and innumerable small wax candles about the head stones or boards of the graves, deposit a liberal lunch of choice eatables and drinkables, designed for the spirits of the departed; recite propitiatory prayers to their savior (Josh), and otherwise show themselves sacredly mindful of the welfare of their dead.[43]

While reflecting certain religious duties, these activities served another important purpose. They enabled Chinese pioneers in Montana to maintain a cultural and spiritual link with family and clan members in China. It was unfortunate that various Sinophobic groups in the country would use the very strength of these enduring Chinese customs as a weapon against the immigrants. All too often Americans viewed Chinese social and cultural practices as "proof" that these immigrants could never be assimilated into American society. Some critics even claimed that because of their different ways and values, Chinese immigrants posed a direct threat to the traditional social order in America.

White Montana's response to Chinese immigration largely reflected contemporary regional and national attitudes. Although Chinese settlers in Montana were never the victims of the kind of mass violence that erupted in Rock Springs, Wyoming, in 1885 and along the Snake River in 1887, they were physically and mentally abused and politically exploited well into the early twentieth century.[44] It was not unusual to hear about individual Chinese being harassed or beaten in many nineteenth-century Montana communities.[45] Moreover, even before Montana became a state in 1889, lawmakers in the territory passed and attempted to pass laws discriminating against Chinese residents, including one aimed at ownership of mining properties.

A typical example of these anti-Chinese sentiments was expressed in an 1872 law that established a special tax, or "license," on Chinese laundries. In one form or another, this law remained on the books well into the twentieth century.[46] Discrimination against the Chinese became even more pronounced once Montana achieved statehood. In the decade or so after 1889, Montana judicial decisions systematically upheld a number of anti-Chinese laws. "By 1902," writes historian John R. Wunder, "the doors to economic opportunity and cultural equality for Chinese Montanans had been closed with appropriate legal fanfare." On March 3, 1909, the final insult was added when the state legislature passed an anti-miscegenation law prohibiting interracial marriage—a law directed against black Americans and Japanese immigrants as well as against the Chinese.[47]

Why was such animosity directed toward the Chinese, especially when they represented one of the most peaceful and diligent groups in Montana? Nineteenth-century critics of Chinese immigration often emphasized that the Chinese introduced tremendous social evils into Montana. Yet, as a group, the Chinese were much more law-abiding than many whites were. Between 1900 and 1918, only six Chinese residents of Montana were sent to the state penitentiary, four of them for the same crime. This does not necessarily indicate that Montana's Chinese communities were crime free, but the evidence does argue against the stereotypical view of Chinese communities as places "teeming" with "tong wars" and "hatchetmen."[48] Some Chinese did have an opium habit (partly because of the Western world's role in expanding the opium trade during the early nineteenth century), but "authorities generally agree that the Chinese were able to exercise better control over opium than most white miners could over whiskey, and that they seemed no better or worse for the habit."[49]

Opponents of Chinese immigration also cited the "economic" threat posed by Chinese workers. During the city-wide boycott against Chinese merchants and laborers in Butte from 1897 to 1899, union leaders in the mining city frequently referred to unfair labor competition. Such notions, however, were largely fictitious.[50]

The Chinese community took boycott leaders to court in Fay Hum vs Frank Baldwin, *eventually prevailing in federal court. Shown here is a hearing in the case held in Butte, circa 1898.* COURTESY MONTANA HISTORICAL SOCIETY, HELENA, 940-905.

To begin with, the Chinese often did the kind of work that many white workers refused to do. Moreover, when the two groups did compete for the same type of job, the Chinese, who were usually excluded from most white-controlled labor unions, were often forced to accept lower wages. The few times when Chinese workers did attempt to strike for higher wages, they found themselves caught between a hostile management and an indifferent general public.[51]

Ultimately, the overriding reason behind the anti-Chinese sentiment in Montana and the rest of the American West was racism—a racism based on cultural stereotypes as well as skin color. It was unfortunate for these Chinese pioneers that their migration to America occurred at a time when racism was especially fashionable in the United States. In fact, the animosity directed toward the Chinese coincided with similar attitudes and acts of violence against black Americans. As the country became increasingly industrialized and urbanized, minorities often became convenient scapegoats for other groups who felt "victimized" by rapid economic and social changes.[52]

An 1893 editorial published in a Butte newspaper gave voice to this racism: "The Chinaman is no more a citizen than a coyote is a citizen, and never can be." After making obligatory references to cheap labor and opium, the scathing editorial continued:

> The Chinaman's life is not our life; his religion is not our religion. His habits, superstitions, and modes of life are disgusting. He is a parasite, floating across the Pacific and thence penetrating into the interior towns and cities, there to settle down for a brief space and absorb the substance of those with whom he comes into competition. His one object in life is to make all the money he can and return again to his native land, dead or alive. His very existence in our midst is an insult to our own intelligence. Pestilence and disease follow in his wake, no matter what sentimentalists say to the contrary. Let him go hence. He belongs not in Butte.[53]

These racist and stereotypical attitudes were not confined to Butte, but were prevalent in many Montana communities during the late nineteenth century.[54] The power and popularity of such racial sentiments help to explain the ease with which the Montana legislature and the federal government could pass so many discriminatory laws aimed at the Chinese. These laws not only limited economic opportunities and cultural equality for Chinese pioneers, but they also effectively shut off the flow of new arrivals from China. Without new, especially female, emigrants, the once-vibrant Chinese communities of the intermountain states were bound to disappear.

Several important observations can be made from this rather brief description of the Chinese experience in nineteenth-century Montana. First of all, one is struck by the great diversity of occupations that the Chinese pioneers pursued in Montana. They did not limit themselves to placer mining or railroad building, but were willing to try almost any occupation that might allow them to achieve financial security and independence. Ultimately, the ability of the Chinese to branch out into new lines of work was limited not so much by their own prejudices and cultural habits as by the prejudices of the larger white community.

One of the most important aspects of the Chinese experience was their contribution to the economic development of nineteenth-century Montana. Chinese pioneers were an integral part of the infant mining industry in the territory, helping to pump thousands of dollars into the local economy while exploiting resources that other miners often ignored. The Chinese role in building the Northern Pacific Railroad was of tremendous value to the future development of the state, as the railroad made possible the greatest growth in the state's history, from 1890 to 1920. In Montana's budding urban communities, Chinese entrepreneurs provided valuable services to non-Chinese as well as Chinese patrons. Taken as a whole, these contributions played a crucial part in transforming Montana from a primitive, isolated patchwork of localities into an increasingly sophisticated, urbanized, and economically prosperous society.

As these Chinese pioneers contributed to Montana's economic development, they also built a complex and semi-permanent subcommunity of their own. This subcommunity often stressed traditional ties of clan and region, which were reinforced through participation in various cultural and religious activities. Unfortunately, the same customs that gave Chinese pioneers a sense of identity and purpose were used by critics to "prove" that Chinese immigrants were "polluting" America's cultural values and social order. Such attacks made it difficult for non-Chinese Americans to comprehend the richness and subtleties of Chinese customs and traditions.

This inability or unwillingness to appreciate the value of Chinese contributions was a direct result of the racial attitudes of the day. In that sense, the reaction of many white Montanans to the presence of Chinese settlers was all too typical of broader national and regional patterns. Montanans generally supported the passage of federal laws prohibiting Chinese immigration to America. At the local level, Montanans passed a series of state laws, which were upheld by the state supreme court, that intentionally discriminated against Chinese Montanans. These prejudices were so pervasive that recognition of the Chinese role in the development of modern Montana would come only after most of the Chinese pioneers and their descendants had left the state.

This essay originally appeared in *Montana, The Magazine of Western History,* Winter 1988.

Robert R. Swartout, Jr., is Professor Emeritus of History at Carroll College in Helena. In addition to publishing numerous books and articles on American-East Asian Relations, he is the editor of Montana Vistas: Selected Historical Essays *(1981); co-editor, with Harry W. Fritz, of* The Montana Heritage: An Anthology of Historical Essays *(1992); and co-editor, with Harry W. Fritz and Mary Murphy, of* Montana Legacy: Essays on History, People, and Place *(2002). His most recent book is* Bold Minds & Blessed Hands: The First Century of Montana's Carroll College *(2009).*

NOTES

1 See Elmer Clarence Sandmeyer, *The Anti-Chinese Movement in California* (Urbana: University of Illinois Press, 1939); Alexander Saxton, *The Indispensible Enemy: Labor and the Anti-Chinese Movement in California* (Berkeley and Los Angeles: University of California Press, 1971); Stuart Creighton Miller, *The Unwelcome Immigrant: The American Image of the Chinese, 1785-1882* (Berkeley and Los Angeles: University of California Press, 1969); Robert Edward Wynne, *Reaction to the Chinese in the Pacific Northwest and British Columbia, 1850-1910* (New York: Arno Press, 1979). In calling for greater attention to the Chinese experience itself, it is not my intention to dismiss the valuable contributions that works such as these have made to our understanding of U.S. history. The American response to Chinese migration is clearly an important historical issue and will be dealt with later in this essay.

2 Excellent recent examples include Liping Zhu, *A Chinaman's Chance: The Chinese on the Rocky Mountain Mining Frontier* (Boulder: University Press of Colorado, 1997); Anthony W. Lee, *Picturing Chinatown: Art and Orientalism in San Francisco* (Berkeley: University of California Press 2001); Marie Rose Wong, *Sweet Cakes, Long Journey: The Chinatowns of Portland, Oregon* (Seattle: University of Washington Press, 2004); Sue Fawn Chung, *In Pursuit of Gold: Chinese American Miners and Merchants in the American West* (Urbana: University of Illinois Press, 2011).

3 To see how the Montana experience fits into a broader, international context, see Michael H. Hunt, *The Making of a Special Relationship: The United States and China to 1914* (New York: Columbia University Press, 1983), especially chapters 2, 3, and 7; Shih-shan Henry Tsai, *China and the Overseas Chinese in the United States, 1868-1911* (Fayetteville: University of Arkansas Press, 1983).

4 Hunt, *The Making of a Special Relationship*, pp. 63-64; Jack Chen, *The Chinese of America: From the Beginnings to the Present* (San Francisco: Harper & Row, 1981), pp. 6-9; Frederic Wakeman, Jr., *Strangers at the Gate: Social Disorder in South China, 1839-1861* (Berkeley and Los Angeles: University of California Press, 1966).

5 Chen, *The Chinese of America*, pp. 35-124; Gunther Barth, *Bitter Strength: A History of the Chinese in the United States, 1850-1870* (Cambridge, Massachusetts: Harvard University Press, 1964), pp. 32-49; Kil Young Zo, *Chinese Emigration into the United States, 1850-1880* (New York: Arno Press, 1978), pp. 81-92.

6 The three regions were San-I (Sam Yup in Cantonese), Si-I (Sze Yup in Cantonese), and Xiang-shan (Hueng-shan in Cantonese; later renamed Chung-shan). See Hunt, *The Making of a Special Relationship*, pp. 61-62.

7 See June Mei, "Socioeconomic Origins of Emigration: Guangdong to California, 1850-1882," in *Labor Immigration under Capitalism: Asian Workers in the United States before World War II*, ed. Lucie Cheng and Edna Bonacich (Berkeley and Los Angeles: University of California Press, 1984), pp. 219-247.

8 Hunt, *The Making of a Special Relationship*, p. 61; Chen, *The Chinese of America*, pp. 10-13.

9 Hunt, *The Making of a Special Relationship*, p. 63.

10 Chen, *The Chinese of America*, pp. 15-29; Barth, *Bitter Strength*, pp. 50-76; Zo, *Chinese Emigration into the United States*, pp. 114-145.

11 See Ping Chiu, *Chinese Labor in California, 1850-1880: An Economic Study* (Madison: University of Wisconsin Press, 1963); Saxton, *The Indispensable Enemy*; Sucheng Chan, *This Bittersweet Soil: The Chinese in California Agriculture, 1860–1910* (Oakland: University of California Press, 1989); Wynne, *Reaction to the Chinese in the Pacific Northwest and British Columbia*; James Morton, *In the Sea of Sterile Mountains: The Chinese in British Columbia* (Vancouver: J. J. Douglas Ltd., 1974); Jeffrey Barlow and Christine Richardson, *China Doctor of John Day* (Portland: Binford & Mort, 1979); John R. Wunder, "Chinese in Trouble: Criminal Law and Race on the Trans-Mississippi West Frontier," *Western Historical Quarterly* 17 (January 1986), pp. 25-41.

12 The four most significant articles published on the Chinese presence in nineteenth-century Montana are Larry D. Quinn, "'Chink Chink Chinaman': The Beginnings of Nativism in Montana," *Pacific Northwest Quarterly* 58 (April 1967), pp. 82-89; John R. Wunder, "Law and Chinese in Frontier Montana," *Montana, The Magazine of Western History* 30 (Summer 1980), pp. 18-30; Stacy A. Flaherty, "Boycott in Butte: Organized Labor and the Chinese Community, 1896-1897," *Montana, The Magazine of Western History* 37 (Winter 1987), pp. 34-47; Laura J. Arata, "Beyond the 'Mongolian Muddle': Reconsidering Virginia City, Montana's China War of 1881," *Montana, The Magazine of Western History* 62 (Spring 2012), pp. 23-35, 90-93.

13 U.S. Department of the Interior, Census Office, *Eleventh Census of the United States, 1890: Population, Part I* (Washington, D.C.: Government Printing Office, 1895), pp. 29, 439; U.S. Department of Commerce, Bureau of the Census, *Fourteenth Census of the United States, 1920: Population, Volume III* (Washington, D.C.: Government Printing Office, 1922), pp. 574, 577.

14 Michael P. Malone and Richard B. Roeder, *Montana: A History of Two Centuries* (Seattle: University of Washington Press, 1976), pp. 50-55.

15 Rossiter W. Raymond, "Statistics of Mines and Mining in the States and Territories West of the Rocky Mountains," 41st Cong., 2d sess., 1870, H. Ex. Doc. 207 (Serial 1424), p. 260.

16 Montana Territory, Legislative Assembly, *Laws, Memorials, and Resolutions of the Territory of Montana, Seventh Session* (Deer Lodge, Montana: James H. Mills, Public Printer, 1872), pp. 593-596; Montana Territory, Legislative Assembly, *Laws, Memorials, and Resolutions of the Territory of Montana, Eighth Session* (Helena: Robert E. Fisk, Public Printer, 1874), p. 97; Wunder, "Law and Chinese in Frontier Montana," pp. 24-25. The original law stated: "No alien shall be allowed to acquire any title, interest, or possessory or other right to any placer mine or claim, or to the profits or proceeds thereof, in this territory."

17 Rossiter W. Raymond, "Statistics of Mines and Mining in the States and Territories West of the Rocky Mountains," 42nd Cong., 2d sess., 1872, H. Ex. Doc. 211 (Serial 1513), p. 292.

18 See Randall E. Rohe, "After the Gold Rush: Chinese Mining in the Far West, 1850-1890," *Montana, The Magazine of Western History* 32 (Autumn 1982), p. 18.

19 Most Chinese miners in Montana worked small placer claims, either individually or with various partners. Generally speaking, the Chinese did not play an important role in the development of industrial mining in Montana, partly because employers were reluctant to hire them and partly

because there were fewer Chinese left in the state by the time industrial mining came into its own around the turn of the century.

20 Chen, *The Chinese of America,* pp. 65-77; Tzu Kuei Yen, "Chinese Workers and the First Transcontinental Railroad of the United States of America," (Ph.D. diss., St. John's University, New York, 1977).

21 "First Across the Northwest—The Northern Pacific," MS, 5, President's Subject files, Northern Pacific Railway Company Records, Box 515, Minnesota Historical Society Archives, St. Paul [NP Records].

22 Newspaper clipping, October 28, 1882, Secretary Scrapbooks, 1866-1896, Box 4, Vol. 25, NP Records.

23 Ibid.

24 Ibid.

25 Anderson to Harris, August 7, August 31, 1886, Letters Received, Registered: President and Vice President (1882-1893), President's Department, Box 19, NP Records; *Weekly Missoulian,* February 16, 1883.

26 *Eleventh Census of the United States, 1890: Population, Part I,* p. 439.

27 *Helena City Directory, 1890* (Helena: R. L. Polk & Company, 1890), pp. 465-466.

28 See Paul Ong, "An Ethnic Trade: The Chinese Laundries in Early California," *The Journal of Ethnic Studies* 8 (Winter 1981), pp. 95-113. Although laundries were labor-intensive businesses, they did require some capital. In California, "investments ranged from $400 to $1,600, with the average being about $800" (p. 101).

29 *Butte City Directory, 1900* (Butte: R. L. Polk & Company, 1900), pp. 689-690.

30 Lewis and Clark County Tax Lists, 1870, 1890, Montana Historical Society Archives, Helena [MHSA]; Rose Hum Lee, *The Growth and Decline of Chinese Communities in the Rocky Mountain Region* (New York: Arno Press, 1978), pp. 155-165.

31 Hunt, *The Making of a Special Relationship,* pp. 65-73; Zo, *Chinese Emigration into the United States,* pp. 131-139.

32 U.S. Department of the Interior, Census Office, *Ninth Census of the United States, 1870: Population, Volume I* (Washington, D.C.: Government Printing Office, 1872), p. 609; *Tenth Census of the United States, 1880: Population* (Washington, D.C.: Government Printing Office, 1883), p. 545; *Eleventh Census of the United States, 1890: Population, Part I,* p. 488; *Twelfth Census of the United States, 1900: Population, Part I,* (Washington, D.C.: Government Printing Office, 1901), p. 492.

33 Normal male-female relations were skewed even further because an un-usually large percentage of the Chinese women in the American West in the nineteenth century were employed as prostitutes. See Lucie Cheng, "Free, Indentured, Enslaved: Chinese Prostitutes in Nineteenth-Century America," in *Labor Immigration Under Capitalism*, ed. Cheng and Bonacich, pp. 402-434.

34 (Butte) *Weekly Inter Mountain*, November 23, 1882.

35 Lee, *The Growth and Decline of Chinese Communities*, p. 263.

36 Chinese Masonic Temple banner, March 3, 1876 (Virginia City), Montana Historical Society Museum, Helena. Regulations translated by Fr. John Wang of Missoula. Sue Fawn Chung's recent study contains an excellent description of the role that Chinese fraternal organizations and district associations played in the lives of many Chinese immigrants. See Chung, *In Pursuit of Gold*, pp. 18-28, 96-103.

37 Ibid.

38 Lee, *The Growth and Decline of Chinese Communities*, pp. 226-232.

39 Quoted in ibid., p. 229.

40 See ibid., pp. 273-280.

41 *Helena Weekly Herald*, February 15, 1872.

42 See *Weekly Missoulian*, June 17, 1881.

43 *Helena Weekly Herald*, April 8, 1869.

44 See Robert R. Swartout, Jr., "In Defense of the West's Chinese," *Oregon Historical Quarterly* 83 (Spring 1982), pp. 25-36; David H. Stratton, "The Snake River Massacre of Chinese Miners, 1887," in *A Taste of the West: Essays in Honor of Robert G. Athearn*, ed. Duane E. Smith (Boulder, CO: Pruett Publishing Company, 1983), pp. 109-129; R. Gregory Nokes, *Massacred for Gold: The Chinese in Hells Canyon* (Corvallis: Oregon State University Press, 2009).

45 See *Helena Weekly Herald*, May 31, 1883, September 24, 1885; *Helena Daily Herald*, January 26, 1870; (Butte) *Tribune Review*, August 4, 1906; *Great Falls Daily Tribune*, December 20, 1903; *Livingston Post*, December 6, 1906; (Miles City) *Yellowstone Journal*, April 5, 1884; (Quigley) *Rock Creek Record*, June 13, 1896; (Deer Lodge) *New North-West*, December 23, 1881; (Butte) *Weekly Miner*, December 27, 1881, August 7, 1891; (Butte) *Semi-Weekly Miner*, October 3, 1885; *Butte Daily Miner*, October 2, October 3, 1893; (Butte) *Daily Inter Mountain*, August 24, 1901; *Anaconda Standard*, January 21, March 8, 1892, January 8, 1893, September 5, 1899.

46 Montana Territory, Legislative Assembly, *Laws, Memorials, and Resolutions*

of the Territory of Montana, Seventh Session, p. 589; State of Montana, *The Codes and Statutes of Montana, 1895, Vol. I* (Butte: Inter Mountain Publishing Company, 1895), p. 562; State of Montana, *The Revised Codes of Montana, 1907, Vol. I* (Helena: State Publishing Company, 1908), p. 807. Although Chinese were not specifically named in the law, female-operated laundries and, later, steam-type laundries were exempt from paying the tax. These descriptions were synonymous with white-operated laundries. The intent of the law was obviously discriminatory.

47 Wunder, "Law and Chinese in Frontier Montana," p. 30; William L. Lang, "The Nearly Forgotten Blacks on Last Chance Gulch, 1900-1912," *Pacific Northwest Quarterly* 70 (April 1979), p. 57.

48 Records of the Montana State Board of Prison Commissioners, 1887-1962, RS 197, MHSA. Regarding the so-called "tong wars," a valuable corrective is Arata, "Beyond the 'Mongolian Muddle'."

49 W. Eugene Hollon, *Frontier Violence: Another Look* (New York: Oxford University Press, 1974), p. 89.

50 Members of the Butte Chinese community eventually took the boycott leaders to court. See *Hum Fay et al. vs. Frank Baldwin et al.* Records, MC 43, MHSA. Local newspapers gave the case extensive coverage, especially the *Anaconda Standard,* the *Inter Mountain,* and the *Butte Miner.* The Chinese won the case in the federal courts in May 1900, but they received no damages to cover their financial losses. See *Butte Miner,* April 4, 1899; *Daily Inter Mountain,* May 19, 1900; and United States District Courts (U.S. Circuit Court-Montana), Final Record, Case #40, RG 21, National Archives—Seattle Branch. For an outstanding study of the entire affair, see Flaherty, "Boycott in Butte," pp. 34-47.

51 See Yen, "Chinese Workers and the First Transcontinental Railroad," pp. 129-131; Chen, *The Chinese of America,* pp. 74-75.

52 See especially Saxton, *The Indispensable Enemy,* and Luther W. Spoehr, "Sambo and the Heathen Chinee: Californians' Racial Stereotypes in the Late 1870s," *Pacific Historical Review* 42 (May 1973), pp. 185-204.

53 *Butte Bystander,* February 11, 1893.

54 As early as 1871, a Missoula reporter declared: "The Chinaman lands upon our shores a serf, and remains so. He clings to his idolatry and heathenism with the tenacity of life; lives upon less than the refuse from the table of a civilized man, and devotes his sister to the basest lusts of humanity. . . ." *Missoula Pioneer,* June 22, 1871. For similar comments, see, for example, *Yellowstone Journal,* April 5, 1884; *Livingston Post,* December 6, 1906; *Anaconda Standard,* January 4, 1903.

Jewish Merchants and the
Commercial Emporium of Montana

~ *Delores J. Morrow*

The communities that sprang up in Montana almost overnight as a result of the placer mining boom created a wide variety of economic opportunities for scores of new arrivals in the Northern Rockies. While many newcomers filed mining claims in hopes of striking it rich, still others, as Delores Morrow notes in the following essay, "sought to dig not riches from the earth but profits from the diggers." In fact, some of the most successful entrepreneurs in early Montana history were those who figured out how to provide essential services to others engaged in the difficult and risky task of placer mining. Commercial activities covered a broad spectrum, from saloons to houses of prostitution, from laundries (often owned and operated by Chinese) to hardware stores. Although almost completely forgotten by today's Montanans, a key segment of this early commercial activity was made up of Jewish merchants who had come West in search of economic opportunities.

Jewish immigrants began arriving in America as early as the 1650s, but their numbers remained quite small—no more than a few thousand—until the mid-nineteenth century. Then, beginning in the 1820s and lasting up to the outbreak of the Civil War, a new wave of immigration broke on America's shores. The two largest groups to arrive during this period were the Irish (in many cases driven out of Ireland by the potato famine) and German-speaking peoples from central Europe. Included within the latter group were thousands of German Jews who had made the decision to emigrant to the United States. Indeed, the influx was so great that the Jewish population in New York City alone grew from just 500 in 1825 to approximately 40,000 in 1860. Nor did these new arrivals confine themselves to East Coast cities, as is sometimes assumed. By 1860, the Midwest city of Cincinnati had a German Jewish population of roughly 10,000. When gold was discovered in California, many Jewish merchants, including Levi Strauss, headed to San Francisco to explore commercial opportunities in that booming port.

The Jewish merchants who came to Montana, and especially to the community of Helena, in the 1860s and 1870s were thus part of a national network of merchants providing badly needed services to the rough-and-tumble settlements of the placer mining frontier. Specializing in the retail sale of clothing, dry goods, and tobacco, many Jewish merchants would also on occasion provide financial services that were in short supply on the frontier. While their record of success was mixed, as was true for most all entrepreneurs working in such a fluid environment, these early Jewish pioneers played a crucial role as Montana evolved from a collection of temporary mining camps into a settled community structure.

A t the close of the year 1877, the *Helena Daily Herald* gave front-page coverage to a directory of the town's businesses, schools, institutions, and societies. All six of the clothiers listed in the business section of this directory were Jews, and Jewish merchants monopolized the sale of other goods, including firearms and tobacco. Despite the numerous Jewish tradesmen recorded in its business columns, the newspaper accompanied its directory with a historical sketch that described Helena in 1877 as "the centre and distributing point for a happy and prosperous commonwealth, bound together by the amenities and civilization of Christian people."[1]

Although this publication chose to ignore the presence of

non-Christians in the territory, Jews played an important role in its settlement. Montana's Jewish pioneers were distinctive, not only for their religious practices, but also for their choice of occupations. Most Jews in Montana gold camps were merchants who "sought to dig no riches from the earth but profits from the diggers."[2]

Between 1862 and 1875, Montana placer mining produced nearly $134,000,000 worth of gold.[3] A substantial portion of this wealth passed through the hands of local bankers, merchants, and saloonkeepers; many of these entrepreneurs, particularly in Helena, were Jews. They controlled a large part of the town's retail trade and served as distributors of manufactured goods to people in other mining camps. Through their widespread business and family connections, Jews often were able to overcome problems endemic to frontier merchants and to maintain prosperous businesses that survived the gold rush.

In addition to supplying goods to their customers, Jewish merchants performed needed financial services; they exchanged gold dust for coin, contracted loans, and extended credit to other business concerns. Through their role as economic middlemen, distributing both goods and capital, Helena's Jewish pioneers encouraged commercial development in the town and influenced Helena's safe transition from gold camp to "Commercial Emporium of Montana."[4]

The discovery of sizable gold deposits on Grasshopper Creek in 1862 touched off Montana's first placer rush. This strike and richer ones at Alder Gulch in 1863 and Last Chance Gulch in 1864 drew thousands of goldseekers to the territory. Included in this migration were hundreds of Jews "attracted by the potentialities of the new region by the rumors of wealth or motivated by the spirit of adventure."[5] Next to Alder Gulch, Helena (Last Chance Gulch) had the richest gold deposits in Montana. This camp soon topped the other camps in population and importance and counted among its inhabitants the largest number of Jewish immigrants.[6]

During Montana's placer boom (1862-1870), more than 160 Jewish men lived and worked in Helena.[7] Most of these Jews were single, in their twenties and early thirties, and recent immigrants from Germany and central Europe, primarily Bavaria, Prussia, and Poland.[8] The majority listed their occupations as merchants and clerks, but

there were also butchers, tailors, saloonkeepers, bankers, and assay-
ers (see Figure 1, page 139). Many came from families of tradesmen
or had learned their mercantile skills as apprentices in businesses in
Europe. Others began their merchandising careers in America, working for relatives already established in business or peddling goods in
towns along the Atlantic coast and in mining camps in the West. For
over sixty percent of these men, Helena was not their first gold camp
experience[9] (see Figure 2, page 140).

During the early years of Helena's settlement, Jewish merchants
dominated the retail sale of general merchandise and clothing in the
camp. In its directory of city businesses, published February 28, 1867,
the *Helena Herald* listed seventeen Jewish dry goods and clothing
merchants to three Gentiles in the same business:

Dry Goods and Clothing[10]

Ladies' Dry Goods Emporium. 36 Bridge street S Levy.
W Weinstein & Bro. 26 Bridge street, clothing store.
I Haas. 20 Bridge street, clothing store.
J Helfer & Co. 15 Bridge street, clothing establishment.
Poznainsky & Behm. 13 Broad [Bridge] street, dry goods
and clothing.
Lavenburg & Co. 11 Bridge street, Temple of Fashion.
Ellis & Bros. 18 Bridge street, dry goods and clothing.
Honest Charley's auction and commission store, 16 Bridge street.
I Harris. Bridge street opposite Main. Dry goods and clothing,
miners' outfitting store.
Emanuel & Co. Cor Main and Bridge streets, clothing,
boots, and shoes.
G Goldenburg [*sic*] **& Co.** Cor Main and Bridge streets,
California clothing store.
J P Nohm. West Main street, west side, dry goods and clothing.
Loeb & Bro. 8 Main street, clothing merchants.
Remish & Stenzel. 20 Main street, pioneer cheap John auction store.
Gens [*sic*] **& Klein.** 28 Main street, clothing, boots, and
shoes, cigars and tobacco.

John How. 73 Main street, dry goods, groceries, and hardware.
L Blumenthal. 43 Main street, clothing, tobacco.
J C Levy. Main street, clothing, tobacco.
A. Cohen. 5 Main street, clothing, boots, and shoes.
John Morris & Bro. 3 Main street, clothing, boots, shoes, etc.

Two of the Jewish clothing stores, Gans and Klein, and J. C. Levy, also sold tobacco and cigars. After clothing and dry goods, tobacco products were the most popular merchandise carried by Jewish retail outlets. Three of the six tobacco store owners enumerated in the newspaper's directory were Jewish.[11] Almost exclusively, Helena's pioneer residents purchased dry goods, clothing, and tobacco from Jewish merchants.

Not all the business conducted by Helena Jews was confined to the retail trade. Some Jewish merchants expanded their operations to include wholesaling, while others, including Gumpert Goldberg and the Morris brothers, had two places of business, one wholesale and one retail.[12]

Jewish wholesalers urged merchants in neighboring gold camps to purchase their goods in Helena, offering their prospective customers numerous inducements: prompt service, low prices, and large selections of merchandise. One clothing and dry goods store, Loeb & Bro., promised "Orders from the Country promptly attended to,"[13] while another Jewish wholesale merchant, A. Weinshenk, announced his purchase of "the largest stock of ladies' dress goods ever brought to Montana" and offered to sell it to his retail buyers for very attractive terms. His advertisement read: ". . . He [A. Weinshenk] will not be undersold. Country dealers will do well to give him a call at his wholesale house."[14]

Some "country dealers" were Jewish merchants from other mining towns who depended on Helena's wholesalers and journeyed there several times each year to purchase their merchandise. Their visits occasionally drew attention in the local newspapers.

Charles Blum, that genial and popular Deer Lodge dry goods merchant, is over on both business & pleasure—purchasing

Four of Helena's successful businessmen pose in their finest garb: from left, Henry Klein,
Herman Gans, Louis Gans, and Herman Richter.

M. A. ECKERT. COURTESY MONTANA HISTORICAL SOCIETY, HELENA, 944-439.

such minor articles in his line as will insure him the most complete stock on the West Side, and shaking the hands of friends on every corner. . . .[15]

Jewish merchants kept their ties with relatives and friends engaged in merchandising in other parts of the country. They used these ties to set up beneficial trading contacts, not only to build up their existent retail and wholesale businesses, but also to open new stores in other camps. For example, Charles Blum and several of his contemporaries, including William Weinstein and William Copinus, had operated clothing and dry goods stores in Helena in the 1860s.[16] When they moved their mercantile establishments to other locations in Montana, they retained their connections with Helena wholesalers and friends.[17]

Many Helena Jewish merchants depended upon Jewish business associates both in Montana and in the trading centers of New York and San Francisco. They participated in merchandising networks consisting of brothers, cousins, and friends in shifting partnerships. It was through such partnerships and trading contacts that many Jews found business success in Helena and the West.[18]

A number of Helena's early general merchandise and tobacco stores were owned by Jewish men in partnerships with their brothers. In 1867, at least four of the seventeen Jewish-owned dry goods and clothing stores and one of the three Jewish-owned tobacco stores listed in the newspaper directory were family operations.[19] Also, at this time there were some Jewish firms identified only as Emanuel and Company or G. Goldberg and Company that were partnerships between either brothers, relatives, or Jewish friends.[20] One such store, for example, Lavenberg and Company, was owned by Alexander Lavenberg and his brother Isaac.[21] Four Helena dry goods and clothing stores—Auerbach Brothers, Loeb and Brother, Morris Brothers, and Sands Brothers— were owned in the late 1860s by Jewish brothers and continued to operate under these partnerships throughout the 1870s.[22]

Several stores run by Jewish merchants in Helena were branch operations or affiliates of firms in Denver, San Francisco, and New York. Often the merchants who managed these stores were related by blood or marriage to their partners in Helena and to their business associates in these larger cities. Morris Brothers, for example, was one Helena general merchandise store that was owned by three Jewish brothers and was operated initially as a branch house. In the 1860s, John, Moses, and David Morris were operating a dry goods store in Denver. They decided to expand their operation by opening two mercantile stores in Montana—one at Virginia City and one at Helena. John Morris ran the Virginia City store until 1863, when a fire destroyed the Morris's business in Denver, and his brothers joined him in Montana. Eventually, the whole family moved to Helena and sold out its Virginia City interests.[23] By 1867, the Morris brothers operated one general store in Helena and had announced the opening of another store, a wholesale business, which they owned in partnership with their brother-in-law Gumpert Goldberg.[24] John Morris sold out his interest in the business in 1869 and moved to Cincinnati, Ohio, and, soon after, Mr. Goldberg was reported living in Corinne, Utah. In 1879, Morris Brothers, owned by David and Moses Morris, was still in operation on Main Street in Helena.[25]

Another firm with family trading connections was Koenigsberger and Brother, a branch of the Koenigsberger family firm in San Francisco. In 1867, this store was operated by Philip and Sebastian Koenigsberger, who sold cigars and tobacco at 13 Main Street.[26] Evidently, it was a successful business, because on December 4, 1873, the *Helena Weekly Herald* noted the departure of one of its owners, Sebastian Koenigsberger, and his wife on a six-month vacation to Europe.[27]

On January 9, 1874, just one month after their departure, a fire destroyed numerous buildings in Helena, and Koenigsberger and Brother suffered losses totaling $35,000.[28] This fire, which occurred during the economic depression that followed the Panic of 1873, may have prompted the Koenigsbergers to close their business in Helena.[29] Sebastian never returned to Montana after his vacation, and in April 1874 Philip Koenigsberger also took his leave, returning to San Francisco.[30]

Success for Jewish businesses in Montana was not guaranteed by family or business connections, but the more prosperous firms in Helena in the early years were those whose owners kept in close contact with their relatives and friends engaged in merchandising in other cities. Both Auerbach Brothers and Sands Brothers were family operations that used their mercantile connections to their advantage and set up personal ties with their suppliers in New York and San Francisco.

Auerbach Brothers was a general merchandise store established in Helena around 1869 by two Bohemian immigrants, William J. and Leopold Auerbach.[31] The Auerbach brothers had relatives and friends in San Francisco, so they planned any personal visits in that city to coincide with their trips to purchase goods for the Helena store. In 1872, the *Helena Daily Herald* announced the departure of Leopold Auerbach on a buying trip to San Francisco and commented at length on the firm's ability to purchase quality California goods for the Helena market because of its connections.

> The Auerbach Bros. are among the most considerable shippers to this Territory of California goods, and for several years past have done a large and lucrative trade in the metropolis, and in many of the mining camps east and west of the range. The firm purchase[s] the great bulk of their merchandise from first hands—their teas, coffees, sugars, and other staple gorceries [sic] from the importers direct, and the various products and manufacturers of California, so popular in all of the mining and agricultural sections of the interior, from the leading firms in Frisco. . . .[32]

Leopold Auerbach set up permanent residence in San Francisco in the late 1870s, giving Auerbach Brothers a full-time buyer to attend to its purchasing needs.[33]

The Sands Brothers firm in Helena had its family and business connections in Denver and New York. Its owners, Abraham and Julius Sands, were Polish immigrants who had spent their early years in America engaged in merchandising in New York. When the brothers came west during the gold rush, they established a mercantile business in Denver and sent for their younger brother, Morris, to join

The Sands Brothers' store held a prime commercial location at 46 South Main Street, downtown Helena. COURTESY MONTANA HISTORICAL SOCIETY, HELENA, 953-089.

them. In the late 1860s, Abraham and Julius started a general merchandise house in Bannack, Montana, and later transferred this business to Helena.[34]

In 1870, all three brothers were living in Helena and Julius Sands was making buying trips to the East.[35] In order to improve their connections with eastern wholesalers, Julius Sands became the resident buyer for Sands Brothers in New York and attended to all the firm's purchases. He returned to Montana on yearly business trips, but left the management of the Helena store to Abraham and Morris. This arrangement proved advantageous to the firm, and by the late 1870s Sands Brothers was one of Helena's largest and most prosperous wholesale and retail stores.[36]

Unlike the successful Sands Brothers' firm, many Jewish-owned Helena businesses did not survive the placer boom; consequently, little is known about their owners or their family connections. Surviving records indicate, however, that Helena Jews engaged in a variety of business partnerships and operated commercial enterprises that were not owned exclusively by family members. Some Jews formed business associations with Gentiles, and others opened businesses with Jewish partners who were not relatives. The exact number of enterprises with this type of ownership is difficult to determine because few of these partnerships remained intact long enough to leave any record of their participants.[37]

Jewish merchant Louis Remish, for example, engaged in a short-lived Jew-Gentile partnership. On February 21, 1867, just months after he was elected one of the trustees of the Hebrew Benevolent Society, Louis was identified by the *Helena Herald* as one of the owners of Remish and Stenzel, a clothing business. The newspaper also announced the expansion of the firm to include a branch store in the Salmon River country.

> Remish & Stenzel—These enterprising wholesale & retail clothing dealers on Main Street, have recently shipped from their house here, and from their branch in Virginia [City], some $20,000 worth of ready made first class clothing to the new Salmon River mines, where they have a large store already completed to receive them.[38]

Not long after this announcement, Louis Remish relinquished his share of the business, and on April 18, 1867, the firm publicized his withdrawal from the partnership. Two months later, Louis was operating his own clothing store, Remish and Company, "one door below Wells, Fargo & Co.'s Office on Main St."[39]

During the early years of the gold rush, many Helena businessmen, both Jew and Gentile, engaged in a series of partnerships and business associations. The unpredictability of economic life in the gold camps made the operation of any enterprise a risk; newspapers of the period frequently reported business closures, partnership dissolutions, and costly losses suffered as a result of the frequent fires in Helena. Some merchants ended their business partnerships and moved away from Helena to seek more lucrative business locations, while others remained in the camp and tried to stay in business, entering one partnership after another. In boom towns of doubtful longevity, most businesses faced a precarious future, and Jewish-owned enterprises were no exception.

Isaac Marks and Moe Edinger were two Helena Jewish businessmen whose early business affiliations reflect the uncertainties of the placer period. On February 28, 1867, the *Helena Herald* listed Isaac Marks and his partner, Moe Edinger, as the proprietors of Our Sample Room, a liquor store on Main Street.[40] Three months later, the same newspaper announced the retirement of Mr. Edinger from the business and the addition of a new partner, W. J. Carnduff.[41] In the city directory of the following year, Marks and Edinger are listed once again as partners, but this time in another liquor business, the "Branch Saloon, Ike & Moe Proprietors, Main Street, Helena."[42] By 1870, Isaac Marks was the only member of this partnership still operating a saloon business in Helena. Moe Edinger was reported by the newspaper to be selling clothing at Cedar Junction, another placer camp.[43]

Like his contemporaries, Ben Falk had a series of business partners during his pioneer years in Montana. In 1865, he moved to Helena from British Columbia and opened a meat market on Wood Street.[44] During his first full year in business, Falk entered and ended at least two separate ownership arrangements involving the Empire Meat Market.[45] Despite these successive partnerships, the market remained in operation and by 1868 Ben Falk was its sole proprietor.[46] Falk ran the market successfully until April 28, 1869, when a fire swept Helena and destroyed numerous buildings, including his store. Following this disaster, Falk abandoned his business interests in Helena and moved to New York.[47]

Fires and fluctuating partnerships were not the only conditions that disrupted business activity in Montana's mining camps. A more significant risk to stable commercial operations in Helena was the practice of buying and selling goods on credit. Few merchants traded on a strictly cash-and-carry basis. Most sold merchandise to miners, prospectors, and retail customers on credit. Often the merchants were badly under-capitalized and were themselves credit customers of wholesalers in New York and San Francisco. On the frontier, success in merchandising "required a skill, the luck of being in the right place at the right time, adequate capital, and a line of credit."[48] The latter two ingredients were crucial elements for the prosperity of Helena's Jewish merchants, and lack of them precipitated bankruptcies and business failures.[49]

Many Jewish merchants preferred dealing with cash customers and used persuasive newspaper advertising to attract them to their stores. In 1870, Julius Sands, for example, ran numerous small ads in the *Helena Daily Herald,* including the following: "Buyers at wholesale and retail are invited to buy goods at their own prices, for cash." The Sands Brothers firm also offered to their customers "a special discount of *five per cent* on all *cash* purchases."[50] Most Helena merchants started their businesses by selling goods "cheap for cash," but later extended their operations to accommodate credit customers.[51]

Julius Basinski was one Jewish merchant who established a successful credit business with several Helena Jewish firms. At the age of twenty-two, he emigrated to the United States from Poland and lived four years in New York before deciding "to leave for the Montana Mining fields."[52] Soon after his arrival in Helena in 1870, Basinski realized that he did not have sufficient capital to open a business, one that could compete with the mercantile firms already operating in the camp. He presented a letter of introduction to the Sands brothers, but was unsuccessful in securing a clerkship in their store. Finally, with the assistance of Jacob and Dave Goldberg, Jewish clothing merchants, Basinski met a local cigar dealer with whom he transacted business.

Discouraged by his prospects in Helena, Basinski investigated other business locations and decided to move to Radersburg, a mining town about fifty miles south of Helena. He operated a candy and cigar store in that community and returned to Helena periodically to replenish his supply of goods. Basinski retained his contacts with the Goldberg brothers, and with their assistance established credit with some of Helena's leading business houses. According to his own account, he received liberal credit terms from Sol Holzman and Brother, Morris Brothers, L. Auerbach and Brother, Gans and Klein, and Koenigsberger and Brother, but "these credits were accepted only with one understanding—they are not to hurry me with the payments and [I] will remit to them as fast as business would justify." This credit arrangement proved satisfactory for all concerned, and Basinski operated a successful business in Radersburg for several years. Finally, the community's lack of growth forced Basinski to seek new opportunities elsewhere. He moved his goods first to Bozeman and later to Miles City, where he remained in the general merchandise business until the 1890s.[53]

Montana retail merchants were not always good credit risks. Some fell behind in payments to their Helena wholesalers and received threatening letters asking them to come forward and settle past due accounts.[54] Others were unable to pay for their purchases because of mismanagement or the loss of goods in a fire, and they became the subjects of court action.[55] Occasionally, too, a merchant had no intention of repaying his bills and deliberately defrauded his creditors.

On May 29, 1868, the *Helena Montana Post* published a story about Abe Polak, a Jewish merchant "with an eye more to his own pecuniary interest and comfort than to that of his creditors." According to the newspaper, Polak had been employed at Louis Remish and Company for some time when he decided to embark on a peddling expedition. He purchased $3,000 worth of goods on credit from several local firms and left Helena to peddle his merchandise in other mining camps. Polak wrote his creditors once from German Gulch and reported his progress, but nothing more was heard from him until news reached Helena that he had "shook the dust of Montana soil from his feet and into the faces of those who had befriended him."[56] He had sold his goods and was attempting to leave the territory without paying his creditors when he was robbed. The *Helena Daily Herald* reported the incident with a vindictive tone:

> Tit for Tat—Abe Pollock [Polak] . . . lost eight hundred dollars by the late robbery of the overland coach, near Pleasant Valley. We are informed that he had disposed of the goods and purchased a ticket for Salt Lake, with the intention of defrauding his creditors out of the money which had realized from the sale thereof. This is what we would call 'tit for tat.'[57]

The editor of the *Helena Montana Post* also published his own version of the story—describing the stagecoach robbers as "agents of retributive justice."[58] Understandably, local newspaper editors were sympathetic to the losses of the town's merchants and were quick to publicize any events that jeopardized business operations in the community.

Helena merchants suffered losses in their credit dealings, not only with retail customers, but also with their own wholesalers. Occasionally, a Jewish merchant failed to pay his debts and experienced a tightening of his credit by his wholesalers in New York or San Francisco. Mitchel Block was one Helena merchant who encountered difficulties with his creditors. Less than a year after his costly experience with Abe Polak, the *Helena Weekly Herald* reported Block's latest misfortune:

> Persuant [*sic*] to instructions received in this city from New York and San Francisco house[s], the wholesale clothing establishment of M. Bloch [Block], Main Street, Helena, was closed last evening by writ of attachment to recover the sum of $27,000.[59]

Helena Jewish merchants took risks when selling or buying goods on credit, but they realized the importance of such financial arrangements. During these years of recession and recurring fires, many merchants had minimal capital resources, so they had either "to find credit or face bankruptcy."[60]

Jewish merchants had more difficulty obtaining credit than non-Jews because credit investigation agencies like Dun and Company usually considered Jews a poor credit risk. Jewish "religious affiliation more often than not carried with it the automatic assumption and assignment of 'poor' or 'not good' for credit." To obtain a favorable credit rating, a person must possess "character" as well as assets. Dun and Company investigators often scribed the latter to Jews, but not the former.[61] Helena merchant Alexander Lavenberg, for example, was described by a Dun and Company agent as "Very hard pay. 'L' lives here with a woman not his wife. He is a very hard case."[62]

Such negative "character" reports meant that Jews received low credit ratings and often were denied access to credit and loans from customary lending institutions. To overcome ethnic and religious prejudice that often barred them from credit, Helena Jews had little choice but to borrow money from relatives and Jewish business associates. Without this credit network, Jewish merchants would have lacked the capital to open or expand business operations in the West.[63]

While Helena's Jewish merchants usually relied upon other Jews for credit and loans, they did not confine their financial transactions to their coreligionists. Gold was the medium of exchange in Montana in the 1860s, and miners depended upon merchants and saloonkeepers to convert their gold dust into coin and credit. Helena's Jewish merchants and their non-Jewish colleagues set the value for gold dust circulating in the camp, converted that dust into currency, and safeguarded valuables.[64] Jews who accumulated enough money from merchandising also made loans to individuals and invested their capital in other business enterprises.

Some Helena Jewish firms, including Auerbach Brothers, offered short-term, personal loans at comparatively low interest rates to both individuals and other firms.[65] Occasionally, the recipients of these loans were neighboring businesswomen, whose not so respectable occupations made access to credit from conventional sources difficult. Dry goods merchants Alexander and Selig Lavenberg extended mortgages to several of the camp's pioneer prostitutes and profited from these transactions. Jewish restaurateur Edward Zimmerman, on the other hand, suffered losses when his mortgages to Helena's fancy ladies went unpaid.[66] If they were fortunate, Jewish merchants who were loaning money received their payments when their notes were due, and they used interest obtained from such loans to expand their merchandising activities or to pursue other investment opportunities.

Some Jewish merchants chose mining as an outlet for their investment capital. The earliest lode records for Lewis and Clark County verify the involvement of Helena's Jewish pioneers in mining ventures.[67] Louis Behm, a dry goods and clothing merchant on Bridge Street, recorded two placer mining claims, one on February 24, 1865,

*From left, Meyer Gensberger, Alex Reed, and Ike Gensberger stand in front
of the Gans & Klein store with their wares on display.*
COURTESY MONTANA HISTORICAL SOCIETY, HELENA, 953-086.

at the mouth of Grizzly Gulch and the other on May 2, 1865, in the Green Horn Lode.[68] Two other merchants, David and Moses Morris, recorded ten claims in Lewis and Clark County between April 12, 1867, and September 19, 1867.[69]

In addition to mining, ranching was another enterprise that appealed to Jewish investors. In 1867, the Morris brothers purchased ranch land in Lewis and Clark County and soon were engaged in raising stock. That same year, Louis Gans and Henry Klein, Helena clothing merchants, bought land for farming and raising livestock.[70] Other Jewish firms, including Sands Brothers and Greenhood and Bohm, invested in ranch properties and cattle, horses, and sheep. From these initial investments, several Jewish merchants gradually increased their ranching interests, until, by the 1880s, they had extensive agricultural holdings throughout the territory.[71]

The Jewish merchants who settled in Helena during the gold rush were influential participants in the business life of the territory. They specialized in the retail sale of clothing, dry goods, and tobacco, and served as distributors of these items to local residents and people in other mining camps. As businessmen, Jews had an interest in the future of the community. They worked to solve civic problems and to promote cultural activities.[72] Jewish merchants also provided financial services badly needed in the region, offering credit to customers, loans to entrepreneurs, and investment capital to developing industries. An examination of Jewish involvement in Montana's early mercantile trade reveals both the difficulties of merchandising on the frontier and the unique aspects of the Jewish merchant experience in the West.

Figure 1.
Occupations of Helena Jews, 1868, 1879*

Occupations	Number in 1868	Number in 1879
Assayers	4	2
Auctioneers	1	-
Bankers	5	2
Barbers	1	-
Bookkeepers/Accountants	1	2
Butchers/Meat Markets	2	1
Cashiers	1	-
Clerks/Salesmen	4	1
Express Agents	1	-
General Operators	1	-
Grocers	1	-
Hide and Fur Dealers	1	-
Hotel Proprietors	1	3
Loan Officers	-	-
Manufacturer's Agents	-	-
Merchants	42	-
Clothes	1	13
Crockery/Glassware	-	2
Dry Goods	-	3
Fruits/Confectionery	-	-
Hardware	-	-
Miners	2	-
Pawnbrokers	-	-
Peddlers	1	-
Physicians	-	-
Ranchers	-	-
Restaurant Proprietors	-	-
Saloon Keepers/Liquor Dealers	4	1
Tailors/Dressmakers	3	1
Tobacconists/Guns and Liquors	-	4
Not Listed	1	1
Total Number	78	36

(2 with residences out of state)

*From *Business Directory of the Metropolis* (Helena, MT: 1868);
Montana Business Directory, 1879.

Figure 2.
Previous Residences of Helena Jews, 1868*

Place	Number
United States	1
California	31
Colorado	8
Idaho	3
Illinois	1
Kansas	4
Louisiana	1
Nevada	1
New York	11
Oregon	3
Pennsylvania	3
Texas	1
Utah	1
Virginia	2
Washoe**	1
Foreign Countries	
Germany	1
Poland	1
Prussia	2
Not Listed	2
Total Number	78

*From *Historical Sketch and Essay on the Resources of Montana: Including a Business Directory of the Metropolis* (Helena, MT: Herald and Job Printing Office, 1868).
**As listed in *Business Directory of the Metropolis.* Possibly Washoe County, Nevada, but this cannot be confirmed.

—◊◊◊—

This essay originally appeared in *Montana and the West,* edited by Rex C. Meyers and Harry Fritz, Pruett Publishing Company, 1985.

Delores "Lory" Morrow is the manager of the Photograph Archives at the Montana Historical Society Research Center. She received her bachelor's and master's degrees in History from the University of Montana. Morrow has written numerous book reviews and articles on Montana photographers and photograph collections. She wrote her master's thesis on Helena's Jewish community and has contributed essays about Montana's Jewish history to several books, including "The Children of Israel," in Religion in Montana: Pathways to the Present, *ed. Lawrence F. Small, vol. 2.*

—◊◊◊—

NOTES

1   *Helena Daily Herald,* 31 December 1877, p. 1. This essay was adapted from the author's master's thesis, "A Voice from the Rocky Mountains: Helena's Pioneer Jewish Community, 1864-1889" (Missoula: University of Montana, 1981). There are three other historical studies on Jews in Montana: Benjamin Kelson, "The Jews of Montana" (M.A., Montana State University, 1950); Patricia L. Dean, "The Jewish Community of Helena, Montana: 1866-1900" (B.A., Carroll College, 1977); and Julie L. Coleman, *Golden Opportunities: A Biographical History of Montana's Jewish Communities* (Helena, MT: SkyHouse Publishers, 1994).

2   Peter R. Decker, "Jewish Merchants in San Francisco: Social Mobility on the Urban Frontier," *American Jewish History* 68 (June 1979), p. 396.

3   *First Annual Report of the Bureau of Agriculture, Labor, and Industry of Montana for the Year Ended November 30, 1893* (Helena, MT: 1893), p. 287.

4   *Helena Daily Herald,* 31 December 1877, p. 1.

5   Benjamin Kelson, "The Jews of Montana," *Western States Jewish Historical Quarterly,* Vol. III, 1 (January 1971), p. 114.

6   Ibid., Vol. III, 2 (April 1971), pp. 170-189.

7   This figure includes only those men who arrived in Helena between 1864 and 1871 and are known to be Jewish by their identification as such in

local newspapers or through their membership in the Hebrew Benevolent Society and their contributions to the Alliance Israelite Universelle, a relief organization set up by French Jews in 1860.

8   U.S. Department of Commerce, Bureau of the Census, *Ninth Census of the United States, 1870.* Thirty-nine of the fifty-eight Jewish males listed had been born in Bavaria, Prussia, or Poland.

9   *Historical Sketch and Essay on the Resources of Montana: Including a Business Directory of the Metropolis* (Helena, MT: Herald and Job Printing Office, 1868); U.S. Manuscript Census, 1870.

10 *Helena Herald*, 28 February 1867, p. 1. Stenzel of Remish and Stenzel is not known to be Jewish. Two merchants, J. P. Nohm and John How, are not Jewish. Honest Charley's auction and commission store might have been owned by a Jewish merchant, either Charles Friedman or Charles Blum. Both were merchants in Helena at this time and not identified with a particular store.

11 Ibid. W. Brown, M. Goldman, and Koenigsberger and Brother were all Jewish.

12 *Helena Herald Supplement*, 26 June 1867, p. 2.

13 *Business Directory of the Metropolis* (Helena, 1868), p. 169.

14 Ibid., p. 135.

15 *Helena Weekly Herald*, 9 October 1873, p. 7.

16 *Business Directory of the Metropolis* (Helena, 1868), pp. 139, 141; *Helena Herald*, 28 February 1867, p. 1.

17 *Helena Daily Herald*, 14 June 1878, p. 3. William Weinstein moved to Philipsburg and William Copinus moved to Butte.

18 Robert E. Levinson, *The Jews in the California Gold Rush* (New York: KTAV Publishing House, Inc., 1978), pp. 32-35; William Toll, "Fraternalism and Community Structure on the Urban Frontier: The Jews of Portland, Oregon—A Case Study," *Pacific Historical Review*, 47 (August 1978), pp. 372-378.

19 *Helena Herald*, 28 February 1867, p. 1. The family-owned dry goods and clothing stores were W. Weinstein and Brother, Ellis and Brothers, Loeb and Brother, and John Morris and Brother. The only family-owned tobacco store was Koenigsberger and Brother.

20 Ibid.

21 *Helena Daily Herald*, 27 March 1871, p. 3; *Deer Lodge New Northwest*, 1 June 1888, p. 3.

22 *Montana Territory History and Business Directory, 1879* (Helena, MT: Fisk Brothers, Printers and Binders), pp. 142, 152, 153, 157.

23 Michael A. Leeson, ed., *History of Montana: 1739-1885* (Chicago, IL: Warner, Beers and Company, 1885), p 1238; Joaquin Miller, *An Illustrated History of the State of Montana* (Chicago, IL: Lewis Publishing Co., 1894), p. 202; *Progressive Men of the State of Montana* (Chicago, IL: A. W. Bowen and Co., 1902), pp. 764, 1742.

24 *Helena Herald,* 28 February 1867, p. 1; *Helena Herald Supplement,* 26 June 1867, p. 2.

25 *Helena Herald,* 12 February 1867, p. 3; Ibid., 6 April 1877, p. 3.; *Montana Business Directory,* 1879, p. 153.

26 *Helena Herald,* 28 February 1867, p. 1.

27 *Helena Weekly Herald,* 4 December 1873, p. 7.

28 Leeson, *History of Montana,* p. 717. In the earlier 1869 fire, the *Helena Weekly Herald* reported that Koenigsberger and Brother suffered losses of $5,000, 6 May 1869, p. 7.

29 Michael P. Malone and Richard B. Roeder, *Montana: A History of Two Centuries* (Seattle, WA: University of Washington Press, 1977), pp. 130, 142.

30 *Helena Daily Independent,* 15 April 1874, p. 3.

31 Neither brother's name is listed in the 1868 Helena city directory. Both are listed in the Hebrew Benevolent Society minutes; William was elected to the society on 3 December 1869, and Leopold was elected a trustee of the society on 3 June 1869. Hebrew Benevolent Association of Helena Records, 1865-1943. Manuscript Collection 38, Montana Historical Society Archives, Helena, Montana. Only William Auerbach is listed in the 1870 census.

32 *Helena Daily Herald,* 14 February 1872, p. 3.

33 William Auerbach to Leopold Auerbach, 1877. L. Auerbach and Brother Papers, 1868-1880, Manuscript Collection 125, Montana Historical Society Archives, Helena, Montana. *Montana Business Directory,* 1879, pp. 142, 161.

34 Leeson, *History of Montana,* pp. 1249, 1351-1352; *Progressive Men of the State of Montana,* p. 398; *Business Directory of the Metropolis* (Helena, MT, 1868), p. 155.

35 *Helena Daily Independent,* 15 December 1910, p. 5; U.S. Manuscript Census, 1870; *Helena Daily Herald,* 23 July 1870, p. 3.

36 *Helena Daily Herald,* 18 May 1877, p. 3; *Montana Business Directory, 1879,* p. 157; *Progressive Men of the State of Montana,* p. 398.

37 A notable exception to this statement was the Stadler and Kaufman live-stock firm. In the early 1870s, Louis Kaufman formed a partnership with Louis Stadler to provide meat for the gold camps. They went into the

stock-raising business and opened a butcher shop in Helena. Their partnership was continuous until the death of Mr. Kaufman in 1933.

[38] Hebrew Benevolent Association of Helena Records, 1865-1943, 3 December 1866; *Helena Herald Supplement,* 21 February 1867, p. 1.

[39] *Helena Herald,* 18 April 1867, p. 2; Ibid., 19 June 1867, p. 5.

[40] Ibid., 28 February 1867, p. 1.

[41] Ibid., 9 May 1867, p. 1.

[42] *Business Directory of the Metropolis* (Helena, MT, 1868), p. 94.

[43] U.S. Manuscript Census, 1870; *Helena Daily Herald,* 11 February 1870, p. 3. Cedar Junction was located in the Cedar Creek (Montana) mining district just south of the present-day town of Superior, in Mineral County, about 60 miles west of Missoula.

[44] Helen Fitzgerald Sanders, *A History of Montana,* 3 vols. (Chicago, IL: Lewis Publishing Co., 1913), Vol. 2, p. 1160.

[45] *Helena Montana Radiator,* 27 January 1866, p. 4; *Helena Herald,* 20 December 1866, p. 3.

[46] *Business Directory of the Metropolis* (Helena, MT, 1868), p. 94.

[47] *Helena Weekly Herald,* 6 May 1869, p. 7; Sander's *A History of Montana,* p. 1160. A summary of Helena's early fires is presented in Leeson's *History of Montana,* pp. 712-718.

[48] William M. Kramer and Norton B. Stern, "Early California Associations of Michel Goldwater and His Family," *Western States Jewish Historical Quarterly* 4 (July 1972): 195.

[49] Levinson, *California Gold Rush,* pp. 21, 52-53.

[50] *Helena Daily Herald,* 10 February 1870, p. 3; Ibid., 29 December 1875, p. 3.

[51] *Helena Herald,* 6 December 1866, p. 1.

[52] Julius Basinski Diary, 1883-1925, Biographies file, 14 pages, p. 3, American Jewish Archives, Cincinnati, Ohio.

[53] Ibid.; Robert E. Levinson, "Julius Basinski: Jewish Merchant in Montana," *Montana, The Magazine of Western History* 22 (January 1972): 60-68.

[54] Letterpress Book, 31 October 1876-12 March 1877, L. Auerbach and Brother Papers, 1868-1880.

[55] Helena's Jewish merchants brought their complaints with customers, other merchants, and freighters before Montana's courts. Jews frequently used Montana's legal institutions and expected that their cases would be judged seriously and equitably. Note the number of Jewish plaintiffs in the

proceeding accounts in the Helena newspapers of the period: *Helena Herald,* 14 March 1867, p. 5; Ibid., 4 April 1867, p. 1; *Helena Herald Supplement,* 4 April 1867, p. 1; *Helena Daily Herald,* 9 March 1870, p. 3. For an examination of the treatment that other minorities received in Montana's courts, read John R. Wunder's article, "Law and Chinese in Frontier Montana," *Montana, The Magazine of Western History* 30 (July 1980), pp. 18-31.

56 *Helena Montana Post,* 29 May 1868, p. 8. Polak is listed as one of the Helena Jewish contributors to the Alliance Israelite Universelle, *Cincinnati Israelite,* 17 April 1868, p. 6.

57 *Helena Daily Herald,* 28 May 1868, p. 8.

58 *Helena Montana Post,* 29 May 1868, p. 8.

59 *Helena Weekly Herald,* 25 February 1869, p. 7.

60 Decker, "Jewish Merchants in San Francisco," p. 398.

61 Ibid., pp. 398-399.

62 R. G. Dun Reports, Vol. I, Montana and Nevada Territories, p. 240.

63 Decker, "Jewish Merchants in San Francisco," p. 398-402.

64 Leeson, *History of Montana,* p. 704.

65 William Auerbach to Leopold Auerbach, 21 February 1877, p. 272, L. Auerbach and Brother Papers, 1868-1880.

66 Paula Petrik, "Capitalists with Rooms: Prostitution in Helena, Montana, 1865-1900," *Montana, The Magazine of Western History* 31 (April 1981), pp. 30-34.

67 The first lode records are listed under Edgerton County and are housed in the Office of the Clerk and Recorder, Lewis and Clark County, Helena, Montana. The county name was changed in 1867.

68 Lode Record A, Lewis and Clark County, 24 February 1865, p. 6; Lode Record B, Lewis and Clark County, 2 May 1865, p. 7, Office of the Clerk and Recorder, Lewis and Clark County, Helena, Montana.

69 Lode Record C, Lewis and Clark County, pp. 242, 273, 274, 275, 291.

70 Ranches and Ditches, Record C, Lewis and Clark County, pp. 30, 264.

71 *Helena Daily Herald,* 16 May 1874, p. 3; Leeson, *History of Montana,* p. 1214-1215; *Progressive Men of the State of Montana,* p. 255, 376, 398-399; Miller, *An Illustrated History,* p. 203, 574.

72 Morrow, "Helena's Pioneer Jewish Community," pp. 62-108. This chapter discusses Jewish civic and cultural activities in Helena. It includes Jewish involvement in issues of concern to the mercantile community.

The Socialization of Uncertainty:
The Ancient Order of Hibernians
in Butte, Montana 1880-1925

⁓ *David M. Emmons*

By the late 1870s, the placer mining boom that had put Montana on the map was rapidly waning, and with it, Montana's future seemed to be in doubt. But two new developments were underway that would change the face of Montana. The first was the coming of the railroads. In 1881, the Utah & Northern Railroad, a branch line of the Union Pacific, reached Butte; in 1883 the Northern Pacific Railroad was completed across the entire breadth of Montana. Other lines were soon to follow.

The second important development was the rise of industrial mining, made possible, at least in part, by the railroads, which could bring in the heavy equipment needed for quartz mining and could then be used to ship the ore to various smelters and markets. The earliest efforts in industrial mining had focused on gold and silver production, but by the 1880s that focus would shift to the mining of a new metal—copper.

Marcus Daly's discovery of fabulously rich copper deposits and his creation of the Anaconda Copper Mining Company would help to make Butte, Montana, one of the most important industrial centers in the entire West. Irish-born Daly was eager to employ his follow countrymen—whether they came directly from Ireland or from the copper mining districts of northern Michigan—to work in the mines of Butte and in the newly built smelter located in the town of Anaconda. Indeed, the

Irish came in such large numbers that they soon dominated the economic, political, and social structures of both communities.

As noted by award-winning historian David M. Emmons in the following essay, a large percentage of first-generation Irish workers in Butte were quick to join an Irish fraternal organization known as the Ancient Order of Hibernians (AOH). Emmons argues that they did so in part to confirm their ethnic solidarity as Irishmen, but also to gain employment opportunities and to secure financial benefits should they be either injured or killed while on the job. (In many respects, the AOH was similar to the social organizations that Chinese immigrants would establish in America to reinforce ethnic solidarity and provide communal benefits for all members.) In the case of the Irish, attitudes had changed by the second decade of the twentieth century. For second-generation Irish Americans, as well as for the next wave of young Irish workers coming to America, ethnic identity was not necessarily their primary concern. Buffeted by the wind of the new industrial age, they identified increasingly with their fellow blue-collar workers, regardless of one's ethnic background, rather than with the Irish elites who ran the Anaconda Copper Mining Company.

The copper mining city of Butte, Montana, was for its workforce a place of multiple horrors. Built on untimbered hills at an elevation of 5,000 to 6,500 feet, the city was described as looking like a "gigantic ship wreck."[1] Even the climate conspired. Winter temperatures routinely reached thirty to fifty degrees below zero. Headframes and hoisting platforms, smokestacks and slag heaps were scattered randomly over a landscape as urban as any in America. The residential neighborhoods adjacent to the mines consisted of densely packed frame homes, boarding houses, saloons, and churches. All reflected the wildly mixed ethnicity of the city. Narrow, unpaved streets took residents into the center of Butte to, among other imposing structures, the Hennessy Building, on whose sixth floor the giant Anaconda Copper Mining Company (ACM) had its corporate headquarters.

Mine headframes loom above a neighborhood in Butte, circa 1939.
ARTHUR ROTHSTEIN, COURTESY LIBRARY OF CONGRESS, LC-DIG-FSA-8A11183.

The people of Butte spoke of the "sixth floor" in the hushed tones befitting reference to a company having near total control over the city and its working families. There can have been few more unlovely industrial settings anywhere than that offered by the world's greatest mining city.

Despite the harshness of the place and its status as a corporate fiefdom, by 1910, 10,000 men from almost everywhere were making a precarious living by taking copper ores from Butte's 900 miles of underground drifts. Their wages were the highest in industrial America; nothing less, it may be assumed, would have been enough to keep them there. Butte's mines were worlds of their own. Underground temperatures were seldom below 85 degrees Fahrenheit, the humidity seldom below ninety percent. The work was physically punishing and uncommonly dangerous. Figures for the years 1899-1906 show 1.14 mine accident deaths per 1,000 men working in the United Kingdom; 1.07 in Germany; 0.75 in Belgium; and 2.02 in France. In the period 1909-1911, India's mine fatality rate was 1.18; Russia's 0.98; the notoriously dangerous Transvaal's 4.29. From 1893 to 1906, the Butte rate was 4.72; in 1896, it was 9.3.[2]

To these grim figures must be added those enumerating death and permanent disability from silicosis and tuberculosis. Mortuary records from 1906-1907 show 277 miners who died of respiratory disease. The average age at time of death was 42.7 years. The youngest to die was twenty-two; seventy-five others were under forty. Between 1916 and 1919, of 1,018 Butte miners studied by the U.S. Bureau of Mines, 432 (52.5 percent) had miners' consumption; another sixty-three had tuberculosis. A Butte physician testified before a federal commission that the rate of consumption death in Butte was "something appalling. . . . Butte is worse than any place I know of." Another said simply that "the slaughter of the miners of Butte . . . is a disgrace to this country." Mine accidents killed between fifty and a hundred men in Butte every year; respiratory disease killed thousands.[3]

The work was hot, hard, and deadly. It was also a hostage to the apparent whimsy of labor and commodities markets. There were extended shutdowns in 1893, 1903, 1907-1908, and 1917-1921. Every American mining town lived on sufferance—of the corporations that ran them and the supply of ore that sustained them. If anything, Butte was less wobbly and unsteady than most, but despite its greater staying power, living and making a living there were at best insecure, for jobs were easy to get but hard to keep. They paid well but they snuffed out lives with a regularity and a randomness that devastated workers' families and affronted workers' dignity. The culture of work and the social forms it created reflected the unsteadiness both of the town and of the lives of its labor force.[4]

In terms of both numbers and influence, the Irish were Butte's dominant ethnic group. They got to the place earlier than anyone else, and they filed what amounted to a proprietary claim on the town. Their influence, however, was never sufficient to buy them immunity from the hazards of living and working in what they called, "Butte, America." Like all of industrial America, it was, at first glance, an unlikely place to find the rural Irish. There is much debate on the characteristics of the Irish immigration and on the natural selection processes at work in it. What are needed are "points of entry" into the mental worlds of nineteenth-century peasantry from the West of Ireland. Almost by definition, however, they reveal more of the minds of those who did not emigrate than of those who did. For the Irish of the diaspora, the most accessible point of entry is provided by studying them in their new homes.[5]

On the basis of both Irish and Irish-American evidence, a case can be made that nineteenth-century Irish immigrants were among the world's most socially insecure and anxious people. It could not have been otherwise. The social and economic forces that drove them from Ireland were almost totally mysterious to them, and often misrepresented. They had been, in the most literal sense of the words, out of work in Ireland. The insecurities of making a living in America thus haunted them more than most. If their emigration were to have meaning, it had to bring some order to a frighteningly disordered world. It had, in other words, to provide them with social footholds.[6]

Their sense, however exaggerated, that England had driven them from their homes, that they were literally exiled, also contributed to what may be called the unsettling of the American Irish. Add to this their vaunted sociability and their deep and tenacious attachment

The crew at the Never Sweat Mine in Butte enjoys a rare moment of leisure above ground, circa 1902. COURTESY MONTANA HISTORICAL SOCIETY, HELENA, LOT 26, BOX 2, F2.

to place and a formula emerges: the American Irish sought safe and steady work at a wage that would allow them to build an ethnic enclave replicating the social and political worlds they had left behind. Quite literally their refuge and their strength, such an enclave prevented their atomization and quieted their terrors. To borrow the language of Gwendolyn Mink, it "socialized uncertainty." It also, however, allowed the American Irish to act out their nationalist fantasies by playing the role of exiled warrior and assailing England—the cause of their exile and, as such, the ultimate source of their fears.[7]

Butte offers a perfect example of this pattern. The Irish presence in Butte arose from two sources. First, by the 1880s, when Butte began its push toward world leadership in the production of copper ore, Irish immigrants and their sons had accumulated years of experience as hardrock miners either in Ireland or elsewhere in the American West. Second, Marcus Daly, the man who moved Butte toward

Irish-born Marcus Daly found wealth in America as one of Butte's "Copper Kings."
COURTESY MONTANA HISTORICAL SOCIETY, HELENA, 941-879.

copper mining and the founder of the Anaconda Company, was himself Irish-born, Roman Catholic, and an Irish nationalist of advanced Anglophobic views. So were most of his friends and corporate associates. The Anaconda Company, from its boardrooms to the depths of its mines, was dominated by "exiles of Erin." Some of the richest men in Butte were Irish; so were some of the poorest; and so were many thousands in between.[8]

Butte's Irish associations reflected this social fragmentation in the ethnic community. The largest of them, and arguably the most important, were the three divisions of the Ancient Order of Hibernians (AOH), a Catholic association open to those of "Irish birth or descent." The overwhelming majority of its up to 1,200 members were working miners, but that point must be interpreted with care. For example, Marcus Daly was also a member; so were the three Irishmen who succeeded him as president of the Anaconda Company, most of Butte's Irish shopkeepers and professionals, and almost every one of the Butte Miners' Union Irish officers. This last is a particularly important connection. Between 1885 and 1914, of 180 union officers, 145, a remarkable eighty percent, were Irish. Of the ninety-four Irishmen who served in these 145 positions, sixty-four, or sixty-eight percent, were members of the Ancient Order of Hibernians. Their management of union affairs *necessarily* reflected this involvement in the world of Butte's Irish enclave.[9]

As important as this middle- and upper-class and union representation was the fact that, until about 1905-1910, hardrock mining required not just a recklessness born of desperation but also great skill. Butte's "practical miners," a phrase much favored by them, thought of themselves as artisans. They were stable men and they lent stability to the entire community. Butte miners spent their working days

The bronze statue of Marcus Daly was crafted by Irish-born artist Augustus Saint-Gaudens, who died shortly before its unveiling in 1906. The statue was originally placed near the intersection of North Main and East Gagnon streets, but now greets visitors to the campus of Montana Tech on West Park at Montrose Avenue.

ARTHUR ROTHSTEIN, COURTESY LIBRARY OF CONGRESS, LC-USF33- 003097-M1.

performing industrial tasks beyond the capability of most in places few others would have dared go. It was these Irish artisans who supplied the AOH with its leadership and sense of purpose.[10]

But Butte's Irish were not just displaced artisans. They were also exiled warriors. The AOH sprang from agrarian radical Whiteboy origins in Ireland, and the American divisions retained a dedication to Irish Home Rule. It collected considerable sums of money for Ireland; its members listened to more than a few speeches filled with nationalist "sunbustery"—Irish code for the rhetoric of the bar-room patriots. But for every dollar the AOH collected for Ireland, it collected many hundred for Ireland's sons in Butte. For all its patriotic ardor, it took most seriously that part of its character that required it to show "friendship, unity, and true Christian charity." In essence, the AOH was a "voluntary cooperative," an ethnic friendly society, overwhelmingly working-class in membership, operating as a nationalist club.[11]

In important ways, the Butte AOH resembled the fraternities described by Mary Ann Clawson. It had elaborate rituals and uniforms, it displayed its strength in parading, and it was based in significant measure on shared artisanal values. It differed from Clawson's fraternities in its ethnic exclusiveness—it was not so much a "constructed brotherhood" as the organizational expression of an existing one—in its working-class dominance, and in the fact that it had a clear political agenda unrelated to American interests. The AOH, in other words, attracted men who were conscious of both their Irishness and their working-class status, and conscious as well of the obligations that attended both.[12] Yet, Ireland was nothing if not remote, and working-class resistance to capital was potentially injurious to the cause of Ireland—and of Butte's facsimile of it—as well as subject to wildly conflicting ideas regarding tactics and goals. What was immediate and not subject to nuanced interpretation was that the uncertainties of their world—whether defined by their Irishness or by their standing as Butte miners—could be combatted only communally. Toward this last function—the socialization of uncertainty—the Irish miners turned the Ancient Order of Hibernians.

The Ancient Order of Hibernians never wanted for things to do. It offered everything from an informal dating service to a missing

The plaque at the AOH Hall at 321-323 East Commercial Street in Anaconda lists the officers of the local chapter's building committee.
COURTESY LIBRARY OF CONGRESS, HABS MONT,12-ANAC,1-U-;-11.

person's bureau. It was part of the chain migration process. It fought the stage Irishman and the nativist American Protective Association (APA). It send "nurses"—members from the same Irish village—to care for dying brothers. Wakes were a specialty, as were flowers and Celtic crosses on graves, and fervent resolutions of condolence. To these essentially social services must be added mutual aid of a more immediate and tangible kind. The AOH Minute Books are filled with references to raffles, drawings, and money drives to aid members—or their widows and children—in need of assistance. They even paid off the mortgages of miners' widows.[13]

All of this was in addition to the regular AOH sick benefits of eight dollars per week and a regular death benefit of $100 to $500 for those willing to pay extra "premiums." Sick benefits began the second week of any member's disabling illness or injury. They continued for up to thirteen weeks, though members whose injury or illness required a longer rehabilitation routinely reapplied, waited out the first week, and were put back on benefits. The usual precautions were taken: a physician's certificate had to accompany the application; a "visiting" or "sick" committee waited on the claimants and confirmed that they were unable to work; and no benefits were paid when the injury had resulted from fighting or drunkenness. Occasionally a cost-conscious AOH treasurer would complain that overly compliant doctors— almost always Irish, though one was identified as a "Quaker"— were conspiring to defraud the benefits fund by not reporting pre-existing illnesses, but the AOH emphasized providing relief rather than strict accounting.[14]

It is doubtful that the Butte Irish community could have survived without these benefits. Eight dollars was less than half a miner's weekly wage, but joined with the eight dollars in benefits paid by the Miner's Union, it was enough to ride out the weeks without work. There were many of those weeks—as the sick benefit accounts indicate. In 1896, the AOH paid out sick benefits alone of $1,884; in 1899, $2,549; in 1903, $2,572; in 1911, $2,712. There were years, 1904 and 1910, for example, when one in every five AOH members collected some sick benefits. In 1908, AOH Division 1 reported that it was "in good shape except the Death Benefit fund is a little short on account of the number of deaths during the last quarter." Two years later, Division 2 sponsored a dance "to build up the treasury which has suffered badly since the first of the year on account of the death of five of our brothers." The total for the nineteen years for which records are complete between 1885 and 1911 indicates that Division 1 alone paid out $30,496 in sick benefits and another $7,800 in death benefits.[15]

There is more to this story than this communal assumption of risk. Under the best of circumstances, Butte was a dangerous town; no man who went underground, regardless of ethnicity, could dodge all the hazards of his work. The Irish miners, however, seemed doubly vulnerable. Their work exposed them to the "deadly dust," fine particles of silicate rock that tore at their lungs and left them vulnerable to a variety of respiratory diseases, including tuberculosis. Their Irishness may have left them more susceptible than any other group to its ravages. Butte miners called tuberculosis and silicosis "the miners' con," "the Galen giggles" after the sanatorium in nearby Galen, or simply, "rocks on the chest." The doctors called it "phthisis." The Irish knew only that they caught it more often and with deadlier consequences than anyone else in town.[16]

A 1912 County Health Department report on tuberculosis made clear the selective nature of the disease and the extent of the Irish miners' risk of contracting it. Of 465 tuberculosis victims from Silver Bow County between 1908 and 1912, 270 were Irish-born men. In other words, approximately ten percent of the population supplied fifty-eight percent of the tuberculosis deaths. There was some idle and mean-spirited speculation as to cause. Some said the Irish drank more than anyone else; others said they lived in worse neighborhoods. The first may have been true, if ultimately unprovable; the second was demonstrably false. Neither is particularly relevant. Part of the problem of interpreting the data arises from the fact that the survey did not distinguish between tuberculosis and silicosis—the first a bacteriological disease, the second an occupational disease with symptoms identical to those of tuberculosis. These were highly politicized diseases. Capital preferred a bacteriological label, labor an occupational, including the even more revealing "miners' consumption." The Board of Health report reflected capital's bias.[17]

The Irish deaths were probably from silicosis; explaining them requires an understanding of Irish work histories, not formal training in epidemiology. That work history was unique. Like the Cornish, Irishmen arrived in Butte early; unlike the Cornish, they stayed late, through the corporate consolidations of 1901, 1906, and 1910. Thus, individually and collectively, they suffered a longer exposure to silicate dust than any other ethnic group. In addition, their greater work experience—particularly after the departure of the equally experienced Cornish—meant that they spent more time working at the face of drifts where the exposure was greatest. Theoretically, the Irish supplied fifty-eight percent of the county's deaths from "TB" between 1908 and 1912 because fifty-eight percent of the miners with more than ten tough years in the mines were Irish. Silicosis, not tuberculosis, was their particular curse, but that fact placed as great a burden on the AOH's efforts at mutual assistance as an epidemic of tuberculosis.[18]

The Ancient Order of Hibernians' other major responsibility was to find for their members the jobs that often maimed and killed them. There is a grim irony in that, but it was one played out in many of America's industrial cities. The AOH was a central part of an Irish miner's enclave; that enclave was dependent upon Irishmen finding and keeping work. It fell, then, to the enclave to find the jobs necessary to its own survival. To an extent, the enclave was itself an employer of last resort. Hibernia Hall, for example, from its janitors and snow shovelers to its coal haulers, ice suppliers, lawyers, and band conductors, hired only Irishmen. All were on retainer to the enclave and its associations. So, to a certain and unofficial extent, were city and county officials. Irish and AOH dominance of the local Democratic Party ensured the Irish access to jobs as school teachers, firemen, and policemen—and as ward bosses, city councilmen, and mayor.[19]

The jobs that counted, however, were not in Hibernia Hall or City Hall but underground, and the Irish would seek their share of these as well, whatever the risks that inhered in them. This involved vocational training for those Irish without well-practiced work skills. New AOH members bound for the mines were taught more than handshakes and passwords; they were schooled in the recondite arts of their trade and in the various stratagems necessary to survive it. It also involved, as John Bodnar has written, "cooperating with the more powerful" by negotiating with the men who controlled the jobs in the interest of getting a portion of them for one's own ethnic group. This ordinarily involved immigrant workers begging favors of native managers. In Butte, however, both supplicant and lord were Irish, and both were determined to sustain the enclave. One Irishman counted over 100

Irish hiring officers in the Anaconda Company mines, and most of those were AOH members. The bishop of Montana noted proudly that "many of our richest mine owners are Catholics and Irishmen." Butte miners even referred to waste rock from Anaconda properties as "Protestant ore." In such an environment, ethnic job preference became the ultimate form of fraternal mutual aid.[20]

The result was a world turned upside down. For the first twenty years of its corporate life, Anaconda, the largest producer of copper in the world, closed its mines on such exclusively Irish holidays as St. Patrick's Day, the all-Irish societies' picnic, and even, on one occasion, the birthday of Robert Emmet, the martyred Irish patriot. It built handball courts in the change rooms of its "Irish" mines, posted job notices in Gaelic, and permitted Irish nationalist fund-raisers to solicit underground. These were not insignificant favors. More important than all of them, however, was the preference given Irish job applicants. The Montana legislature commented on it, marveling at the extent of Irish "clannishness;" the American Protective Association moaned that "'NO ENGLISH NEED APPLY' was virtually posted on the doors of the Anaconda syndicate of mines," and that English and native-born miners were "insulted and treated with contempt by the Irish bosses." The APA exaggerated, but not by much.[21]

The Hibernians understood their power; they may even have understood how uncommon it was. David Ryan, an AOH officer, commented in 1908 that "so many of our members are in a position to give employment." Ed Lawlor agreed, pointing out that one of the chief benefits of AOH membership was the chance "to know those who are in a position to give employment." The AOH had a varied agenda; it provided a chance for "exiled" Irishmen to play the patriot game; it provided social diversion; it offered a kind of health insurance; and it served as an employment bureau. Of all of these, however, the most important, at least if its use as a membership lure is any indication, was the last. Those Irish not in the AOH simply did not count. Walter Breen, himself a hiring officer, said that he "would as soon get a job for a Cousin Jack as an Irishman not in the AOH." This reference to Cornishmen, among the Irish's most ancient and intractable foes, was instructive. Thomas Kealy used an even more heavily laden analogy.

Cornelius "Con" Kelley served as president of both the Anaconda Company and the Montana Power Company. KAIDEN KAZANJIAN STUDIOS, COURTESY MONTANA HISTORICAL SOCIETY, HELENA, 943-062.

"Fallen away Hibernians" were deserving of no consideration. "They were scabs," said Kealy, "worse than scabs." The Irish exile, in other words, had to seek out his refuge and embrace it, for it would not automatically find him. As for the "few grumblers" who were not placed "through this organization," said John J. McCarthy, a mine foreman and former union officer, "let them join the 'Birds and Animals' organizations and see how many jobs they will secure for them."[22]

It would not have been many. Indeed, few fraternal associations anywhere, Masonic lodges included, can have had the influence of the Butte AOH. Hibernian job committees met routinely with ACM hiring officers, themselves AOH members. When Con Kelley, fourth president of ACM and an active Hibernian, referred to a "community of interests" between capital and labor in Butte, his comment bespoke ethnic more than class cooperation, and ACM's interests were well served by these ethnic sweetheart deals. The company took comfort in knowing that its associational Irish workers, according to a local priest, "towered above the average Irishman, morally, socially, and economically." It took even greater comfort, however, in knowing that stable Irishmen in the AOH were unlikely to strike or take other job actions and risk losing the jobs their careful negotiations had secured for them. Cooperation with the more powerful, at least in Butte, could be made to seem like fraternal good will, or class collaborationism, or both.[23]

Whether this fraternal role was countercultural, in the sense of being oppositional, or merely supplied an alternative vision is less important than that the role constituted a communal and noncompetitive approach to dealing with the uncertainties of an industrial working class. The enclave embraced mutualism, cooperation, communalism, what later Catholic and Irish thinkers like Father J. C. Harrington and Monsignor John Ryan came to call "distributism." Ugly and imprecise, the word nevertheless says something important about the Irish Catholic working class, in Butte and elsewhere. Drawing on his reading of Pope Leo XIII's 1891 encyclical *Rerum Novarum*—though at times the reading was loose if not creative—Harrington insisted that the "social teaching of the . . . Church is irreconcilable with . . . Capitalism," an extreme statement of the case perhaps, but, for all that, a useful description of what David Montgomery called "a spirit of mutuality [among American workers] . . . a collectivist counterculture in the midst of [a] factory system." Ryan wrote similarly that a system of cooperation "has a greater claim to the title of Catholic than any other. . . . It . . . and not . . . present-day capitalism . . . is in harmony with Catholic . . . social principles. . . ." This sounds a lot like what the historian Alan Derickson called "an ethic of mutualism [that] shaped the lives of union miners." The voluntary cooperation and social welfare programs of Butte's AOH provide a classic example not only of that mutuality but also of the uses to which it could be put when the circumstances were right. Butte was what other American Irishtowns would have been had those others obtained the same power-sharing opportunities.[24]

There was, however, a false note in the way these themes were played out by Butte's dominant Irish association—false, at least, to those who listen for the sounds of interethnic class harmony. The Irish enclave was steeped in Irish nationalist values, but there was an obvious "symbiotic relationship" between Irish nationalism and workers' rights, to borrow from the language of Eric Foner. There was a symbiosis between Irish worker and interests, but only if the workers were themselves Irish, and associational ones at that—only if in the Gaelic word, they were of the *muintir*, meaning everything from family, folk, and tribe to party, religious order, and community. The Hibernians *had* learned well the Catholic social teaching that arose out of *Rerum Novarum*—but they applied its countercultural proscriptions with a fine ethnic selectivity. AOH collectivism did serve as a cultural antidote, for it challenged at least some of capitalism's control of workers' lives and its presumed hegemonic authority over working-class values. But it challenged as well the idea that multi-ethnic worker organizations were the more appropriate and "natural" place to combat—or at least bargain with—the capitalist world view.[25]

This, then, was an Irish miner's alternative culture that had arisen from lessons learned on Irish farms and in Butte's underground mines. It was worker and Catholic only in so far as Butte's Irish were both. Its commitment to Irish nationalism, though not entirely symbolic or cosmetic, was subordinated to taking care of the needs of Butte's Irish miners and their families. It paid bills, offered vocational instruction, and found its members employment; it then nursed, waked, and buried them, and cared for their families. It helped create staying power and helped propel the survivors of a brutal industrial system into positions of power. It offered in its program of social services what secular reformers called the "cooperative commonwealth." Indeed, its control of the labor force and its influence over worker holidays even gave it and its working-class constituency unprecedented leverage over production. It spoke to a uniquely Irish world view that comported poorly with industrial America's celebration of competitive individualism and just as poorly with labor's demands for worker control. Members of the Ancient Order of Hibernians were, in part, what their charter and their remembered pasts required them to be—an intensely exclusionary, almost tribal, fraternity of the passionately Irish. But men of every class, both the buyers and sellers of labor, fit that description. It was the Hibernians' affection and support for one another in the interest of steady employment and enclave survival that most closely defined them. Living—and dying—in Butte made greater demands on their time and their resources than did the cause of Ireland.

That interclass affection and support distorted the labor market and put Butte on the long road to worker solidarity. In this context, the system of ethnic mutual aid in Butte provides partial confirmation of Mink's argument that old labor in the American Federation of Labor, much of it immigrant, behaved most uncharitably toward new immigrants. When the Ancient Order of Hibernians' control of the Butte Miners' Union is recalled, and when the similarities between the policies of the Butte Miners' Union and those of the AFL are noted, support for Mink's thesis becomes even clearer.[26] The problem arises when it is also recalled that the "old laborers" in Butte's AOH excluded not only new immigrants but non-affiliated Irish as well, that the Butte Irish, in other words, were both old labor and new immigrants.

These later Irish, as with all of the "new immigrants," got to town after 1905. They were not of the *muintir* nor of the West of Ireland, and they would transform Butte's Irish world, including the AOH. They were not like those Irish who had preceded them to Butte. They were more politicized—more than a few of them radicalized—by developments in Ireland. They came from different parts of the island, and Ireland was a place where county origins were taken seriously and frequently invoked. Most important, few of them had any work skills. By then, they did not need them. New technologies had reduced the demand for stable, experienced hand drillers able to use black powder and nitroglycerine. Hardrock mining went from being a craft to being a job that consisted of tending a machine while it dug holes.[27]

The Anaconda Mining Company was still Irish run, but, as the AOH learned to its dismay, it no longer depended on fraternal good will in building a skilled and dependable workforce. In 1908, the Hibernians sent a job committee to see ACM boss John D. Ryan in "the employments interests of the Order." For thirty years, AOH job committees had been greeted cordially and sent home happy. This time, Ryan accorded the solicitors "a very chilly reception, . . . thanked [them] for calling on him," and promised them nothing. Perhaps, one prominent Irishman commented on hearing of Ryan's new attitude, "it was not wise any more to be too Irish."[28]

The old Irish had lost their privileged place in Butte. Their positions were being taken not by miners but by thousands of strong men willing to take heavy equipment underground. There was literally a world of difference between the two work cultures—and significant tensions between the holders of each. The dissimilarities between the Irish immigrant generations also played on this emerging intra-ethnic feuding. The Irish-born among the new immigrant workers found their companions among the second generation of their own age—and these sons of the old immigrants did not share their fathers' fraternal instincts. One Hibernian described the young Irish, both immigrant and second generation, as "contumelious" and said that they "ridiculously scorned" the AOH.[29] There was also less of the exile about these new Irish; they had little need of refuge and no willingness at all to seek it in interclass fraternities and the social "arrangements" that distinguished them. One older Hibernian explained that younger Irish spurned the AOH because they feared that what was said "at meetings [was] being repeated on the 6th floor." That, of course, was precisely the point. Older Irish gloried, in fact, that there was no need to repeat on the "6th floor" what was said in meetings for the simple reason that the "6th floor" was so well represented at the meetings. To the younger Irish, AOH job committees were both demeaning and, in the new industrial environment, ineffectual. Even had they retained their usefulness, job preferences for associational Irish meant fewer jobs for those not in the associations—Irish included.[30]

Some parts of the miners' world had not changed. "Miners' con" was still ubiquitous, more so, in fact, than it had been when hand drills were being used. But the young Irish were not committed to Butte and its enclave. They were more willing to assume their own occupational risks. Like most unskilled workers, they had no intention of remaining in that occupation—or in Butte—longer than was necessary and certainly not long enough to catch the "Galen giggles"—or, it would seem, to join the AOH. In 1914, the average underground laborer worked 137 days; in 1917 that average dipped to 53 days; in 1918 to 38. No figures are available before 1914, but impressionistic evidence suggests that, for say 1905, individual miners had worked for three to three and a half years.[31]

Injury remained a constant hazard—in June 1917 a fire incinerated 165 men in the Speculator Mine—but on this point there were new elements in the industrial calculus. One was workmen's compensation, passed in Montana in 1915, a system which, for all its inadequacies, paid better than $8 a week for thirteen weeks. Another was worker militancy. The younger Irish were not so much anti-associational as they were anti-AOH, which meant anti-BMU as well, for the two organizations in the minds of many—new Irish included—were the same thing. In 1914, these new Irish joined with other dissidents to destroy the old Butte Miners' Union, an "obsolete

Labor issues sometimes led to violence, as when the Miners' Union Hall in Butte was ripped apart by a bomb in June 1914.
WESTPHAL, COURTESY MONTANA HISTORICAL SOCIETY, HELENA, 946-114.

union," said one radical, run by and for AOH Irishmen, said another. In 1917, younger, more radical Irish formed an organization of their own, the Pearse-Connolly Irish Independence Club. This was no friendly society dispensing social welfare but a radical Irish workers' club which shared office space with the striking Metal Mine Workers Union, the Finnish Workers Association, and the Industrial Workers of the World. Among the demands of each of these groups was that the mines be made safer and the work day shorter. They would close down the mines to enforce these and other demands—whatever the cost in job security. Closed mines were preferable to wakes, death benefits, and flowers on Irish graves.[32]

The consequences of these new attitudes were far-reaching. Sweetheart deals between ACM and the Ancient Order of Hibernians for job preference for the associational Irish—and the Butte Miners' Union complicity in those deals—could not survive this new industrial order. Job preference was attacked from all sides. The new unions demanded that any "discrimination against any group . . . be resented by the men on the job." The new, self-consciously progressive state government formed equal opportunity employment agencies. The new corporate managers, in an effort to bring scientific management to the mines, drastically changed their hiring and personnel policies. The needs of specific ethnic groups were not a part of the new dispensation.[33]

Similarly, the corporation and the state assumed far greater responsibility—and authority—over matters of worker safety and worker health. Whether it was the ACM's Safety First campaign or state workmen's compensation, the role of friendly societies—and to an extent, of the conservative unions—was significantly diminished. The result was a greater sense of worker rather than ethnic solidarity than had existed under the old rules. This was not something commonly sought either by corporations or by the state, but among the ultimate and ironic consequences of the decline of ethnically selective voluntarism was the idea of interethnic industrial unionism of a distinctly Congress of Industrial Organizations sort.[34]

Events far removed from Butte also played a role in the decline of the Hibernians and the voluntaristic social welfare they represented. As far as the Wilson administration was concerned, all Irish-American associations were suspect, and it refused to distinguish among Hibernian, Clan-na-Gael, or Pearse-Connolly clubs. The first two were guilty of colluding with the Germans in demanding an independent Ireland, and the last shared in this crime, then compounded the treachery by embracing the cause of revolutionary socialism and consorting with Wobblies and Reds. The Great Red Scare had about it elements of a great green scare.[35] Add to this events in Ireland itself. The Rising of 1916 gave rise to the Anglo-Irish War. Butte's Irish were as divided on these events as the mend of women of Ireland, but the event that sundered Butte's Irish community—as it did Ireland—was the Irish Civil War of 1921-1923. It was difficult for the community to recover, and impossible for the associations. Internally divided, betrayed and persecuted by the Wilson administration, shattered and heartbroken by Ireland's Civil War, Butte's Irish enclave retreated and turned inward. The social welfare programs of its nationalist associations,

The once-proud entrance to the AOH Hall in Anaconda serves as a faded reminder of the order's glory days. COURTESY LIBRARY OF CONGRESS, HABS MONT,12-ANAC,1-U-;-9.

particularly the AOH, were casualties of demoralization and declining memberships. The Hibernians fell from a membership of 1,200 in 1905 to fewer than 100 by 1925. Like the heady nationalism of its earlier years, AOH sick and death benefits and job committees were relics of a communal past. Neither had any contemporary relevance. The Irish were no longer exiles and there was no refuge.[36]

Butte's miners, Irish or not, drifted alike through the 1920s.

The Butte Miners' Union was gone, and so by 1920 were its rivals and successors. There are no records of the Pearse-Connolly Club after 1922. Old men—and not very many of them—ran the established Irish organizations, including the AOH. There was nothing of the last hurrah about the fall; government agencies did not usurp the social welfare functions of voluntaristic private associations. The "socialization of uncertainty" among Butte's Irish was not taken away from them; it went by default. It had no place in a new industrial system dominated by a mobile labor force whose protection, beyond that provided by its mobility, was mandated by the state, demanded by more militant unions, and offered up as gestures of magnanimity by corporations.[37]

This essay originally appeared in *Éire-Ireland,* Volume 29, No. 3, 1994.

David M. Emmons received his Ph.D. from the University of Colorado in 1969, two years after he joined the History Department at the University of Montana. He is the author of many articles and three books: Garden in the Grasslands: Boomer Literature of the Central Great Plains *(1969);* The Butte Irish: Class and Ethnicity in an American Mining Town, 1875-1925 *(1989), and* Beyond the American Pale: The Irish in the West, 1845-1910 *(2010).* The Butte Irish *was awarded the Statue of Liberty/Ellis Island Prize and the Robert G. Athern Prize, and was runner-up for the Donnelly Prize.*

NOTES

1   The author wishes to thank the Irish American Cultural Institute for the generous grant that made additional research for this article possible. The shipwreck reference is from Gertrude Atherton, *Perch of the Devil* (New York: A. L. Burt, 1914), p. 57. For an account of the Anaconda Company and its power, see Michael Malone, *The Battle for Butte: Mining and Politics on the Northern Frontier* (Seattle: University of Washington Press, 1981).

2 For the number of men working in Butte, see Works' Project Administration, *Copper Camp: Stories of the World's Greatest Mining Town* (New York: Hastings House, 1943), p. 21; U.S. Industrial Commission, *Mining Conditions and Industrial Relations at Butte, Montana.* Sen. Doc. 415. 64th Cong., 1st sess. *Final Report and Testimony,* vol. 4 (Washington, D.C.: Government Printing Office, 1915), p. 3687. On wages, see Butte Chamber of Commerce, *Resources of Butte: Its Mines and Smelters* (Butte: Intermountain Printers, 1985), pp. 7-10; Clarence Long, *Wages and Earnings in the United States, 1860-1890* (Princeton: Princeton University Press, 1960), pp. 121-166; Industrial Commission, *Conditions,* p. 3712; David M. Emmons, *The Butte Irish: Class and Ethnicity in an American Mining Town, 1875-1925* (Urbana: University of Illinois Press, 1989), pp. 23-24 and notes. For the miles of drifts, see Montana, Bureau of Agriculture, Labor, Industry, *Report, 1912* (Helena: Independent Pub. Co., 1912), pp. 275-278. Temperature and humidity figures are from Silver Bow County, Board of Health, "Report on Sanitary Conditions in the Mines and Community, Dec., 1908-April, 1912," (typescript in Montana Historical Society), pp. 6, 9, 10, 15, 25, 26. Death statistics are from Mark Wyman, *Hardrock Epic: Western Miners and the Industrial Revolution, 1860-1910* (Berkeley: University of California Press, 1979), p. 115; Montana, Dept. of Labor and Industry, *First Biennial Report, 1913-1914* (Helena: Independent Pub. Co., 1915), p. 297; the *Montana Socialist* (Butte), May 25, 1913.

3 Silver Bow County, Mortuary Records, 1906-1908, Butte-Silver Bow Public Archives. Industrial Commission, *Conditions,* p. 3978; Bureau of Mines, David Harrington and A. V. Lanza, *A Preliminary Report of an Investigation of Miners' Consumption in the Mines of Butte, Montana, Made in the Years 1916-1919,* Technical Paper 260 (Washington, D.C.: GPO, 1921), pp. 12-14. For an overview of occupational hazards in the western mining regions, see Alan Derickson, *Workers' Health, Workers' Democracy: The Western Miners' Struggle, 1891-1925* (Ithaca: Cornell University Press, 1988), pp. 28-56.

4 For mine shutdowns, see Emmons, *Butte Irish,* pp. 135-136, 141, 142, 226, 242-244, 260, 267, 302, 364-373, 383, 398-402, 408. On May 13, 1916, the U.S. Navy ran an advertisement in the *Montana Socialist* comparing the safe and steady work offered by the Navy with the hazardous and uncertain work of the mines.

5 The "points of entry" reference is from Robert Darnton, *The Great Cat Massacre and Other Episodes in French Cultural History* (New York: Basic Books, 1984), p. 7. One of the most revealing for the purpose of understanding—or at least being able to carry on a conversation with—the nineteenth-century Irish is Peter O'Leary (Peadar Úi Laoghaire), *My Story:*

Reminiscences of a Life in Ireland from the Great Hunger to the Gaelic League, 1915, trans. Cyril Ó Céirín (New York: Oxford University Press, 1987). See also the collections of Irish folk tales and stories by Padraic Colum, *A Treasury of Irish Folklore* (New York: Crown Publishers, 1967), and W. B. Yeats, *Fairy and Folk Tales of Ireland* (1888, 1892; rept. New York: Macmillan, 1983).

6   Emmons, *Butte Irish,* pp. 61-87. Kerby A. Miller, *Emigrants and Exiles: Ireland and the Irish Exodus to North America* (New York: Oxford University Press, 1985), pp. 427-435, 441-444, 556-568. See also Miller, "Emigration, Capitalism, and Ideology in Post-Famine Ireland," in *Migrations: The Irish at Home and Abroad,* ed. Richard Kearney (Dublin: Wolfhound Press, 1990), pp. 91-108. On the general fear of unemployment and its consequences, see Alexander Keyssar, *Out of Work: The First Century of Unemployment in Massachusetts* (Cambridge: Cambridge University Press, 1986). See also Herbert Gutman, "Work, Culture, and Society in Industrializing America," in *Work, Culture, and Society in Industrializing America: Essays in American Working-Class and Social History* (New York: Vintage, 1976), pp. 13-16.

7   On the "exile motif," see Miller, *Emigrants, passim.* Gwendolyn Mink, *Old Labor and New Immigrants in American Political Development: Union, Party, and State, 1875-1920* (Ithaca: Cornell University Press, 1986), p. 239.

8   Emmons, *Butte Irish,* pp. 13-40.

9   The *Montana Catholic* (Helena) referred to AOH as the "refuge of the exile," June 10, 1899. AOH, *Convention Proceedings, Anaconda, Mt, 1910* (ts). Daly's membership is noted in AOH, Div. 1, Minute Books, July 7, 1886. General membership data, including names, addresses, occupations, etc., are from AOH, Membership and Dues Ledgers, 1881-1925. All from the Irish Collection, microfilm copy, University of Montana, hereafter cited thus: UMIC. Butte Miners' Union (BMU) officers were listed in R. L. Polk, *Butte City Directory, 1884-1915* (Butte: R. L. Polk, 1884-1915).

10 See the comments by Judge Jeremiah Lynch in the *Montana Socialist,* Aug. 25, 1917. Emmons, *Butte Irish,* pp. 155-156, 221-248.

11 For the origins and history of the AOH, see *Irish-American Voluntary Organizations,* ed. Michael Funchion (Westport, Conn.: Greenwood, 1983), pp. 51-60 and John O'Dea, *The History of the Ancient Order of Hibernians and Ladies' Auxiliary,* 4 vols. (Philadelphia: AOH, 1923). Voluntary societies are discussed in Roy Lubove, *The Struggle for Social Security, 1900-1935* (Cambridge: Harvard University Press, 1968), pp. 1-10, 17, 21, 24; Mary Ann Clawson, *Constructing Brotherhood: Class, Gender, and Fraternalism* (Princeton: University Press, 1989), *passim.* See also U.S. Commissioner of

Labor, *Workmen's Insurance and Benefit Funds in the United States, 1908, Twenty-Third Annual Report* (Washington, D.C., Government Publishing Office, 1909).

12   Clawson, *Constructing Brotherhood*. See also Derickson, *Worker's Health*, pp. 57-85.

13   The dating service took the form of dance classes held in Hibernia Hall. See Hibernia Hall, Board of Trustees, Rent Ledgers, July 31, 1894-Dec. 31, 1911. For missing Irish bureau, see AOH, Div. 1, Minute Books, Nov. 3, 1897. For evidence that AOH was part of the migration chain, see Membership and Dues Ledgers and Minute Books. Older members "witnessed" the initiation of new men known to them for many years. For the AOH war on APA and stage Irishmen, see, for example, Div. 1, Minute Books, April 3, 1895; Feb. 19, 1896; Feb. 4, 1903; March 30, April 6, May 25, 1904; Dec. 20, 1905; Div. 3, Dec. 18, 1905; Jan. 7, 1907; March 23, 1908; March 8, 1909; Oct. 1 1910; Sept. 12, 1914. The *Butte Independent,* the city's Irish newspaper, carried stories on the stage Irish on Aug. 13 and Sept. 10, 1910. "Nurses" are identified in AOH, Div. 1, Minute Books, March 15, 1886; Nov. 6, 1889; Dec. 3, 1890. For examples of wakes, AOH, Div. 1, Minute Books, Nov. 16, 1898; Div. 3, Minute Books, March 11, 1907. The MS Census for both 1900 and 1910 are filled with Irish-born widows (no evidence that husbands had been Irish, but 93 percent of Irish marriages were with other Irish) who owned their homes free and clear and listed no occupation. There are literally scores of references to drawings and raffles in aid of destitute members in the AOH Minute Books. All UMIC. For examples and notes and for evidence of Irish marriage patterns, see Emmons, *Butte Irish*, pp. 82, 111-112, 160-166.

14   For the policy of sick and death benefits, see AOH, *Constitution*, 1886 (Philadelphia: AOH, 1887). AOH, Div. 1, Minute Books, 1884-1908; Treasurer's Reports, 1909-1911; AOH, Physician's Certificates, 1904-1911, UMIC. See also Industrial Commission, *Conditions*, p. 3837.

15   Dollar amounts are from AOH, Div. 1, Minute Books, 1884-1908; Treasurer's Reports, 1909-1911. For examples of financial difficulties as a consequence of sick and death benefits, see AOH, Div. 1, Minute Books, Feb. 6, 1901; AOH, Silver Bow Co. Board of Directors, Minute Books, April 30, 1908; AOH, Div. 2, to AOH, Div. 1, June 1, 1910, Correspondence, UMIC.

16   "Deadly dust" is from David Rosner and Gerald Markowitz, *Deadly Dust: Silicosis and the Politics of Occupational Disease in Twentieth-Century America* (Princeton: Princeton University Press, 1991).

17   Board of Health, "report," pp. 1-3, 7, 15-17, 20-21, 24.

18   The Cornish left Butte after the consolidations because those corporate

reorganizations limited the practice of contract mining, a practice that enabled the Cornish to double their wages. Emmons, *Butte Irish,* p. 239. René and Jean Dubos argue that the Irish were genetically vulnerable to tuberculosis. That may or may not be, but it would have no bearing on silicosis deaths that arose from the nature of their work, rather than some genetic predisposition. See *The White Plague: Tuberculosis, Man, and Society* (Boston: Little, Brown and Co., 1952), pp. 192, 193. My discussion of this issue benefitted enormously from information provided me by Prof. David Rosner of the City University of New York.

19 When it was suggested by a physician that men with "miners; con" be quarantined in Butte as they were in Michigan, Dan Sullivan, an Irish miner, answered that that would "deprive needy men of bread and butter." Industrial Commission, *Conditions,* p. 3939. For Irishmen on retainer to Hibernia Hall, see Hibernia Hall, Board of Directors, Report for the Year 1909, Board of Trustees, Report for the Year Ending Dec. 31, 1912, Financial Reports, UMIC. For Irish dominance of the local Democratic Party, known as the "Dalycrats," see Emmons, *Butte Irish,* pp. 97-103. On the Irish and Democratic "machines" nationally, see Steven P. Erie, *Rainbow's End: Irish-Americans and the Dilemmas of Urban Machine Politics, 1840-1985* (Berkeley: University of California Press, 1988), pp. 1-66.

20 For vocational lessons, see Wayland Hand, "The Folklore, Customs, and Traditions of the Butte Miner," *California Folklore Quarterly,* 5 (1946): 158; Joseph H. Duffy, *Butte Was Like That* (Butte: by the author, 1941), p. 298; WPA, *Copper Camp,* pp. 186-189. The "cooperating with the more powerful" quote is from *Workers' World: Kinship, Community and Protest in an Industrial Society, 1900-1940* (Baltimore: John Hopkins University Press, 1982), p. 65. Hugh O'Daly counted the hiring officers. See "Life History of High O'Daly" (unpaged ts, 1945, in possession of Prof. Kerby Miller), p. [156]. The comment by Bishop John Brondel was reported in the *Catholic Sentinel,* Oct. 3, 1885, in Brondel Papers, Diocese of Helena Office, Helena, Montana. The "Protestant ore" reference is from Hand, "Folklore," p. 167.

21 For examples of holiday mine and smelter closures, see AOH Div. 1, Minute Books, July 31, 1885; July 7, 1886; March 13, 1889; Aug. 22, 1894; June 26, 1895; March 10, 1897; March 9, 1898; July 10, 1901. The handball courts are shown on Sanborn's *Fire Insurance Map of Butte, Montana, 1900.* Irish job notices in Gaelic were mentioned to me by Father Sarsfield O'Sullivan, Interview, Nov. 19, 1985. Fund-raising for Irish organizations is noted in Robert Emmet Literary Association (RELA), Minute Books, Aug. 3 and 10, 1899; Feb. 8 and 15, 1900; Feb. 18, 1904; AOH, Div. 1, Minute Books, Jan. 2, Aug. 7, 1901. The legislative comments were reported in the *Helena Independent,* Feb. 20, 1889. The APA lament was in its newspaper, *The Examiner* (Butte), June 15, 1895; see also the issues of Feb. 27,

March 19, April 19, Oct. 31, 1896. For further evidence that Irish mines and Irish miners was not the usual pattern, see Derickson, *Workers' Health*, pp. 57-60.

[22] All of the quotations are from AOH, Div. 3, Minute Books. David Ryan's is from Oct. 5, 1908; Lawlor's from Sept. 21, 1908; Breen's from March 30, 1908; Kealy's from July 9, 1910; McCarthy's from April 19, 1913. McCarthy's job and union involvement are noted in Polk, *City Directory*, 1908.

[23] Kelley's comment was made to the Industrial Commission, *Conditions*, p. 3866. The priest's remarks are from AOH, Div. 3, Minute Books, Dec. 21, 1908, UMIC. The BMU never struck during its thirty-six-year history, 1878-1914. See Emmons, *Butte Irish*, pp. 221-248.

[24] Eric Foner, "Class, Ethnicity, and Radicalism in the Gilded Age: The Land League and Irish-America," in *Politics and Ideology in the Age of the Civil War*, pp. 150-200 (New York: Oxford University Press, 1980), J. C. Harrington, *Catholicism, Capitalism, or Communism* (St. Paul: E. M. Lohmann Co. 1926), p. 114. David Montgomery, "Labor in the Industrial Era," in *The U.S. Department of Labor History of American Workers*, ed. Richard B. Morris (Washington, D.C.: Government Printing Office, 1976), p. 121. Ryan, "Introduction," in Ryan and Joseph Husslein, *The Church and Labor* (New York: MacMillan Co., 1924), pp. xvi-xvii; this volume also includes the text of *Rerum Novarum*, pp. 57-94. Derickson, *Workers' Health*, p. 57. See also Francis L. Broderick, *Right Reverend New Dealer: John A. Ryan* (New York: Macmillan, 1963). For an overview, see James Terence Fisher, *The Catholic Counter Culture in America* (Chapel Hill: University of North Carolina Press, 1989), pp. 1-24.

[25] Foner uses the "symbiotic relationship" comment in "Land League," p. 176. For the meanings and importance of *muintir*, see Ó Céirín, "Introduction" to O'Leary, *My Story*, p. [11].

[26] Mink, *Old Labor, passim*. See also Erie, *Rainbow's End*, pp. 25-106.

[27] For a discussion of the "new" Irish and the differences between them and the old, see David M. Emmons, "Faction Fights: The Irish World of Butte, Montana, 1875-1917," in *The Irish World Wide: History, Heritage, Identity*, vol. 2, *The Irish in the New Communities*, ed. Patrick O'Sullivan (Leicester: Leicester University Press; New York: St. Martin's Press, 1992), pp. 82-98. Wyman, *Hardrock*, pp. 12, 84, 88-90; Emmons, *Butte Irish*, pp. 238-239.

[28] Ryan's comment is from AOH, Div. 3, Minute Books, Jan. 8, 1910; O'Meara's remark is from RELA, Minute Books, April 28, 1910, IMIC.

[29] See Emmons, *Butte Irish*, pp. 261-263. The quotations are from a letter from John D. Sullivan to Patrick Kenny, Sept. 17, 1911, Correspondence, UMIC.

30 AOH, Div. 3, Minute Books, Oct. 30, 1915, UMIC.

31 Figures on days worked from Ralph Brissenden, "The Butte Miners and the Rustling Card," in *American Economic Review,* 10 (1920), pp. 770, 771.

32 By this time, declining enrollments had forced the AOH to cut its sick benefits from $8 to $5 per week. The first radical quoted was Industrial Workers of the World (IWW) organizer Arturo Giovannitti. His remarks are from the *Miners Magazine,* July 9, 1914. The remark about Irish Catholic, that is, AOH, dominance of the conservative wing of the BMU was from an unidentified radical in the Western Federation of Miners (WFM), *Proceedings, 20th Annual Convention, Victor, Colorado, 1912* (Victor: WFM, 1912), p. 260. For the Pearse-Connolly Club, see Emmons, *Butte Irish,* pp. 359-366, 374-378, 384, 385, 398, 399, 401, 403, 405.

33 Butte Mine Workers' Union, "Grievances, June 30, 1914," in WFM, *Proceedings, 21st Convention, 1st Biennial, Denver, 1914* (Denver: WFM, 1914), p. 56; *Miners Magazine,* July 16, 1914. Brissenden, "Rustling Card." Emmons, *Butte Irish,* pp. 272-277, 283, 366, 373, 381-383.

34 On Safety First at ACM, see Isaac Marcosson, *Anaconda* (New York: Dodd, Mead, 1957), pp. 142-156. Alan Derickson discusses these changes under the heading "The New Paternalism," *Workers' Health,* pp. 189-219. On the self-conscious progressivism of the Democratic Party in New York, see Robert F. Wesser, *A Response to Progressivism: The Democratic Party and New York Politics, 1902-1918* (New York: New York University Press, 1986), pp. 218-219. See also *The Uses of Charity: The Poor on Relief in the Nineteenth-Century Metropolis,* ed. Peter Mandler (Philadelphia: University of Pennsylvania Press, 1990). The Montana Democratic Party went through a similar transformation from the embrace of nonjudgmental voluntarism to state-sponsored social reform. See Jules Karlin, *Joseph M. Dixon of Montana,* part 2 (Missoula: University of Montana Publications in History), pp. 1-104. See also Erie, *Rainbow's End,* pp. 67-106. Mary Ann Clawson discusses the decline in fraternalism nationally in *Constructing Brotherhood,* pp. 259ff. For the Congress of Industrial Organizations, see Thomas Goebel, "Becoming American: Ethnic Workers and the Rise of the CIO," *Labor History,* 29 (Spring, 1988), pp. 173-198.

35 The Wilson administration suppressed three Irish-American newspapers and kept up an active surveillance on suspect Irish-American organizations. Emmons, *Butte Irish,* pp. 384-386, 404-406. Dennis Clark, *The Irish in Philadelphia: Ten Generations of Urban Experience* (Philadelphia: Temple University Press, 1973), pp. 151-152; John Devoy, *Recollections of an Irish Rebel* (New York: Charles Young, 1929), pp. 469-471. For government activities in Butte, see Burton K. Wheeler to Thomas Gregory, Sept. 16, 1918, Dept. of Justice file 195397-1; J. Edgar Hoover to Col. A. B. Cox,

Aug. 21, 1920, Dept. of Justice file 195397-6, National Archives, microfilm copy. Montana Council of Defense, Minute Books, Sept. 9, 1918, Montana Historical Society.

[36] AOH, Membership and Dues Ledgers, 1903-1925; AOH, Quarterly Reports, 1908-1928, UMIC.

[37] AOH, Membership and Dues Ledgers, 1903-1925; AOH, Quarterly Reports, 1908-1928, UMIC. Gwendolyn Mink writes that the failure of voluntary organizations created a "social welfare vacuum in the United States." *Old Labor,* p. 253.

Windmills in Montana:
Dutch Settlement in the Gallatin Valley

— Rob Kroes

The coming of the railroads and the forced placement of Native Americans onto isolated reservations helped lead to the greatest of all booms in Montana history: the homestead boom. Thousands of would-be farmers poured into Montana from across the country and around the world. (Between 1900 and 1920, the state's population more than doubled, from 243,329 to 548,889.) Many of the immigrant farmers came from distant lands in Europe, including large numbers from Sweden, Norway, Germany, and Russia. One special group of new arrivals chose to settle on the western side of the Gallatin Valley; these were the Dutch immigrants from the Netherlands who would establish family farms and build the small settlements of Manhattan and Amsterdam.

It is important to remember that all immigrants bring with them cultural values and traditions from their countries of origin, which provide them with a sense of who they are as human beings. In certain instances, some of these values and traditions may fade with time as immigrants adjust to their new social and cultural environment, although this tendency is likely to be much stronger among the American-born children of immigrants. The Dutch who came to the Gallatin Valley provide us with an example of how such values can persist over an extended period of time.

Why were these Dutch settlers able to maintain an especially strong sense of their own cultural uniqueness? Perhaps it was brought about by the rather isolated nature of their settlement in southwestern Montana. But there may have been more at work here that just geography. Historian Rob Kroes argues: "To the Dutch residents of the west Gallatin Valley, religion formed the overarching dimension of their society. Their social order was based on their conviction to be a Covenanted People, secure in their links to a distant country where their fathers had first seen the light." He goes on to suggest that "the traditional language of religious debate, which had fostered many a church schism in the Netherlands, served to give expression to the community's endeavor to protect its Dutch heritage against American encroachments."

The names on the mailboxes along the road leave no doubt. Here, in a valley in the American West, live people of Dutch origin. We see the names of Flikkema, Alberda, Sinnema, Weidenaar. In a few cases, one is briefly misled by an Anglicized spelling, but there are always helpful residents to confirm one's hunches that Cole used to be Kool and Fisher, Visser. In his front yard, one resident has proudly planted the road sign of Amsterdam that until recently, soiled and tilting, had indicated a stop on the nearby railroad spur. The spur has fallen into disuse and its tracks have been removed, yet the need for a marker has remained. There is no denying it: We are in Amsterdam, Montana.

For over three centuries, Dutch immigrants came to America by the tens of thousands and in a number of separate waves. They first arrived during the seventeenth century, settling in what was then known as the New Netherlands, and they left a lasting imprint on American society. One of the oldest religious denominations in the United States, the Reformed Church in America, is an offshoot of the Reformed Church of the Dutch Republic. A second influx of

Dutch immigration, a great wave compared to prior immigrations, began in the late 1840s. It would bring a large number of the so-called Seceders (an orthodox breakaway from the official Reformed Church) to America, along with their religious leaders. A second variety of Dutch Reformed life was founded in America: the Christian Reformed Church, with its center in Grand Rapids, Michigan.

The Christian Reformed Church in particular received a strong infusion of members from a third wave of Dutch immigration at the turn of the twentieth century. In the Netherlands, under the charismatic leadership of Abraham Kuyper, a new religious awakening had occurred that was very much an emancipation movement of the lower class. Many immigrants, freshly under the influence of this movement, came to America to reinforce the ranks of the Christian Reformed Church. Their trek across the continent and their subsequent settlement on what was then the frontier—in the Dakotas, Nebraska, Montana, Washington, and California—made the church into a truly nation-wide denomination. One such area of settlement was the western Gallatin Valley in Montana.

In Amsterdam, Montana, live a group of people who clearly value the preservation of a history that ties them to the Netherlands. They have married mostly within their own group; they are not just neighbors, they have also become relatives. They have an uncanny sense of the kinship networks that tie them together, and they are aware of their separate identity. In conversations with residents of Amsterdam, they refer to outsiders as "Americans," as if they have not been Americans themselves for a long time. The great majority of them have joined a church that spans the continent but whose members are almost exclusively of Dutch descent.

They live scattered across the fertile, hilly area in the western part of the Gallatin Valley. There is no clear center of settlement that is even remotely similar to Dutch villages or small towns. Yet, to someone hovering over the area on a Sunday morning, the community would become clearly visible. It is like a spider's web in the early morning light. Like so many dewdrops, the army of cars converging on the church show the structure of the social web, its center, its connecting points, its reach.[1]

At an elevation of some 4,200 feet, the Gallatin Valley is surrounded by mountains. The natural scene is dramatic, and so is its history. This is Lewis and Clark country. Three rivers—which these early explorers named after Madison, Gallatin, and Jefferson—rise in the nearby mountains and meet here to form the mighty Missouri. Long ago, the valley was the bed of a lake that has long since vanished; the soil is fertile and drains well. The central part of the valley is relatively flat, but toward its edges, in broad undulating movement, it rises into an attractive, hilly landscape. All around there is a view of the mountains. The memory of early explorers lives on in the local geography, in the name of the Bridger Mountains and the town of Bozeman, the main urban center in the valley. Although settlers came to the valley in the 1860s, the Gallatin was really opened up for settlement by the construction of a railway line in the 1880s.

In about 1890, Henry Altenbrand, the son of a German immigrant and president of the New York and Brooklyn Malting Company, selected the Gallatin Valley as a good place to grow malting barley. Until that time, the only barley fit for malting had come from Canada, but Altenbrand had his mind set on changing that. In 1888, he had been the driving force in getting the tariff on malting barley raised from ten to thirty percent. That gave him the protection he needed to start the cultivation of high-grade malting barley in the United States. He ordered from Germany 2,000 bushels of the famous Saale barley, which he planted in a number of selected areas. As it turned out, only the barley crop grown on irrigated land in the Gallatin Valley was satisfactory. In fact, it had even shown an improvement compared to the original seed material.

Altenbrand proceeded in grand manner. In 1889, together with a number of East Coast brewing and railroad interests, he set up the West Gallatin Irrigation Company to build an irrigation network that would take water from the Gallatin River across the hilly land to the southwestern part of the valley. A pier of stones, stretching into the river like a bent arm, still leads the water to the headgate of the irrigation system. From there it follows the natural contour of the land, through the main ditch and a number of laterals to the Highline Canal and the Lowline Canal systems, which were built with different inlets on the river and would eventually have a total combined length of over 100 miles. There were a number of problems with the system during the early years. At times the loose banks of the ditch would wash out, blocking the flow, and sometimes they would break, undermined by gophers. Worse, the canals would dry up too early in the growing season.

All this effort, of course, served the purpose of growing malting barley. From the county records in Bozeman, it appears that the irrigation company acquired large tracts of land from the Northern Pacific Railroad in 1892 and 1893. Brought under irrigation, they produced so well that the first crops of barley caused a sensation in Europe. In 1893, the Imperial Ministry of Agriculture in Berlin, Germany, dispatched a staff of experts to the Gallatin Valley to report on conditions there.

In 1890, Altenbrand and a number of brewers from the East founded the Manhattan Malting Company. Located on the railway line, immediately to the north of the irrigation area, they built a malting house for the processing of at least part of the harvest. The remainder was shipped East by train to be sold there or exported. Manhattan was the little railway town that grew around the malting operation.

The report to the Imperial Ministry of Agriculture mentioned ten families "of Hollanders" that as early as 1891 had settled on land of the West Gallatin Irrigation Company. These families were mostly of Frisian origin and had first settled in America in the older settlement areas of Michigan and Iowa. They had probably heard about the new opportunities in Montana from Reverend A. Wormser, a man who was to play an important role in attracting Dutch settlers to the Gallatin Valley. Of Dutch origin himself, Reverend Wormser worked for the Board of Domestic Missions of the Presbyterian Church in America and was well-connected among the Dutch immigrant population in Michigan and Iowa. In 1891, as an agent for the West Gallatin Irrigation Company, his job was to recruit Dutch farmers, in America as well as in the Netherlands, and to encourage them to settle in the valley.

Reverend Wormser's timing could not have been better. The number of emigrants leaving the Netherlands for America in search of

The Manhattan Malting Company's grain elevator, shown here circa 1894, could hold 275,000 bushels of wheat. F. JAY HAYNES, COURTESY MONTANA HISTORICAL SOCIETY, HELENA, H-3184.

work or land was on the rise again. Emigration was predominantly from rural areas, where jobs in agriculture had diminished due to mechanization and modernization and where there was no alternative industrial employment. In addition to these poor and landless emigrants, there was a smaller contingent made up of the sons of well-to-do farmers. They left the Netherlands because of the lack of land and farming prospects.

There were rather marked differences among the emigrants in terms of their available cash resources. Pieter Alberda and Pieter Van Dijken, both from Bedum, are registered on the emigration lists as "well-to-do"; others, such as Jacob Kimm from Bierum and Harmannus Klugkist from Bedum, are listed as "less-well-off." None of those who got ready to move to Manhattan was registered as "needy." Yet, these differences do not tell us much. We do know that during the early years there were

Reverend T. Vander Ark, pastor of Churchill's Christian Reformed Church, moved his family into the new parsonage when it was completed in 1916.
COURTESY MONTANA HISTORICAL SOCIETY, HELENA, PAC 79-59.1.

no laborers or farmhands; all were from the relatively small upper stratum of landholding rural families. Also, there were intricate links of intermarriage. Pieter Alberda's wife, for instance, was a Klugkist, and the pages of the genealogy of the old, elite Wigboldus family at the National Archives in Groningen contain a number of names that also occur among the first group of Groningen emigrants to Montana. Thus, for instance, two of the three Van Dijken brothers who migrated to Montana in the 1890s were married to a Wigboldus. As the emigration lists also tell us, the Montana group was not homogeneous in religious terms when its members left the Netherlands. Some belonged to the established Dutch-Reformed Church; others, like Alberda or Kimm, appear as Christian-Reformed, that is, members of more orthodox break-away churches.

For all practical purposes, however, these settlers acted as a cohesive group after they arrived in the Gallatin Valley. When the Dutch immigrants had to move outside their own small circle, as they did when making formal transactions such as acquiring a homestead or becoming citizens, they selected their official witnesses from among their own community. Over and over again, the same Dutch names appear in the official records. There are only a few exceptions, as in the case of Arien Doornbos, who was among the later arrivals and was the last to acquire a homestead at what was then the far western corner of the Dutch settlement area. His only Dutch neighbor, John Weidenaar, and two of his American neighbors appear as witnesses on his naturalization and homestead documents.

Shortly after their arrival in the Gallatin Valley, most of the Dutch immigrants filed their homestead applications accompanied, as required by law, by their applications for citizenship. At the time of naturalization, after the statutory five years of residence had lapsed, the new citizen had to declare "that he will support the Constitution of the United States of America, and that he doth absolutely and entirely renounce and abjure all allegiance and fidelity to every foreign Prince, Potentate State or Sovereignty whatever, and particularly to," in this case, "Wilhelmina Queen of the Netherlands."

Some Dutch settlers bought land from the irrigation company. Jacob Kimm, for instance, although registered on the emigration lists as "less-well-off," never bothered to apply for a homestead but bought land directly from the irrigation company. Pieter Van Dijken did likewise. Pieter Alberda and Lambertus Van Dijken did both, taking out a homestead and buying land in an adjacent section. In all cases, these settlers must have arranged an installment purchase; according to records at the Gallatin County Courthouse, the company land bought by the settlers was not registered in their names until five or six years after the purchase.

The ledgers of the Manhattan Malting Company show that agricultural production in the west valley rapidly took off. In November and December 1894, the company recorded the barley crops of P. Alberda, J. Balda, J. Braaksma, W. Broekema, A. Brouwer, J. P. Van Dijken, L. Van Dijken, P. P. Van Dijken, J. R. Kimm, W. Koning, J. TeSelle, and J. Weidenaar. Payments ranged from $400 for TeSelle to $85 for Weidenaar. Kimm, Brouwer, and Alberda received incomes of about $370. According to Pieter Van Dijken, the son of one of the early settlers who worked for Kimm, Kimm harvested thirty-five bushels of oats per acre in 1894. From about the same time, there is a report—perhaps overly roseate—from D. J. Walvoord, the teacher at the valley's country school near the old cemetery. He reported that crop returns for October 1894 were approximately forty-five bushels of barley per acre.

Walvoord was from the Dutch community of Cedar Grove in Wisconsin, and his October 12, 1894, report appeared the following year in Wisconsin's *Sheboygan Herald.* It is a clear example of that general repertoire of writing that must have made Dutch immigrants in the older settlement areas in the East and Midwest aware of possibilities farther west. As Walvoord put it:

> I was met at Manhattan by Reverend Wormser and Reverend Van den Hoek of Chicago, who was here on his second trip, and who since his first visit has been an enthusiastic admirer of Montana climate, fertility of soil, and beautiful scenery. (I may state right here, that fertile as our own good state of Wisconsin is, I never saw such fields of grain and other produce. In every direction could be seen fields of golden and heavy grain still in the shock. Everybody I met was abundant in praise of irrigation, by which a large crop is secured year after year.) One of the farms we visited was the one belonging to Jan TeSelle, who was formerly of Cedar Grove, and lately of Sioux County, Iowa. They had threshed 3,500 bushels of grain from 120 acres, part of which had been plowed for the first time last spring, and not a foot of which had been under cultivation for more than two years.

Walvoord also mentioned his visit to the farm of Reverend Derk E. Deuninck, Van den Hoek's friend and colleague. Deuninck had recently acquired a homestead himself, south of the TeSelle place, and had bought additional land from the irrigation company. Walvoord concluded: "I have decided to spend the winter here, and have been engaged to teach a district school, soon to be opened in the settlement." It was a personal note that could only enhance the appeal of his report.

The Gallatin Valley was a prodigious producer of wheat. Here farmers use a tractor and horses to bind or "shock" wheat into bundles.
ALBERT SCHLECHTEN, COURTESY MONTANA HISTORICAL SOCIETY, LOT 32, B1F11 04.

The documents pertaining to the acquisition of land and the case files concerning homesteaded land revealed much of the early settlement history of the west Gallatin Valley. A total of twenty-six Dutch immigrants filed for a homestead in the valley and acquired land. Doornbos was the last receiving title to his land in 1912. The settlement pattern forms a relatively continuous band that follows the irrigation network of the Highline and Lowline canals, stretching from the hills area in the south toward Manhattan, where the land begins to level off. Dutch homestead land is concentrated at both the southern and northern ends of this band of settlement. The area in between was mostly farmland bought directly from the irrigation company or from earlier, non-Dutch homesteaders. Two cores of settlement formed in the valley: one in the hills, the other around Churchill and Amsterdam.

The small world that Pieter Van Dijken described in 1894 in a letter to the Netherlands was the beginning of the community in the hills.

His daily world really ended at the somewhat more northerly farm of Jacob Kimm on Godfrey Creek, just south of Churchill. It took him over an hour to get there, and he got home only for the weekends. Religious meetings, mostly bible reading, were held at his Uncle Pieter's place, but at the insistence of Reverend Wormser, a Presbyterian congregation was formed that met in a nearby school. The congregation was named Second Holland Presbyterian Church.

The more northerly group at first oriented itself more toward nearby Manhattan and found some work in town. J. H. Bos, for instance, had his homestead in the area in addition to a blacksmith shop in town. The First Holland Presbyterian Church was also in Manhattan. The first pastor to serve both groups was pastor-farmer Derk Deuninck. Somewhat later, his friend and colleague Van den Hoek would join him, an emeritus from Chicago. Like Deuninck, Van den Hoek was quick to apply for a homestead, slightly to the east of the southern core of settlement.

In this way, the early Dutch immigrants in the west Gallatin Valley were organized within a church of essentially Anglo-Saxon origin. It may have been as good a solution as any. Both doctrinally and organizationally, English Presbyterianism is close to the Dutch-Reformed Church, and the early ministers—Wormser, Deuninck, and Van den Hoek—were all Dutch-born and thoroughly familiar with Dutch traditions and teachings. Yet, this arrangement would only be transitional.

In yet different ways, two spheres of organized social life appeared in the valley, imposed by the geographical dispersal of the settlers. Because of poor transportation, schools had to be close to the pupils' homes, and parents could petition the county government to organize their neighborhood into a separate school district. It was not long before a number of one-room schools were established across the entire area of settlement. In the more southerly District 52, the so-called Little Holland District in the hills, the Weidenaars, the Braaksmas, Broekema, Veltkamp, Alberda, Balda, and, later, Cornelius Lucas, Sam Dijk, and G. Van der Ark sat on the local school board. The teachers were also Dutch. The board of District 34, at the northern tip of Godfrey Canyon near present-day Churchill, was composed of those who had settled there, such as Lambertus Van Dijken (who had bought land nearby) and his son Pieter, Jacob Kimm, and one non-Dutch resident, Amos Walrath. To the north, in District 30, there was the Heeb School, named after a farmer in the area. There, Henry TeSelle and, later, Garret Te Hennepe (from the province of Gelderland in the Netherlands who had arrived in the valley by way of Wisconsin) together with non-Dutch residents sat on the school board. At the far north, in District 3 in Manhattan, the role of the non-Dutch residents is predominant, but the Dutch community is still represented by J. H. Bos. Toward the western edge of the Dutch settlement, two school districts were formed at the behest of Arien Doornbos. District 8 in particular showed a gradually increasing Dutch character to its school board, reflecting the westward expansion of Dutch settlement. This movement into the western part of the valley gathered momentum during World War I, when agricultural prices were high and rainfall was relatively abundant.[2] People moved beyond the irrigated area to take up dry farming on land that, for the most part, they had leased.

Some ten years earlier, a clear need for a consolidation of the community around one center of religious life had made itself felt. As Pieter Van Dijken remembered it about sixty years later, religious life in the community had begun to stagnate, especially in its more isolated branch in the hills.[3] But there was also dissatisfaction among those who lived near Manhattan. At the time, services in the Presbyterian church there were held only in English and were conducted by a pastor from Bozeman. In the summer of 1902, a missionary from the Classis Orange City, Iowa, of the Christian Reformed Church visited the area and held services in both the Hills School in the south and the Heeb School in the north. He was a moving force behind consolidation. In 1903, nineteen families and five single men, from both north and south, founded a Christian-Reformed congregation. The membership of the first consistory reflected the consolidation of the community. The first elders were J. H. Bos, A. Elings, and W. Broekema; the first deacons were E. Bos and J. Braaksma. The northern and southern parts of the valley were equally represented.

One of the group's first constitutive acts concerned building a church on Church Hill in the center of the settlement, halfway between north and south. The church was to be a clear beacon, a guiding light that would turn the dispersed settlers inward upon themselves, inspiring a sense of their own vital center and their common tradition. At the same time, the church would also serve as a demarcation, setting the community apart from its American environment. The congregation had a rapid increase in its numbers, mainly because of the many new settlers who came to the valley before World War I. In 1904, the Christian Reformed Church counted forty families in its membership; in 1908, there were fifty; and in 1913, there were ninety families in the congregation.

The first act of consolidation was followed by others. It was not long before this group of Dutch settlers decided to set up its own denominational school system. Financially, they were taking a daring step. They would have to continue to support public schools in addition to shouldering all of the costs of their own schools. There is a sense of the symbolic dimensions of this organizational withdrawal from the established forms of American society in the realization that the Dutch were already in relative control of their public school districts. Yet, as they saw it, that was not enough. They were still not free enough to educate their children in a Christian setting. Their first school was built close to their church, at the center of the settlement on Church Hill. But distance affects schools differently than it does church-going. With only one Christian school, consolidation had only a limited effect in the area of education. But when the county government closed the public school in the hills in 1909, parents set up a Christian school there as well. They kept it going until 1920, when drought and low prices forced them to close it down, at least temporarily.

In 1904, the strategy of separate, denominational schools was adopted in the west Gallatin Valley. On May 12, the first general meeting was held of the *Vereeniging ter oprichting en instandhouding van Christelijk Onderwijs, op Gereformeerden Grondslag,* the Association for the Founding and Maintenance of Christian Education on a Reformed Basis. The association, with members from all across the Dutch settlement, was established for this purpose: "The object of the Association is the founding and maintenance of Christian schools of a Reformed nature in our area, to the extent that there are members."

Thus, these people took up a Dutch tradition of religious life that went back as far as the Synod of Dordrecht of 1618-1619, when Calvinism in the Netherlands received its characteristic Dutch imprint.

It is interesting that in this process of consolidation in church and school, little emphasis was placed on preserving the Dutch language. In the General Meeting of Members of April 1909, for instance, the group decided that teaching would be in Dutch only during the first year of school. "In the other grades Dutch will be taught for half a day every week. Bible classes too will be in Dutch. All other subjects will be taught in English." What remained of a Dutch education apparently left much to be desired, according to the school board's report in 1910 that the school mistress in her Dutch classes mixed "English and Dutch too much." In 1914, the group considered whether bible classes should be taught in English. And in 1919, it was decided to translate the "Statutes of the Association" into English. In 1924, in an amended version of the Statutes, the association agreed to "abolish Dutch in the first grade." Gradually, step by step, the next generation was moving away from its linguistic heritage.

Thus, during the early twentieth century, a consolidation of the community had occurred around the institutions of church and school. But we must not overstate the point. Not everyone involved in the movement went along in every respect. There were those who joined the new church congregation but did not send their children to the Christian school. Others stopped supporting Christian education altogether. Still others stood completely aloof from the consolidation of the Dutch community, having begun to mingle with their non-Dutch neighbors instead. Most of those in this last group probably lived in or near Manhattan, like the Fabriek family, or the Presbyterian minister Van den Hoek and his banker son, or Chris Buitenhof, who would become a wealthy apiculturist. The process of consolidation never included all of the Dutch settlers in the valley. We would do well to conceive of consolidation as a strategy of ethnic survival, with its advocates and activists, vying for cultural hegemony within their community with those who put less emphasis on ethnic cohesion.

The 1920s and 1930s were a high point in this contest of rival affinities. Those years were times of hardship and depression in agricultural life, yet the tensions were expressed in language that centrally concerned the sense of identity of this Dutch-Calvinist group. In a collection of letters sent to relatives and friends in the Netherlands, J. R. Kimm and his wife, Willemina Omta, one of the central families of the west Gallatin Valley community, there are telling references to the cultural clash occurring in the settlement.

During the 1920s, religious revivalists were active in the immediate vicinity of the Dutch settlement. Their appeal had not gone unheeded among the Dutch. One influence was a revivalist preacher named Lyness, who made some early conversions among people on the fringe of the Dutch community. There were other cases as well, where an outside call found a willing response within the community, leading to the formation of small church groups composed of Dutch and non-Dutch believers. It is this response within the Dutch community that can help us understand the religious conflict within the community that resulted in a long-drawn and high-pitched debate over the proper definitions of their own pure faith. This was not a matter of a united front of the Dutch confronting the outside world. A rift had begun to open up, cutting right through the community.

Elsewhere in America, a schism had already occurred among Dutch Americans, beginning at the center of Christian-Reformed life, Grand Rapids, Michigan. There, in 1924, the Reverend Hoeksema and a number of his followers had been expelled from the Christian Reformed Church because of their deviant doctrinal teachings. The news had reached Montana through reports and polemical writings in the journals of the Christian Reformed Church—the *Wachter* and the *Banner*—through personal letters, and through the formal meetings of the regional church Classis, where consistory members from Churchill were delegated. In 1926, Kimm mentioned the unrest in his letters:

> In the area of church and school there is much commotion, among the Hollanders in the United States. Church teachings are being preached in a way as if man has it in his power to do much through good works. Well, we know better than that. On our own we can do nothing but through God's grace. There are already 11 congregations that have left the Chr Ref church,

partly expelled, and in other places congregations are being organized, separate from the Chr Ref church, which for the time being have the name of the protesting church. Well, the protesters are much purer in their teaching and preaching than the Chr Reformed. Recently we had Rev. Bultema from Muskegon here. That is another fine speaker, but of course he was not allowed to speak in the church, so it had to be in a school house. He has preached six times, 3 times English and 3 times Dutch. Always a large audience, for a sparsely populated country. Always the school brimming over with people. you may have read about Bultema; and also about Danhof, Hoeksema, and others. Would it all were to God's honor and our salvation.

People like Hoeksema, Danhof, and Bultema were uncompromising in their return to some of the old doctrinal tenets of Dutch Calvinism, especially in such areas as the doctrine of predestination and God's covenant with His Chosen People. God's sovereign grace, as these theologians saw it, was not open to arrangement with such as hoped to win His kind-heartedness through good works. Kimm's wife Willemina described the religious dispute in a December 1930 letter:

There is turmoil here in every area, church and school. Many people leave church who have come to different views. There are alien preachers here, and there they come to see the light, they say. They find the preaching more appealing. There is a whole awakening going on. They can tell what the Lord had done to their souls. They do not believe in child baptism anymore, nor in many other things. That is why they can no longer go to church here. The millennium is all they can talk about. They have themselves baptized again in the river. It is a strange world nowadays. . . . But I think it is good for all of us. People talk much more about God's Word than before.

The Kimms' social position gave them a certain distance in their observations of the change going on in their community. The economic depression presented no personal emergency for them, and they were never alarmed about signs of decay or slippage, in the outside world or in their own midst. They observed the turmoil in the church with relative equanimity, satisfied to know where they stood themselves. In 1932, in perfect detachment, Kimm overlooked the increase in religious diversity:

> There is a lot going on here among the Hollanders. Marvel, marvel! Near us we have the Reformed church. A mile west of us [in Amsterdam] the free evangelical association. In Manhattan town, another evangelical variety, and then the presbyterian church also controlled by Hollanders. Two brothers-in-law of Henry Kimm's wife [his daughter-in-law] do services there as elders, not reading, but leading.

In this astute observation, Kimm knew that the diversity in the community did not diminish the fact that "Hollanders"—friends, relatives, and in-laws—were on either side of every fissure. These people were still held together, even though they had gone their separate ways in religious matters.

Undoubtedly, then, it is not church and faith that have kept the Dutch community together in the Gallatin Valley, but what might be called an ethnic consciousness. That sense of a common heritage has enabled the community to transcend its religious divisions and to draw a wider, more encompassing circle that helps define their sense of identity. Yet, that circle gives no exhaustive definition of their identity. At best, their sense of ethnicity—of their Dutchness—is no more than a vague sentiment that affects behavior in certain areas, in their choice of friends, or in their selection of marriage partners—and sometimes not even there. There is always a wide, gray zone where an ethnic community tends to blur into its environment. But if we move inward from the margin toward the center, ethnicity becomes more of a guiding force, leaving its imprint on an increasing number of institutions that have an unmistakably ethnic character. Looked at in that way, we have another vantage point from which to consider the role of the church in this Dutch community.

To Dutch residents of the west Gallatin Valley, religion formed the overarching dimension of their society. Their social order was based on their conviction to be a Covenanted People, secure in their links to a distant country where their fathers had first seen the light. In a very special, Providential sense, they are in a line of Dutch descent connecting them to the Synod of Dordt, to the Secession, and to Kuyperianism—as to so many high points in a history of Dutch Calvinist orthodoxy—rather than to such accidental places on the map as Friesland or Groningen or Zeeland. They are securely connected to an old promise of collective salvation. At the same time, they are part of a tradition that is forever intent on deviation and false prophets. They brought with them to Montana an age-old virtuosity, defending and defining the "true church." They saw signs, they spoke a language, which could divide them against themselves yet could also set them apart from any environment that stood in a different tradition. In Montana's Gallatin Valley, their environment was no longer Dutch, but American, and their constant alertness could take on the "ethnic" appearance of a defense of their heritage against Americanization. If they felt it was necessary to draw a line through their own community in order to achieve a clear and unambiguous demarcation from the environment, that is what they did. Remarkably, however, the overall effect was for people on either side to carry on their fight, not unlike soccer teams after a kickoff. There was a unity of discourse, a continued interaction, a frenetic involvement in a fight whose rules and nuances were known only to them. In this rather intricate way, it can be argued that religion has been a factor of the continued communal existence of this Gallatin Valley community, in spite of schisms and fights.

Interestingly, the traditional language of religious debate, which had fostered many a church schism in the Netherlands, served to give expression to the community's endeavor to protect its Dutch heritage against American encroachments. Religion served as a border-protecting device. Most potently, the debate over God's grace being general, extending to all of creation, or including only His Chosen People drew a hard line in the defense and definition of a Dutch-American identity in the midst of an American environment. The Christian-Reformed community broke up in 1939 over precisely that issue, with the hardliners withdrawing upon an uncompromising position of special grace. They were in the world, but not of it, and they withdrew within a narrowly defined ethnic bastion, leaving the doubters to fend for themselves. Looking at the lines that were drawn and that set up the contending parties within the community who were struggling to control the definition of their identity, an outside observer may be tempted to see it as a mere epiphenomenon. He could set out on a reductionist quest for the real interests underlying the surface conflict. Yet, no clear underlying lines of fissure can be seen. It is not a matter of hidden class conflict. There are rich and poor, tenant and farmer, on both sides of the dividing line. Nor is it a matter of periphery versus center. Again, there is a mixture of both on either side.

Therefore, the outsider may be well-advised to interpret the language of their conflict as a meaningful expression of the disagreement as the contenders saw it. Clearly, the language of theology, pitting special grace against general grace, helped them define their collective identity. But if we try to look at the conflict through their eyes, we must also return to the initial question: Can religion have been the ingredient of this community's continued cohesion if it was also an element of fissure? There is, it seems, a dialectical answer to this quandary.

Sociologists and anthropologists have already reminded us of the integrating function of conflict. Therefore, rather than trying to reduce the religious conflict to its assumed "real" causes, we are well-advised to look at it in terms of its functions. One main actor in the conflict, the Reverend Bernard Kok, who came to the west Gallatin Valley in 1938 as a missionary fire-brand minister of the Protestant Reformed Church to work toward a schism, pounding away on the theme of God's particular grace, used one tactical device that clearly worked to integrate rather than to divide the Dutch community. Trying to expose the local Christian Reformed Church establishment as half-hearted backsliders who had neglected the cause of Christian education, he actually shamed the entire community into a renewed effort to support and expand the Christian school. Both religious camps left in his wake worked together harmoniously toward that goal. An element of integration was as much a result of his efforts as the church split that he had effected.

In a much more general sense, it appears that the raging conflict over fine points of religious doctrine had served to draw the entire community closer together. Spending their mental energies on a religious conflict of which all the participants could see the implications and ramifications, they were kept from dividing along more secular lines precisely at a time of economic hardship. Their common quest was to find sense and significance in their trials and tribulations and in language that they understood, looking at temporal events in the light of God's plans. Whatever the outcome, they were acting out a highly stylized and linguistically articulate conflict of which they, and they alone, knew the rules. Both contending parties were busy fighting over a religious tradition that left them revitalized as a community—in America, but not (quite) of it.

The Dutch settlement in Montana is especially interesting in the context of the history of the American West. Much of the history of the West is still written in a mainstream, Anglo-Saxon mold. The history of the Dutch settlement in the Gallatin Valley may serve to remind us of the ethnic dimension to the settling of the West; ethnic enclaves are not just a feature of the urbanized, immigrant East. In addition, the rhetoric of the frontier is often cast in terms of rugged individuals, powerfully sustained by the availability of free land. The history of the Dutch settlement in the Gallatin Valley demonstrates how the success of this community, and many others, depended on a combination of homestead history and large-scale capitalist development ventures. Perhaps the most important thing we can learn from the history of this one settlement is the way in which an idea like ethnic cohesion has been expressed in meaningful language and significant social strife in the West. We are made aware of the intricate relationship between religion and ethnicity and of the complex dialectics between conflicts and schisms on the one hand and cultural and social continuity on the other.

This essay originally appeared in *Montana, The Magazine of Western History,* Autumn, 1989.

Rob Kroes, who received his Ph.D. from the University of Leiden, the Netherlands, in 1971, is Professor Emeritus and former chair of the American Studies program at the University of Amsterdam. He is also Honorary Professor of American Studies at the University of Utrecht and past president of the European Association of American Studies (1992-1996). He is the founding editor of two series published in Amsterdam: Amsterdam Monographs in American Studies *and* European Contributions to American Studies. *He is the author, coauthor, or editor of thirty-seven books. Among his recent publications are* If You've Seen One, You've Seen The Mall: Europeans and American Mass Culture *(1996);* Predecessors: Intellectual Lineages in American Studies *(1998);* Them and Us: Questions of Citizenship in a Globalizing World *(2000); and* Straddling Borders: The American Resonance in Transnational Identities *(2004). With Robert W. Rydell he coauthored a book entitled* Buffalo Bill in Bologna: The Americanization of the World, 1869-1922 *(2005). His most recent book is* Photographic Memories: Private Pictures, Public Images, and American History *(2007). In 2012 he coedited, with Jean Kempf, a special issue of the* European Journal for American Studies, *on "War and New Beginnings in American History."*

NOTES

[1] This article is based on the research for Kroes's book *The Persistence of Ethnicity: Dutch Calvinist Pioneers in Amsterdam, Montana* (University of Illinois Press, 1992). In the Netherlands, the Rijksarchiefs in both Leeuwarden and Groningen hold important collections of letters and emigration records. School board records and church consistory and church classis records are all held on microfilm in the research collection of Calvin College in Grand Rapids, Michigan. Local records at the county courthouse in Bozeman and at the Montana Historical Society in Helena provided additional information. Responses

to newspaper advertisements in the Netherlands as well as the generosity of members of the Dutch settlement in the Gallatin Valley made large holdings of private material, such as letters and diaries, available for my research.

2   For figures concerning annual precipitation and wheat prices from 1892 to 1935, see Meinte Schuurmans, *The Church and Assimilation in an Isolated Nationality Group: A Study of the Role of the Christian Reformed Church in the Dutch Community near Manhattan, Montana* (M.A. thesis, Michigan State College of Agriculture and Applied Sciences, 1941), p. 88.

3   He wrote this memoir on the occasion of the fiftieth anniversary of the Christian Reformed Church in Churchill. See *High Country News,* March 31, 1976.

'Greetings From This Coalvillage':
Finnish Immigrants of Red Lodge

— *Erika Kuhlman*

As suggested by the rise of copper mining in Butte, Montana, the pace of the industrial revolution occurring in the United States following the Civil War was breathtaking. By 1900, for example, the nation was producing more steel than England and Germany combined. The ranks of the ever-expanding workforce could not be met by simply attracting native-born Americans off the farm and into the city. To fill this gap, American factories, mines, and smelters increasingly turned to immigrant labor. Between 1877 and 1890, 6.3 million new immigrants arrived in the United States, many of whom quickly joined the expanding industrial workforce. While the number of immigrants tapered off a bit in the 1890s, due in part to the Crash of 1893 and its aftermath, the flow accelerated once more after the turn of the century. From 1900 to 1914, an average of 1,000,000 immigrants came to America each year, a figure that would not be matched until the late twentieth century.

Included among these new immigrants were tens of thousands of Finns, drawn to the United States by potential job opportunities, but also pushed out of Finland because of dramatic economic changes occurring in that country. One such Finn was Mikael (Mikko) Marttunen, who arrived in Red Lodge, Montana, in 1910. The community of Red

Lodge was tied to the production of coal, which was a key element in America's new industrial order. It had become a major enclave not just for foreign workers, but for Finnish workers in particular.

Erika Kuhlman's fine essay reminds us that not all immigrants coming to America's shores achieved their dreams of success. Frequently arriving without technical skills or a command of the English language, workers such as Mikko Marttunen were often forced to accept the most dangerous and lowest-paying positions within the new industrial workforce. It was quite natural that unskilled workers such as those laboring in America's forests, mines, and factories would be drawn to the ideology of socialism (this would be especially true of those Finns who had been part of a communal system in Finland), but their very embrace of socialism would serve to further alienate them from mainstream American society. Immigrants like Mikko Marttunen— often overworked, underpaid, and single—ended up living between two worlds, those of Finland and the United States, but never fully a member of either.

"If only now all the Finnish people would pray together for the end of the war and peace for all people. At night in peace we sing; in war, all wail. Joy breaks forth in peace; in war, nothing but complaints." Thus did Emilia Aronen, a Finnish peasant woman, invoke the faith of the Finns to end the First World War in writing to her immigrant son, Fredrik Mikael (Mikko) Marttunen, in Red Lodge, Montana.[1] Her pleas for peace went beyond concern over the grief that swept war-torn Europe. Emilia Aronen's supplications also reflected the sentiments of Finnish families writing to their immigrant sons and daughters living in America. Wartime disrupted the exchange of letters between the two countries, and unfavorable travel conditions delayed the promised return to Finland of immigrants making temporary homes in the United States.

For Mikko Marttunen, a socialist coal miner working in Red Lodge, the First World War and working conditions in Montana altered his

The Rocky Fork Coal Mines near Red Lodge were the site of a fire that killed eight miners in 1906. COURTESY MONTANA HISTORICAL SOCIETY, HELENA, 950-573.

political views and changed his personal plans. Mikko understood the European conflict as a war waged by capitalist nations vying for the world's resources. Growing increasingly disgusted with what he considered a senseless loss of lives in Europe, he immersed himself ever deeper in the socialist movement in America. Lack of economic opportunity also pushed him toward socialism. Mining coal in Red Lodge did not yield the financial rewards he had sought when he emigrated to the United States in 1910. Disillusioned, but conscious of his role as a worker, Mikko dropped his initial goal of earning money mining Montana coal to purchase farmland in Finland, and threw himself into Finnish-American socialism.

The letters Mikko Marttunen wrote to his mother in Kauhajoki, Finland, reflected the hopes and dreams of many immigrants and the sorrow they felt being separated from their families during wartime.

In his letters, Mikko described his adjustment to American culture, his disillusionment as an immigrant worker, his hopes for change as a result of union activity, and his increased class-conscious reaction to the war.

Mikko also discussed what he saw as the shortcomings of America's capitalistic economy, which resulted in the impoverished condition of many foreign-born workers. Although they recruited foreign laborers, industrial leaders also sought to control workers to attain maximum productivity and secure the highest profits possible from their factories, mills, and mines. As a result, immigrant workers like Mikko experienced disillusionment. Mikko stayed in the United States after the war, growing increasingly radical in ideology as he became more disillusioned with the unchanging plight of labor and the frustrations of the Depression. As time went on, his letters revealed the downhill course of his life from hopeful expectations to disappointment and bitterness.

America's powerful capitalistic economy attracted 229,000 Finns between 1894 and 1920. Coming to America in search of material gain, they left behind a desperate economic and political situation in Finland. Finland's industrialization brought increased land consolidation and mechanized agriculture to its hinterlands. Wealthy landholders bought up smaller farms, converting into tenants those farmers still willing to work the land. Until 1906, landless Finns had no voice in government, and landowners could and did raise rents arbitrarily, forcing tenants off their farms. In trouble economically and without legal protection, many tenant farmers in Finland emigrated to the United States, hoping to make enough money to return to Finland to buy farmland.[2] Like many Finns, Mikko emigrated because he could not live independently in Finland without the money necessary to buy land and establish himself as a farmer. At his confirmation into the Finnish Lutheran Church, Mikko confided in his mother and told her of his plans to emigrate. His ideas startled his mother, although she realized his situation was desperate. "I can't figure out what it was that made you want to move to America soon after you finished confirmation school," his mother wrote many years later. "Though I have to admit that it was pretty miserable [on the family farm] at that time.

Residents of the Suomela Boarding House in Red Lodge gather outside the wash house.
COURTESY CARBON COUNTY HISTORICAL SOCIETY AND MUSEUM, RED LODGE.

There is really nothing to envy about those times." With no prospect of owning land, Mikko left the family farm and joined others at a co-operative dairy farm in nearby Karijoki. Seven years later he departed for the United States.[3]

Mikko joined millions of European immigrants in supplying labor to American industry. At first he worked cutting timber for the iron mines at Bessemer, Michigan, where many of his countrymen were already at work. The Quincy Mining Company of northern Michigan's copper country had solicited Finnish miners in Norway since the 1860s to replace workers lost to the American Civil War. By the turn of the century, Michigan had become the starting point for immigrant Finnish laborers.[4] Working as a logger did not yield Mikko the economic gains he had anticipated, however, and he did not stay long in Michigan. He had worked only fourteen days during his two-month stay at the iron camp when he decided to leave the Midwest for Red Lodge, Montana. As he explained to his mother in 1911, he left the Michigan logging camp primarily for financial reasons:

> The work in the lumber camps near Bessemer ended at Christmas. They didn't need anyone else except drivers and loaders who would load the logs on trains. Since mining activities in Bessemer were not very good, work was getting less and less and jobs were not to be had, we decided to come here to the coal mines and see how it would go here. We left Bessemer on Tapani Day [St. Stephen's Day, December 26] morning at 6 o'clock and got here on Wednesday, the 28th, about noon. The trip was almost 2,000 miles and the ticket cost $27. Here the wages are much better than in Michigan and here we don't need to fear mine explosions, because here there is no exploding gas.

Mikko was unaware that a fire in a Red Lodge mine four years earlier had killed eight miners.[5]

Mikko arrived in Montana by train and, once in Red Lodge, followed a pattern similar to that of other Finnish immigrants. Like others before him, he depended upon Finns already established in a Red Lodge boarding house that catered to Finnish-born miners. Mikko then followed his housemates to the coal mines and relied on them to introduce him to a variety of social activities. As Mikko reported to his mother:

> I don't have much to tell but the usual that I am healthy and work at the mines. I spend my evenings in many ways, sometimes at the boarding house sometimes at the candy shop other times in dances or at parties at the Workers' Hall.

Mikko socialized exclusively with other Finns in Red Lodge and complained about the lack of female companionship. "There are so few girls here, because we haven't gotten any new ones from Finland for some years, and all the ones that have been here for a while are married."[6]

Like nearly half of his fellow Finns in Red Lodge, Mikko did not speak English. Instead, he spoke his native language and relied on communicating with his compatriots to adjust to the community and his new job. When he first arrived in town, Mikko worked shifts in the mines with a Finnish-born partner, bought clothing at a Finnish-owned dry goods store, and, after he stopped advocating temperance, drank his fill at the Finnish saloon. So it was that Mikko, like hundreds of his compatriots, could go for months, even years, without learning English. Immigrants from other countries settled in Red Lodge, as well, but the Finnish enclave was larger and functioned as a community all its own, isolated from the rest of the community.[7] The isolation allowed Red Lodge Finns to practice their customs in the manner they wished and keep traditions alive. Until anti-socialist and nativist sentiments peaked during World War I, Finns expressed their cultural values without fear of repression.

Despite insulation in the Red Lodge enclave, Mikko encountered values very different from the ones he had known in rural Finland. About sixty percent of Finns who immigrated to the United States between 1893 and 1920 came from agricultural backgrounds. Close attention to the seasons and the weather, recognition of holidays coinciding with seed-time and harvest, and hard work with little material reward characterized farm life in Finland at the turn of the century. Once arrived in America, however, Finnish immigrants had to cope with new values and norms, some of which arose from an urban industrial society. Despite their isolation in the protective ethnic enclave of Red Lodge, Finnish immigrants found themselves exposed to American values where they worked—in the mines.[8]

Mikko reflected on the differences between farm life in Finland and what he found in Red Lodge in a December 1912 letter home in which he described local Christmas celebrations. In rural Finland, Christmas festivities lasted well beyond Christmas day, but in American industrial towns like Red Lodge, Mikko discovered that work continued as usual:

In honor of the Christmas season I am writing you a few lines. I didn't go to work today. I decided that it isn't too much if

*Men pause with their picks and lunch pails before a shift at the Eastside Mine,
Red Lodge. The mine produced an average of 100 tons of coal per day.*
COURTESY CARBON COUNTY HISTORICAL SOCIETY AND MUSEUM, RED LODGE.

I celebrate Christmas for two days in Finland they celebrate
it for a week. Christmas was celebrated here on the Eve at
the Temperance Hall, as well as at the Socialists' Hall, with
Christmas trees, speeches, songs, poetry reading, and plays.
There was no Christmas sermon offered to the Finns since the
church, which has served the Finns here for years, just stood
there cold and dark. There is no minister nor any religious activities. Isn't this a pagan place? What do you think?[9]

On the farm in Finland, Mikko had known the seasons and paid
close attention to the calendar of holidays. In Montana, things were
different. "Here," in Red Lodge, he wrote to his mother in 1913, "one
does not notice whether it's Sunday, [or] whether it's a holiday; it's
always work and restless activities, so here one doesn't even follow the
almanac very much."[10]

Money also took on a new meaning for Mikko. At the cooperative dairy farm in Finland, Mikko had traded for, borrowed, or made what he required and had sometimes needed to ask his mother for money. As he wrote in one letter from Karijoki in 1904:

> What about that loan? Is there any hope of getting one? And how much? I don't have any money nor will there be any money from the dairy yet. . . . And also, will I be getting those cattle to fatten up from Kauhajoki? I would appreciate a speedy response, and if possible some assistance. That is if you haven't forgotten your son.[11]

Once in America, however, Mikko drew wages with some regularity, and soon realized the difference it made in society:

> I haven't lost my money in card games either, though card games seem to be a common vice, not just among young men but also among family men. There is one observation that I've made both about myself and others and that is the longer you're here the harder it is to save money. There seems to be so many different ways one can be tempted into throwing money away one penny after another. In America, one thing I've discovered is true: you can have anything if you have money. But another truth is that you can't get anything unless you have money."[12]

Despite an initial resolve to save their earnings, immigrant Finns often scrimped less and consumed more. Saving money eluded immigrant laborers like Mikko because of high expenses. Describing his financial condition to his mother, Mikko wrote:

> I am on day wages in the mine, as a timber man, for which I get $8.39 a day. It seems like good wages except that living costs have risen in the same proportion as the wages. For example, last month food cost $35.65, and I pay $12 for my room a month, and if I have a suit made I have to pay about $50, laundry cost $1.50 a month, a cost which I have to spend each

month. If I have a suit pressed at the tailors, I have to pay $2, and so on. So there seems to be plenty of tricks to bleed away the wages from the workers. It takes a lot of denial and will power to be able to save anything. And after one is here in the U.S. for awhile it is difficult to pinch pennies. . . . It certainly isn't time to think about my return to Finland since I haven't even started getting rich yet.[13]

Despite such expenses, expectations for significant savings remained high. Both Emilia and Mikko hoped to make their lives in Finland more comfortable with the money Mikko earned in the United States. Emilia asked Mikko to send money, and he warned her sternly that cash would not be forthcoming immediately. In a January 1912 letter, he expressed his fear of being stranded in a town where work was not available. "Tell me if you think I have been a spendthrift," he told his mother. "I have thought that when I have over $200, I will send the amount to Finland and I will always have that to fall back on. Life here is unstable; one can be laid off at any time and if one doesn't have money he can't even move to another community."[14]

As time went on, Mikko grew more enthusiastic for union activities and for Finnish-American socialism. Like immigrant workers elsewhere, he found that the supply of workers often exceeded demand and drove down wages. Growing dissatisfied, Mikko believed American capitalists were responsible not only for inequities in Red Lodge, but also for the First World War. The ill treatment of Finnish workers during the Finnish Civil War also altered his attitude toward capital and labor. He found himself drawn to working-class politics and socialism because he believed that organized effort was the best way to effect social change. Moreover, the right of free expression in America encouraged those already attracted to radical politics to employ in Red Lodge the socialistic customs of communal living and cooperative businesses they had known in Finland.[15]

For Finns, socialism was not merely a political philosophy but a way of life. They cultivated both the mind and the body toward a communal lifestyle. Finnish-American socialist halls reverberated with readings of socialist literature, poetry, and plays. In Red Lodge,

performers with the socialists' gymnastics club even worked together
to promote fitness and exhibit human strength.[16]

Because they saw economic disparity as the root of all human
conflict, Finnish socialists attempted to dissolve economic classes
by instituting cooperatively run businesses. Co-ops, like the Kalena
Co-op in Red Lodge, attempted to create economic democracy. They
belonged to the people who consumed the products sold, and their
control was distributed among members in proportion to how often
they used the service. Co-ops had the added benefit of neutralizing
the competitive individualism that American culture tended to promote, an individualism that Finns thought incompatible with genuine
democracy. Faced with harsh economic conditions, Finnish socialists
organized to improve their situation, and communal living and cooperative businesses became two of their most significant contributions
to American society.[17]

Mikko lived at a Finnish boarding house, was the bookkeeper at a
cooperatively run diner, and supported the Socialist Party. His sympa-
thies lay with the proletariat, both in Finland and in the United States,
and he was proud of his political affiliation. In 1912, he wrote to his
mother hopefully:

> Here in America, socialism is gradually getting a stronger foot-
> hold. Just recently in the presidential election held in November,
> the socialist candidate got more than a million votes while in
> the 1908 election the socialists got only 428,000 votes. Here in
> Red Lodge last summer the Finnish socialists built a magnifi-
> cent hall that came to cost almost $20,000. The Socialist Party
> in this country is the only party that looks after the interests
> of the workers, and I wonder if any other party in Finland has
> the interest of the workers at heart—at least I don't think so.[18]

Mikko also participated in Finnish Workers' Hall meetings, sang in
the men's chorus, and acted in Finnish plays. Social activities such as
these were typical of Finnish communities all over the United States,
and in that sense American Finns were one large community. Mikko
received letters from Finnish workers throughout the United States,

During the summer of 1912, Finns held "building bees" to construct a workers' hall in Red Lodge. COURTESY CARBON COUNTY HISTORICAL SOCIETY AND MUSEUM, RED LODGE.

and their correspondence revealed the similarities between the activities of Red Lodge's Finnish socialists and those in other western Finnish communities. "Here the Socialist Society is very active," wrote one Finnish friend named Wilho from Astoria, Oregon.

> The chorus is a good organization and a damned good drama group which has some really good actors. Last Sunday they presented the play "Devil" and it went extremely well. There is a big hall here where they can present big plays, and they make quite a bit of money.[19]

Moreover, what Mikko's friends told him strengthened his convictions about the broad appeal of class-conscious politics and socialism. From Diamondville, Wyoming, for example, Jussi Luoma wrote to Mikko about the hard times Finnish immigrants faced there, about the organizations they formed, and the central role communal groups played in the Finnish community. Luoma also hinted at the divisiveness among Finnish Americans; not all Finns felt the same attraction to radical politics. "Warm greetings from me here," wrote Luoma,

> . . . from this desolate mining town where a handful of Finns fight for their existence. A small divided group we have here. Radicalism has been around here but it hasn't been as strong as it is in Montana. But on the other hand, we have had a temperance person here who has carried his hate of the activities of the socialists to the extreme. They have control of the hall, through whose activities they try to suffocate our activities by charging us unreasonably high rents. We, however, have presented our side of the matter and I think that we can get them to be more kindly disposed to us. I heard that our people's activities are pretty much in a state of rest there now [in Red Lodge]. A zealous pioneer is lacking, and what can you do about that at the drop of a hat?[20]

Western immigrant communities undoubtedly aided the Finns' transition from their native lands and economies to the ways of the United States. Ethnic enclaves like the Finnish community in Red Lodge, however, also became a base for radical politics that threatened to interrupt the smooth operation of industries. In Red Lodge, as in Astoria and Diamondville, Finnish temperance advocates and socialists quarreled. Mikko joined the local temperance group early on but later turned toward socialism. In replying to his mother's fears concerning his drinking in 1911, Mikko wrote: "You are afraid that Kalle [a Finn also from Kauhajoki] will teach me to drink and run around. It's useless to worry since I have decided to teach Kalle to stop drinking and squandering—and Kalle plans to let me." Mikko added: "Don't worry that I will put my money into liquor since I am able to pass the door of a bar without feeling any twinge of temptation." A year later, Mikko wrote: "The temperance society has in recent years been increasing its activity, and has just recently set up a men's choir and mixed choir." By 1916, however, Mikko's attitudes were changing. "You don't have to worry about me turning into a drunk, because that I have not done yet, though I'm not a total abstainer, either." Mikko's attitudes toward alcohol shifted as his political views became more intense. He never spoke of temperance again after World War I.[21]

With the end of the war in Europe, Finland enjoyed an improved economy, which beckoned many Finnish immigrants to return home. Describing his own fortune, Antii Kaura in Kauhajoki, Finland, wrote encouragingly to Mikko:

> I am involved in business undertakings and in some of them I succeed and in others I don't—the latest case is less frequent. Among my businesses is the flourmill which up to now has been doing all right. But it is weaker today since we are at the mercy of German raw material and the storehouses are depleted. On the other side of the coin, the shoelace factory is in the heyday since no laces are available from the outside and in Finland there are only two factories. . . . Before I end this letter, I want to give you a bit of advice. Come back home and buy a place and become a farmer. It would be so much better than working so hard under the ground or wherever in a foreign land.[22]

Emilia Aronen had pressured her son to return home even before the war ended. His absence caused her much grief and hardship, both emotionally and financially. She told him of her loneliness and of the physical illnesses that plagued her after Mikko left for America. Although she had married for a second time before Mikko emigrated, her union with Matti Aronen was not a happy one. Living on a farm with Aronen and his children, she complained of her husband's laziness and of his children's selfish demands on her time. When tragedy struck a neighboring farm in 1916, Emilia sought to become a matchmaker and secure a better future for herself and her son.

> Well, listen, I have a little matter to tell you about: a terrible thing has happened here. The young man who was master of the Luoma-Aijo place shot himself in July, a month ago, and now they are going to have an auction. The couple didn't have any children and so the relatives of the deceased get to inherit

half of the property except for a fifth of their half of the house which belongs to the wife. Everything except for that fifth is to be split in half—the heirs number 16—so it will be necessary to have a sale. There is a lot of land according to the assessment. It has a good house in the middle of the land; it isn't too far from the county road, a kilometer. A good gravel road to the place goes over the fishing bridge. The Mrs. will not sell her half at all. So I thought why not, when the other half goes up for auction, shouldn't we try to get the other half, and then you can combine it with the widow's half. She is a healthy handsome person who is capable of all sorts of work in the house and outside. And as a person, she is very pleasant and happy. We were there yesterday visiting and I came to the conclusion that we could get a good house that would need little work—but work you have to do wherever you are. There was an exceptionally fine well in the middle of the yard, and the water is good. Come back from America and become the master of this house. It isn't too early to create your own future.[23]

Though she never had much money, Emilia worried increasingly over how to provide for herself when Matti Aronen died in January 1919. She counted on Mikko to take care of her when he returned, and her hopes for his return were kept alive by mention of his possible return. Unable to make up his mind, Mikko see-sawed endlessly over the question of returning to Finland or remaining in Red Lodge. He continued on in Montana for the same reasons he became a Finnish-American socialist—his faith in unionism, his views on American involvement in the First World War, and his perception of the political situation in Finland.

As early as 1898, Red Lodge coal miners had formed a union local of the Western Federation of Miners in hopes of gaining higher wages and better working conditions.[24] The union membership roster included men from various European countries, many of whom had come to the United States without specific skills and had to accept work in the lowest-paying positions. Not long afterward, Red Lodge miners affiliated with the United Mine Workers of America,

Membership in the United Mine Workers of America union was ratified in certificates such as this one dating from 1899. COURTESY LIBRARY OF CONGRESS, LC-DIG-PGA-01953.

a powerful national union. Affiliation with the UMWA gave the miners more leverage, for they could strike nationwide and paralyze mine operations throughout the nation. Although radical Finnish workers believed in union organizing, affiliation with the UMWA had

drawbacks. National union officials controlled the union's negotiations with operators and limited worker freedoms. In 1919, the
UMWA went on strike when management kept wartime wages in
effect until the Senate ratified the Versailles Treaty.[25]

In a letter to his mother the following summer, Mikko described
progress made during the strike as well as his skepticism about union
leadership.

> Well, we were on strike last winter—all soft coal miners, about
> 450,000 men, from the beginning of March to the middle of
> December, but we didn't win hardly anything, since our lead-
> ers cheated us just when a complete victory would have been
> possible in a few days. This kind of thing embitters the workers,
> but at the same time it teaches them to organize better. I was
> still out of work after the strike, only in the middle of April did
> I finally begin to work.[26]

Immigrants respected the power unionism represented and hoped
the union might bring the economic rewards they had hoped for
when they emigrated. In Red Lodge, as in other Finnish communities, Finnish socialist halls served as headquarters for unionizing.
In Red Lodge, Finnish immigrants opened the Kalena Co-operative
Mercantile Association on the first floor of Red Lodge's Labor Temple,
built in 1909. The association aided union activity, but the UMWA
began losing power by the 1920s. As mine owners closed union mines
in northern states and opened non-union mines in southern states,
the UMWA's most potent weapon—the strike—became less effective.[27] In 1922, the UMWA struck to gain access to company records
to prove that workers were not receiving fair pay. At the close of the
strike, Mikko reflected:

> Thus for almost five months all the organized miners of coal
> stood united behind the strike. 610,000 were involved. A cou-
> ple hundred thousand non-union miners dug the coal, but it
> was not enough to meet demand, so the coal barons gave in to
> demand and we were able to go back to work with old wages

and conditions, despite the coal barons' plan to lower the wages by $3 a day and to break the union. The unanimity of workers prevented this.[28]

Mikko praised UMWA's strength in the face of company threats to dissolve the union. The fact that union access to records was not achieved did not dampen his faith. As Mikko noted, workers had grown tired of the strike and were pleased simply to get their jobs back.

Despite setbacks, Finns and other immigrant miners held tightly to the promise of unionism. Immigrant miners typically worked at the most dangerous and lowest-paying jobs in the mines, while native-born Americans held preferred jobs as electricians, engineers, timbermen, and drivers. The census manuscripts of 1900 and 1910 for Red Lodge and Carbon County show that a majority of those who worked underground, where work was most dangerous, and a majority of those injured or killed were of foreign birth.[29]

Mikko's class-conscious attitudes, developed from his union membership, were intensified by the nationalistic prejudices expressed toward foreign-born peoples in small Montana towns during World War I. The atmosphere in Red Lodge grew tense during World War I as over-zealous patriots, businessmen, and mine owners, all of whom supported the war effort, criticized socialist miners and immigrants, who opposed American involvement in the war. Finnish anti-war activists suffered persecution from native-born Americans not only because of their socialist activities, but also because of their radical union activities. Radical Finns in Red Lodge, for example, supported the Industrial Workers of the World, a union that set itself against American involvement in the war and favored control of industries by workers.[30]

Correspondence between Mikko and his mother during the war years slowed considerably. Mail delivery was sluggish, and Mikko confided that he did not feel like writing when he knew a letter would not reach its destination for months, if at all. Both Emilia and Mikko found solace in music, however. Emilia wrote of joyous song during peacetime, while Mikko found diversion and release from the anguish of war in his choral activities. "We have started a man's chorus this spring and tomorrow evening we will have a concert that we hope will be a success. We just sing, although dark forces tear up the world—we sing away the burdens from our shoulders."[31]

Although they both agonized over the inconveniences of delayed mail and restricted travel, Emilia and Mikko differed in their personal reactions to the war. While Emilia invoked prayers for peace, Mikko theorized about wartime conditions:

> We are having bad times in America now. The capitalists or money-men say it is on account of the war, but I believe that if there wasn't a war, it would be worse. The countries that are warring in Europe have bought from this country hundreds of millions of dollars worth of guns and ammunition. . . . That great and terrible war doesn't seem to end. On the contrary, it seems to draw more and more countries into the conflict.[32]

Mikko agonized even more over the turn of events in Finland. The 1918 Finnish Civil War, fought between bourgeois and communist forces, shaped the political attitudes of Finnish immigrants throughout the United States, and Mikko's perception of the political atmosphere after the bourgeois triumph persuaded him to stay in the United States. The bourgeois victors had taken as prisoners thousands of communists who Mikko saw as fellow protestors against the capitalist order. Describing his views in a letter home in 1920, he wrote:

> It's terrible to imagine being there in Finland nowadays. I can just imagine how thousands of pale workers languish in crowded and filthy prisons slowly dying from disease and starvation. I can see workers being transported from their homes . . . and shot like dogs without an investigation . . . and all this because they had the courage to demand themselves justice and bread. Where is justice now in Finland? At the tip of a bayonet. Even the African cannibal is shocked with the 'civilization' of your white heroes.

Events in his Finnish homeland had intensified Mikko's class-conscious attitudes.[33] After the war, Mikko abandoned his plan to return to Finland. Writing to his mother in 1922, he explained:

> I've always thought that I will come and at least visit Finland, but because of the miserable civil war the conditions in Finland are such that I really don't feel like going there. A couple from here visited Kalajoki and they described the conditions in there as very bad. There is a bitter class hatred smoldering in the minds of the workers. Even in work places one can't hear any other names than 'red' and 'murderer' . . . the Finnish government has arranged plunder trips to Estonia and East Karelia. There seems to be enough funds for such things, but not for helping the starvation in Russia, even the workers have been denied the permission to voluntarily collect money for the starving, innocent children, not to mention the adults. Government behavior like that is condemned, and the sword of Damocles hangs heavy over the head of it.[34]

Because of his immigrant status, Mikko identified both with the working classes in the United States and the proletariat in Europe, which encouraged his belief in the idea of a worldwide working-class revolution. Accordingly, as his class consciousness heightened, he felt isolated both from his homeland and from his adopted country. He did not live in Finland, but he never became an American citizen either, and consequently he could not participate fully in either society. The largest hurdle keeping Mikko and other Finns from integrating fully into American society was language. Finnish is a unique language belonging to the Finno-Ugric group. Its only close relative is Estonian, and it differs markedly from English. Because Finns did not hear English spoken in their enclaves, they did not learn it easily. As fewer Finnish immigrants arrived in the United States after World War I, however, ethnic enclaves began breaking up. Contact with the larger society increased for many foreign-born immigrants who, like J. F. Koski, grew frustrated with not having mastered the English language. Writing from Lava Hot Springs, Idaho, in 1937, Koski began:

Greetings, man, Mike, although this letter writing goes rather clumsily with a pencil, because I haven't really written much of anything in 20 years except for my name once in awhile. . . . I just thought that I would scratch out a letter to you also; I wrote already to Waino and to Eemeli Autio last week. In the pool I have noticed—it would be easy to make friends with all the women, and with the men, since in the pool we really feel as if we are all on common ground, and equal no matter what nationality or color—if I only didn't have language difficulties. There are no other Finns here but me, but there are Americans, Japanese, Mexicans, Yugoslavs and Indians, and we are just like people living under the same roof, like at Riipi's boarding house. There have not been any Negroes in the pool so I can't say what kind of psychological effect they might cause. But, for example the young Japanese girls are just as lovely as the white ones. . . . As interesting as life is here, life still seems quite lonesome when because of lack of English I can't mix with the Americans. My English is so poor that I don't feel like trying to use it for anything except the essentials. It makes me mad sometimes in that pool when a young pretty girl, or woman, seems to encourage me to come to talk to her. I have already met three such persons, who were so forward that they didn't wait but took the initiative; and you can imagine what kind of situation developed for a man of my personality. I have many times cursed under my breath that I never took it upon myself to learn the language as soon as I came to this country.[35]

The exclusiveness of the Finnish enclave and its social distance from outsiders also became a disadvantage for Finnish socialists. Isolation kept the radicals from spreading their views, while prejudicial and repressive attitudes kept native-born Americans from hearing their ideas. As a consequence, Finns like Mikko failed to initiate the changes they sought. In his letters after the war, Mikko described a dwindling Finnish community. Many Finnish radicals had been chased out of Red Lodge, while others gave up mining and purchased farms. In his letters after the war, Mikko described the changes:

Well, I have lived in this same house, which is owned by Fiina Hakala's Kalle and his wife, for over 12 years—I'm not much of a mover. Last winter I moved into a new boarding house, since because of layoffs they had to quit the Rientola cooperative boarding house. I am now eating at the Suomela (Finnish) boarding house which is the only cooperative boarding house in town. When I came here at the end of 1910, there were 6 or 7 Finnish boarding houses and in Rientola there were over 80 men, right now in Suomela there are about 70, but 20 men of other nationalities. The world war and decrease in immigration from Finland has created the situation that the majority of Finns are family men who live in their own or in rented houses. Pretty soon I am going to get tired of boarding house life and will begin to board with a wife as it is the custom to say here.[36]

Emilia Aronen died in 1926 after sixteen years of pleading with her son to return home. Mikko returned to Finland for a visit after receiving word of her death. While there, he settled his financial affairs and those of his mother. He also collected the letters he had written to her over the years and brought them back to the United States. Upon returning to Montana, he settled in Butte where he peddled socialist literature in the Finnish enclave for the Työmies (Workingman) Society, a Finnish-American workers' organization based in Superior, Wisconsin. The society began publishing a newspaper called *Työmies* in 1900. Published initially by the Finnish Socialist Federation, the paper reflected the political conflicts within the Finnish-American community and was caught up in the split between moderate and leftwing socialists during the 1920s. Finnish socialists divided over the role the consumers' cooperatives should play. Moderates felt that the co-ops should remain neutral politically. The communists, believing the co-ops were replacing ideology with economic interests and thereby hindering the workers' revolution, wanted to take them over and use them as a source of financial aid. *Työmies* eventually became the voice of the Finnish-American communist party.[37]

Remarkably, the "Americanization" programs following World War I and the decline in emigration from Finland during the 1920s did not weaken the solidarity of Finnish-American workers during the 1930s. Members of Työmies still chose to express their political opinions within the context of the Finnish community, rather than in an American political group. The longevity of a foreign-language political group like Työmies in the United States indicates the extent of the Finnish-American community's isolation and the tenacity of Finnish enclaves in the United States.[38]

Still, Mikko's involvement in the Työmies society reflected the downhill course of his life in Montana. By the time he moved to Butte, he was in his forties and battling periodic unemployment, ill health, and a drinking problem. His situation had changed little since he first arrived from Finland. The chronic unemployment that had hindered him in his early years as an immigrant had followed him to Butte. Unable to find steady employment, he found solace in an ideology that offered the foreign laborer a chance to control his own future. The circumstances of Mikko's death are unknown, except that he died while in the United States.

Mikko's experiences reflected the paradox inherent in the lives of Finnish immigrant socialists: They lived in isolation from the rest of society, but they wanted to change conditions for laborers of all nationalities. Clearly, Mikko's economic options were constrained by a combination of the low wages and unemployment that periodically plagued the U.S. economy and by his decision to remain in the Finnish enclave. Although Mikko did not achieve the material success he dreamed of, the significance of his experiences is reflected in the values his letters communicated and in how life in America did not always live up to the expectations of those who came here. Mikko wrote of injustice in American society, and he worked toward its correction. He expressed eloquently a sympathy for the worker, an intolerance for the futile suffering and atrocities of war, and a special joy for the comfort he found in communal living. His contribution, the same made by thousands of Finnish immigrants, was in the work he did to help industrialize the United States and in the heightened class and ethnic consciousness he brought to his fellow laborers on the western mining frontier.

—∿∿—

This essay originally appeared in *Montana, The Magazine of Western History,* Spring 1990.

   Erika Kuhlman received her bachelor's and master's degrees from the University of Montana, and her Ph.D. from Washington State University. She teaches history at Idaho State University in Pocatello. Her books include Petticoats and White Feathers: Gender Conformity, Race, the Progressive Peace Movement, and the Debate over War *(1997);* Reconstructing Patriarchy after the Great War: Women, Gender, and Postwar Reconciliation between Nations *(2008); and* Of Little Comfort: War Widows, Fallen Soldiers, and the Remaking of the Nation after the Great War *(2012).*

—∿∿—

NOTES

1   Emilia Aronen to Mikko Marttunen, Kauhajoki, Finland, January 25, 1915, correspondence of Mikko Marttunen, 1904-1939, author's collection, Missoula, Montana. Unless noted otherwise, all correspondence to or from Mikko Marttunen was translated from Finnish into English and is part of the author's collection. See also Ralph J. Jalkanen, *Faith of the Finns* (East Lansing, Michigan State University Press, 1972).

2   A. William Hoglund, *Finnish Immigrants in America, 1880-1920* (Madison, University of Wisconsin Press, 1960), pp. 13-16; John I. Kolehmainen, "Finland's Agrarian Structure and Overseas Migration," in *Agricultural History,* 15 (January 1941), pp. 41-48; Al Gedicks, "Finnish Immigrants in Michigan," in *Politics and Society,* 7 (Spring 1977), pp. 127-156.

3   Emilia Aronen to Mikko Marttunen, May 9, 1920.

4   Hoglund, *Finnish Immigrants,* p. 9.

5   Mikko Marttunen to Emilia Aronen, January 20, 1911. Aune Arlene Poutio Harris, "The Coal Mines," in Shirly Zupan and Harry Owens, *Red Lodge: Saga of a Western Area* (Billings, Montana, Carbon County Historical Society, 1979), pp. 129-139.

6   Mikko Marttunen to Emilia Aronen, December 2, 1920.

7   1910 Census Population Schedule, Carbon County, M-299, National Archives, Washington, D.C. On "little Italy" and other immigrant groups, see Zupan and Owens, *Red Lodge,* pp. 177-179.

8   Herbert G. Gutman, *Work, Culture and Society in Industrializing America* (New York, Vintage, 1977), pp. 19-32, 43-45; Hoglund, *Finnish Immigrants*, pp. 9, 24-25.

9   Mikko Marttunen to Emilia Aronen, December 25, 1912.

10 Ibid., July 21, 1913.

11 Ibid., April 23, 1904.

12 Ibid., March 20, 1916.

13 Ibid., November 20, 1923.

14 Ibid., January 27, 1912.

15 On the predisposition of Finnish immigrants to radicalism, see Al Gedicks, "The Social Origins of Radicalism Among Finnish Immigrants in Midwest Mining Communities," in *Review of Radical Political Economics*, 8 (Fall 1976), pp. 1-31. On transformation of ethnic consciousness to class consciousness among miners in immigrant communities, see Gedicks, "Finnish Immigrants in Michigan," pp. 127-156.

16 Aune Arlene Poutio Harris, "The Red Lodge Finns," in Zupan and Owens, *Red Lodge*, pp. 179-187.

17 On Finnish and other co-operatives, see H. Haines Turner, *Case Studies of Consumers' Co-operatives* (New York, AMS Press, 1968), p. 14. On Finnish-American socialism, see Walfrid Jokinen, "The Finns in the United States: A Sociological Interpretation" (doctoral dissertation, Louisiana State University, 1955), p. 150.

18 Mikko Marttunen to Emilia Aronen, December 25, 1912.

19 Wilho to Mikko Marttunen, August 17, 1918.

20 Jussi Luoma to Mikko Marttunen, February 8, 1916.

21 Mikko Marttunen to Emilia Aronen, January 20, 1911, January 27, July 18, 1912, March 20, 1916.

22 Antii Kaura to Mikko Marttunen, October 5, 1916.

23 Emilia Aronen to Mikko Marttunen, August 23, 1916.

24 See Philip S. Foner, *History of the Labor Movement in the United States*, 4 vols. (New York, International Publishers, 1947-1965), IV, pp. 490-495.

25 The exact year of Red Lodge affiliation with UMWA is unknown, although it may have occurred as early as 1898. See Harris, "The Coal Mines," pp. 129-139; and Erika Kuhlman, "From Farmland to Coalvillage: Red Lodge's Finnish Immigrants, 1890-1920" (master's thesis, University of Montana, 1987), pp. 74-75.

26 Mikko Marttunen to Emilia Aronen, August 22, 1920.

27 On European immigrant loyalty to the UMWA, see Foner, *History of the Labor Movement*, III, p. 267, IV, p. 491. On decline of UMWA because of regional competition, see Morton S. Baratz, *The Union and the Coal Industry* (New Haven, Yale University Press, 1955), p. 61.

28 Mikko Marttunen to Emilia Aronen, October 29, 1922.

29 On employees' positions at the mines and their nations of birth, see the 1910 Census Population Schedule for Carbon County, M-299. For lists of mining accident victims and their nationalities, see Inspector of Coal Mines, annual and biennial reports (Helena, Independent Printing Office, 1903-1910).

30 Kuhlman, "From Farmland to Coalvillage," pp. 91-103.

31 Mikko Marttunen to Emilia Aronen, June 18, 1915.

32 Ibid.

33 Mikko Marttunen to Emilia Aronen, April 1, 1920. On Finnish-American reactions to the Finnish Civil War, see Auvo Kostianen "The Tragic Crisis: Finnish American Workers and the Civil War in Finland," in *For the Common Good*, Michael G. Karni and Douglas J. Ollila, Jr., eds. (Superior, Wisconsin: Työmies Society, 1977), pp. 219-221.

34 Mikko Marttunen to Emilia Aronen, October 29, 1922.

35 J. F. Koski to Mikko Marttunen, August 19, 1937.

36 Mikko Marttunen to Emilia Aronen, November 20, 1923.

37 For a discussion of Finnish communists, Työmies, and cooperatives, see John I. Kolehmainen and George W. Hill, *A Haven in the Woods: The Story of the Finns in Wisconsin* (Madison, State Historical Society of Wisconsin, 1951), pp. 136-137.

38 Ibid.

Fire in the Hole:
Slovenians, Croatians,
and Coal Mining on the Musselshell

～ *Anna Zellick*

By the beginning of the twentieth century, the complexion of America's—and Montana's—ethnic communities was changing. Not only were immigrants coming in record numbers; they were also coming from different places. Through most of the nineteenth century, the vast majority of America's immigrants had come from western and northern Europe. After the turn of the century, more and more came from eastern and southern Europe. Just as that change was occurring, the last of the great transcontinental railroads—the Chicago, Milwaukee, St. Paul & Pacific Railway—was being constructed up the Musselshell Valley in central Montana. The arrival of the Milwaukee Road and the establishment of Roundup as a regional rail center created an immediate demand for coal. As it turned out, coal was readily available in nearby underground seams. A rush of coal miners into the Musselshell country was soon underway; many of those miners were Slovenians and Croatians looking for new economic opportunities of their own.

As the late Anna Zellick vividly recounts in the following essay, southern Slavs from Croatia and Slovenia soon made up a sizable percentage of the population in Musselshell County. Like other recently *arrived ethnic groups of this era, they faced daunting challenges: limited funds, significant language barriers, sometimes hostile local officials, and dangerous working conditions, especially in the underground mines. Yet they often met these challenges in an impressively successful fashion. They were able to mold satisfying lives for themselves for many reasons, including strong family ties, an explicit sense of community that featured ethnic grocery stores and saloons, and the establishment of fraternal organizations that were similar to those supported by other immigrant groups such as the Chinese, Irish, and Finns. Some of them, due to ties with their places of birth within the Austro-Hungarian Empire, were persecuted by nativist Montanans during the First World War. Yet such challenges notwithstanding, most of the Slovenians and Croatians living in the Musselshell Valley had successfully adapted to the broader American culture by the 1930s, and, in the process, helped to build much of twentieth-century Montana.*

In 1906, W. W. Taylor, general superintendent of mines for the Chicago, Milwaukee, St. Paul & Pacific Railway—the Milwaukee Road—and A. A. Morris were in the Bull Mountains near Billings, Montana, prospecting for coal. After a long hard day, they stopped at a rancher's house, where they spent the night. Over supper, the rancher told them of wading in the Musselshell River to retrieve a duck he had shot and of seeing a ten-foot vein of coal near Old Roundup. His discovery and its subsequent development by the railroad triggered one of the most extensive coal mining booms in Montana. It also resulted in the birth of new Roundup. Dubbed the "Miracle City of the Musselshell," the new railroad and coal mining town quickly eclipsed what had been a stockmen's center for thirty years.[1]

Among the hundreds of men and women who came to the coal mining settlements in the Musselshell River Valley were Croatians and Slovenians. Croatia and Slovenia are neighboring republics in former northwestern Yugoslavia, two of the six republics that comprised the country. The word "Yugoslavia" means South Slav, as distinguished from eastern or western Slav. Although their peoples speak different languages, Croatia and Slovenia share many traditions, including an overwhelming adherence to Roman Catholicism. Often called Austrians because of their inclusion in the Austro-Hungarian Empire, even after Yugoslavia became an independent nation in 1918, these South Slavs converged on the Musselshell Valley from a number of areas.[2] Some came from other Montana mining communities such as Aldrich, Lehigh, Red Lodge, East Helena, Anaconda, and Butte. Others came from mining towns in Wyoming and Utah, and still others came directly from what was Yugoslavia.

Opportunity and ethnic ties attracted South Slavs to Montana. What they encountered in the coal mining settlements along the Musselshell River was a mixture of hard times, danger, and tragedy, of social pleasures and, at times, relative prosperity. Although coal mining eventually declined in the area, the legacy of their ethnic distinctiveness lingers on. What follows is a consideration of why they made their homes in Roundup, Klein, and other nearby coal mining communities, what sort of lifestyles they established, and what contributions they made to the social fabric of south-central Montana in the early decades of the twentieth century.

The Chicago, Milwaukee, St. Paul & Pacific Railway began mining coal along the Musselshell in 1907, before the railroad company's track even reached Roundup.[3] As the railroad extended westward across Montana, it needed high-grade coal to fuel its locomotives. In addition to the railroad, various communities along the line needed coal as well. Entrepreneurs quickly organized the Roundup Coal Company, which in 1908 opened the Number Three Mine just west of present-day Roundup. Other mines such as Keene, Collins, Davis or No. 4., Jeffries, Carpenter Creek, Prescott, Northern, and Gildroy also were developed to take advantage of the high-grade Bull Mountain coal. By 1918, 600 men worked at the Number Three Mine producing 600 tons of coal daily, and annual production reached 530,000 tons. By 1929, the Number Three was reputed to be the largest commercial mine in Montana, supplying enough coal to load one railroad car every twelve minutes.[4]

When the Number Three Mine opened in 1908, however, the new

Roundup was still a cowboy's settlement, a place where stockmen organized annual roundups. Blessed with level ground and good drainage, the new Roundup seemed to be an instant city. "Every day," the *Roundup Record* reported in 1908, "new buildings are going up." In time it became a modern place. New structures had indoor plumbing and electricity, while the community boasted of paved streets, cement sidewalks, and electric street lights. By 1917, Roundup had ninety buildings, and the local newspaper noted optimistically:

> Increase in size is the most easily proven miracle. The most sensitive proof is that of the eyes—just look at the town. Every business block shows by its appearance it is new, and the smell of fresh varnish still persists in nearly all the residences.[5]

Roundup was a city of more than 3,000 people by 1920, but most of its foreign-born workers lived in a section called "Camp Three." Located close to the mine, Camp Three emerged early on and had a population of 800 by 1910. Most of its residents were Croatians and Slovenians, although English, Scotch, Irish, Italian, and Polish immigrants also settled there. South Slavs typically lived in small frame houses, and most of them were prodigious gardeners with productive vegetable gardens. Slovenians called Camp Three "Trbovlje" after the hometown of several South Slav immigrants. The community had a school, grocery store, saloon, and Union hall.[6]

To foreign-born immigrants like Frank Gruden, the opportunities must have seemed unlimited. Gruden emigrated directly from his native Mala Vas (near Ljubljana) in Slovenia to join his brother-in-law, Louis Vidic, who had moved to Roundup a short time earlier. Vidic came to Roundup from Aldrich, Montana, where he also had mined coal. In moving to Roundup, Gruden and Vidic joined a growing number of South Slavs attracted to the area by an abundance of work. Gruden estimated that when he arrived in 1912, South Slavs constituted one-third of Roundup's population, including 200 Croatians and 150 Slovenians. Gruden was employed first as a maintenance man and then as a muleskinner at the Number Three Mine, whose vein measured nearly six feet thick. He walked fifteen miles to the mine every day, worked from 7 A.M. to 3 P.M., and earned 17½ cents an hour. Gruden worked deep in the mine, two and one-half miles from the main entry, where he shoveled coal into three-ton cars. He piled coal to one foot above the top of the car, then used mules to pull the car to the main entry, where it was hoisted up a half-mile slope to the surface.

Other South Slavs settled elsewhere along the Musselshell River. Some went to a second community called Klein, three and a half miles south of Roundup near the Republic, or Number Two Mine. Klein was named after M. L. Klein, postmaster and saloon owner in Old Roundup. Operated by the Republic Coal Company, a subsidiary of the Milwaukee Road, the Number Two Mine opened in March 1909 and at first supplied coal solely for the railroad. Producing between 2,000 and 3,000 tons of coal a day, the mine required a large workforce. The tents and shacks that sprang up near the mine during the first year were soon replaced by gray, four-room houses, built and owned by the Republic Coal Company. The company constructed 300 homes to house the nearly 1,400 residents and collected $10 a month rent on each house.[7] At the opening of the gulch below Klein was Republic, which had a grocery store and two saloons, one with a hotel. South Slavs came to Republic, and to Farreltown and Gibbtown, two other communities that sprang up between Republic and Camp Three. South Slavs represented the largest number of foreign-born people in Musselshell County in 1920 and quickly earned reputations as energetic and courageous workers.[8] Matt Broze, for example, emigrated to the United States in 1886 at age twelve from Bribir, a town in Croatia known for its stonemasons. Like most of the "Bribirci" who settled in Lewistown, Winifred, Winnett, Great Falls, Black Eagle, Anaconda, Butte, East Helena, and Red Lodge, young Broze became a stonemason. With thirty of his stonemason countrymen, he worked in Yellowstone National Park during the late 1890s and helped build coke and bread ovens in Big Timber and Cokedale. When the Croatian stonemasons split up in 1911, Broze went to Billings, where he heard about opportunities in Roundup. In the company of a good friend, Frank Rom, Broze set out on foot and reached Klein, forty miles distant, in three days. Broze and Rom got jobs at the Number

Smoke pours from the stacks at the Republic "Number Two" Mine near Klein, circa 1909.
C. T. LUPTON, COURTESY U.S. GEOLOGICAL SOCIETY, LCT00039.

Two Mine, and Broze later filed on a homestead twenty-six miles south of Roundup.

Broze set up housekeeping with his wife, Catherine Antonich Broze. He had married Catherine in Bribir in 1899 on one of his return trips to Europe. For nearly eight years, he worked in the mine during the week, then walked to his homestead on the weekend to be with his wife and family. Working and living on the homestead and caring for her family was a harsh experience for Catherine Broze. She had the help of a devoted husband and children, but the work was simply too much for her. One morning, her young son, Vincent, found her dead in her bed. She was thirty-eighty years old. Sick at heart, Matt Broze held on to his homestead but moved his children to Farreltown, where he could keep his job as a miner and maintain a home.[9]

Joseph and Augustina Rački, a young Croatian couple, experienced similar conditions. Immigrants from Fiume, the Račkis settled on a homestead twenty-five miles north of Roundup. Joseph found a job as a muleskinner in the Number Three Mine. Rather than walk as Broze did, he bicycled home every weekend to be with his family. Working the homestead soon became too much for Augustina and the Rački children, however. In 1918, with the help of her oldest son, Peter, she loaded her six children and their meager belongings in a hayrack and moved to Camp Three to be with Joseph in his one-room shack. Sixty years later, a daughter, Frances Rački Zickovich, recalled:

> We were as poor as church mice. We had a large garden, made sauerkraut in a fifty gallon barrel. Mother made her own seed from the garden and flower plants. We, kids, baby sat our cow, fed the pigs and the chickens brought in from the homestead. Since the land around dad's shack bordered on the Musselshell River, we even raised our own geese and ducks. We did all the work while dad worked in the "soup bone" mine, the nickname we gave the Number Three. Work there wasn't quite as steady as in the "T-Bone" mine, the nickname we gave to the Republic in Klein. Mind you, we were so poor, we even had to steal our coal by picking up the chunks that fell along the railroad track from moving cars.[10]

The South Slavs applied themselves energetically to coal mine work. They were, in the words of a Bair-Collins mine official, "Dependable, trustworthy. . . . A good worker." Their reward was good pay. Anton Krasevec, for example, earned $20 to $30 a day under the contract system used in the Roundup mines at that time. Eldest sons customarily followed their fathers into coal mining, and sons and fathers were often paired in the work. When young Alois Broze joined his father, Matt Broze, in the mine in 1922, for example, they earned together $25 a day. Nick Zickovich worked with his father Pete for five years, earning as much as $15 a day for loading coal into cars in the Number Two Mine. The added income helped South Slav families, but the boys paid a heavy price, for they could not hold full-time jobs and go to high school as well.[11]

Work in the Roundup mines was rewarding, but it was also dangerous. Unlike the coal mines in Red Lodge and Bear Creek, the mines in Roundup did not have gas or firedamp, but they did have unstable rock. Falling rock killed many South Slav miners. Fred Sporer, a twenty-year-old worker who had a reputation for steadiness, was crushed and killed instantly by fallen rock in 1916. According to evidence submitted at a subsequent inquest, Sporer "must have become paralyzed by fright as his companions leaped to safety, and Sporer would only have had to move eighteen inches to either side to escape." In another incident, Antone Kristan, a native of Austria who had worked in Roundup ten years, was killed by a rock weighing between three and four tons. Rescuers found it necessary to use jacks to lift the "huge" rock off Kristan's body.[12]

Deep-shaft mining was especially dangerous. The cage and the vertical shaft at the Number Two Mine at Klein, for example, posed many hazards. Installed when the mine opened in 1909, it was reputed to be one of only two deep shafts in western coal mines. Dropping 387 feet into the earth, it was operated at first by a steam engine and in later years by electricity. The shaft was the scene of many accidents. In 1913, for example, thirty-two-year-old Marko Popovich was killed instantly when he tried to cross the cage as it was being lifted to the surface and fell to the bottom of the shaft. The coroner's jury returned a verdict of carelessness as the cause of the accident.[13] Fatalities and serious injuries resulted from other types of mishaps as well. Carl Mihalovich, a nineteen-year-old Croatian, lost his right leg below the knee after being caught between two coal cars. Paul Hemovich, a twenty-nine-year-old Croatian, met his death in 1922 when he slipped and fell under a moving car while trying to unhitch an unmanageable mule.

Some accidents resulted from a new mining method called the "longwall system." Introduced in the 1920s, it was used for a limited period in the Number Two Mine in Klein. Using the longwall system, miners worked near walls that were too large to support. Steve Piok, Joe Popish, and William Otaski died in 1927 when rock fell on them. Three other miners—John Sudan, Walter Yakovich, and Tony Ballal—also were injured in the same accident, which prompted the state's Industrial Accident Board to send a telegram ordering immediate discontinuance of the longwall method of mining. The Republic Coal Company complied and discontinued use of its two large mechanical loaders.[14]

The system used in most mines was known as the room-and-pillar method. Coal was mined in rooms located away from the entries, and ceilings to the rooms were propped with timbers for safety. To loosen the coal, black powder was wrapped in paper and placed in hand-drilled holes in a wall of coal. The explosive was then ignited by means of an attached fuse. Before lighting the fuse, the miner in charge shouted three times "Fire in the Hole!" This was the signal to all the others to get out of the area before the blast occurred. No one returned until the thick smoke cleared, which usually took several hours. In the early years of coal mining, when Slavic miners first arrived in south-central Montana, practically everything was done by hand. It was enormously difficult and dangerous work and remained so even after the mines were mechanized.

In an era before Social Security benefits and unemployment compensation in Montana, South Slavs relied on their own institutions for support. Private fraternal and benevolent societies provided much-needed assistance. Slovenians who arrived in Roundup from Aldrich in 1910, for example, brought with them a charter granted by the Slovenska Narodna Podporna Jednota, an organization headquartered in Illinois. Miners paid $1.25 per month and received death benefits of $600 and sick benefits of $1 a day. The Slovenska Lodge also provided other benefits, such as financial assistance and personal nursing care when illness struck the miners who lived alone. The Slovenska Lodge secretary's book was audited every three months, and minutes of the group's meetings were recorded in Slovenian.[15]

Croatians had lodges and societies that offered similar benefits. The "Sv. Srce Isusove," or Sacred Heart Lodge number 384, affiliated with the National Croatian Society, was organized in Roundup in 1909. "BanJelacic" Lodge 65 of Klein, believed to have been organized about the same time, was affiliated with the Croatian League of Illinois. Later, in 1931, Roundup's second lodge, the "Montana Stars," No. 775, was organized. As an affiliate of the Croatian Fraternal Union of America, it was disbanded officially in 1981.[16]

Miners took special pride in their lodges, which, in addition to providing benefits, also prescribed certain standards of behavior. The "Zivila Ilirija" Lodge number 114, for example, met every third Sunday

Members gather for a meeting of the Croatian Brotherhood in 1948.
CULVER STUDIOS, COURTESY MONTANA HISTORICAL SOCIETY, PAC 2002-51.3.

at 4 P.M. in the UMW Local 2866 Hall in Camp Three. If a member did not attend, he was fined 50 cents. Last rites were regarded with utmost importance, and lodge members were fined $1 if they failed to attend a funeral. In fact, it was customary for two or three lodge members at a time to attend a wake, usually held in the home of the deceased. Each lodge had its own flag, which could cost up to $20 and was carried by a flag bearer at the head of the procession from the home of the deceased to the cemetery. A particularly solemn occasion, the services often called for music, which was provided by the lodge's band. Lodge members also were encouraged to visit the sick and care for the poor.

The South Slav community provided communal support in other important ways, especially when times were difficult. Summer months and a slackening demand for coal always pinched wages, but the most trying times came during several miners' strikes between 1917 and 1935. South Slav families lived frugally and had productive gardens, but they also had to rely on their good credit at the local stores

Lucas Zupan with his son Robert show off their first delivery truck, a Model T Ford,
in front of the Zupan Store at Camp Three, west of Roundup.
COURTESY MONTANA HISTORICAL SOCIETY, HELENA, PAC 90-67.

operated by fellow South Slavs. In Klein, the Gorsich Brothers—
Frank, Tony, and Joe—ran a store that catered to South Slav miners.
The Gorsich brothers first settled in East Helena and opened a store
there, but a fire destroyed the enterprise in 1919, and they moved on
to Republic, near Klein.

They considered the Klein area the state's best prospect for a
Slovenian grocery store. Subsequent success confirmed their thinking. After 1924, Frank Gorsich maintained the store by himself, using
the back of the building for his home. Gorsich was able to establish
a strong clientele in Farreltown and Gibbtown, as well as in Klein,
where the company store had burned and not reopened. Gorsich
hired young John Cebull to walk house to house through the camp
every morning and solicit grocery orders. Cebull phoned in his orders
and Gorsich got the boxed groceries to his customers by afternoon.
It was all done on credit, for Gorsich knew that the miners would pay
when they could.[17]

Lucas F. "Luke" Zupan, meanwhile, opened a store in 1927 in Camp Three and operated it with his wife Ann Scufsa Zupan until their retirement in 1966. Zupan had joined his father in the mines in 1914 at age fourteen, but he lasted as a coal miner just two and one-half days. Not happy with getting bruised by falling rock, he got a job as a clerk at the Marshall Store, a general merchandise business that sold nearly everything, including farm machinery. In 1922, he took on a bakery route for the Blue Ribbon Bakery, delivering house to house in Roundup, Riverside, Old Roundup, Gibbtown, Farreltown, Republic, and Klein. He saved enough in the next five years to open a grocery.[18]

The Zupan Store in Camp Three stocked groceries and other necessities. Here, Joe Zupec, a family relative, holds Robert Zupan, ready to ride. COURTESY MONTANA HISTORICAL SOCIETY, HELENA, PAC 90 67.

Zupan became the Camp Three merchant. He extended credit to all miners regardless of nationality and treated newcomers and established customers in the same fashion. Like Gorsich, Zupan extended credit because he knew and understood the miner. He knew that even when the mines were running there would be days of no work. As state coal inspector, Ed Davies, noted, the mining camp whistle held meaning not only for the day's end but also for the following day's beginning:

> One blast indicates that there will be no work on the following day. Three blasts mean that the mine will operate the next day. As the time for the whistle approaches, all other things are forgotten in the homes of the miners. Everything comes to a standstill; there is a strain, a suspense—then the whistle ends it all for another twenty-four hours.

The miner's life was one of constant uncertainty, something Zupan understood.[19]

When not working, South Slav miners found spirited familiarity in the saloon culture of their communities. Coming from a country where wine, *rakija*, and *slivovica* were as important as bread, Croatians and Slovenians made drinking and saloons integral parts of their lives. They owned and operated several of the approximately seventy saloons that sprang up in Republic, Gibbtown, Farreltown, Klein, Roundup, and Camp Three. For South Slavs, the saloon was a place for visiting. Off-limits to women, it functioned as a social center for men. When Frank Gruden arrived in 1912, for example, and no one met him at the depot, he went directly to the saloon. There, he could converse with someone in his own language and alert his relatives to his arrival in Roundup.

Saloonkeepers ranked high in the South Slav social hierarchy. Frank Preshern, who settled in Camp Three about 1910, was typical. In addition to dispensing liquor, he performed many other duties and services. He acted as an interpreter and loaned money—any amount from $5 to $100—without interest. He served as a character witness for those applying for citizenship and kept their valuable papers in his safe. He also provided meals to strangers, served as a pallbearer, and posted bond for those who got into trouble with the law. Because he was one of the first people in the area to own an automobile, a 1918 Buick touring car, he even drove his friends and customers to Billings.[20]

South Slav social life was not limited to male-centered saloon culture, however. Men joined with wives, mothers, daughters, sisters, and sweethearts in various social activities, including singing and dancing, weddings, and other celebrations. Wedding parties were known to last several days. Accompanied by music provided by the wind flute, tamburitsa, and accordion, Croatian dancers twirled their partners at incredible speed. When they performed the kolo, a favorite dance done indoors or outdoors, they sometimes danced for hours, linked hand-to-hand in a circle, and sang traditional songs.

During Prohibition, when cars were more available, South Slav miners were known to travel to visit and socialize with their countrymen in other towns. In 1927, for example, several carloads of

Roundup Croatians called on the homesteader Croatians of Lewistown and celebrated with them for several days. In contrast to their Lewistown hosts, who were deep in debt and struggling to meet monthly payments on Federal Land Bank loans, the miners of Roundup were well dressed and had nice cars. Some even brought fishing rods. The "rich" Roundup visitors seemed like dudes. Unlike their Lewistown kinfolk, Roundup Croatians received paychecks every two weeks. Whether they lived in towns or settlements, or on ranches, South Slavs enjoyed liquid spirits. It was tradition.

When the Volstead Act brought nationwide prohibition in 1920, many South Slavs faced a difficult decision. Although the act made the manufacture, sale, or transportation of alcohol a federal offense, the law was largely disobeyed in South Slav mining communities. Saloons in Roundup and the surrounding communities went undercover, serving Slav and non-Slav customers alike. Saloons were popular because, as the *Roundup Tribune* commented, the average resident "had not yet learned the trick of turning fruit and malt into moonshine and beer."[21]

South Slavs willingly risked operating stills in their houses because they thought it was their right. As long as they did not sell it, they saw no wrong in making spirits for their own use. Some did sell the alcoholic drink they made, however, often because they were in need of money. As a result, South Slavs figured prominently in raids on local residents, such as one by sheriff's officers in 1922. On a Saturday evening late in May, Sheriff Chris Rusch, carrying a long list of names and accompanied by his deputies, eagerly awaited Train Number 16. The train brought eight federal officials, who helped Rusch arrest fourteen alleged offenders of the Volstead Act that night. Nine more people were charged by the following Monday morning. In addition to the arrests, the *Roundup Tribune* reported confiscation of liquor.

There was white mule that later tested as high as 111 and was as clear as denatured alcohol and almost as strong; there was red wine and brown wine, beer that carried bead and beer that was still in the making—drinking liquor manufactured possibly from every known material and every known process.

The jail lobby took on the appearance of a wholesale distributing center, the *Tribune* commented, and by Monday noon, the sheriff made public the names of twenty-three persons, ten of whom were South Slavs.[22] Matt Polich, well-known Roundup businessman and restaurant owner, was one of those charged. He challenged his arrest for bootlegging, however, and was acquitted. So thrilled with the verdict, Polich astounded his lawyers by kissing them on the right cheek in open court, shocking judge, jury, and spectators. "Seldom has such an exhibition of Slavic emotionalism taken place in America," the press commented. "A few thoughtless persons openly guffawed and brought an admonition for order in the courtroom."[23] Polich was found guilty of other charges connected with the raid, however, and sentenced to ninety days in jail and a $500 fine.

After serving forty-five days, Polich appealed his convictions to the Montana Supreme Court and to the State Board of Pardons, but was unsuccessful in both appeals.

In another incident, Sheriff T. G. Beazley was removed from office in 1926 for his connection with a South Slav bootlegger. Beazley apparently had borrowed money from Nick Vranish, a Croatian bootlegger. When a dispute ensued over the payment, Beazley lost his office because he had failed to enforce prohibition laws and was found guilty of misfeasance. Beasley's conviction was later overturned on a technicality.[24]

South Slav women were also offenders. Older women especially enjoyed porridge (natrena kasha) with wine instead of milk, claiming that wine gave them added strength. The custom survived from the old country, where wine was served routinely with meals. Mrs. Joe Butorac was sincere as well as honest when she testified in her own defense in 1931, saying she had to have liquor on hand because her husband was ill and required whiskey. With her daughter acting as interpreter, she added that she was weak because she had given blood for one of her husband's transfusions and needed her wine to regain her "vitality."[25]

Steeped in the tradition of wine and spirits, some Slavs indulged to excess. Sometimes it ended in tragedy, as it did in 1912, when twenty-three-year-old Boza Davich killed his chum, George Keserich, by hitting him in the back of the head with a hand axe.[26] This incident and others equally grotesque encouraged public criticism of Slavs. Anglos saw Croatians and Slovenians as social inferiors, and residents of uptown Roundup regarded themselves superior to those living in Camp Three and other South Slav settlements.

Despite being depicted as social inferiors, or perhaps because of it, South Slavs showed strong loyalty to their adopted country. As residents of the Austro-Hungarian Empire, South Slavs had been a downtrodden people. They had come to the United States, in part, to escape that oppression.[27] For that reason, naturalized citizens in the South Slav community were among the first to join U.S. armed forces when the United States entered World War I in April 1917.

The first draft from Musselshell County had a distinctly foreign-born cast. Thirty-eight of those drafted were from Austro-Hungary, two from Serbia, twenty-nine from Greece, twenty-eight from Italy, and eleven from Sweden. Portions of the military roster read like a Slavic directory—Yunek, Bublich, Failkaska, Legerski, Loplich, Peta, Bozoksoki, Sekarach, and Takoch. Those who were not citizens at the outset of the war had to register as aliens. "Not a single Austrian," the *Roundup Record* reported, "has claimed exemption as an alien citizen . . . and they have all offered their services."[28] South Slavs supported the American war effort in other ways as well. They bought liberty bonds and made contributions to the Red Cross and the YMCA war-fund drives. In the third liberty bond drive in Musselshell County, for example, Klein alone raised $62,000. One Roundup newspaper reported that "practically every miner in the camp purchased bonds," while another claimed that Klein "is the nearest 100% community in Musselshell County."[29]

South Slavs in Montana also sought to show their loyalty by obtaining U.S. citizenship, but doing so was not always easy. Some applicants had to try again and again to convince the federal naturalization examiner and the local district judge that they had sufficient knowledge of the U.S. Constitution and government to qualify for citizenship. On one occasion, only twenty-six of fifty applicants were granted their final papers. Even women who did not have to obtain citizenship papers as long as their husbands or fathers were naturalized revered the concept of citizenship. But some women actually had their citizenship taken away from them. Rose Timinich, Mary Merhar, and Evangeline Francis Pogachar, for example, lost their citizenship when they married husbands who were aliens, even though two of the women had been born in Montana. If they sought to recover their citizenship, they had to reapply, declare their intent to become citizens, and take the oral examination.[30]

Language also was a barrier to citizenship. Frank Gruden remembered paying a teacher 50 cents an hour for private lessons in English in the teacher's home. In about 1915, Gruden was one of twenty students in a private class conducted in the Union Hall at Camp Three by a Slovenian teacher who charged $5 a month. In Klein, two teachers held English classes three nights a week at the school. But the most common way South Slavs mastered the language was to learn English informally from someone who could speak it. Ann Scufsa Zupan, for example, having taught English to Finnish immigrants in her native town of Ely, Minnesota, helped many other people in Roundup to learn English, and without pay.[31] Because they did not have to take citizenship examinations, however, many Slovenian women never learned English.

Nonetheless, the demands for patriotic behavior during the war were often extreme. Vince Oset, a Slovenian who defended another miner charged with questionable attitudes toward American war efforts, was confronted by enraged miners and "presented a pitiable picture" when they finished with him. Oset had to be jailed for his own protection. As a result of the altercation, the local union stipulated that only English was to be spoken at the mine. Slovenians also proclaimed their support of the American war effort. In a public meeting, more than 300 Slovenians from Roundup, Klein, and other mining camps called for the overthrow of German-Austro-Hungarian militarism before any peace conference took place.[32]

Despite such evidence of loyalty to American war aims, the first cases to be tried in Musselshell County under Montana's repressive 1918 sedition law involved Croatians and Slovenians. Martin Ferkovich, a Croatian miner at Carpenter Creek, was sentenced from ten to twenty years hard labor at the state penitentiary for expressing opposition to American policies:

This government cannot take me. I would kill the first guy who
tried to take me. Austria is my country and I won't fight against
her. I wouldn't shoot my own brother; I would shoot someone
else first. The government didn't do right, they did not give me
my citizenship papers. The Kaiser was all right; he never bothered me. The Kaiser didn't bother this country.[33]

Another miner at Carpenter Creek, Joseph Hocevar, a Slovenian
by birth but a naturalized American citizen, received a sentence of
six to twelve years in prison for comparing the U.S. government
unfavorably with the German and Austrian monarchies and for criti-
cizing President Woodrow Wilson. Underscoring the mixture of
loyalties, Joseph Broze, a Croatian, was a juror in the Hocevar case.
Two other Slovenian miners at Carpenter Creek, Tony Kocheva and
Paul Ungerer, also were jailed for disrespectful remarks about the
federal government and for gleefully celebrating German victories.
Anton Kurbish, a Slovenian saloonkeeper at nearby Absher, was jailed
and his saloon closed because of his critical comments.[34]

In an attempt to make their views on the European political situation better known, a number of Roundup-area Slovenians announced
in April 1918 that they belonged to the Slovenian Republican Alliance,
an organization of Slovenians in the United States working for an
independent Jugoslav republic. Slovenians living in Hungary and
Italy constituted a group entirely separate from Austrian Slovenians.
Consequently, one and a half million Slovenes were divided against
their will. Because of that, South Slavs in Montana wanted their kinsmen liberated from the "iron claw" of Austrian control and united
with all Slovenians in a free republic.[35]

However much South Slav immigrants adjusted themselves to new
ways and conditions in south-central Montana, it was their children
who felt the full impact of Americanization. Perhaps nowhere was
this more true than in the schools. In Roundup, the school term began immediately as work was progressing on the Number One Mine
in 1907-1908. The school opened with only a few children, but by the
end of the term, 42 students were attending.[36] Fergus County School
District 55 was soon organized and had more than 200 students.

The school population grew phenomenally. A four-room school-house was built in summer 1908, and three years later an eight-room stone building was erected and employed eight teachers. Soon 500 students were attending, many of them from South Slav families. An elementary school had been opened at Camp Three by 1914, as an accommodation to children of miners' families.[37] Predominantly Catholics, some Slovenians and Croatians preferred to send their children to St. Benedict's Catholic Parochial School, built in 1923 under the direction of Father Thomas Hennessy.

Like Roundup, a school was established quickly in Klein. By 1911, School District 12 in Yellowstone County counted 448 students. A high school also opened, and the two schools were housed in the same build-ing, which became a well-known landmark along the highway between Roundup and Billings. A gymnasium was added about 1924, funded by miners' contributions. Administered by the school, the gymnasium was used for community events as well as school activities.[38]

South Slav youngsters were able students. Unlike many of their parents, they mastered the English language easily and quickly. Their names appeared in local newspapers for scholastic achievements in spelling, writing, typing, bookkeeping, and other contests. As the boys excelled in various sports, the rivalry between Roundup and Klein teams in football and basketball escalated and was likened to that which prevailed between the University of Montana and what was then known as Montana State College. In one football game played in eight inches of snow, neither Roundup nor Klein scored. The wet ball became an oval of ice, as difficult to punt as it was to hold.[39]

Also important to Americanization was the growing sense of connection these people had with the world beyond south-central Montana. The railroad provided one such link. Twice daily the east-bound and westbound passenger trains ("The Olympian") rolled through Camp Three. Trains not only transported passengers and coal, they also hauled strange cargos from faraway places. On one occasion, two freight trains, each pulling twenty-five baggage cars filled with 10,000 bales of raw silk, went through Roundup. The silk was on its way east from Yokohama, Japan, by way of Seattle to be "spun into thread woven and manufactured into cloth," according to the *Roundup Record*, which also declared the shipment the largest of its kind on record.[40]

Coal mining remained an important industry in south-central Montana throughout the first half of the twentieth century. By the 1920s, however, competition from other sources of fuel were affecting the industry's vitality as well as the local economies of communities like Roundup and Klein. As early as 1916, W. J. Swindlehurst, Montana's labor commissioner, noted:

> The development of huge hydro-electric power plants, the substitution of electricity for steam power in the mines and smelters, the electrification of the Butte, Anaconda and Pacific and 450 miles of the Chicago, Milwaukee and St. Paul railways in Montana have resulted in a decreasing demand for large quantities of coal.[41]

Subsequent reports also forecast decline. Coal mine inspector George N. Griffin wrote in his 1924 report to the Industrial Accident Board:

> I regret to have to report that the past year has been one of the worst from a business standpoint. Notwithstanding the fact that no serious disturbances have affected the coal mines of the state, the production shows a decrease as compared with other years.

Griffin cited an increasing use of electricity and natural gas generally, and of oil to power the railroads, as reasons for declining production. The opening of the lignite mines in eastern Montana and western North Dakota also hastened the decline of coal mining along the Musselshell River.[42]

Griffin's successor, Ed Davies, was equally pessimistic in 1926:

> The coal mining industry of the nation as a whole has been seriously depressed for a number of years. The consumption of coal has not kept pace with our industrial development. . . .

Sam and Mary (nee Pipinich, left) Zellick, emigrated from Serbia and Croatia, respectively. They homesteaded ten miles east of Lewistown in the early 1900s. Shown here are Anna (center), her brother George, and an unidentified woman.
COURTESY LEWISTOWN PUBLIC LIBRARY, CENTRAL MONTANA HISTORICAL PHOTOGRAPHS, 01456.

The effect has been broken time in the industry, resulting in decreased annual earnings and a lowering of the living standards of the miners. If it could be arranged so that the mines would close down for a definite period during the slack season, some of the miners could, during the period, seek other employment. But, unfortunately, it is impossible to make such an arrangement and in consequence the miners must stay around camp waiting for the mine whistle to call them to work.[43]

Mine owners tried to counteract the competition with modernization. The Number Three and Number Two mines at Klein underwent complete overhauls in 1928 and 1930, respectively. Greater efficiency and faster production, however, meant fewer jobs. The workforce at the Number Three Mine was reduced from 600 to about 150, and at Klein from 525 to about 200. Miners like Nick Zickovich had to find jobs elsewhere. When Zickovich lost his job at Klein, he went to the Prescott and Northern coal mines to work as a machinist and hoist operator. Declining markets eventually spelled the end of coal mining on a large scale in Roundup and Klein.

Although the mines declined and the first-generation South Slavs passed away, their contributions to Montana's economic and social development lived on through their descendants, in the history of the communities they lived in, and in their burial grounds. One passes two cemeteries between Roundup and Billings on U.S. Highway 87. One among many similar tombstones reads: "TUKAY POCIVA GREGORI ZOBEC ROJEN 1865 V RIBNICI UMERL 2-10 OKTOBRA LETA 1927 NAJUMRA POCIVA," which in English translates to: "Here rests Gregory Zobec born 1865 in Ribnici died 2-10 October year 1927 may he rest in peace." South Slavs like Zobec mined the coal to buy the land, the fence, and the gate for their final resting places. Their markers, like those farther south on the same highway, testify to an important chapter in the history of Montana.[44]

This essay originally appeared in *Montana, The Magazine of Western History,* Spring 1990.

The late Anna Zellick, a native of Lewistown, Montana, played a crucial role in establishing the field of ethnic studies in Montana. She received her bachelor's and master's degrees in American History from the University of Chicago. In addition to the essay reprinted in this volume, her publications included "They Carved Their Hopes in Stone and Helped Build a Montana City," Montana, The Magazine of Western History *28 (Winter 1978); "Patriots on the Rampage: Mob Action in Lewistown, 1917-1918,"* Montana, The Magazine of Western History *31 (Winter 1981); and "Childhood Memories of South Slavic Immigrants in Red Lodge and Bearcreek, Montana, 1904-1943,"* Montana, The Magazine of Western History *44 (Summer 1994).*

NOTES

[1] *Roundup Record,* March 29, 1912.

[2] [The original publication of this note predates the dissolution of Yugoslavia that began in 1991.] Of 23 million people in modern Yugoslavia, only 2 million refer to themselves as "Yugoslavs." The remainder use their precise ethnic identity or the designation "South Slav." See George J. Prpić, *South Slav Immigration in America* (Boston: Twayne Publishers, 1978), pp. 21-31.

[3] Interviews with Frank Gruden, July 6, 7, August 3, 4, 1982, March 13, 1983.

[4] Ibid.; Rudolph J. Cebull, "History of Coal Mining in Musselshell County," *Roundup Record-Tribune,* Golden Anniversary issue, April 3, 1958; *Roundup Record,* October 7, 1910; *Roundup Record-Tribune,* January 3, 1930.

[5] *Roundup Record,* April 3, 1908, December 14, 1917.

[6] *Fourteenth Census of the United States, 1920.* Population (XI vols., Washington, D.C.: Government Printing Office, 1921), I:504; *Roundup Record,* January 7, 1910; interview with Elsie Koncilya Lynch, July 7, 1982.

[7] Cebull, "History of Coal Mining"; *Roundup Tribune,* June 5, 1919.

[8] *Fourteenth Census* I:586.

9   Interviews with Alois Broze, July 26, December 11, 18, 1988; interviews with Vincent J. Broze, July 2, August 28, 1988; interview with Ludwig Broze, July 2, August 28, 1988; Anna Zellick, "The Men From Bribir, They Carved Their Hopes in Stone and Helped Build a Montana City," *Montana, The Magazine of Western History*, 28 (Winter 1978), pp. 44-55.

10   Interviews with Frances and Nick Zickovich, July 8, 1987, January 16, 1989.

11   Interview with Lillian Gildroy Kirkpatrick, February 3, 1987; interviews with Anton Krasevec and Anton Krasevec, Jr., July 11, August 29, 1983.

12   *Roundup Record*, February 4, 1916, March 18, 1926.

13   *Roundup Record*, April 11, 1913; *Roundup Tribune*, April 10, 1913; Cebull, "History of Coal Mining." Attributing carelessness to miners involved in accidents was common until the 1930s. See James Whiteside, "Coal Mining, Safety, and Regulation in New Mexico, 1882-1933," *New Mexico Historical Review*, 64 (April 1989), pp. 159-184.

14   *Roundup Record*, February 21, 1919, September 1, 1922; *Roundup Tribune*, October 20, 1927.

15   Interviews with Frank Gruden, July 6, 7, August 3, 4, 1982, March 13, 1983.

16   Lodge 65 transferred into Lodge 384 in March 1930; Lodge 384 transferred into Lodge 775 in 1952; Lodge 775 transferred into CFU Lodge 84 of Anaconda in 1981. Bernard M. Luketich, president of the Croatian Fraternal Union of America, Pittsburgh, Pennsylvania, to author, June 2, 1987, March 2, 1989.

17   Interview with Frank Gorsich, December 18, 1988; interview with John Cebull, January 16, 1989.

18   Interviews with Lucas F. Zupan, June 9, 1987, March 4, 1988.

19   Jerome G. Locke, *Eleventh Annual Report of the Industrial Accident Board for the Twelve Months Ending June 30, 1926* (Helena: State of Montana, 1926), p. 75.

20   *Roundup Record*, July 27, 1928; interview with Tony Preshern, August 4, 1982.

21   *Roundup Tribune*, August 3, 1922.

22   *Roundup Tribune*, June 1, 1922.

23   *Roundup Tribune*, December 6, 7, 13, 1923, January 31, 1924.

24   *Roundup Record*, February 19, November 26, December 17, 1926.

25   *Roundup Record-Tribune*, February 5, 1931.

26   *Roundup Record*, August 2, 1912; *Roundup Tribune*, August 1, November 22, 1912.

27 George J. Prpić, *The Croatian Immigrants in America* (New York: Philosophical Library, 1971), pp. 89-100.

28 *Roundup Record,* November 26, December 14, 1917, January 4, 1918.

29 *Roundup Record,* April 12, 1918; *Roundup Tribune,* April 18, January 11, 1918.

30 *Roundup Record,* November 11, 1921.

31 *Roundup Record,* October 8, 1914; *Roundup Tribune,* May 12, 1929; interview with Ann Scufsa Zupan, March 4, 1988.

32 *Roundup Record,* June 14, May 2, 1918.

33 *Roundup Record,* September 20, 1918.

34 *Roundup Record,* February 21, 1919, May 3, April 19, 1918.

35 *Roundup Record,* April 26, 1918.

36 *Roundup Record,* February 6, 1914.

37 Ibid., October 23, 1914.

38 Figures obtained from the Yellowstone County Superintendent of Schools; interviews with Alois Broze, July 26, December 11, 18, 1988.

39 *Roundup Tribune,* October 24, 1929, November 25, 1926.

40 *Roundup Record,* January 16, 1926.

41 W. J. Swindlehurst, *Second Biennial Report of the Department of Labor and Industry 1915-1916* (Helena: State of Montana, 1916), pp. 5-6.

42 George N. Griffin, "Coal Mine Inspector's Report," in Jerome G. Locke, *Ninth Annual Report of the Industrial Accident Board for the Twelve Months Ending June 30, 1924* (Helena: State of Montana, 1924), p. 24.

43 Locke, *Report of the Industrial Accident Board, 1926,* pp. 75-76.

44 *Roundup Tribune,* June 22, 1927. Miners made contributions through five local UMW unions for the land, fence, gate, and upkeep.

Danske i America:
Danish Immigration in Beaverhead County, Montana—A Case Study

~ Rex C. Myers

Scandinavians—specifically, Swedes, Norwegians, and Danes—comprised one of the largest groups of immigrants to come to the northern tier states stretching from Wisconsin to Washington during the late nineteenth and early twentieth centuries. Between the end of the U.S. Civil War and the onset of the First World War, some 3,000,000 Scandinavians made their way to the United States. To a much greater degree than such groups as the Irish, Chinese, or Italians, they tended to settle in rural areas and take up agrarian pursuits. Within the overall population of Scandinavians who came to the United States during this period, roughly ten percent, or 300,000, were Danes. While this was a relatively modest number compared to some other immigrant groups, it represented a significant percentage of the total population back in Denmark.

In the following essay, historian Rex Myers provides readers with a detailed case study of a Danish community that arose in Beaverhead County of southwestern Montana during the height of Danish emigration to America. Myers reconstructs the story of this community by drawing upon U.S. census records, family survey results, and church records. He notes that Danish immigrants, in general, "spread more widely, and assimilated more readily and thoroughly than any other

*European or Scandinavian nationality. They learned English more quick-
ly, became naturalized citizens at a higher rate, [and] married outside
their ethnic group more often."*

*And yet these general tendencies did not prevent the Danish set-
tlers in Beaverhead County from shoring up their own strong sense
of ethnic identity. As the Danish population in the area grew in the
early twentieth century (due largely to the use of chain migration),
leaders in the community looked for ways to strengthen the bonds
that held them together as a unique group of people. Two institutions
would soon be established to serve that purpose: the First Evangelical
Lutheran Church, whose minutes were recorded in Danish until 1920;
and a fraternal organization known as the Danish Brotherhood Lodge
#273. The Danes of Beaverhead County had discovered that they could
embrace the benefits of becoming American while still celebrating the
heritage of their ancestors.*

In December 1983, Danish Brotherhood Lodge #273 in Dillon,
Montana, celebrated its seventy-fifth anniversary. Nearly 200 members, friends, and descendants of original Danish settlers gathered to
celebrate the Diamond Jubilee with a banquet and dance. Danish flags,
memorabilia, and "Kiss Me, I'm Danish" buttons abounded, as did a
sense of being part of a larger, pioneering legacy. Twenty-five years
later, lack of membership numbers and interest obviated any hope for
a centennial celebration.[1] Statistically, Danes never comprised a large
segment of the county, the state, or the nation as a whole (see Table
1). Yet in the first decade of the twentieth century, Danish numbers
in southwestern Montana reached a "critical mass," creating ethnic
institutions to support the heritage that would last for almost 100
years. The process generally typified historical patterns identified in
Danish immigration, providing a case study in process and pattern,
at the same time highlighting a small patch in the colorful design of
America's ethnic history.[2]

American immigration records of Danish arrivals began in 1820

TABLE 1: Characteristics of Population, Foreign Born and Danish Foreign Born

	Total Population	Total Foreign Born	Percent Foreign Born	Total Danes	Percent of Population	Percent of Foreign Born
1870						
Montana	12.616	7,979	36.2	95	0.75	1.19
Beaverhead Co.	722	228	31.0	—	—	—
Madison Co.	2,684	901	33.6	6	0.22	0.66
1880						
Montana	27,638	11,521	41.7	190	0.69	1.65
Beaverhead Co.	2,712	830	30.6	18	0.66	2.17
Madison Co.	3,915	1,029	26.3	21	0.54	2.04
1890						
Montana	89,063	43,096	48.4	683	0.77	1.58
Beaverhead Co.	4,655	1,216	26.1	32	0.69	2.63
Madison Co.	4,692	945	20.1	15	0.32	1.59
1900						
Montana	243,329	67,067	27.6	1,041	0.43	1.55
Beaverhead Co.	5,615	1,250	22.3	76	1.35	6.08
Madison Co.	7,695	1,261	16.4	31	0.40	2.46
1910						
Montana	376,053	91,644	24.4	1,943	0.52	2.12
Beaverhead Co.	6,446	1,164	18.1	143	2.22	12.29
Madison Co.	7,229	1,018	14.1	42	0.58	4.13
1920						
Montana	548,889	93,620	17.1	2,990	0.54	3.19
Beaverhead Co.	7,369	1,035	14.0	121	1.64	11.69
Madison Co.	7,495	845	11.3	57	0.76	6.75

Source: U.S. Bureau of the Census, Decennial Censuses of the United States, 1870, 1880, 1890, 1900, 1910, 1920. Respective *Population* volumes.

and documented fewer than 200 annually for most years until the American Civil War. During the second half of the nineteenth century, the flow increased, with a sustained crest from 1882 to 1892 (topping 11,000 annually for 1882 only), with another rise between 1903 and 1907 (albeit with only an 8,970 annual peak in 1905). By 1910, Bureau of Immigration statistics reported 258,053 Danish émigrés during the ninety-year period—a small total compared to overall European immigration or even figures from other Scandinavian countries (two and a half times as many from Norway and nearly five times more Swedes came to the United States during the same period).[3]

Demographic studies from both sides of the Atlantic give texture to any purely statistical compilation. Using Danish government data on 172,000 emigrants from 1868 through 1900, Kristian Hvidt identified characteristics of the outflow.[4] Although numerically smaller than emigration from most European countries, Danish emigration losses were relatively larger when compared to the national population. Urbanization and land reform processes in Denmark delayed the outward demographic "push" (compared to other Scandinavian countries) and affected two particular segments of the population: rural laborers, 43.2 percent of the emigration; and urban domestic and industrial workers, 25.6 percent.[5] It was, generally speaking, a young people's movement (65.5 percent between fifteen and twenty-nine years of age), with few families (33 percent) and more men than women (61 percent vs. 39 percent).[6]

Coming later than most mass emigration from northern Europe, the Danish movement lacked the strong "pull" of established ethnic communities in America (accounting for diminished overall numbers in Hvidt's view), but the influence of feedback and chain migration should not be discounted: fully one-third of all Danes who immigrated to the United States did so on pre-paid tickets, and 55 percent who left Denmark listed specific communities of destination.[7]

By 1870, an agrarian Danish "heartland" had developed in the midwestern United States centering on Iowa, Wisconsin, and northern Illinois.[8] Generally, however, Danes spread more widely and assimilated more readily and thoroughly than any other European or Scandinavian nationality. They learned English more quickly, became naturalized citizens at a higher rate, married outside their ethnic group more often, and were less apt to cluster about their national church (Danish Lutheran) than any group of immigrants.[9] But, like other ethnics, Danes did form mutual aid institutions. A Danish language press developed beginning in 1872,[10] and in 1881 former Danish veterans organized the Danish Brotherhood. By 1920, there were more than 350 lodges in the United States, and three in Canada, with total membership exceeding 21,000. Lodges provided fraternal support, life insurance, and other social aid to their members.[11]

Into the pattern of national growth and population movement, Montana came relatively late. A placer gold rush of the early 1860s sputtered out quickly, replaced by a substantial silver boom begun in the mid-1870s and transformed into a copper bonanza a decade later. Economic prosperity attendant to the latter two minerals brought railroads, population, and urban growth, which, in turn, supported agricultural expansion. Farming and ranching began in Montana's western valleys and backfilled to the eastern plains—first with livestock in the 1860s, and later in a substantial homestead rush begun shortly after the turn of the twentieth century.

Reduced to textbook simplicity, the ethnic influx which accompanied Montana's economic growth distilled into urban mining combinations of Irish, Cornish, and southern Europeans—best typified, perhaps, in St. Patrick's Day pasties and the Serbian Orthodox Church in Butte. The agrarian counterbalance is extant in Scandinavian and northern European influences surviving in town names like Amsterdam, Lothair, and Dagmar, as well as in multiple Lutheran churches, which would constitute Montana's second-largest religious denomination.[12]

Danish pieces fit variously into Montana's ethnic quilt. Scattered Danes appeared in major and minor mining camps from the 1870 census forward, in concentrations varying according to the size of the camp itself. Individually identified, they tended to be single men, often rooming with other Danes, but seldom with family ties which would indicate stability.[13] Agricultural pockets of Danish settlement appeared three-fold. An initial concentration grew in western Montana's Deer Lodge Valley from 1870 forward, a vestige of the Morrisite schism in the Mormon church.[14] Chronologically, the next area of activity sprouted in the Ruby and Beaverhead Valleys a decade later and is the focus of this essay.[15] The third center for Danish settlement and influence resulted from a deliberate colonization effort by the Danish Lutheran Church of Iowa and North Dakota. It began in 1906 and took root in Montana's northeastern counties around the community of Dagmar.[16]

Southwest Montana's valleys attracted livestock men and farmers early on. Geography and history made the origins of agriculture in this region less than accidental. Sheltered behind a loop in the Continental Divide, the Beaverhead and Ruby drainages are protected from extreme winter weather. The same mountains gather snow and feed a network of streams that water the broad valleys year-round, providing feed for stock and irrigation potential for farming. Historically, Montana's first placer gold discoveries bracketed the agricultural districts in Beaverhead and Madison Counties with strikes at Bannack (1862) and Virginia City (1863). In the burgeoning gold camps, farmers and ranchers found ready markets for their produce, and their respective industries grew. Johnny Grant used the area as open range for cattle and horses as early as 1850; the Poindexter and Orr ranching partnership thrived along Blacktail Deer Creek by 1864; and John F. Bishop brought in Montana's first commercial sheep operation during 1869.[17]

Niels Christiansen began Danish settlement in the Ruby Valley. Born in Denmark about 1846, he came to the United States in 1861, farmed in Missouri, and then joined the early influx of placer miners to Montana, trying his luck in Virginia City during 1864 and 1865. He abandoned his effort in 1866 and settled near present-day Sheridan, Montana, to begin farming along one of the creeks that fed the Ruby River. Two years later, he married sixteen-year-old Caroline Crane, from Illinois. Eventually they had six children, and Niels Christiansen lived in the Ruby Valley until his death in 1923.[18] Christiansen had significance to Danish immigration in southwestern Montana beyond a purely genealogical entry. In the 1870 census, Montana counted only ninety-five Danes. Madison County had only six and Beaverhead County, none.[19] Niels Christiansen began a process at a specific location. He was the only married, Danish farmer in either Madison or Beaverhead Counties in 1870. He extolled the region's virtues, diffusing that information back to Denmark and attracting other Danes to his specific locale. The result became apparent in the 1880 census. Twenty-one Danes had congregated in Madison County by that year—eleven along the Ruby Valley near Sheridan. Four of those were Niels Christiansen's parents and two sisters. All eleven Ruby Valley Danes belonged to some family group (married, related to, or living with a family), and engaged in farming or related industries.[20]

Danish presence in Beaverhead County took on permanence by 1880 in much the same fashion as Madison County a decade earlier. Names of only eighteen Danes appeared on the census rolls that year; nine were employed on Utah and Northern Railroad construction crews then pushing their way through the Beaverhead Valley; eight held down a variety of jobs associated with mining camps throughout the county. Only thirty-year-old Lars Hansen engaged in agriculture along the Beaverhead River north of present-day Dillon.[21] He married several years later (Abbie from Kentucky) and raised a family on his farm.[22]

Niels Christiansen and Lars Hansen fit national patterns of Danish immigration. They came to the United States as young, single men, fifteen and eighteen years of age, respectively; each followed a pattern of chain migration to the Midwest and then to Montana; both engaged in farming; both married non-Danish women; and, in the case of Christiansen (where religious affiliation is available), he abandoned the traditional Lutheran church for the Episcopal. Also typically, they were pioneering members of their ethnic group who undoubtedly disseminated information and provided a geographic nucleus for Danes who followed them.

What these two men began, grew in the decades following 1880.[23] Perhaps because the Ruby Valley was not as wide, or perhaps because settlement patterns radiating out from Virginia City's mining boom peopled the Ruby earlier than the adjacent Beaverhead drainage, two changes in Danish settlement occurred between 1880 and 1900. Danes began to congregate more heavily in Beaverhead County; in addition to farming, these Scandinavian immigrants turned to sheep ranching (as had non-Danes like John Bishop), using not only open bench land adjacent to the river, but also surrounding hills and mountains. By 1890, Beaverhead County had thirty-two Danish born; Madison County, fifteen.[24] A decade later, numbers had risen to seventy-six and thirty-one, respectively.[25]

"Date of Immigration" data from the 1900 manuscript census document the process of community growth among Danes that took place in Beaverhead County from 1880 through 1900.[26] The population influx, still clearly male dominated, intensified beginning in 1888 and peaked between 1896 and 1900 (see Table 2). This surge approximated

TABLE 2: Danes in Beaverhead County by the Year of Arrival in the United States

	1900 Manuscript Census[1]	1900 Manuscript Census[1]	1910 Manuscript Census[2]	1910 Manuscript Census[2]
	Males	Females	Males	Females
Pre-1880	5	4	4	0
1880–1885	7	2	2	2
1886-1890	10	1	12	2
1891-1895	11	5	8	3
1896-1900	20	4	20	5
1901-1905	--	--	33	11
1906-1910	--	--	30	11
No date given	3	4	6	1

[1] 78 Total
[2] 150 total includes seven individuals who listed their nationality as German-Danish
Sources: 1900 and 1910 Manuscript Census tables for Beaverhead County

the national rise in Danish immigration, delayed, in all probability, by some step migration through the Midwest. More important than sheer numbers was the composition of those statistics and their geographic dispersion across the landscape.

In 1880, Beaverhead County had only six family units with one or more Danish parents; only five of those had children present—eleven children total. Richard Frank, a twenty-seven-year-old working on the Utah and Northern grading crew, was the only Danish male head of a household. All five other family groups had a non-Danish husband and a Danish wife. By 1900, the number of family units with one or more Danish parents more than tripled, as did the number of children present within those households (see Table 3).

A second phenomenon of Danish community composition appeared in the extended families that developed by 1900. In addition to brothers and sisters clearly identified on census rolls, Danish farmers and stockmen employed newly arrived Danes in significant numbers. Thirty-one-year-old Oster J. Peterson, a farmer/stockman along Blacktail Deer Creek, illustrated the process. His twenty-two-year-old wife immigrated in 1898, his brother in 1897, sister-in-law in 1900, and five of the six employees working for Peterson were Danes with immigration dates ranging from 1895 to 1900.[27]

TABLE 3: Family Composition among Danish Foreign Born in Beaverhead County

	Men	Women	Family Units[3]	Family Units w/ Children	Total Children	Family H & W Danish	Family H only Danish	Family W only Danish[3]
1880	11	7	6	5	11	0	1	5
1900[1]	56	20	21	16	32	9	5	4
1910[2]	109	41	41	34	83	24	13	4

[1] Manuscript Census information for the 1890 census is not available.
[2] 150 total includes seven individuals who listed their nationality as German-Danish.
[3] Includes widows.

The economic pattern begun in 1870 in Madison County amplified in Beaverhead by 1900. Of seventy-six individuals on the census, fifty-six (seventy-four percent) worked or lived in farming/ranching households. Thirteen (seventeen percent) had urban occupations and seven listed no occupation or were widowed. None of the urban households employed newly immigrated Danes. Clearly, motive and opportunity to encourage other Danes to settle in Beaverhead County, and to provide them with a livelihood, rested with the Danish foreign born in agriculture.[28] A new urban center for the valley also appeared after the 1880 census: Dillon. Born of the railroad, this community quickly grew as the new county seat and trade center for the region.[29]

Geographic patterns strengthened sociological and economic ones. Early ranchers and settlers (like Poindexter and Orr and those associated with the mining rush around Virginia City) claimed much of the prime bottom land along the Beaverhead and Ruby Rivers. Land left open to homesteading for the Danes—relative latecomers to southwestern Montana—lay on the benches or the outer rims of the valleys. In particular, Danish settlement concentrated in the voting precincts and enumeration districts known as Barrett's, Blacktail, Dillon, and Bishop in Beaverhead County. Not surprisingly, these lay adjacent to the Ruby Valley concentrations of Danes in Madison County.[30]

Finally, between 1880 and 1900, new leaders emerged in the Danish community. Oster J. Peterson was one, along the Blacktail. To the north, in Bishop precinct, Rasmus Henningsen enhanced both the size and permanence of the Danish community. Henningsen, who arrived in the United States at the age of fifteen in 1886, settled in Beaverhead County not long thereafter, and by 1900 had married Marie (also from Denmark) and brought over his two younger brothers, as well as another Dane to work for him.[31] In Dillon, Jasper Nelson (born 1866, immigrated 1889) established himself initially as a bartender and later as a grocer, serving as an urban contact for the growing number of Danes along the Beaverhead.[32]

SOUTHWEST MONTANA: 1900–1910

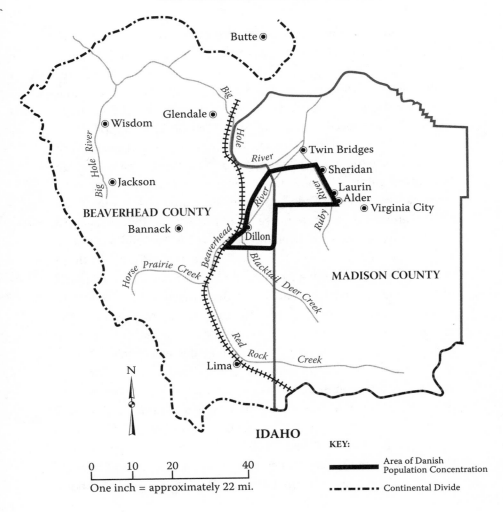

KEY:

▬▬▬▬ Area of Danish Population Concentration

▪—▪—▪—▪▪ Continental Divide

0   10   20   40

One inch = approximately 22 mi.

The 1880s and 1890s served as prelude to a substantial Danish in-flux into Beaverhead County during the first decade of the twentieth century. By 1910, 143 Danes resided in Beaverhead County—150 if we include individuals who listed themselves as German-Danish. Not only did the increase represent a near doubling of the county's Danish population, it took on additional significance given the county's rela-tively sparse population as a whole and the generally modest increase in the number of county residents.

Patterns of social, economic, and geographical population dis-persion extant in 1900 intensified during the next ten years. Table 2 demonstrates that the flow of Danish men increased by fifty percent over 1896-1900 levels, while the influx of women more than doubled. Nonetheless, figures indicate a greater percentage of men and a lower percentage of women than national averages for Danish immigrants. Furthermore, Danish males, who arrived singly prior to 1900 brought over or met newly arrived Danish women. The number of families with at least one Danish parent increased to forty-one: twenty-four with both parents Danish; thirteen with Danish male and non-Danish female; three where the wife was Danish and husband was not; and one widow. More important, as an indication of permanence and a sense of community, thirty-four of those households had children—in all, eighty-three children (see Table 3).

The Oster J. Peterson and Rasmus Henningsen families typified the exponential nature of Danish population growth. In 1910, Peterson and his wife had four children and two recently arrived Danish farm-hands in their employ—different individuals than the five Danes he employed in 1900. Peterson's brother, Peter C., and his Danish-born wife, Caroline, had three children and brought her fifty-three-year-old father to live with them. Two of Oster Peterson's employees from 1900, Erik Hansen and Fritz Jensen, remained in the county, but moved out on their own. Hansen had a Danish wife and three children, a twenty-one-year-old Danish female household servant, his brother, and two employees—all recently arrived from Denmark. Jensen did not marry, but owned his own farm and employed one Dane. Rasmus Henningsen continued to operate his ranch in Bishop precinct, where he and his wife raised three children and employed

Haying at the Peterson Ranch (here, circa 1935) featured use of the "beaver slide" stacking mechanism, a common system in the Big Hole and Beaverhead Valleys.
COURTESY MONTANA HISTORICAL SOCIETY, HELENA, PAC 80-61, BOX G-R.

two Danish immigrants. His younger brother, Hans, remained in the county, but had not married as of 1910. He worked for Erik Hansen. Jasper Nelson still ran his grocery store in Dillon, married a Dane thirteen years younger than himself, and had two children.[33] The newly arrived also assimilated rapidly. Only thirteen of the 150 Danes did not speak English: six who arrived in 1910, four in 1909, two in 1908, and Erik Hansen's wife, who arrived in 1902.[34]

Three factors not reflected in the manuscript census united the Danish community beyond strictly nationalistic or language ties. First, the Beaverhead County community actively recruited new residents from the homeland. Men like Hans Anderson, who began his ranching career near Henningsen as a young man of twenty in 1896, made trips back to Denmark and personally escorted immigrants to southwestern Montana. In particular, on a 1905 trip, he brought back five single women, all of whom had married by 1910.[35]

Second, with such specific recruiting, most immigrants between 1900 and 1910 came directly to Beaverhead County (not the product of step migration, like many of their predecessors). Of thirty-three Danes for whom family histories are available, twenty-four came directly to the county; seven stopped for varying periods in the Midwest (Wisconsin, Nebraska, Minnesota, Illinois, and Iowa); one went first to California; and no specific information is available for the remaining individual.[36] Third and finally, in common with other ethnic groups, many of Beaverhead County's Danes returned to their specific area of birth and brought back not only family, but also friends and neighbors. In the case of this county, that particular locale in Denmark was the island of Aero. Again, using data obtained from the thirty-three family histories, fourteen immigrants came from Aero, ten from undetermined provinces, and the remaining nine from communities all over Denmark.[37] Hvidt observed that the emigration flow from this small island reached only modest intensity, which suggests that Beaverhead County's concentrations of Aero Danes was somewhat unique and contributed to a sense of unity in southwestern Montana.[38]

As with the previous decade, most (eighty percent) Beaverhead County Danes in 1910 engaged in farming or stock raising, while concentrations along Blacktail Deer Creek, in or around Dillon, and in the Bishop precinct intensified. Sixty-six percent of total Danish residents resided in those areas. Among Madison County's forty-two Danes, eighty-one percent farmed/ranched, and fifty-five percent lived along the Ruby River from Alder to Sheridan.[39] These economic and geographic concentrations added to an increasingly stable, family-oriented ethnic community, and a common sense of origin. Between 1905 and 1910, these traits produced a "critical mass" among Beaverhead County's Danish residents[40] that manifested itself in the formation of two ethnic institutions—a Lutheran Church and a Danish Brotherhood Lodge—which solidified the sense of group identity.

On March 4, 1906, Dillon's Baptist, Presbyterian, and Methodist-Episcopal churches cooperated to sponsor revivalist Ray L. Palmer in leading a week-long spiritual rejuvenation.[41] Lutheran Pastor H. O. Svare of Anaconda traveled to Dillon to witness the event, but his visit had more specific denominational goals. Among those attending

Danish Brotherhood Lodge Halls served as community centers in far-flung corners of Montana. Here, farmers meet at the hall in Dagmar, circa 1938.
HENRY B. SYVERUD, COURTESY MONTANA HISTORICAL SOCIETY, HELENA, PAC 77-94.

the revival in the Presbyterian church building were a number of Danes with their families. "These young married people, parents of young children, needed a church home to rear their families in, and for their own spiritual strengthening."[42]

With Pastor Svare serving as recording secretary, this group drafted a twenty-three-article constitution for the First Evangelical Lutheran Church. Svare took notes in Danish, and Article VI in the document specified worship services in the 1685-1688 Danish form, to be conducted in Danish or English—whichever language the congregation and minister agreed to use. The group went on to support the purchase of several lots for a building; to elect three trustees, a secretary, and a treasurer; and to ask Pastor Svare to serve their fledgling congregation as his time and church finances permitted—particularly at Christmas, Easter, and Pentecost.[43] Both church services and business meetings continued irregularly until the church grew to a point where it could afford a full-time pastor in 1930 and a permanent building in 1934.[44] Important for the Danes, however, was the initial coming together as a common interest community to organize a church.

TABLE 4: Leadership in Beaverhead County's Danish Community

Officers in Danish Brotherhood (age)	Occupation	Residence	Date to U.S.	Married/ Single	Officer Lutheran Church
Hans Christensen (30)	Laborer	Bannack	1904	Single	
Jens Christensen (53)	Farmer	Dillon	1901	Widowed	XX
Jens H. Christensen (29)	Farmer	Blacktail	1900	Married	XX
Hans Henningsen (28)	Farmer	Bishop	1900	Single	
Rasmus Henningsen (40)	Farmer	Bishop	1886	Married	
Laurits Jensen (30)	Farmer	Dillon	1899	Married	
Hans Dehr Madsen (?)	Farmer	Red Rock	1904	Married	XX
Hans K. Madsen (29)	Farmer	Red Rock	1900	Married	
Albert Mikkelsen (33)	Farmer	Bishop	1900	Single	
Hans Mikkelsen (31)	Farmer	Bishop	1900	Married	XX
Jasper Nelsen (44)	Merchant	Dillon	1889	Married	XX

Sources: Danish Brotherhood Lodge #273, Minute Books; First Evangelical Lutheran Church, Secretary's Minute Books; 1910 Manuscript Census, Beaverhead County.

In 1908, Danes talked of another ethnic organization—a Lodge of the Danish Brotherhood. Members of the Lutheran congregation, along with other interested Danes, met north of Dillon at the community park on a regular basis to celebrate Danish and American holidays and to enjoy a good time.[45] Leaders codified the friendship and fraternity in 1908 with the formation of Danish Brotherhood Lodge #273.[46] They remembered this as an effort "to preserve and promote their Danish heritage and to strengthen family unity and probably to combat those terrible homesick blues . . . ."[47]

Membership books opened October 3rd, when twenty-five men signed their names to membership. The roster revealed a mature core of leadership within Beaverhead County's Danish community. A comparison of the Danish Brotherhood's first slate of officers with manuscript census data and Lutheran Church minute books indicates that key leaders were established in the county. They were married, farmers near Dillon, and active in both church and fraternity (see Table 4).

Oster Peterson signed the Brotherhood's membership book first, Rasmus Henningsen second. By the time Dillon's chapter received its formal charter in December, membership numbered thirty-one, and at decade's end, minute books showed forty-one men current with their dues and fully enrolled in the Brotherhood's insurance program.[48] Meetings took place the first Saturday of each month in the I.O.O.F. Hall. On New Year's Eve, 1908, seventy-five men and women (with their children) met at the ranch home of Peder C. Peterson, in the Bishop precinct, to celebrate the new year, the new Brotherhood charter, and the new sense of ethnic community they had brought to Beaverhead County. *The Dillon Examiner* observed "all had a royal good time, as the Danish people in Beaverhead county know how to have."[49]

Over time, sons and grandsons added their names to Lodge #273's membership. The high watermark for the lodge may have come with the seventh-fifth anniversary celebration in 1983. Time took its toll on first- and second-generation members. By the 2010 Census, there were no first-generation Danes in Beaverhead County. In the U.S. Census Bureau's 2007-2011 American Community Survey, only 303 of Beaverhead County's 12,313 residents listed Danish heritage.[50] Interest in Lodge #273 declined in the twenty-first century to only "two or three really active" members.[51] First Lutheran continues Sunday services and Sunday school, both in English, for worshipers now generations removed from their ancestors who felt its services necessary.

Indeed, the region's Danes have so integrated into southwestern Montana that in 2013 the Beaverhead County Chamber of Commerce director did not know they had ever been there. In retrospect, however, their story is a national one writ locally. Danes came later to American immigration history. Montana's growth, likewise, occurred late in frontier development. It is not surprising that Danes from agricultural backgrounds found the broad valleys of the Ruby and Beaverhead attractive for their crops and livestock. Initially, among their numbers came single men to assess the region and put down roots. In turn, they induced others of their nationality to come until the process compounded itself in a growing, vibrant ethnic community.

Their arrival peaked with the second wave of Danish immigration into the United States during the first years of the twentieth century. That was part of the national pattern, too, as they encouraged men and women from their own locale to join them in the United States, to learn America's language and ways, and to share with them in the agricultural largess the land had to offer. Perhaps more than their brothers in the Midwest, Beaverhead County's Danes married other Danes and attended the Lutheran Church on a regular basis; but like their counterparts elsewhere, they congregated in agricultural pursuits, and when their numbers reached that critical point, a sense of community awareness developed. The result was two typical institutions to support ethnic identity: a Lutheran church and a fraternal organization. Their story contributes to the ethnic diversity of Montana's settlement and is a microcosm of the formation and maintenance of ethnic communities on the American frontier as a whole.

This essay was originally presented at the Pacific Northwest History Conference in Bellingham, Washington, in 1984.

Rex C. Myers teaches history and geography part-time at Northwest College in Powell, Wyoming. He worked on the history of Danes in Beaverhead County when he was a faculty member at the University of Montana—Western, and has published articles in Montana, The Magazine of Western History, South Dakota History, Great Plains Quarterly, *and* Journal of the West.

NOTES

1. Conversation with Randall Tommerup, October 31, 2013. As of 2011, the U.S. Census Bureau reported 303 individuals claiming Danish ancestry among Beaverhead County's population of 12,313. Danes constituted the eighth-largest ethnic group behind Germans, English, Irish, Norwegians, French, Scots, and Swedes. No Madison County residents reported Danish ancestry. U.S. Census Bureau, "Total Ancestry Reported," 2007-2011 American Community Survey 5-Year Estimates, Beaverhead County, Montana.

2. Historians and geographers alike have worked with ethnic movements in the American West, and the literature is somewhat extensive, although

little has been done specifically on Danes. Frederick C. Luebke provided an overview of the process and bibliography in his article "Ethnic Minority Groups in the American West," in Michael P. Malone, ed., *Historians and the American West* (Lincoln: University of Nebraska Press, 1983). John C. Hudson's "Migration to the American Frontier," *Annals of the Association of American Geographers*, 66, 2 (June, 1976), pp. 242-265, provides a geographer's perspective to the process. Two articles in Birgit Flemming Larsen and Henning Bender, eds., *Danish Emigration to the U.S.A.* (Aalborg, Denmark: Danish Worldwide Archives, 1992), are helpful in understanding the historiography of Danish settlement in the United States: Erik Helmer Pedersen, "An Outline of the Historiography of Danish Emigration to America," pp. 190-196, and John Mark Nielsen and Peter L. Peterson, comp., "A Danish-American Bibliography," pp. 210-218. A preponderance of material focuses on the Danish heartland in the American Midwest, with little material relating to Montana.

3   William P. Dillingham, comp., *Reports of the Immigration Commission. Abstract of the Reports of the Immigration Commission*, Vol. I (Washington, D.C.: GPO, 1911). William Dillingham, comp., *Statistical Review of Immigration, 1820-1910*, Vol. 3, *Distribution of Immigrants, 1850-1900* (Washington, D.C.: GPO, 1911).

4   Kristian Hvidt, *Flight to America: The Social Background of 300,000 Danish Emigrants* (New York: Academic Press, 1975), is extremely useful in understanding the nature of the Danish population that moved to the United States. Frederick Hale, ed., *Danes in North America* (Seattle: University of Washington Press, 1984), compiled letters of Danes who immigrated to the United States. He cited no Montana Danes, and his overviews mirror Hvidt's conclusions. Elliott R. Barkan looked broadly at immigrants in the American West, including Scandinavians, concluding that while they adapted to their new homeland, they also maintained ties with places of their birth. "American in the Hand, Homeland in the Heart: Transnational and Translocal Immigrant Experiences in the American West," *Western Historical Quarterly*, 35:3 (Autumn, 2004), pp. 331-354.

5   Ibid, pp. 103-122.

6   Ibid, pp. 71-80.

7   Ibid, pp. 167-175, 198.

8   John H. Bille, "A History of the Danes in America," *Transactions of the Wisconsin Academy of Sciences, Arts and Letters*, Vol. XI (March, 1896), 12. Utah also had a substantial number of Danes because of early Mormon missionary work in Denmark and Scandinavia; the first translation of the *Book of Mormon* into a language other than English was into Danish in 1845. William Mulder's *Homeward to Zion: The Mormon Migration from*

Scandinavia (Minneapolis: University of Minnesota Press, 1957), discusses this issue. Niels Peter Stilling and Anne Lisbeth Olsen, *A New Life: Danish emigration to North America as described by the emigrants themselves in letters 1842-1946* (Aalborg, Denmark: Danes Worldwide Archives, 1994), also identifies the Danish "heartland" in the United States and discusses Mormon migration.

9   George R. Nielson, *The Danish Americans* (Boston: Twayne Publishers, 1981), pp. 10-14; Hvidt, pp. 167-175.

10   Paula Noel Twelker, "Ethnic Communities in Western Settlement." Unpublished M.A. Thesis (University of Washington, 1978). Twelker discussed ethnic newspapers in the United States.

11   Nielson, pp. 174-175. *Danske i America* (Minneapolis: G. Rassmussen Publishing Company, 1908), Vol. I, Part II, p. 222. The Danish Immigrant Museum, "The Danish Brotherhood," www.danishmuseum.org/the-danish-brotherhood (October 29, 2013). Six Brotherhood Lodges formed in Montana between 1901 and 1916: Butte, Big Sandy, Dillon, Dagmar, McCabe, Sidney. The Dillon and Dagmar lodges still exist officially, although Dillon's lodge has only "two or three" active members and admits to filling out annual paperwork to keep the lodge official. Conversation with Lodge #273 President Randall Tommerup, October 31, 2013.

12   Michael P. Malone, Richard Roeder, and William L. Lang, *Montana, A History of Two Centuries*, rev. ed. (Seattle: University of Washington Press, 1991), provides the best overview of Montana's history, but devotes scant space to the state's immigration patterns in Chapter 14, "A Social and Cultural Profile," pp. 348-355.

13   U.S. Bureau of the Census. Manuscript Census of Montana, 1870. Butte, as a large urban area focused on copper mining, had sufficient Danish population to form Montana's first Brotherhood in 1901; see Danish Brotherhood materials at the Danish Immigrant Museum.

14   C Leroy Anderson deals with the Morrisites in his book *For Christ Will Come Tomorrow: The Saga of the Morrisites* (Logan: Utah State University Press, 1981). Mulder provides general background on Danish immigrants who were involved in the movement, as do Stilling and Olsen, pp. 158-160.

15   Transportation routes from the Oregon/California trail and from Utah to the Morrisite settlement in the Deer Lodge Valley pass through Beaverhead County. Scattered Danish settlers with Utah backgrounds appear in 1880, 1900, and 1910 manuscript census records. Ties appear to be circumstantial, and not the result of deliberate colonization. At best, they are difficult to substantiate.

16   Material available on Danish settlement around Dagmar includes Arthur

C. Larsen, *Next Year Will Be Better* (Sioux Falls, SD: Augustana College, n.d.); and Bertha Josephsen Anderson, "The Life History of Mrs. Bertha Josephsen Anderson," in *The Bridge*, VIL1 (1983). Joni Justice, ed., *The Dagmar Diamond Jubilee Book, 1906-1981* (Dagmar: Dagmar Historical Society, 1981), also has information on the community. Gerald Zahavi, "Who's Going to Dance with Somebody Who Calls You a Mainstreeter": Communism, Culture and Community in Sheridan County, Montana, 1918-1934," *Great Plains Quarterly*, 16:4 (September, 1996), pp. 252-286, discusses Danish and Norwegian "farmer-based radicalism" in the Dagmar area. Dagmar celebrated its centennial in 2006 with a parade and variety of festivities, but not a centennial history. Nathanael and Volmer Lutheran churches provided focal points for Dagmar's Danish community. Records of the latter congregation are collection OPVELCA7a3_79 in the Archives and Special Collections ELCA Region 1 Archives, at Pacific Lutheran University of Tacoma, WA. Danish Brotherhood Lodges at Dagmar (1910), McCabe (1914), and Sidney (1916) owe their numbers and origins to the breadth of this northeast Montana colonization effort.

[17] Kimberly Brown, *Historical Overview of Dillon District, Bureau of Land Management* (Boulder, CO: Western Interstate Commission for Higher Education, 1975), has background information on the history of Beaverhead and Madison Counties. Malone, Roeder, and Lang also deal with the general livestock history of Montana.

[18] Madison County History Association, *Pioneer Trails and Trials, Madison County, 1863-1920* (Great Falls: Madison County History Association, 1976), p. 444. 1870 Manuscript Census, Madison County.

[19] 1870, 1880 Manuscript Census, Beaverhead County, Madison County.

[20] 1880 Manuscript Census, Madison County.

[21] 1880 Manuscript Census, Beaverhead County. Census districts were not clearly defined in the 1880 census. For the story of Dillon's founding, see Stanley R. Davison and Rex C. Myers, "Terminus Town: The Founding of Dillon, 1880," in *Montana, The Magazine of Western History*, 30, 4 (Autumn, 1980), pp. 16-29.

[22] 1900 Manuscript Census, Beaverhead County.

[23] The 1890 Manuscript Census is not available and leaves a void in what was, undoubtedly, an important period in the growth of the Danish community in southwestern Montana. All subsequent data is taken from the 1900 or 1910 Manuscript Census returns for Beaverhead and Madison Counties.

[24] U.S. Bureau of the Census, *Report on Population of the United States at the Eleventh Census, 1890*. Vol. I, Part I (Washington, D.C.: GPO, 1895), p. 641.

25 U.S. Bureau of the Census, *Twelfth Census of the United States, 1900.* Vol. I, Population, Part I (Washington, D.C.: GPO, 1901), p. 591.

26 1900 Manuscript Census, Beaverhead County. The author realizes that the date of immigration listed on the manuscript census may not correspond with the date of arrival in Beaverhead County, but data from Danish family history questionnaires (discussed below) indicate the process was relatively direct during the last decade of the nineteenth and the first decade of the twentieth centuries.

27 1900 Manuscript Census, Beaverhead County.

28 Ibid.

29 Davison and Myers.

30 1900 Manuscript Census, Beaverhead County.

31 Ibid.

32 Ibid. Interview with Otto Christensen, Dillon, Montana, December 2, 1983. "Danes oral history interviews, 1984," OH 633, Montana Historical Society.

33 1910 Manuscript Census, Beaverhead County.

34 Ibid.

35 Christensen Interview. Interview with Axel Madsen, Dillon, Montana, March 23, 1984, OH 633.

36 Biographical questionnaires submitted to all members of Danish Brotherhood Lodge #273 in 1983. Twenty-five questionnaires were returned containing information on thirty-three separate Danes who immigrated to Beaverhead County. See "Danish Settlement in Beaverhead County, 1983," SC 2439, Montana Historical Society.

37 Ibid. According to Hvidt, Aero does not figure prominently in overall Danish emigration data.

38 Hvidt, p. 47.

39 1910 Manuscript Census, Beaverhead and Madison Counties.

40 Luebke, p. 394.

41 *The Dillon Tribune,* March 2, 1906.

42 *First Evangelical Lutheran Church History, 1906-1981* (Dillon: Privately printed, 1981), p. 1.

43 First Evangelical Lutheran Church, Secretary's Minute Books. These books were kept in Danish until 1920.

44 *Church History.* There is no complete list of members during the period

from 1906 to 1930. Danish Brotherhood questionnaires indicate that Beaverhead County Danes tended to belong to the Lutheran Church in significant numbers. Of the thirty-three individuals covered, twenty-seven were active in the Lutheran Church.

45 Interview with John Anderson, Alder, Montana, February 13, 1984, OH 633.

46 Organized in 1881 to provide fraternity and insurance for its members, the Danish Brotherhood typified a plethora of associations formed nationally in the late 1800s and early 1900s. See note #11, and Alvin J. Schmidt and Nicholas Babchuck, eds., *Fraternal Organizations* (Westport, CT: Greenwood Press, 1980), pp. 3-5, 80-81.

47 *Danish Brotherhood Lodge No. 273, 1908-1981, Dillon, Montana, History* (Dillon: Privately printed, 1981), p. 1.

48 Danish Brotherhood Lodge #273, Secretary's Minute Book.

49 *The Dillon Examiner,* January 6, 1909.

50 U.S. Bureau of the Census, "Total Ancestry Reported," 2007-2011 American Community Survey 5-Year Estimates. Seven other ethnic groups within Beaverhead County had larger numbers: German, English, Irish, Norwegian, French, Scotch, and Swedish.

51 Tommerup.

Creating a New Community in the North:
Mexican Americans of the Yellowstone Valley

— Laurie Mercier

The unprecedented numbers of immigrants who came to American between 1900 and 1914 created a backlash against immigrants—especially those who did not come from western or northern Europe—by the start of the First World War. The passions unleashed by the war and the political conservatism that arose in the United States during the 1920s led Congress to pass the highly restrictive National Origins Quota Act of 1924. While these political developments were occurring in Washington, D.C., the Yellowstone Valley of eastern Montana was experiencing a different type of transformation: the establishment of a major sugar beet industry. The Yellowstone Valley had rich farmland and a necessary supply of water, the latter thanks in large measure to federal reclamation projects. The one thing that the valley did not have was an adequate supply of labor; cultivating sugar beets, after all, was a labor-intensive enterprise.

Fortunately for the sugar beet growers, and firms such as the Great Western Sugar Company, Mexicans were exempted from the quotas that were put into place by the 1924 federal law. Consequently, an increasingly large number of Mexican laborers began to move northward across the Rio Grande in the 1920s to fill the ongoing need for unskilled workers in the American West. Of course, many of the workers who eventually settled in the Yellowstone Valley were, in fact, Mexican Americans, born and raised in such states as Texas and California. It was the need for work, and often their prior experience as migrant field hands, that brought them to Montana. As the decades passed, many Mexican-American families made the decision to settle permanently in the Yellowstone Valley. They also began looking for better-paying, more secure jobs—including those connected with the railroads and sugar beet plants—that would take them beyond the sugar beet fields. In addition, Mexican-American men who served in the U.S. armed forces during World War II returned home with a greater sense of their rights as American citizens.

The following essay by historian Laurie Mercier effectively demonstrates the value of using personal interviews to preserve history—in this case of a largely working-class community—that might otherwise be lost through the passage of time. The story of this particular community also reminds us of the dilemma that almost all ethnic groups in Montana have faced as they transition into the second and third generations: how to preserve cultural and social traditions within one's ethnic group while also working to be part of the larger society.

The Yellowstone River wets the richest agricultural lands in eastern Montana. Since the early twentieth century, irrigation projects and the nation's sweet tooth have made sugar beets the most profitable and enduring crop grown. Unlike agricultural products such as grain and livestock, which demand little more than the labors of a single family, sugar beets required an army of temporary workers to thin, cultivate, and harvest the persnickety roots. Mexican Americans have provided much of this essential labor, yet their contributions have gone unheralded. This essay traces the history of the Mexican Americans who came to the Yellowstone as seasonal workers and created a vital ethnic community, which has persisted despite years of economic hardship, discrimination, and cultural and social change.

The Great Western Sugar Company, in Billings (here, circa 1930s), was a major employer in the area. COURTESY MONTANA HISTORICAL SOCIETY, HELENA, 941-126.

Long before Montana became a state, Hispanic explorers, trappers, miners, and vaqueros were among the first non-Natives to visit the region. After the United States annexed the northern half of Mexico in 1848, many Latin Americans continued to migrate to the north, but it was not until the 1920s that Mexico's dramatically increasing population and an expanding western U.S. economy combined to persuade millions of residents to seek work across the border. By 1930, more than 1,000 Mexicans and Mexican Americans had come to the Yellowstone Valley.

Federally financed reclamation projects transformed the arid West in the early 1900s, including the Yellowstone Valley, where Billings capitalist I. D. O'Donnell and other local businessmen invested in growing sugar beets, an expensive and labor-intensive crop. They incorporated the Billings Sugar Company in 1905 and built one of the largest sugar beet factories in the world the following year. A dozen years later, during the height of wartime agricultural demand, the Great Western Sugar Company bought the factory and encouraged area farmers to plant beets instead of wheat. Beets became a profitable investment up and down the Yellowstone, and Great Western became Montana's (and the nation's) largest sugar producer. Holly Sugar Company also built factories in the region at Sidney in 1925 and at Hardin in 1937.

Profitable sugar beet production required a reliable supply of low-cost labor, which the Montana labor market could not supply. Sugar companies began to recruit from areas where labor was more abundant and from groups of people who had been denied access to other kinds of employment. In 1921, Great Western's Labor Bureau in Denver recruited 385 beet laborers from "southern points" in Texas, California, Colorado, and Mexico for Montana farms. Two years later, the company reported that most of the 500 workers they imported were "of the Mexican type," the beginning of a seven-decade reliance by the beet industry on cheap labor from the American Southwest and Mexico. Government and industry worked together to maintain this employment niche for Latinos. Even when many Americans clamored for immigration restrictions in 1924, for example, growers lobbied for unrestricted movement of Mexican labor and Congress exempted Mexicans from new immigration quotas.

The Great Western Company cultivated its dependence on two ethnic groups to tend valley beets. In 1924, it brought to Montana 3,604 Mexicans and 1,231 German Russians to harvest a record 31,000 acres that year. But the company had different long-range plans for each ethnic group. Great Western loaned money to its German-Russian growers, hoping to attract their peasant relatives, who could provide temporary labor for thinning and harvests and eventually become tenants and even landowners. This Company encouragement, along with kinship ties, community acceptance, and ready adjustment to Montana's climate, probably explains why seventy-seven percent of the German workforce remained in the Billings district that winter, a sharp contrast to just twenty-five percent of the Mexicans. Company actions reflected American racial assumptions that European immigrants made more capable landowners than Mexicans, who many insisted were more suited to agricultural labor than farming.

The racist underpinnings of American culture, together with restrictive legislation and hiring practices, hindered Latino economic mobility, and the low wages made agricultural labor a family endeavor. Families migrated and worked together as a unit and sold their collective labor to farmers. This pattern of family migration and family wage-work shaped the character of the Yellowstone's Latino community and helped maintain fairly equal male-to-female ratios. It also stimulated the growth of a settled community. Sugar companies, which sought to maintain a stable workforce, promoted family settlement by providing transportation, labor contracts, and housing for families.

The Great Western and Holly Sugar companies created colonias near their factories to encourage Mexican workers to "winter over" in Montana. In 1924, the Great Western Company invested in improvements in the Billings colonia, which housed forty-two families. Mexican laborers built ten new adobe apartments, cindered streets, extended the water line, constructed a drainage ditch, and leveled and planted grass on the compound grounds. Severo "Sal" Briceno came with his family to Billings in 1928, and he recalled that the forty-odd adobe homes of the colonia each had one bedroom, a woodstove, and an outhouse. Briceno's family of nine spread into two of the small homes. Residents were responsible for upkeep, and the factory donated tar to patch pervasive leaks in the flat roofs. An outdoor water faucet served every five houses, and when temperatures dipped, Briceno remembered, "we'd have to go out there and make fires around it to unfreeze it."

As in other industrial labor arrangements, settled families fostered a stable workforce, and the colonias helped families remain and survive on their meager wages. Colonia residents could raise chickens, pigs, and gardens to supplement their diets. The company also created a winter jobs program on the factory grounds, believing that in the spring "there would not be a big debt hanging over [farmworkers'] heads, making them more willing to work in the territory rather than to leave . . . in order to get away from their debts." The colonia provided a clinic and school for migrant children and unified the Latino community. Esther Rivera recalled that her father, Fred Duran, "used

Many Montana sugar beet workers lived in adobe houses such as these, circa 1939, part of Great Western Company holdings near Hysham, east of Billings.
ARTHUR ROTHSTEIN,
COURTESY LIBRARY OF CONGRESS,
LC-USF34- 027399-D.

to talk about the colonia all the time. Everybody knew everybody. The people really hung together."

As the colonia provided the immigrants with a sense of community, it also isolated them from other residents, while their growing numbers also aroused prejudice. The Great Western Company campaigned against the baseless fears directed at its Latino labor pool. During the 1920s, the Company's annual reports emphasized that Mexican laborers had "solved the farm labor problem," that many were U.S. citizens, and that they were skilled workers. These reports concealed the racial tensions that predominated in white Billings.

During the first half of the century, people who spoke Spanish or who were perceived as "Mexicans" faced great discrimination in Billings. Sal Briceno recalled that Latino children could not participate in the annual Kiwanis Easter egg hunt in South Park: "They had men on horses riding around that South Park kicking us out. There were a lot of kids that wanted candy, but they'd kick us out." Latinos were banned from the public swimming pool, segregated in theaters, and not allowed in restaurants. Signs above some Billings business doors read, "No Mexicans or dogs allowed." Mexican Americans knew racism's unwritten rules and the boundaries of acceptable behavior. Robert Federico's four aunts and mother had vivid stories of "where they could go and could not go." If they could endure stares and taunts, for example, they could venture into the local skating rink. But most places, such as bowling alleys, were off-limits. Sal Briceno noted "they [whites] would have kicked me in the head with a bowling ball" if he had ventured there. Barred from most stores, Mexican Americans were dependent on their farm employers to do their shopping.

Farmworker families usually came as part of a crew or group of families recruited. Robert Rivera's family was part of a trainload of Californians who were recruited and promised "opportunities" in

Tending and harvesting sugar beets was backbreaking work. In 1939, the U.S. Farm Security Administration sent photographer Arthur Rothstein to Treasure County to document agricultural conditions after a decade-long drought.
ARTHUR ROTHSTEIN, COURTESY LIBRARY OF CONGRESS, LC-USF33- 003274-M4.

Montana during the 1920s. Once in Billings, farmworker families often stayed at the St. Louis Hotel on Montana Avenue across from the depot, while they waited for the Great Western Sugar Company to match them with farmers and take them to the farms. The Riveras and other families, who wintered over for beet planting in the spring, stayed in the colonia until the Company transported them once again to Custer, Hysham, Belfry, Joliet, and other places where farmers needed labor. The Company also arranged credit at the local grocery until workers were paid and brought farmworkers back to the colonia at the end of the beet season. But with limited earnings, families faced many a grim winter. Rivera recalled that his family and most others took their beet earnings to Sawyer's on 29th and invested in bulk groceries:

> That's where most of the people traded, and if they had 300 to 400 dollars to spend on groceries for the winter, they would buy

in big lots, flour by the 100-pound, coffee by the 25-pounds, lard by the 50-pounds, and as much groceries as they could afford, they'd take in provisions for the winter. Of course when that was gone, that was it.

Some migrant workers developed lasting relationships with farmers and sought to renew their associations each spring, while some other families remained with farmers throughout the year and helped in feeding cattle and mending fences during the winter while they waited for the beet season to begin. As Robert Rivera noted, these arrangements helped sustain farmworker families and also initiate permanent resident status:

> If they wanted you to stay, a lot of times they would offer you the place to stay for the winter if you wanted to. Then the men would work for them . . . which was better than moving back to the colony, because once you moved back there was nothing to carry you through the winter.

Mutual friendships often developed between female farmworkers and owners because of shared concerns about children's welfare, or for female companionship on isolated farms. Farm women frequently helped with childcare, dispensed advice, and supplied eggs and other farm products to supplement their workers' earnings. Maria Cantu usually took her children with her to the fields, but when it was too cold, she often left them with the female farm owner, whom she fondly remembered: "This lady was just like my mother. She was nice and so sweet." Esther Rivera recalled that a farm woman taught her mother "how to cook American food, she learned how to do everything there. She let her have her own garden spot to raise a garden, so we were very fortunate there."

The beet cultivation cycle changed little over time. In mid-April, farmers began planting; workers hoed and thinned from late May to mid-July. Until farmers began mechanizing and applying herbicides in the 1950s, many migrant families remained over the summer to weed and through the fall to harvest and top the beets. The stoop labor and distinctive tools—a short-handled hoe for thinning and a curved knife for topping—also remained the same. "You worked backbreaking long hours," Esther Rivera recalled, "everything was done by hand." It was arduous work, as Sal Briceno remembered, but there were few choices. "The work was hard, [but] you had to do it, you had no alternative." As Esther Rivera remembered it, "both parents really working day and night to keep eight of us children going. You didn't think anything of the work because it was your way of life."

Latino parents often had to care for young children while they worked, and children assisted as soon as they were old enough. Dora Cantu recalled that her father always carried an extra hoe in the car; when one of his children reached eight or nine years, he enticed

A young worker hoes a row of sugar beets in Treasure County, circa 1939. ARTHUR ROTHSTEIN, COURTESY LIBRARY OF CONGRESS, LC-USF33- 003275-M1.

them to "help mom out" so they could go home early. Her mother distracted her children from the drudgery by telling folktales, which often featured children and animals and emphasized cooperation and sharing, crucial themes in the lives of families dependent on the contributions of all their members to survive.

Economic realities also forced many married women to do fieldwork, sometimes on the days when they went into labor and gave birth. As in most American families, the "double day" prevailed for female farmworkers, extending work into the evening: "Father would sit down, mother would cook, she would wash clothes . . . no one questioned it, all the women were in the kitchen, all the men ate."

When possible, families sacrificed women's critical field labor to manage the household, to cook, and to care for young children and boarders. Ruth Contreraz remembered her mother "practically cooking all day long" to feed her family and ten male boarders who helped her husband work beets. Women often raised gardens and chickens for food, and created clothing and household goods from available materials, such as feed sacks. Many women found time also to make functional products more attractive. "I don't know how she found the time," Esther Rivera recalled of her mother's determination to create beauty in her family's home:

> She made the quilts, she made our clothes, she made home-made cheese, she made everything from scratch, plus she always had time to embroider every pillowcase . . . and had everything fancy. I guess that was their way of expressing . . . having something beautiful for themselves.

The 1930s depression halted recruitment of Latino laborers, and the government even deported many to Mexico, including U.S. citizens. In the Yellowstone, opposition to the employment of migrant workers compelled the Great Western Company to hire local workers before hiring outsiders. The Company also agreed to employ "solos" from outside the district to discourage families from "remaining and becoming a charge on relief." This reversal of the Company's earlier promotion of family settlement resulted in a reduction of wintering employees from 221 in 1935 to 173 in 1937.

Spurred by labor demonstrations across the nation during the 1930s, many farmworkers protested poor wages and working conditions. Yellowstone farmworkers, like other agricultural workers, faced numerous obstacles in labor organizing. Often without supportive communities and dependent on individual growers for jobs, farmworkers were vulnerable to companies and growers, who could retaliate by ejecting rebellious families from housing, refusing to pay back wages and transportation, and importing replacement workers. Nonetheless, from 1934 through 1937, Beet Workers Union strikes and threats of strikes periodically interrupted thinning and harvests, reminding sugar producers of the workers' importance. In 1937, the Yellowstone Growers' Association and beet laborer representatives settled on a piece rate of $21.50 per acre, or $9.50 for thinning, $2.25 for hoeing, $1.35 for weeding, and $0.70 per ton for topping.

Second World War production demands and labor shortages generated new calls for Mexican and Mexican-American agricultural workers, but new opportunities in defense work on the West Coast, armed services recruitment, and other industry jobs beckoned the nation's Latinos. In the Yellowstone Valley, the percent of acres thinned by local Mexican-American farmworkers steadily declined during the war years, from forty-four percent in 1941 to just nine percent in 1946. Sugar companies and growers frantically pursued workers from the Southwest, and increasingly from Indian reservations, local high schools, German prisoner-of-war camps, and the Japanese-American internment camp at Heart Mountain. With fewer resident Latino families interested in farm labor, Great Western resumed its recruitment efforts, soliciting by mail and by personal visits to Mexican-American prospects in California and Texas.

Wartime demand was so great that Western growers and agricultural industries in 1943 pressured Congress to create the "bracero" program, Public Law 78, which allowed farmers to employ Mexican nationals to harvest crops. Under the program's agreement with the Mexican government, employers paid transportation and living expenses, provided individual contracts, and promised not to undercut existing wages. From 1943 through 1946, the Great Western's Billings district relied on Mexicans to thin up to thirty percent of its beet fields, and top up to half its crop in the fall when labor was even more difficult to procure.

After the war, farmers accelerated their demand for beet labor and the sugar companies assisted. Santos Carranza began his thirty-three-year career as a labor recruiter for Holly Sugar Company in Sidney during the war. As field office supervisor, Carranza traveled to Texas each spring and distributed cards announcing Montana employment needs, located workers, and advanced money for the trip north where he linked families with lower Yellowstone farmers. After 1963, when Congress terminated the bracero program, companies continued recruiting workers to assure contract farmers of sufficient labor.

Many migrant workers in the Yellowstone Valley sought permanent jobs and better livelihoods, and some actually purchased farms. Anastacio and Brigida Carranza brought their family to the lower

Yellowstone from Colorado in 1925 to work beets, and ten years later they managed to buy their first beet farm near Sidney. Maria Cantu and her husband came to the Yellowstone Valley in 1951 with a south Texas contractor's team that worked Great Western's fields in Colorado and Montana. Maria wanted to keep her children from a life on the road, so despite the hardships, she insisted that her family find a way to stay in Montana. The Cantus felt lucky to find year-round employment with the same Worden-area farmer for eleven years. They saved and purchased a small farm in 1962, while they continued to thin and harvest beets for area farmers. To supplement the family income, Mr. Cantu periodically worked during harvest, loading beets on trains at Pompey's Pillar, Worden, Huntley, Shepherd, and Park City, and also during the winter at the sugar factory.

Farmworker families generally left agricultural work for better-paying, steady jobs as soon as they could. As Robert Rivera explained: "The Spanish people would work the fields and work their hearts out trying to make a living, but there was nothing in return, nothing like social security or retirement." But it was not easy to find alternative work. Workers occasionally were hired to "work the beet cars" in the wintertime, unloading beets for factory processing. "It was hard work, cold, working through the night," as Robert Rivera reported, "but then it meant that you had a better chance to go through the winter." Still, widespread discrimination limited opportunities for Mexican Americans, as Sal Briceno remembered, because "they'd get white people for the better jobs." Race was a factor in finding any kind of employment: "There was a lot of discrimination in those days. If you were of Mexican descent, you couldn't do nothing."

Mexican-American women often took wage jobs to ensure their family's survival. Esther Rivera believed that Mexican-American men—not unlike the men in the larger society—felt "embarrassment if your wife worked" outside the home, before social mores began to change in the 1970s. But economic realities often defy popular ideals. Robert Rivera remembered that his mother had to work "out of the home," cleaning hotels to provide for the family. And Mexican-American women also faced discrimination. Esther Rivera recalled that there was considerable employment discrimination during the

1940s and 1950s. She had taken a business course in high school in 1949, for example, but when she sought advertised jobs, the doors were often closed. "I applied for jobs all over town and I couldn't get anything, so I had to take a dishwashing job."

Landing a job with the Northern Pacific Railroad or a Billings factory was often Mexican Americans' first real break. "Most of your Spanish people here in Billings," Robert Rivera believed:

> . . . since they started working for the railroads, that's what really made a better life for them, because they got steady work, and they got pretty good pay, and the majority bought their little house and moved up, educated their children, and they got retirement from the railroad.

Ralph "Chino" Armendariz was one such success story. He came with his father to the Yellowstone in 1936 to work beets, and in 1939 he was hired as a section laborer for the Northern Pacific, where he worked until he retired in 1964.

The Second World War was a watershed period for the nation's Latinos. When veterans returned to their communities and sought non-agricultural jobs, many insisted on equal treatment. Robert Rivera and his five brothers, who served in the military while many of the area's Euro-American residents received deferments to work in agriculture, felt strongly: "I've fought for this country, and my brothers have fought for this country, and we feel like we belong here just like anybody else." Rivera became an ironworker and welder, while his brothers became carpenters. Sal Briceno chose to drive a Yellow Cab after his release from service, and Ynes Contreraz worked at Pierce Packing Company from 1948 to 1982, receiving several promotions and feeling no discrimination. Contreraz believed that discriminatory practices at local businesses discouraged Mexican applicants, but "when younger people saw Pierce hiring Mexicans, they knew they had an alternative to working beets."

Mexican-American young people eagerly sought non-agricultural work. Robert Rivera remembered as a teenager longing for a different life:

I would just say to myself when I was in those fields, "I hope to God I never have to do this again, and as soon as I'm able I'm gonna get out of here and never do this again." And I did.

Esther Rivera claimed that "all" Mexican-American youth were determined not to live farmworker lives:

We just got out the minute we were fifteen or sixteen and didn't have to work in those fields, then you'd do anything else. When I turned sixteen, I applied for my first job at Billings Laundry.

Yellowstone Valley Latinos believed that education was key to attaining the American Dream. Beginning in the 1940s, when many farmworkers acquired their own transportation to "come and go everyday to the beet fields," many families moved to Billings and other towns to secure year-round schooling for their children. "My dad felt that we were not getting enough education," Ruth Contreraz remembered. "They would always tell us, 'you kids have to continue going to school no matter what, so you guys can end up with better jobs.'" Esther Peralez's parents also remained in the Yellowstone Valley so their children could attend school. She recalled a phrase repeated by "everybody's Mexican parent," including her father: "to study so you learn so you're not ignorant like we are." Her father emphasized the importance of education as "what you have to do to get out of [beet work] because I don't have a choice." Parents repeatedly sacrificed and labored long hours, hoping that their children would prosper. Dora Cantu remembered that her mother had been educated in Mexico and had hoped to be a teacher:

That was her dream to be a schoolteacher, and she was denied this. She always dreamed that one of us would be a schoolteacher. From the time that we were little, "you've got to learn, you've got to learn to read, you've got to learn to do this. You don't always want to be out here working beets. . . . Go to school and learn. If you don't, this is the kind of life that you'll have.

Two realities hindered children's education: family economic needs and discrimination. Spring thinning and fall harvesting schedules, for example, placed difficult demands on schoolchildren. Dora Cantu and her sister missed school on alternate days to watch younger siblings while their parents worked beets, and they also adapted work schedules to accommodate school

> We would get up at four o'clock in the morning, we would work until an hour before the bus would come and pick us up. We would be out until six or seven. We would go down to the house, or we would take our clothes to the field with us, change from our work clothes into our school clothes, run and catch the bus, go to school, come home, and then work again until sundown. This was from early spring when they started thinning beets until we got out of school in June. Then in the fall, when they were topping beets, we would get up again in the frost, and we would go out and pile beets. . . . We'd stack them in the evenings, we'd do at least two or three of those rows, enough so Mom and Dad would have enough beets the next day to top. . . . Sometimes it'd be dark when we went home.

Cantu remembered that Mexican-American children, whose parents had a small farm or worked for the railroad, were able to attend school regularly; those who did farm labor often had to drop out. Her parents emphasized the importance of school, so despite the interference of farm labor, she struggled to learn, even though she missed out on important instruction—such as how to calculate percentages—that hindered her.

Although parents supported them, many children encountered prejudice from students and teachers. Ruth Contreraz remembered her experience at Garfield School, where the city's Mexican-American students attended classes:

> We were a minority, and we never felt that the teachers defended us in any way. When we got accused of anything, they

would go as far as saying well don't even come back to school if you don't want to. They just did not accept us.

Fights erupted when Mexican-American youth refused to ignore racial slurs, such as "dirty Mexican," or "greaser" and "bean eater." Ruth Contreraz's mother told her to disregard taunts, but she beat up kids who called her names and then feared her mother would discover that she had been fighting. "We were already thinking, 'why don't Mom and Dad stand up a little bit for our rights. . . .' [When] the ones with authority, the teacher and principal, don't defend you in any way or form, even I started hating school." Contreraz "begged" her father to let her drop out of school and go to work. He agreed to allow her to stay out for one year; she never returned. Nonetheless, she insisted that her own children remain in school so they would not "have to work as maids or go through what I had to."

Education provided many Mexican-American parents and youth with a greater awareness of their stake in American society. Ruth Contreraz believed that "with education you start recognizing your rights. . . . The younger parents felt they were going to get their kids educated and they can live where they want, we don't have to hold back anymore." But racism and their children's poor performance in the schools convinced many parents that mere access to education was insufficient. Contreraz noted, "That's when I feel that our parents started thinking, 'no, this is not right, our kids are not getting the education they need.' First it was because we lived in farms, and a lot of the kids had to work, so they would always kind of lag behind." Mexican-American parents began joining PTAs and voicing their complaints.

During the 1960s, many of the Yellowstone's Mexican-American youth, influenced by the Chicano civil rights movements, worked to change social attitudes and increase educational and employment opportunities. Robert Federico, who was inspired by VISTA anti-poverty volunteers while still a student at Rocky Mountain College, began organizing the Latino community to combat discrimination, improve housing, increase voter registration, and promote affirmative action hiring. Esther Peralez, who had worked in Oregon and observed many militant Chicano students demanding equal rights, returned to Billings in the early 1970s and joined Federico and others in mobilizing the Mexican-American community to pressure the city to hire a Chicano school counselor and help more young people enter college. At that time, she recalled, there were many Latino social activities—dances and picnics, and cultural events, such as Cinco de Mayo celebrations—but few organized attempts to challenge the Billings city government and implement reforms.

Latino youth often clashed with their elders over their reform goals and their militancy. Older residents wanted to preserve cultural traditions and promote community events, while younger people wanted social change. "We just did not click," Robert Federico recalled, between "those who wanted to go slower, and those who wanted to move faster." Another activist explained that many preferred working quietly behind the scenes to effect change. "When we have wanted something, we have never done it like they do in the big cities. Hispanics there will raise their fists and are very demanding." Jim Gonzalez, a Mexican-American leader and respected Billings city council member from 1977 to 1985, represented the "old school" belief in working slowly through the system. Federico represented the younger generation's more aggressive assertion of reformist demands and opposition to discrimination. Esther Peralez saw the differences as generational. She remembered her mother's complaints about one young activist: "What is his problem? Things are good now. He should have been here when we were younger, because they wouldn't allow Mexicans in school, they would beat them up. Things are good now." But, as Peralez recalled, her generation's thinking was different. "We were saying, 'no that's not good enough. We shouldn't be thankful. . . . There should be rights that everybody has.'" Still, Peralez and other youth felt "cultural frustration," because "in our culture, you respect your elders, and I was taught that way," even though she disagreed with their tactics.

By the mid-1970s, second- and third-generation Mexican Americans had established several political and cultural associations to improve the welfare of Billings-area Latinos. Since the 1920s, Yellowstone Latinos had organized dances to raise money to help families burdened by hospital debts or victimized by the legal system.

Beginning in the 1960s, community members chartered more formal groups. The Latino Club sponsored cultural events and sought to preserve Mexican history and culture. Concilio Mexicano, composed of educated, middle-class Hispanics, advocated jobs and education programs for their community. The Mexican American Community Organization (MACO) tried to coordinate Mexican-American organizations' activities and responses to crises that affected the larger Latino community. Nevertheless, young and old frequently united on major issues, such as successfully lobbying the city to take action on an incidence of police brutality and persuading the *Billings Gazette* to curb stereotypical coverage of area Latinos.

The Billings South Side neighborhood had long been the heart of the Yellowstone's Latino community. As the traditional home for many of Billings' immigrants and industrial workers, the South Side accepted the new migrants while other neighborhoods did not. They continued to establish permanent homes there, Robert Rivera believed, because they felt "more like being around your own people." Some Mexican Americans who joined the middle class later chose to move away from their South Side roots to other parts of the city. Esther Peralez moved to the Heights, she explained, as part of living out "the American Dream." As someone who grew up in poverty, she wanted "a piece of that pie . . . to have a brand new home made from scratch," instead of the older housing available on the South Side. Esther Rivera's family also moved from the South Side to the Heights, but they missed their former neighborhood and ties they had kept since moving to the valley:

> The minute I could drive I was back down there. We attended all the social functions, we went to the same church . . . [my dad] used to like to go to the Mexican dances. If there wasn't a dance, he'd make one, he'd sponsor one. We never lost contact with our [South Side] friends. . . . My parents were very social. They met all these people at the colonia, and they never forgot them.

The South Side's major landmark, Our Lady of Guadalupe Catholic Church, has played an important role in solidifying the Yellowstone's

Latino community during the last forty years. Most farmworkers were devout Catholics, but poor transportation and Sunday work demands often prevented them from attending church. Nonetheless, families made special efforts to give their children proper religious instruction. Dora Cantu remembered her father working in fields close to the Ballantine Catholic Church when his children needed to take first communion lessons. Yellowstone Latino families attended a variety of Catholic churches, but they desired a setting that nourished their culture. To that end, Sal Briceno helped build the Little Flower Catholic Church on the South Side in the early 1930s. But an increasing white membership in the new church, Briceno felt, soon began "pushing the Mexicans away." Esther Rivera also "never felt like Little Flower was our special church. We always felt like we might be a little in the way." In the early 1950s, as Ruth Contreraz recalled, residents began planning a special ethnic church:

> I think what helped a lot was when a lot of the older Mexican people started talking about how we should have our own church and how we should better our own community. . . . I think all the different circles at St. Ann's and other churches started talking about developing this and that. They would hold meetings and then everyone had their say on what they felt, what they wanted. . . . That's how it started changing.

After its construction in 1952, Our Lady of Guadalupe Church attracted Latinos from Ballantine, Huntley, and other Yellowstone communities as well as the sizable South Side Mexican-American community. "We could attend mass anywhere," Esther Rivera explained, "but there we congregated because we need to keep continuity in the community. You're at home." Other residents, such as Liz Castro, agreed that the church attracted people with ethnic, kin, and neighborhood ties. "Everybody knows everybody, it's just a neat place to be." Esther Peralez tried attending other churches in her Heights neighborhood, but she was drawn back to Guadalupe. "It was like old home week. You fit right in, you know people, it's just a comfortable place. . . . So many places, I'm always the only minority, and I think when is this

ever going to end . . . you can always pick up subtle discrimination. . . .
But going to Guadalupe I always feel comfortable."

In addition to providing for the spiritual needs of the Latino community, the church strengthened ethnic identity, Esther Rivera explained. "Before that, we were unified, but yet kind of distant, each
to his own. But when the church started out, that's when all the
people started thinking more or less alike." The church enhanced
ethnic pride by providing a gathering place for people to organize
cultural events such as Cinco de Mayo and September 16 (Mexican
Independence Day) celebrations. "They used to celebrate . . . in little
surrounding towns like Huntley, Worden, Ballentine," Ruth Contreraz
remembered, "but here in Billings, nothing . . . because there was no
place to get started with it." Since Our Lady of Guadalupe's inaugu-
ration in 1952, Contreraz believed that Yellowstone Hispanics "have
really come a long ways. . . . Now our culture is being recognized,
we have identity, and it's being shared by many other nationalities
besides us." The annual December 12 celebration commemorates
the day when the Virgen de Guadalupe appeared before Mexico's
Juan Diego. After a special mass, the congregation sings to the Virgin
and girls present flowers to the church altar. Celebrants then ad-
journ to the church hall for more singing, refreshments, and piñatas.
Before Christmas, parishioners celebrate another Mexican tradition
in the processions of Las Posadas. Participants reenact Mary and
Joseph's search for lodging and share Christmas greetings, refreshments, and songs.

Before building Our Lady of Guadalupe, Yellowstone Latinos made
both formal and informal attempts to preserve their Mexican heritage. In 1929, Mexican Americans in Billings formed La Honorifica
Mexicana to celebrate fiestas on the important Mexican holidays:
Cinco de Mayo, which commemorates the courageous Mexican defeat of an invading French army in 1862, and the 16th of September,
Mexican Independence Day. At these fiestas, Robert Rivera recalled,
older men in the community would often discuss the history of
Mexico. "They were the ones that really carried the tradition and remembered the customs and everything from the old country. They
tried to teach that to the younger people." Adapting traditions to

Montana's harvest schedule and unpredictable weather, Billings organizers in recent years have combined the May and September commemorations in one August celebration.

Cultural activities, especially with music, took place on a more informal basis among extended families and groups of friends. Sal Briceno recalled, "Everybody used to get together to sing. I don't think there was a Mexican man who didn't know how to sing and play guitar, and dance the *juarabe tapatilla.*" People frequently organized dances, which engaged many area Mexican-American bands, such as Little Joe and the Alegres, Harold Garza and the Rebeldes, and Andy Martinez and the Bandoleros. Other residents have periodically sought to preserve and perpetuate Latino culture. Ruth Contreraz, for example, organized a group of young women to learn and perform traditional Mexican dances.

Food arts are often the most persistent cultural activity among American ethnic groups. Yellowstone Latinos introduced the region to a cuisine that has become a standard feature in many restaurants and households. Many women still proudly prepare dishes and employ methods learned from their Mexican mothers and grandmothers. Maria Cantu described how she makes tortillas from scratch, shunning packaged varieties:

> I don't even use corn meal or masa harina. I plant my own corn, I cook my own corn, I grind my own corn, and I use my own corn. I let the corn dry, and shell it and put it away in a barrel. Anytime I need it . . . I have a machine to grind it. I cook the corn with lime, and it takes the shell off, and I have to watch it until it turns completely white.

For holidays and special occasions, women sometimes joined other female kin and friends to prepare traditional foods. Sal Briceno remembered his mother often joined with three or four families to buy and roast a pig and then make tamales with pork or turkey and spices for holidays. "All the women would get together" to scrape the meat off the skull, and make chicharrones and flour tortillas. A few women combined their culinary expertise with business acumen and opened restaurants in Billings. Hermina Torres, who came to the Yellowstone Valley with her husband in 1940 as migrant farmworkers, opened Torres Cafe in 1963; her daughter, Josie Torres Quarnberg, took over the operation in 1977. Liz Castro and her family operated the El Paso Café during the 1980s. The restaurant opened on South 29th Street, then moved to Montana Avenue to serve "the South Side people."

The Yellowstone's Latino community often faced difficult choices. Sometimes they had to sacrifice cultural identity to obtain greater respect and economic prosperity. Many second- and third-genera-tion Mexican Americans hoped acculturation would engender tol-erance. Sal Briceno, for example, recalled that his family was "more Americanized" and therefore "treated better" by the dominant soci-ety. But assimilation into the larger community often made economic class rather than "race" the significant factor in distinguishing Latinos. Esther Rivera thought that the larger community became more tol-erant when "we became middle class," and that farmworker families became middle class because they "wanted something different for our children," and struggled to attain a more prosperous lifestyle. But the poorer migrant farmworkers were still viewed as the "other," in racial terms, by many non-Latinos in the Yellowstone. Gaining accep-tance and opportunity in the larger community has sometimes been won at the expense of cultural cohesion, which has troubled many Yellowstone Latinos who regret the loss of the Spanish language and other aspects of cultural identity. In this respect, the Yellowstone's Latino community has faced greater obstacles than Spanish-language communities in the Southwest and the nation's larger cities, where the density of ethnic populations has provided a measure of ethnic security and diminished the demand to assimilate. Sal Briceno noted that his children lost interest in traditional Mexican music because "there are so many things that they can do now." Traditional culture was no longer central to their lives. "Their culture doesn't mean any-thing, they're Americans. They consider themselves just as 'white' as anybody else." Intermarriage between the children of Euro-Americans and Mexican Americans, however, has provided a mixed blessing. "So what's happening is our race is getting very diluted." Esther Rivera noted, "You're losing your language, you're losing a lot there. I see it with every generation it's more and more. . . . They don't have memories, they're losing a lot of their culture."

The decline of Spanish as a second language for third- and fourth-generation Mexican Americans alarms many, while some parents remember problems they faced learning English and insist on speaking English to their children. Ruth Contreraz remembered her frustrations as a child trying to learn English in school. "I thought, darn it, when I get married and have children I'm going to talk to them in English. I love my culture, and I'll teach my kids anything to do with my Mexican culture, but English is the important language now. I didn't want my kids to go through that." Families were forced to choose between their language and their children's success. When her older brother failed the first grade because he could not speak English, Esther Peralez's parents resolved to do "whatever we have to do to get you through school," and they "spoke in Spanish, and we spoke in English." Peralez noted that Billings is unusual because so many Chicanos understand Spanish but cannot speak it. "It's sad, but that was the tradeoff in order to survive in these schools." The Yellowstone Mexican-American experience illustrates the dilemma of cultural pluralism in the United States, where "either/or" demands to assimilate to avoid discrimination and enjoy equal opportunity often impede the formation of dynamic ethnic cultures that can play an equal and beneficial role in society.

Economic and educational success eluded many resident Latinos. Augie Lopez, who became Billings' first counselor for Latino students in 1973, found an "astronomical" dropout rate because of a hostile school environment and poverty. But increased bilingual instruction dramatically improved conditions and the retention rate. In 1980, concerned Latinos initiated the Eastern Montana College Hispanic Student Scholarship Fund Board to increase Chicano college enrollment. Esther Peralez, a counselor at Eastern Montana College, lamented that still too few Chicano youth were graduating to college, but since the 1980s area educators have begun to link educational progress to positive ethnic identity and have worked to improve cultural sensitivity. In 1990, Latinos comprised almost half of Garfield School's students, and their parents actively participated in school

A worker checks sugar beets being loaded for processing at the Great Western Sugar plant.
BILL BROWNING (MONTANA CHAMBER OF COMMERCE), COURTESY MONTANA HISTORICAL SOCIETY, HELENA,
PAC 97-61, BOX 3, POWER I-2-B-1149.

activities to foster cultural awareness. At an annual teacher-apprecia-
tion day, for example, they present homemade tortillas and Mexican
paper flowers.

Mexican-American school populations increased in Billings because economic changes made the Latino community more urban
rather than rural. Beginning in the 1950s, when agriculture became
more mechanized and some discriminatory barriers in urban employment lifted, the state's Latinos began moving to Billings. In 1950,
thirty-one percent of Montana's Mexican-born population resided in
urban areas; by 1960, sixty percent lived in cities. By 1980, only two
percent of Yellowstone County's Hispanic residents were involved
in agriculture. This shift in employment patterns reflected general
trends in the Northwest region, as Latino immigrants "settled out"
and moved to larger towns and cities for jobs and the comforts of an
established ethnic community.

The mechanization of the beet industry substantially reduced immigration to Montana. Sal Briceno noted, "We have very few people that come in here now to work beets. Most of it's mechanical now." Merle Riggs, former labor recruiter and agricultural manager for the Billings plant, explained that herbicides greatly reduced the need for hand labor, and allowed "workers that came up here to perform more acres per day." A severe wild oats infestation in the 1950s and 1960s prompted Billings area growers to apply chemicals before other states because they did not have alternative crops to grow. By 1976, an era had ended, when the Great Western Company stopped furnishing transportation for migrant workers, transferring the burden to individual growers and migrant laborers.

In addition to the declining need for farmworkers, declining blue-collar work opportunities discouraged Latinos from settling in the valley. Railroad and packing plant jobs have disappeared, and as Robert Rivera noted, "There was just hundreds of Mexicans working at those [packing] plants, so when those plants shut down, by golly that put a hardship on this town." Esther Rivera agreed that a vital economy was essential to a flourishing Latino community. "A lot of your people have gone and settled elsewhere, and stayed away. Like my aunt and uncle left. We lost a lot of people in our Hispanic community because of the economy, because they will go where the work is."

Despite farm mechanization, beet growers still depend on hand labor. Every spring, about 6,000 migrant farmworkers—mostly Mexican Americans from the Rio Grande Valley of Texas—come to the Yellowstone to work, following a migrant route that takes them on to Oregon to top and bag onions, to Washington to pick apples, and to Minnesota to harvest beans before returning to Texas in late fall. Successful farmworker organizing during the 1960s and 1970s, however, provided families with benefits not available to their predecessors. In 1972, for example, the Montana Migrant Council was established to provide labor, health, housing, and educational assistance to migrant families. Many Yellowstone Mexican Americans, who retained ties with families from Texas, often worked with federal migrant programs. Parishioners at Our Lady of Guadalupe Church have also extended aid to farmworker families, helping newcomers find housing, farm employment, and food. Ruth Contreraz noted, "The Mexicans that were settled already in the Hispanic community were helping the migrants that were coming in . . . because a lot of them knew what it was like to be a fieldworker."

Despite the migrants' importance to the area economy, many Montanans refuse to acknowledge that migrant farmworkers have permanent connections to this place, even though Mexican-American families return year after year to the same area farms. The term "migrant" is a misleading title for many Latino families who loyally return to the valley each spring. Just as many Montana "snowbirds" annually escape winter's icy grip for the warmer Southwest, many Texans routinely join the "migrant stream" to thin beets each cool Montana spring. Some, such as Juan Montes, have been migrant farmworkers for several decades and have not realized their dream for more settled employment or a "piece of land" to farm. Others, who consider Texas their home, continue to work beets during the summer to supplement family incomes. Mario Iracheta, a Texas construction worker, has come to the Yellowstone to work beets since 1952 and has children who were born here.

The persistence of the Yellowstone's Latino community is distinct in the Northwest and Rocky Mountain West. The Hispanic population in Colorado and Idaho, for example, has grown dramatically in the last few decades, but Montana's has remained relatively stable and constant with the rest of the state's population. Scant economic opportunities draw fewer working immigrants to the Big Sky Country, and declining infusions of Spanish-speaking immigrants challenge the established second- and third-generation Billings community to retain links with their ethnic heritage. Yet Latinos young and old in the Yellowstone continue to find meaning in family reunions, traditional celebrations, religious observances, and other social, cultural, and political activities. Like their predecessors, third- and fourth-generation Mexican Americans continue to honor their history and reshape their cultural identity.

The Latinos who moved north to the Yellowstone Valley have left a vital legacy to the area's heritage. The region's agricultural prosperity, according to one former migrant, depended on the essential labor of

Latino farmworkers. "If it hadn't been for the Mexicans, the farmers wouldn't have succeeded." Besides their crucial economic role, Mexican Americans have contributed an enduring ethnic community and enriched the Yellowstone's culture.

Resources on Montana's and the Yellowstone's Mexican-American communities are few. This essay relies to a great extent on the reminiscences of Yellowstone Valley Latino residents. In providing a sense of the past and information on elusive topics such as ethnic identity, oral history interviews are a crucial source of information about people in the twentieth century. Interviewers Linda Lee Hickey, Laurie Mercier, Lynda Moss, Nancy Olson, and Wanda Walker interviewed Sal Briceno, Maria Cantu, Liz Castro, Ruth Contreraz, Ynes Contreraz, Robert Federico, Dora Cantu Flannigan, Esther Peralez, Don Pippin, Merle Riggs, Esther Rivera, and Robert Rivera as part of the Yellowstone Sugar Beet Oral History Project. The project was funded by the American Association of State and Local History and Western Sugar Company, Tate & Lyle, Ltd. The tape-recorded interviews and transcripts are preserved in the Western Heritage Center's archives. An interview with Santos Carranza of Sidney, by Laurie Mercier, is deposited with the Montana Historical Society archives. Also critical to understanding the historical role of Latino beet workers, or betabeleros, were the annual reports of the Billings Sugar Factory and Great Western Sugar Company, produced by factory managers for the years 1917-1950. These records are also deposited with the Western Heritage Center. Clippings and pamphlets in the vertical files of the Billings Public Library, typescripts and reports in the vertical files of the Montana Historical Society library, and articles on the Yellowstone Hispanic community in the *Billings Gazette* (appearing more frequently after 1976) also significantly aided research.

The researcher using census records to estimate Latino populations must use caution. Early classifiers branded Mexican people as a "race," ignoring the diversity found within Mexico and the U.S. origins of many Mexican Americans. Official definitions shifted over time, reflected in the confusing Bureau of Census demarcations that range from a racial category, "Mexicans," in 1930, to a more ambiguous language identity, "Hispanic," in 1990. Since 1970, the census came closer to acknowledging ethnic identity by classifying Spanish-language residents, which included second- and third-generation Mexican Americans, in addition to those born in Mexico. Only seven percent of Montana's Hispanic residents in 1970 and 1980 were foreign born, and close to half were born in Montana, indicating the stability and slow growth of the community. As late as 1990, Montana's 12,000 Hispanics accounted for just two percent of the entire state population. Census records, however, notoriously undercount Latinos and often do not include those who identify with the culture but do not consider Spanish their primary language. This particularly applies to Montana and the Yellowstone, where Spanish is more selectively spoken.

The selected bibliography below indicates the paucity of materials on Latino communities in Montana and the Yellowstone, but these sources will assist those interested in further research. The author extends special thanks to Emily Witcher, Lynda Moss, Wanda Walker, and Dave Walter for their assistance in locating materials, to Esther Rivera for reviewing the manuscript and offering her suggestions, and to the narrators who volunteered their recollections for the WHC oral history project.

—꿈—

This essay originally appeared in *Stories from an Open Country: Essays on the Yellowstone River Valley,* University of Washington Press, 1995.

Laurie Mercier is the Claudius and Mary W. Johnson Professor of History at Washington State University Vancouver (WSUV). Her research explores the intersection of class, race, gender, work, and region, and her recent publications include Speaking History: The American Past through Oral Histories, 1865-2001, *with Sue Armitage (2010);* Mining Women: Gender in the Development of a Global Industry, 1670-2000, *with Jaclyn Gier (2006 and 2009); and* Anaconda: Labor, Community, and Culture in Montana's Smelter City *(2001), which won the Mining History Association's biennial Clark Spence Award for Best Book on Mining History in 2003. She is former associate director of the Center for Columbia River History, a former president of the Oral History Association, former codirector of the*

WSUV Center for Social and Environmental Justice, and codirector of the Columbia River Basin Ethnic History Archive project. From 1981 to 1988, she served as oral historian for the Montana Historical Society.

—⟋⟍⟋⟍—

SELECTED BIBLIOGRAPHY

Adams, Helen D. "History of the South Park Neighborhood." South Park Neighborhood Task Force and Billings-Yellowstone City-County Planning Board, 1978. Pamphlet file, Billings History, Billings Public Library.

Cardoso, Lawrence A. *Mexican Emigration to the U.S., 1897-1931.* Tucson: University of Arizona Press, 1980.

Devitt, Steve. "We Montanans: The Billings Hispanic Community." *Montana Magazine* (September 1987), 6-13.

Gamboa, Erasmo. *Mexican Labor & World War II: Braceros in the Pacific Northwest, 1942-1947.* Austin, University of Texas Press, 1990.

Gutierrez, Robert F. "The Montana Migrant Workers." Typescript, 1982. Vertical file, Montana Historical Society (MHS) Library.

Hispanic Task Force. *Hispanics in Montana: Report to the 47th Montana Legislative Assembly.* Montana Department of Community Affairs, 1980. Vertical file, MHS Library.

Holterman, Jack. "Californios in Far Montana." Unpublished manuscript, 1980. SC 1653, MHS Archives.

Reisler, Mark. *By the Sweat of Their Brow: Mexican Immigrant Labor in the U.S., 1900-1940.* Westport, Connecticut, Greenwood Press, 1976.

Rural Employment Opportunities. Migrant Oral History Project. Interviews by Patricia Nelson. OH 634, MHS Archives.

Slatta, Richard W. "Chicanos in the Pacific Northwest." *Pacific Northwest Quarterly* (October 1979): 155-162.

Spomer, Pete. "History of Sugar Beets." Big Horn County Historical Society Newsletter, n.d. Vertical file, WHC.

George 'Montana' Oiye:
The Journey of a Japanese American
from the Big Sky to the Battlefields of Europe

— *Casey J. Pallister*

Japanese immigrants began arriving in Montana in the 1890s, often recruited by railroad companies such as the Great Northern that were looking for section hands to maintain the new lines constructed across Montana. By 1900, there were 2,441 Japanese living in the Treasure State. The so-called Gentlemen's Agreement of 1907-1908 between the Theodore Roosevelt administration and the government of Japan blocked any further emigration of Japanese laborers into the United States. However, Japanese workers legally residing in the United States could bring their wives to America (many of these women would become known as "picture brides")—at least until 1924, when the National Origins Quota Act essentially halted all immigration from Asia. Because of the inflow of Japanese women up to 1924, Japanese married couples in Montana and elsewhere were able to produce a second generation of Japanese Americans, those known as Nisei.

As the following essay by Casey Pallister makes clear, growing up in Montana was not always easy for the Nisei, or for their parents. Conditions became especially difficult after December 7, 1941. Although Japanese Americans living in Montana were not subject to Executive Order 9066—the order issued by President Franklin

Roosevelt on February 19, 1942, that forced over 110,000 Japanese Americans living on the West Coast, more than two-thirds of whom were American citizens, into quickly constructed concentration camps known as "Relocation Centers"—they were nonetheless confronted with angry stares, racist comments, and, in certain instances, loss of employment.

Confronted with such challenges, an impressive number of young Nesei, including George Oiye of Three Forks, Montana, chose to demonstrate their loyalty by joining the U.S. armed services. Many, including George, became members of the famed 442nd Regimental Combat Team, the most highly decorated unit in the history of the U.S. Army. George Oiye's wartime actions in Europe dramatically illustrate that the definition of what it means to be an American is not determined by one's ethnic background or the color of one's skin, but rather by the strength of one's character and courage under fire.

The Vosges Mountains of France were a gloomy place to be in late October 1944. Tall pine trees and intermittent fog blocked most of the sunlight, while steady, soaking rains muddied the terrain and brought a lasting chill to the air. For the soldiers fighting in the region, dry feet seemed a luxury long forgotten. But for a young staff sergeant and his squad from the 442nd Regimental Combat Team, there were more important things to worry about than the climate: German artillery and more than 13,000 infantrymen were entrenched in the mountains, where, ironically, even the giant pines could be a formidable danger. When hit by German artillery, both tree and shell could explode into a lethal shower of metal and wood.[1]

As the 442nd patrol came within range of the enemy, the staff sergeant brought his men to a halt, awaiting orders from the company commander. It was then he noticed the German tank, moving away over a ridge, the barrel of its gun fixed directly on the patrol. There was no time to react, no time to take cover. In a blinding flash, the 88-millimeter shell tore into the tree next to where the American soldiers stood.[2]

In the fall of 1944, a young soldier from Montana was fighting for his country in Europe. What made George Oiye different than most was his Japanese ancestry and membership in the 442ⁿᵈ Regimental Combat Team, authorized by President Franklin Roosevelt to provide a way for Japanese Americans to join the armed forces. Here, infantrymen of the 442ⁿᵈ hike a muddy road in the Chambois sector of France in late 1944.
COURTESY ARMY CENTER FOR MILITARY HISTORY.

Staff Sergeant George Oiye was lucky that day. As he watched in astonishment, the German shell struck the tree, whizzed harmlessly down its trunk, and spun in place on the ground. Then it lay still. An explosion would surely have killed him and his men, but miraculously, no one was hurt. The twenty-two-year-old from Montana would continue to fight for his country until the war's end.

George served in Italy, France, and Germany, and during his time as a soldier, he liberated towns, stormed enemy positions, and captured prisoners, narrowly escaping death many times. Still, as dramatic as they are, these experiences are hardly unusual in the annals of World War II. Millions of military personnel served during the war; learning about their stories helps broaden our understanding of the war while fleshing out the image of the "American soldier." But what exactly is that image? Readers might assume that George Oiye and his men were Caucasian. The Allied heroes of World War II are seldom portrayed otherwise. In this case, however, the soldiers of the 442nd were Nisei, second-generation Americans of Japanese ancestry. In segregated units, these men fought with a vigor that gained the 442nd a reputation as an elite American fighting force. Collectively, the Nisei soldiers of the 442nd earned more decorations for its size and length of service than any other fighting unit in American history.[3]

George Oiye, who had grown up near Three Forks, Montana, in the 1920s and 1930s, was one of those Nisei.

Although a few Japanese immigrants began arriving in the United States in the 1870s, it was not until the 1880s, when railroads began looking for a new labor force after the passage of the Chinese Exclusion Act of

Even though they were deemed by the federal government to be "enemy aliens," many young Japanese Americans, like other American men and women of their generation, wanted to serve their country during the Second World War. George (above) enlisted in the U.S. Army, then fought in the European theater. COURTESY OIYE FAMILY.

1882, that Japanese immigrants first came to Montana Territory. The Issei (first-generation Japanese Americans) followed the tracks of the Northern Pacific and then the Great Northern railroads eastward from Washington. By 1898, as many as 380 Issei were earning ninety-five cents a day laying track on the Great Northern line between Billings and Tacoma. A few took up small farms. This combination of railroad and agricultural employment opportunities led to a 400 percent increase in Montana's Japanese population between 1890 and 1900: in 1890, the census recorded only 6 Japanese living in Montana, but by 1900, of the 24,326 Japanese living on the U.S. mainland, 2,441 (more than ten percent) resided in the state.[4]

Despite the employment opportunities, life in the Rocky

Mountains proved challenging. Harsh winters were difficult for those raised in the typically temperate climate of Japan, and the short Montana growing season disheartened many Issei who had enjoyed the bountiful harvests of California, Oregon, and Washington. Moreover, Montana had a much higher male-to-female ratio among Japanese residents than its western neighbors (roughly 347 males for every female in 1900). Perhaps the young bachelors who left the state to marry in Japan or on the West Coast found better employment elsewhere and never returned to Montana. Whatever the reason, only 1,585 Japanese remained in the state by 1910.[5]

George Oiye's father, Jengoro Oiye, a farmer from Kyushu, Japan, immigrated to the United States sometime after 1910; in Seattle, immigration officials who found it difficult to pronounce his name listed him as "Thomas" Oiye. The teenager first found work as a vegetable salesman but soon moved on to jobs as a lumberjack, a salmon canner in Alaska, and then a harpoon gunner on a whaling ship. In 1914, having gathered sufficient funds, Tom (as he now preferred to be called) returned to Kyushu to be married to Taka Kimura, the daughter of a sake merchant. As was common among the Japanese, the marriage was prearranged. Within a few months of the ceremony, the couple sailed for Seattle, never to return to Japan.[6]

In Seattle, the Oiyes began to learn English and secured steady employment. Taka opened a rooming house, and Tom started a small fertilizer business, collecting blood from slaughterhouses, drying it, and shipping it to Japan as blood meal. By 1920, they had two little daughters, Peggy and Anita. However, in 1921, a man they would remember as "Mr. Breen" dramatically changed their lives. Although James Breen had sold his mining interests to the Anaconda Copper Mining Company in 1916, he remained the manager of several of the company's mines on the Porphyry Dike along the Continental Divide southwest of Helena, Montana, and he had never abandoned his vision that the Porphyry Dike could be one of the largest gold mines in the world. The smooth-talking Breen convinced the Oiyes to invest in a small mine, the Josephine, on the Porphyry Dike and to move to Montana to work the Josephine and other nearby mines.[7]

In late summer 1921, the Oiye family arrived in Basin, Montana,

George's father, Tom Oiye (left, circa 1917), emigrated from Kyushu, Japan, to Seattle sometime after 1910. He worked a variety of jobs, including as a vegetable salesman, lumberjack, salmon canner in Alaska, and harpoon gunner on a whaling ship. In 1914, Tom returned to Japan to marry Taka Kimura (right, circa 1917). The couple sailed for Seattle within a few months and would never return to Japan.
COURTESY HEADWATERS HERITAGE MESEUM, THREE FORKS.

then proceeded north by wagon to the Porphyry Dike. They established their home in a log cabin along a tributary of Tenmile Creek. It was here, on February 19, 1922, that George Oiye was born.[8]

At the time the Oiyes settled in Montana, the state was in the midst of a deepening economic depression. Drought plagued the state between 1917 and 1925, and some 60,000 people left during the 1920s. Many Japanese were part of that exodus: their numbers dropped from 1,074 in 1920 to 753 in 1930. Those who stuck it out tended to live in closely knit urban communities—usually made up of railroad workers and their families—or, like the Oiyes, in isolated pockets throughout the state.[9]

For two difficult years, Tom worked the mines of the Porphyry Dike. By the time George was two years old, however, his parents realized that their fortune was not to be found along the Continental Divide.[10] In 1924, they moved to Helena and quickly found a home,

In 1936, George began high school in nearby Three Forks, where he was a popular and academically gifted student. COURTESY HEADWATERS HERITAGE MUSEUM, THREE FORKS.

thanks to a fortunate meeting with a local Japanese man who had established a community of stucco-and-tar-paper shacks for Japanese railroad workers along the tracks. Steam was piped in from the roundhouse, to provide heat and hot water. At a time when Japanese Americans were hard pressed to find jobs in the capital city, Tom secured work at the roundhouse, where he spent his days in the pits beneath the locomotives, shoveling mounds of hot ashes. George only rarely visited his father on the job because the noise, steam, and raining ash frightened the child (he recalled a visit to the pits as an experience "not unlike Hell").[11]

The roundhouse job proved too hazardous for a family man. In 1926, the Oiye family, which now included baby Ben, moved to the small town of Trident near the Three Forks of the Missouri River, and Tom found work at the Three Forks Portland Cement Company's cement plant. He worked in the "pack house," where he cleaned, repaired, and filled cement sacks. The job was stable and offered the chance for promotion but was not without its shortcomings. The cement plant was hot and the dust so thick that he returned home each day with reddened eyes and face covered with powdered cement.[12]

The young Oiyes—Peggy, Anita, George, and Ben—attended grammar school in the two-room Trident schoolhouse that stood on the banks of the Missouri. When they were out of class, they spent most of their time by the river, swimming, fishing, or ice skating. "We never lacked anything to do," a playmate of Peggy Oiye's, Georgie Olsen Wellhouser, remembered. She and other children frequently visited the Oiye house. Taka Oiye "was always doing something for us or helping us with something," Wellhouser recalled. Sometimes she

While George was in high school, the family purchased a twenty-three-acre farm along the Gallatin River near Logan. In 1923, Montana had passed legislation that forbade "aliens" ineligible for citizenship from owning land, so the Oiyes bought their farm in George's name, since he was the eldest son and a native-born American citizen.
COURTESY HEADWATERS HERITAGE MUSEUM, THREE FORKS.

would let the local girls dress up in her traditional Japanese clothes; she also gave them lessons in origami. The Oiyes were well thought of in their community of some 200. Taka formed close friendships with many of the women of the community, and Tom earned the respect of the men at the plant. He was quiet and soft spoken but kind and generous, "a good neighbor and a good friend," recalled James Nelson Jr., whom Tom supervised in the pack house.[13]

The Oiye children also prospered in Trident. In 1936, George began high school in the nearby town of Three Forks. In high school, as in grammar school, George was popular and excelled academically. He was cocaptain of the six-man football team and the starting quarterback for the 1939 squad that captured the division title with an undefeated record. He developed a strong work ethic, both in and out of the classroom, and learned the importance of helping one's neighbors. In most ways, George and his siblings, despite their Japanese heritage, were raised no differently than any of the Caucasian children with whom they had grown up. Each of the Oiye children, as Georgie Wellhouser explained, was "just one of the kids."[14]

Even so, George was well aware that he and his siblings were different. As a child in Helena, he was called "funny names" by the local children. Later, George tried to distance himself from his roots by refusing to eat traditional Japanese foods, to adhere to any Japanese customs, or to learn his parents' native language. Though he developed a close relationship with the children of the Itoh family who lived in Three Forks, he kept that friendship private, fearing he would be ridiculed.[15]

During George's high school years, the Oiyes relocated to nearby Logan and put a $250 down payment on a twenty-three-acre vegetable farm along the Gallatin River. Tom stayed on at the Trident factory even while working the farm, and George continued to attend the high school in Three Forks. He dreamed of studying mining at the Montana School of Mines in Butte, but despite his good grades, could not afford the tuition. After high school graduation, he spent a year working on the family farm to earn the $65 he would need to cover the first year's tuition and books at Montana State College in Bozeman. During this year, he gave his free hours to fishing and hunting and became proficient with a rifle, a skill that would serve him well in the future.[16]

In the fall of 1941, George enrolled at Montana State. He quickly joined the school's chapter of the American Society of Mechanical Engineers and the Reserve Officers Training Corps (ROTC) and became captain of the school's rifle team. Though the friends with whom he shared a basement apartment ran out of money after one semester and dropped out of school, George found assistance through the National Youth Administration. Working odd jobs for fifteen cents an hour, he managed to make ends meet.[17]

George's life and that of other Japanese Americans changed dramatically when Japanese aircraft bombed the American fleet at Pearl Harbor, Hawai'i, early on the morning of December 7, 1941. Because of their ancestry and their physical resemblance to the enemy, Japanese Americans were declared "enemy aliens" and prohibited from joining

When the Japanese attacked Pearl Harbor on December 7, 1941, many people immediately viewed Japanese Americans with suspicion. George's eldest sister Peggy was removed from her Los Angeles home and interned at California's Manzanar Relocation Center, shown here in 1943. ANSEL ADAMS, COURTESY LIBRARY OF CONGRESS, LC-A35-6-M-1.

the U.S. military. On February 19, 1942, President Franklin Roosevelt issued Executive Order 9066 that mandated Japanese Americans be evacuated from their homes on the West Coast and relocated to internment camps in the interior.[18]

As residents of a landlocked state far from potential invasion sites, Japanese Americans in Montana were exempt from Executive Order 9066, but they still felt the sting of the anti-Japanese sentiment that quickly spread across the country. In Superior, Montana, an angry mob nearly lynched five Japanese-American railroad workers before the local sheriff placed them under protective custody. Employees of the Milwaukee Road shop in Miles City refused to work until six Japanese-American coworkers were sent home. In Whitefish, business owners adopted a pair of resolutions that called for the firing of Japanese railroad workers and the circulation of a petition to prevent the hiring of Japanese in the area. Japanese-American businesses throughout the state were boycotted, vandalized, or, as was the case in Plentywood, run out of town.[19]

The Oiye family personally felt the repercussions of Pearl Harbor. Tom was forced to quit his job at the Trident plant. James Nelson Jr., who was working with Tom in the pack house at the time, recalled the incident: "Trident was a cement plant and the cement industry was, after a while, declared a war industry, and this was when they started cracking down. . . . They told Tommy he had to quit. . . . I didn't think it was right, and a lot of people down there at the cement plant didn't think it was right, but when Uncle Sam says he had to go, then he had to go." After losing his job, Tom devoted his energy to the vegetable farm, which, luckily, provided sufficient income to support the family. One day, however, the farm caught the attention of a pilot flying over who saw "strange patterns" in the plowed fields. The pilot alerted the FBI, and Tom was briefly jailed due to the accusation of sending messages to the "homeland."[20]

In Bozeman, George tried several times to join the armed forces but was repeatedly refused. In 1943, however, President Roosevelt rescinded the ban against accepting Nisei men into the military.[21] Through the intercession of two professors, Gerry Pesman and Fred Homan, both of whom were of German descent and had faced discrimination during World War I, George was allowed to join the U.S. Army. First, though, he had to provide letters of commendation from five prominent citizens and pass a physical.[22]

Shortly after his induction, George shipped off to basic training. At Camp Shelby, outside Hattiesburg, Mississippi, the new recruit entered a very different world—there were Japanese Americans everywhere, more than he had ever seen in his life. These men were to be part of a special Nisei combat unit—the 442nd Regimental Combat Team—made up of 3,500 Nisei, nearly three-fourths of them from Hawai'i.[23]

Nicknamed "Montana," George rose quickly in rank because of his ROTC training. Although he hoped for an appointment with the 442nd's Engineer Company, he was assigned to its field artillery battalion, the 522nd, whose primary duty was to provide artillery support, through the use of 105-millimeter howitzers, to the infantrymen of the 442nd. Training lasted more than a year. Finally, on May 2, 1944, the 442nd sailed to Europe in a convoy of over fifty ships. Twenty-six days later, "Montana" Oiye and his comrades landed at Bari on Italy's eastern coast, then headed to the front as a part of General Mark Clark's Fifth Army.[24]

In northern Italy, the men of the 522nd quickly proved their expertise in detonating "air bursts"—shells that exploded over their targets, blanketing them with shrapnel. In an attack on Hill 140, a single, well-placed barrage killed more than 100 Germans. When the fighting stalled at the Arno River near Florence, the 442nd pulled back to Naples, and on September 27, 1944, the combat team, including George Oiye, departed for France, to join the 36th ("Texas") Division of the Seventh Army.[25]

By September of 1944, the Seventh Army was steadily advancing up the Rhone Valley toward the last natural border between France and Germany, the rolling hills and dense forests of the Vosges Mountains, where more than 13,000 German infantrymen prepared for battle under Adolf Hitler's orders to hold the region at all costs. Never in history had an army defending the Vosges been beaten.[26]

As the 442nd pushed toward the Vosges, it liberated the town of Bruyères, a crucial transportation center. Here George was selected

For his "cool efficiency" and bravery under fire, the U.S. Army awarded George Oiye, third from right, the Bronze Star. COURTESY OIYE FAMILY.

to accompany a forward observation crew to locate targets for the howitzers and radio the coordinates back to the waiting artillerymen of Company K. The task proved dangerous, as the men fought from house to house with small arms and grenades, but George, with another forward observer, managed to establish an observation post in an old hotel. From there, they directed artillery fire on Hill D, the last major German stronghold near Bruyères.[27]

The hill taken, and both city and countryside now in Allied hands, George returned to battery headquarters "cold, wet, hungry, and pooped" only to be assigned as a forward observer for a mission to rescue a portion of the 141st Infantry Regiment surrounded by German forces east of Bruyères. German captives reported that Hitler had ordered that none of the men in this "Lost Battalion" be taken prisoner. It was up to the Nisei to break through the German lines.[28]

George Oiye and a party of three others set out on reconnaissance, again in support of Company K, marching through the rain. Upon reaching the forest, George and his men followed orders to "dig a foxhole and wait for daylight." It was then that he heard a strange voice. "John, is that you?" he asked his radio operator. The "no" sent chills through his body. Then he heard the voice again. "Comrade, comrade," the German pleaded. Feeling around in the dark, George found the man, who was holding a white handkerchief to indicate his surrender. After escorting his prisoner back to the command post, George returned to the line.[29]

On October 29, General John Dahlquist, the commander of the 36th Division, sent orders to the 442nd to launch an attack the next morning on the one hill that still separated the men from the Lost Battalion. Their officers were to "keep [the Nisei] going and . . . [not] let them stop" until they took the hill. George knew the fight to capture "Banzai Hill" was going to be brutal when he heard the order to fix bayonets. And brutal it was. The well-fortified Germans reduced Company K to seventeen riflemen, plus George and his three men. Other units sustained similar numbers of casualties. By sunset on October 30, the 442nd was reduced to half its strength; in the end, the 442nd suffered more than 800 casualties in rescuing the 211 survivors of the Lost Battalion. George Oiye's "cool efficiency" under fire won him a Bronze Star for bravery.[30]

After the bitter fighting in the Vosges, the men of the 442nd took on the less strenuous duty of guarding the Franco-Italian border along a twelve-mile stretch of the Italian Riviera. In March 1945, however, General Mark Clark of the Fifth Army and General Alexander Patch of the Seventh both requested the support of the hard-fighting 442nd. As a compromise, the 522nd was assigned to Patch, and the remainder of the 442nd to Clark. The 442nd returned to Italy to assault the Gothic Line while George and his fellow artillerymen turned north toward Germany.[31]

Moving fast, the men of the 522nd crossed the German border on March 12 and received assignments to several different units as the Allies pushed deeper into enemy territory. In late March, the 522nd assisted the 45th Division's crossing of the Rhine River near Worms. Even though the Germans were retreating, they were not giving up

Crossing into Germany in 1945, George and battery commander Gus Ratcliffe were patrolling for enemy hideouts when they discovered and captured seventeen German soldiers, partly shown here, and marched them back to headquarters.
GEORGE OIYE, COURTESY OIYE FAMILY.

the fight. While in the area, George and three other soldiers were sent on patrol in search of enemy holdouts. George and the battery commander, Gus Ratcliffe, split from the other two and proceeded up a draw until they came upon what appeared to be a hunting lodge. There they captured seventeen Germans and delivered them safely back to headquarters. Also near Worms, George was strafed by a low-flying fighter plane, was nearly killed by a stray 20-millimeter shell, and was riding in a Jeep when it was hit by a 155-millimeter dud. Still, he survived, crossing the Danube River on April 26, 1945, then proceeding southeast toward Munich with the 522nd.[32]

As German lines broke, scouting parties from the 522nd branched out in all directions in search of any remaining enemy soldiers. In early May 1945, while on patrol, George and several other soldiers discovered lumps in the snow that turned out to be the emaciated bodies of over 100 people clothed in striped prison uniforms, former

During the Vosges campaign, the 442nd, sent to rescue a portion of the surrounded 141st Infantry that became known as the "Lost Battalion," faced the fiercest fighting they had ever seen. The Nisei suffered more than 800 casualties to rescue the 211 survivors of the Lost Battalion. Here the remaining men of the 442nd stand at attention while their citations for bravery are read. COURTESY ARMY CENTER FOR MILITARY HISTORY.

inmates of a sub-camp of the Dachau concentration camp. Although some of the prisoners had already died, George and the others offered the survivors what little food they had. With a Kodak camera he had "liberated" from a German officer, George documented the scene— and was strangely overcome by a sense of his own personal guilt; he felt ashamed to be human.[33]

Germany surrendered on May 8, 1945, and late that fall a portion of the 522nd, including "Montana" Oiye, left Europe, arriving in New York Harbor on New Year's Day, 1946. After being mustered out of the army at Camp Kilmer, New Jersey, on January 4, 1946, George made his way back to Montana. He returned to school, hoping to pick up where he had left off in 1943. However, like many veterans, he found it difficult to readjust to civilian life. Alone in his tiny basement apartment, he suffered flashbacks, often hearing screams or shell bursts. Studying became virtually impossible, and George dropped out of school. He worked as a farmer and railroad hand and spent a lot of time hunting and fishing. Gradually his mind eased and he was able to move on with his life. Even after the war, however, there were many Americans who held on to their dislike of Japanese Americans. George Oiye remembered facing the humiliation of police questioning after he asked to use the phone at a gas station because, to the female employee, he "seemed suspicious."[34]

George left Montana in 1947 and spent a brief time in Arizona before moving on to California. After graduating from the California Aero Tech Institute in Glendale, he entered the aeronautics field. In 1951, he married Mary Sumie Toyoda, with whom he raised two children, Thomas and Nancy. Surviving stomach cancer in the 1970s, he continued his work in the aeronautics industry, and later in the high-tech fields of aerospace and laser engineering. For a few weeks every summer he returned to his old home at the Missouri headwaters, where he enjoyed the company of many of his childhood friends. It was "the salmon's instinct," he said, that drew him back there each year.[35]

In an interview conducted before his death in 2006, George modestly claimed that his proudest achievement in life was "just having been able to make it this far." When he looked back on his experiences with the 442nd, "Montana" Oiye felt that his military service brought him to embrace the ancestry that he had earlier shunned: "If I hadn't been in an all Japanese-American unit, nobody would have known me but Montanans." His service also taught George about being an American. He realized in adulthood that it depended not on race or culture but on love of country.[36]

This essay originally appeared in *Montana, The Magazine of Western History,* Autumn 2007.

Casey J. Pallister was a magna cum laude graduate of the History program at Carroll College. After teaching English for two years in Japan, he earned a Master of Arts in Asian Studies from the University of Oregon, a Master of Arts in History from Northwestern University, and a Master of Education from Montana State University. He currently lives in Sisters, Oregon, with his wife and four sons, where he teaches U.S. and East Asian history at Sisters Middle School.

NOTES

1 Thelma Chang, *I Can Never Forget: Men of the 100th/442ⁿᵈ* (Honolulu, 1994), p. 26; George Oiye, interview by author, San Jose, California, June 26, 2002.

2 Oiye interview.

3 Paul R. Spickard, *Japanese Americans: The Formation and Transformations of an Ethnic Group* (New York, 1996), p. 122.

4 Bill Hosokawa, *Nisei: The Quiet Americans* (New York, 1969), p. 68; Michael P. Malone, Richard B. Roeder, and William L. Lang, *Montana: A History of Two Centuries,* rev. ed. (Seattle, 1991), p. 184; Robert Wilson and Bill Hosokawa, *East to America: A History of the Japanese in the United States* (New York, 1980), p. 68; U.S. Department of the Interior, Bureau of the Census, *Report on the Population of the United States at the Eleventh Census: 1890,* pt. 1, p. 397; U.S. Department of the Interior, Bureau of the Census, *Twelfth Census of the United States Taken in the Year 1900: Census Reports Vol. I: Population,* pt. 1, p. cxxii.

5 U.S. Department of the Interior, *Twelfth Census,* p. 492; U.S. Department of Commerce, Bureau of the Census, *Thirteenth Census of the United States: 1910 Vol. 2: Population 1910: Reports by States, with Statistics for Counties, Cities, and Other Civil Divisions: Alabama-Montana,* p. 1147. California, Oregon, and Washington had between seventeen and thirty males for every female, and even Idaho's ratio was half that of Montana's.

6 Oiye interview.

7 Ibid.; "James Breen Dead," *Helena (Mont.) Independent*, August 12, 1925, pp. 1-2, copy in James Breen folder, Vertical Files, Montana Historical Society Research Center, Helena (hereafter MHS); Edwin A. Mohler, *Cultural Features Found at the Paupers Dream Mine Project Site, Lewis & Clark and Jefferson Counties, Montana* (Helena, Mont., 1987), pp. 1-3. Breen owned and frequented hotels in cities throughout the Pacific Northwest, including Seattle, which may have been how he came into contact with the Oiyes.

8 George Oiye, "The Headwaters Heritage, 1997–1998," p. 1, George Oiye Exhibit, Headwaters Heritage Museum, Three Forks, Montana.

9 Malone, Roeder, and Lang, *Montana*, pp. 280-284; U.S. Department of Commerce, Census Bureau, *Fifteenth Census of the United States: 1930 Vol. 3: Population: Reports by States Showing the Composition of the Population for Counties, Cities, and Township or Other Minor Civil Divisions: Montana-Wyoming*, pt. 2, p. 7.

10 Because of lack of water near the Porphyry Dike mines, little ore could be processed on-site, and plans to construct a rail line to ship the ore to offsite mills were hindered by lack of money and the difficult terrain. Breen died in 1925, and repeated reports of water pollution caused the Anaconda Company to cease operations at the Porphyry Dike the following year. Mohler, *Cultural Features*, pp. 1-3; "James Breen Dead," pp. 1-2.

11 Oiye, "Headwaters Heritage," p. 1. A roundhouse is a collection of large bays, shops, or garages forming a semicircle designed to hold a train engine needing repair or maintenance. In the roundhouse yard, a small section of the tracks intersected on a turntable. When a locomotive needed some work, it would drive to a turntable in the roundhouse yard where the tracks on which the engine sat would rotate, lining up the engine to the appropriate garage.

12 Ibid.; Oiye interview.

13 Georgie Oslen Wellhouser, interview by Penelope Lucas, Manhattan, Montana, May 12, 1983, tape recording, Oral History 531, MHS; James Nelson Jr., interview by Penelope Lucas, Helena, Montana, May 24, 1983, tape recording, Oral History 538, ibid. Taka Oiye's command of English was reportedly impressive, and she later acted as an interpreter and tutor for Japanese living in Montana.

14 Wellhouser interview.

15 Oiye, "Headwaters Heritage," p. 2; Oiye interview.

16 George Oiye, e-mail to author, February 20, 2003; Oiye interview. After the

passage of California's Alien Land Act, which forbade "aliens ineligible to citizenship" from owning land, thirteen other states, including Montana, in 1923, passed similar legislation. As a result, when the Oiyes bought their farm near Logan, it was purchased under George's name, since he was the eldest son and a native-born citizen. Roger Daniels, *Asian America: Chinese and Japanese in the United States since 1850* (Seattle, 1988), p. 139; Son B. Nguyen, "Testing the 'Melting Pot': The Anti-Japanese Movement in Montana, 1907–1924" (History Research Seminar paper, Carroll College, Helena, Montana, 1990), pp. 9-16; Oiye interview.

17   Oiye interview; Oiye, "Headwaters Heritage," p. 8.

18   Wilson and Hosokawa, *East to America*, pp. 189-190, 194.

19   Nguyen, "Testing the 'Melting Pot,'" pp. 9-16; Kevin C. McCann, "Japanese Americans in Montana: A History of Their Presence and Treatment before, during, and after World War II" (undergraduate honors thesis, Carroll College, Helena, Montana, 1982), pp. 21-23. Even though the war acted as a catalyst for discrimination against Japanese Americans in Montana, this discrimination was not new. In 1908, violent attacks on Japanese railroad workers by a group of masked men were reported in Judith Gap. The following year, the state passed an anti-miscegenation bill, forbidding Caucasians to marry those of different races and declaring that marriages "between a White person and a Japanese Person shall be utterly Null and Void." Nguyen, "Testing the 'Melting Pot,'" pp. 9-16.

20   Oiye interview; Nelson interview. Peggy, the oldest Oiye daughter, who was living in Los Angeles at the time of the attack on Pearl Harbor, was eventually interned at California's Manzanar Relocation Center.

21   On February 1, 1943, in announcing the formation of the 442nd Regimental Combat Team, Franklin Roosevelt observed, "Americanism is not, and never was, a matter of race or ancestry." Daniels, *Asian America*, p. 250.

22   Oiye interview. A few Japanese-American guardsmen became translators and interrogators in the Pacific for the Military Intelligence Service even before 1943, and the military kept some National Guardsmen from Hawai'i in uniform after Pearl Harbor but sent them to the mainland, where they trained until 1943.

23   Ibid.; Daniels, *Asian America*, p. 252; Chang, *I Can Never Forget*, pp. 112-113. George, like many mainlanders, had a difficult time getting along with the Hawaiian Nisei. The islanders spoke a pidgin language, combining English, Japanese, and Hawai'ian, that was incomprehensible to mainland Nisei. In addition, they were more likely to understand and follow Japanese traditions than the men from the continental United States. For this reason, they were dubbed "Buddaheads" by the mainlanders. The

"Buddaheads" labeled the mainlanders "Katonks," claiming that was the sound that would be made when a coconut fell on their empty heads. Oiye interview; Chang, *I Can Never Forget,* pp. 112-113.

[24] Oiye interview; 522nd Field Artillery Battalion Historical Album Committee, *Fire for Effect: A Unit History of the 522nd Field Artillery Battalion* (Honolulu, 1998), pp. 31, 33.

[25] 522nd Field Artillery Battalion Historical Album Committee, *Fire for Effect,* pp. 35-36, 117-18; Masayo Umezawa Duus, *Unlikely Liberators: The Men of the 100th and the 442nd,* trans. Peter Duus (Honolulu, 1987), pp. 159-160.

[26] Lyn Crost, *Honor by Fire: Japanese Americans at War in Europe and the Pacific* (Novato, Calif., 1994), p. 170; Keith Bonn, *When the Odds Were Even: The Vosges Mountains Campaign, October 1944–January 1945* (Novato, Calif., 1994), pp. 28, 77.

[27] Oiye interview; *Charlie Battery: A Legend* (n.p., n.d.), p. 95.

[28] Oiye interview; 522nd Field Artillery Battalion Historical Album Committee, *Fire for Effect,* p. 166; Crost, *Honor by Fire,* p. 185.

[29] Oiye interview.

[30] Ibid.; Crost, *Honor by Fire,* pp. 189, 194-195; 522nd Field Artillery Battalion Historical Album Committee, *Fire for Effect,* p. 167; *Charlie Battery,* p. 108; Hosokawa, *Nisei,* pp. 406, 409.

[31] Crost, *Honor by Fire,* 237.

[32] Oiye interview; Chang, *I Can Never Forget,* p. 163; *Charlie Battery,* p. 108; 522nd Field Artillery Battalion Historical Album Committee, *Fire for Effect,* p. 164.

[33] Oiye interview. During the American occupation, George was briefly the "mayor" of a small German town. One of his primary responsibilities there was to prevent displaced persons, mostly former inmates of concentration camps, from taking revenge on German citizens. However, he found it difficult to stop these violent acts of retribution. For instance, there was little he could do the evening he rushed into a house, drawn by an ungodly scream, to find an entire family murdered. Ibid.

[34] Ibid.

[35] Ibid.; George Oiye, e-mail to author, March 24, 2003; Oiye, "Headwaters Heritage," p. 1.

[36] Oiye interview.

Love, Valor, and Endurance:
World War II War Brides Making a Home in Montana

— Seena B. Kohl

World War II took thousands of young Montanans such as George Oiye overseas for the very first time. A select number of these young men fell in love and married foreign nationals while they were serving abroad. These young women, commonly referred to as war brides, thus became an important—if often overlooked—part of America's larger immigration story. Because they usually came as individuals, and settled in the United States in no particular pattern, they have often, until just recently, escaped the detailed attention of historians specializing in the fields of immigration and ethnic studies.

As suggested by Seena Kohl's interviews with several of these women living in Montana, their decisions to marry American servicemen and move to the United States have to be placed within the context of World War II. The uncertainty of the war years, changing social attitudes, and scarcity of food, clothing, and other daily necessities led people to make decisions that they might not have made otherwise. Despite their willingness to take on such a grand adventure, these newest immigrants to Montana faced daunting challenges. How would they adjust to an environment—and a set of social and cultural practices—so different from their own back in Europe or Australia? Moreover, they would have to make these adjustments while being thousands of miles away from their own parents, grandparents, and siblings. They could not draw upon support from their immediate family members, other than their husbands, in times of loneliness, confusion, or heartache. It is worth noting that several of these women became involved with both formal and informal organizations, including the American Red Cross, the YWCA, and the Overseas War Brides Club, as a way of creating a kind of surrogate family. Such connections were especially important in the early years of transition. Another important step that helped these women integrate into the larger society was by joining the local workforce. In seeking employment in the local community, these war brides could not only augment the family income, but could also begin to establish meaningful relationships with other members of that community.

One of the fastest-growing segments of the American population today is comprised of people who might identify themselves as multi-ethnic, whose parents and grandparents come from a variety of ethnic backgrounds. The experiences and remembrances of World War II war brides remind us that this multiethnic and transnational aspect of contemporary society has a long tradition in Montana history.

Not quite fifteen when World War II began, Joyce Butler of Hampshire, England, went to work for a transistor and battery firm—her contribution to the British war effort. At a canteen run by the U.S. Army, Joyce met a GI from Somers, Montana, Russell DeLong, and a whirlwind courtship followed. The pair received the army's permission to marry just before the Normandy invasion, and when the war was over they made plans to move to Montana. As Joyce recalled, "Most people had not heard of Montana. . . . They said, 'If you are going to Montana they will have cowboys and Indians there . . . and they don't have any water in the house, and you will have to go outside to the toilet.'"[1]

Undeterred, Joyce left for the United States with a nine-month-old baby in February 1945. The trip took two weeks in high seas due to

In February 1945, Joyce DeLong and her nine-month-old baby made the long journey from England to join her GI husband Russell in Somers. Here, in her Somers home in 2002, Joyce displays photographs of herself and Russell on their wedding day and on their fiftieth anniversary. SEENA B. KOHL, COURTESY OF THE AUTHOR.

bad weather. The next step was the train trip west, held up for eighteen hours in a blizzard at Wolf Point, Montana. At the Kalispell train station, Joyce was met by her husband, "who said I was the sorriest looking lady he ever saw. . . . It was some experience. . . . When I first came over I cried myself to sleep every night. I thought, 'Why did I do this?' Now I think I didn't make a mistake. . . . I go back to England and I wouldn't want to live there anymore."[2]

Joyce DeLong's story is representative of those told by many women who married GIs during World War II and moved to Montana. For most of these women, Montana was a truly alien place. They had to adapt to the state's open spaces, sparse population, and harsh climate as well as to new families, communities, ways of speaking, and customs. Doing so in the absence of their families, and often while dependent upon a single person, their husband, who also faced a period of readjustment, called for uncommon abilities to deal with hardship. All managed, albeit not without tears. Heroic on a personal level, the narratives are success stories.

But these individual histories do more than offer stories about building satisfying lives: they illustrate the connections between a person's life decisions and the social context in which they are made. For all of these women, their understanding of gender roles, expectations for marriage, and acclimation to hardship underlay the successful transitions to new lives.

More than any other factor, World War II shaped the lives and outlooks of the war brides who came to Montana. To understand their lives, it is necessary to remember how young these women were when the war began. They were, for the most part, twelve to sixteen years old in 1939, and most had graduated at age fourteen from eighth grade. Prior to the war, they would have entered the workforce, continued in technical programs, or continued their formal educations. All that changed with the onset of war. By 1941, the British government was recruiting young women into female service organizations such as the Civil Defense Women's Volunteer Service, Women's Auxiliary Air Force, and the Women's Land Army and directing them to areas with labor shortages.

When the war started, Evelyn "Chub" Tuss was fourteen years old, living with her family in Diehl, a town on the English Channel twenty-one miles from France. She recalled, "You could see France on a clear day. We were called Hellfire Corner. We were bombed, we were shelled, we were machine-gunned. We had warships coming and shooting shells on the beaches. . . . Dad was in the ambulance [service] and mom was too. . . . But when you were fourteen, everybody had to do a job. . . . We were Civil Defense workers. We all had to wear the . . . tin hats. The fourteen-year-olds used the fire hydrants to [put out the] incendiary bombs. We used to climb the roof and put them out—that was our job."[3]

War experiences differed, of course, but there are commonalities among all the participants: scarcity of food, scarcity of clothes, scarcity of recreational opportunities. Scarcity is a relative concept, but all talked about how they and their families learned to "make do."

The experience of war dramatically shaped young people's lives. As Evelyn "Chub" Tuss recalled, "We were bombed, we were shelled, we were machine-gunned." In the midst of this wartime chaos, Frank Tuss courted his future bride, shown here in a field outside her home in Diehl, England. COURTESY EVELYN "CHUB" TUSS.

A comment from Ruth Batchen, who grew up on the outskirts of Liverpool, illustrates: "We were living pretty much as we were living before except for the air raids, the shortage of food. For instance, two ounces of butter a week per person and two ounces of meat per person to eat, so that was hard on my mother trying to, you know, eke out the meals for four of us. And it was difficult, but, you know, you think you can't get by, but you can."[4]

Elvia Stockton, who grew up in a village outside of Paris, was seventeen when Hitler invaded France. Under German occupation, young girls returned to school and she recalled, "We went because we were allowed some biscuits—a kind of dog-biscuit-shaped thing with vitamins. We went for that . . . and of course, there was a little, how do you say, indoctrination. We were supposed to really obey the law and stuff—no food, no way to open your mouth. I mean you just

After the war, Chub Tuss sailed to the United States on the Italian liner, Vulcania, *and crossed America alone by rail for four days and three nights before arriving in Harlowton, where Frank met her train. Here she relaxes in her Lewistown home in 2003.* SEENA B. KOHL, COURTESY OF THE AUTHOR.

knew that you were under very strong pressure. You had to be very, very careful [about offending the Germans]."[5]

In general, the respondents did not elaborate on their memories of hardship. As Doreen Richard, who lived in West Bromage just outside of Birmingham, said of the air raids, it was "just unbelievable if you think back . . . that you lived through that. More unbelievable to think that you could accept it and cope. You'd go to work one morning and you would see your friends' houses down. You'd see them digging bodies out. It was just unreal. It was like it was a nightmare. . . . But I was a teenager and I got kind of brave. Well, most people did."[6]

Perhaps part of "getting brave" was accepting these horrific childhood experiences as normal. The respondents presented their experiences of wartime hardship as just one part of growing up, which, if not forgotten, was not viewed as a primary factor in who they were.

For the women interviewed, meeting one's husband, marriage, leaving one's family, and coming to the United States defined their lives. Their narratives are love stories, framed around gender and a set of expectations of love and marriage. The war years were a time of far-reaching changes in sexual behavior: there was an increase in venereal disease and illegitimate births, and an increase in rates of divorce as well as marriage. In England, there was also the breakdown of a relatively rigid class system, since everyone worked in the war effort.[7] Further, the arrival of U.S. and Canadian servicemen, sometimes called the "peaceful invasion," accelerated these changes.

Initially, American soldiers were, for many, virtually mythological creatures, seen as symbols of hope for an end to the war. They were Santa Clauses who had so much when compared with French populations living under German occupation or with the British armed forces.[8] People made comparisons regarding their better uniforms, their food, and their apparent wealth and generosity toward the families of the girls they dated. (Servicemen learned quickly that the best way to a girl's family's heart was to bring food to dinner.) Marie Houtz, originally from London, remembered that one Christmas, "we were sitting in the dark. We couldn't get any coal. It was cold and all of a sudden there was a knock on the door and it was Earl and he had all these brightly wrapped gifts. We didn't have a Christmas tree or a gift in the house because everything was rationed and my family just fell in love with him. My mother dearly loved Earl."[9]

Elvia Stockton recalled that under the German occupation of France, girls returned to school and "we went because we were allowed some biscuits." Fear of offending German officers remained constant. Elvia later married and moved to Montana after the war, eventually ranching at Grass Range. SEENA B. KOHL, COURTESY OF THE AUTHOR.

In fact, *A Short Guide to Great Britain,* a pamphlet filled with practical advice given to servicemen prior to their arrival, warned that "if you are invited into a British home, and the host exhorts you to 'eat up, there's plenty on the table,' go easy. It may be the family's rations for a whole week, spread out to show their hospitality." Commanding officers began to encourage their men to take official "hospitality rations when they went visiting. . . . Fathers received cigarettes; mothers tinned fruit, ham, chocolate and candies."[10]

Yanks laughed and were fun and for young women, greatly attractive, particularly in a setting where most of the young men had been called off to war. As Irene Owen, from Cheshire, explained, "I think some people would think, 'Why don't you marry someone from your own country.' But I never went out with anyone from my own country. I was only nineteen and I was wanting to go out."[11]

Besides the excitement expected from teenage girls at the arrival of a large number of handsome young men into their communities, the GIs were seen as symbols of hope, or as in Australia, defenders. Beatrice "Pete" Berrenger, from Rockhampton, Australia, recalled, "We welcomed them because Australia was left to fend [for itself]. Britain just kind of wiped us off. Until America came into the war . . . the Japanese were getting mighty close. Americans were very welcome there."[12]

Although all of the respondents noted how fun, attractive, polite, and considerate their future husbands were, not everyone had such positive views of GIs. Peggy Floerchinger remembered, "Oh, there was some animosity with certain people . . . against the American soldier. . . . They came over at a time when we were in dire straits. . . . We had been going without for a long time, and the American servicemen were paid a lot more than the British servicemen. Consequently they were looked upon as show-offs. You know, they've got all this money and especially if a British girl went out with an American, they were stealing British girls."[13]

Such ambivalence toward the Americans was common, and GIs were seen alternately as generous or spendthrifts, friendly or pushy, frank or boastful, slovenly or casual. As Elsie Persicke, originally from London, recalled, "Well, most Englishmen didn't appreciate the Americans being over there because they took the women and then they had more money than our soldiers. . . . And they always had candy and fruit, which we couldn't get."[14]

Less frequently mentioned by war brides was the general feeling that "nice girls" did not go out with U.S. Army men. The common saying in both Britain and Australia was that the "Yanks were oversexed, over-paid, and over here." Along these lines, Joyce DeLong recalled her mother's response to her future husband: "I almost gave my mother a heart attack. She heard through her sisters . . . that 'Joyce is dating a Yank.' . . . They didn't have a very good opinion because of some of the GIs. . . . They had a very bad reputation. I just went ahead and he seemed to be a very nice guy. Fell in love."[15]

In Norma Duff's case, it was her father who objected to her dating an American. The town of Rockhampton, Australia, where Norma lived, had a population of about 30,000, and there were about 60,000 servicemen (this was the Forty-first Division, which included members of the Montana National Guard). Norma's husband, Roy Duff, explained, "He [her father] worked for the U.S. Army, . . . and he worked with the GIs, and all they talked about in the daytime was the girls they had out the night before and that kind of stuff. So he prohibited his daughters from having to do anything with the Yankees."[16]

Norma's mother, on the other hand, was supportive. Norma remembered, "I used to go out with him, and then when I'd come home at night, so my dad wouldn't know who I was with, my mom would stand at the window and move the window up and down to tell me it was time to come inside."[17] Perhaps her mother recognized that for Norma, as for all of the war brides, the desire to date—to have some semblance of a normal life—trumped any familial or community objection.

For Joyce DeLong and the other war brides, falling in love was the easy part. Parental desires, age of consent, and army regulations complicated the decision to marry for all of the respondents.[18] Marie Houtz recalled that although Earl Houtz was twenty-three, he nevertheless had to get permission from his father, who initially opposed their marriage.

In addition to parental permission to marry, army regulations required an appearance before a committee. Marie recalled, "We had to have an interview I think with about six officers, very high-ranking officers, and a chaplain, and they called Earl in and questioned him. Then they called me in and questioned me. Then they called us both in and this is kind of a funny part here—they asked my husband, 'Do you have to marry this girl?' And he said, 'No, sir!' [laughs]. Then the chaplain kept smiling at me. Everyone else was very sober faced and they . . . denied our request to be married."[19] Only after a second letter from Earl's father did they receive permission.

Joyce DeLong recalled a similar experience:

You had to get permission from your commanding officer. Colonel Bell said, "I don't believe in foreign marriages." He said, "If you want to marry her, you go back to the States and

Roy Duff was among the 60,000 U.S. troops stationed in Australia and New Guinea during the Second World War. Norma Duff's father disapproved of her dating Roy, but her mother helped Norma escape his watchful eye. Norma and Roy married on November 8, 1944, in Rockhampton, Australia. LAUREEN STUDIO, COURTESY ROY DUFF.

get your discharge and come back and marry her." Russell [her husband] "didn't like that answer at all. . . . He found out that some of the GIs were getting married to English girls. . . . He went to Colonel Bell and said, "How come you are giving permission to some of these GIs to get married?" "Well, they are expecting a baby, so they have to get married. . . . [T]hey need a marriage license on the birth certificate." Russell said, "Colonel Bell, I think that . . . is discriminating to the girls that don't have to get married." So, [Bell] thought about it. He said, "Soldier, you're right. I will sign the papers.". . . Then, the chaplain came down to see me, to see what kind of girl I was, the house I lived in and everything. He talked to my mother. Finally it did go through that we could get married.[20]

DeLong's colonel was not the only one opposed to foreign marriages. Elizabeth Goff, a refugee from Poland and working for the U.S. Army in Germany when she met her husband, recalled, "He wrote home and told his mom that he met me. And her comeback was, 'Of all the beautiful American girls, why in God's name would you want to bring a foreigner home?' And I never forgot that. When I reminded her, she said, 'Oh my, honey, why do you have such a good memory?' Many thought they [the girls] just wanted to get to America."[21]

In retrospect, the respondents expressed few regrets about marrying. The regrets they did express dealt with leaving their families and enduring some very difficult times. All of the women viewed marriage as an inevitable and hoped-for step. For the most part, however, all of the respondents emphasized that they did not know what they were getting into. All explained that they were young, in love, and could not be assured of a future. As Marie Houtz noted, "You know, it was strange. We didn't think we would live very long because, when we were married, there were still the V-2 rockets coming over and we just didn't think we'd survive. So we didn't think of the future. . . . We just thought we were lucky to be alive that day and maybe by the end of the day we wouldn't be."[22]

Being young and in love also meant that most of the respondents did not think about the difficulties of separating from their families until it was too late. However, when recalling their feelings about leaving their families and country, for the most part, despair was paired with love. The recollection of Chub Tuss illustrates a common feeling. "I knew he lived in Montana. He said, 'Now, love, there are going to be lots of open spaces, but don't worry about it. It's going to be okay.' . . . He didn't have a clue. . . . [I] didn't really know. I just was in love, I guess. I just thought it would be all right no matter where we were."[23]

Elvia Stockton recalled how upset her family was. Leaving the family was "very very difficult. . . . [It was] terrible, terrible, but I was really too full of Bill. . . . We never talked about money or anything. Absolutely none. I guess I was awfully naive. I just didn't expect anything. But then too we loved each other."[24]

Elfriede Johnsen was living in Karlsruhe, Germany, under the U.S. occupation when she met her husband. Her memory of leaving was slightly different. "I didn't feel bad [about leaving my parents]. . . . But I was young and in love and adventurous, so you leave and a new life starts. Only for them [her parents] it was probably very sad, you know. And every time I went back to visit it was very sad on both parts to leave."[25]

For the most part, the respondents were well received by their husband's families and the particular community. Further, for the most part, they felt they had been "told the truth" about Montana. Nevertheless, few imagined the reality of Montana's spaces, mountains, weather, and small population. Chub Tuss recalled the trip west to join her husband in Lewistown in central Montana. She was on a train alone for four days and three nights before she arrived at the station in Harlowton where her husband met her.

[It] was just me. . . . I was so scared [whisper]. Just me, that's all. I tried to make friends with people and everybody was nice. . . . They were really kind and I got off at Harlowton, and I say, "Oh, my Lord!" . . . All I saw was nothing, nothing, nothing! [In the 1940s, Harlowton had a population of 1,897.] I mean land, land, land. . . . You know in England it's so crowded—shoulder to shoulder on the pavement. . . . It was really a shock. It was February and bare. . . . I remember they were all waiting for

me. I'd only been in a car once, we rode bikes . . . and buses.
So going in the car was quite something and then seeing all
that land.[26]

Doreen Richard's husband told her about Montana and his family's
farm, but she remembered wondering:

What is it going to be like? But everyone said to me, "Oh, they
have cars and it doesn't take long to get from one place to another." Hello! I arrived here . . . in Great Falls about December
the sixteenth and I thought that Great Falls was such a small
town. This was so small, and everything. . . . But anyhow we
went to the farm and I thought it all looked alike. . . . It was bar-
ren. Snow. And we'd go along and we would turn the corner, it
was the same. No change. Absolutely none. . . . It went on and
on for such a long time. I said to my husband, "Don't we ever
come to a town?" "Oh yes, we will be coming into Loma very
soon." So I waited and I said to him, "When will we be coming
into Loma?" "Oh, we did" [laughs]. That was it. I hadn't even
noticed it. So, that was my first experience.[27]

Peggy Floerchinger and her husband, Tom, whose family farmed
outside of Conrad, came on the same ship to the United States and
then took a bus to Montana. She remembered, "I didn't see an awful
lot until we got to Montana, which is so wide open. . . . I got to see
the majesty of the state. It was overpowering. It was a little daunting
because I'm a person that needs to have trees and things around me.
When I get out in the open spaces, I'm not at all happy. I'm not very
good out in a wheat field with nothing around me, and I marry a
farmer who is."[28]

There were problems of housing, family relationships, language,
prejudice, loneliness, homesickness, and of learning the ins and outs
of a new culture, from the currency to appropriate behavior. Most of
the new marriages started in the groom's family home, due in part to
the severe housing shortage and to the financial situation of the new
couples. Some, however, were able to find their own place. Elfriede

Sometimes war brides arrived in Montana ahead of their husbands, leaving them to meet their new in-laws, settle into new living arrangements, and begin the often difficult adjustments alone. Dick Vashro met his bride upon her arrival, but for two years Joyce Vashro and her young daughter Mary Ann (shown here in 1945) spent six days each week alone, rooming in a Butte hotel, while Dick worked out of town for a railroad. COURTESY JOYCE VASHRO.

Johnsen remembered her first apartment in Billings. "The housing situation was terrible, so we ended up in a one-room apartment. We had to go through the furnace room that had a coal furnace to get to this one room, and there was a hot plate in the closet that we cooked on. There was a table and a bed. We had to share the bathroom upstairs. It was terrible, but believe me, I didn't mind it because I was in love."[29]

Many of the women had corresponded with their future in-laws and exchanged pictures and presents. However, even where families welcomed the new brides, problems arose. Peggy Floerchinger recalled, "I wasn't thrown into a den of lions, so to speak, so that was good, because I was terribly homesick.... Tom's family was wonderful. They enveloped me, but there were so many changes that I had to make. I was very conscious of the way I spoke . . . or the way I, for instance, laid the table."[30] The first time Chub Tuss met her husband's family was a shock:

I was an only child and we had a nice house—not fancy but a nice house and I came to one with eleven in it and it wasn't clean.... They were Yugoslavian.... [T]hey could speak English, but Grandpa couldn't very much. It was such a small place and . . . you had to give him [her father-in-law] money because that was what was expected.... We lived there six months and then I went and got a place.... They were kind to me, but it was just a shock to come into a house like that, with all those people, after being an only child and spoiled rotten.[31]

Most of the war brides' husbands met their new wives on their arrival; however, in several instances, the women arrived before the men. Both Elizabeth Goff and Marie Houtz arrived in the United States while their husbands were still in Europe. In both cases, the family met them, and they had a place to stay. And even in cases where husbands met their wives, in some instances, circumstances forced them to spend a great deal of time away from home. Joyce Vashro's husband was a railroad employee, and Joyce found herself left alone with her in-laws. She recalled:

Dick had to leave the second day after I got there [Minneapolis] because he had a job back in Montana. So he had to leave, and I stayed there for three months with the in-laws. I tried to make the best of it, but I did feel terribly lonesome for my folks and for the things I was used to. . . . He finally found a place for us to live in Butte. . . . I got to Butte, I thought, 'Oh, my Lord, what have I [done]?' So, I thought, 'Well, Dick will be here. Everything will be fine now and we'll have a good life.' Well, he found a room up on the third floor of this hotel and there was just two rooms and he went out and got some sheets and blankets and some silverware and food, and he got it in all in there and then he said, "Well, I've got to run." And I said, "Where are you running to?" And he said, "I've got to catch the train. I'll see you next Saturday night." This was on a Monday and in those days they worked six days a week, and I hadn't realized that he'd be gone all week.[32]

Joyce Vashro lived in the hotel with her baby for two years.

For many of the women, a generally positive welcome eased the transition to life in America. Often, the arrival of a war bride was, as in the case of Ruth Batchen's arrival in Great Falls, front-page news.[33] For some of the other women, the entire family would be at the railroad station to meet them. Elfriede Johnsen recalled, "Everyone welcomed me in Broadus . . . a very small town of maybe 300 population. Everybody was very nice, very interested. Nobody made any remarks because I came from Germany. They were just awed by seeing probably the first war bride that they'd ever had in that town."[34]

Jung Van Dam, from Korea, who moved to her husband's hometown of Conrad after the Korean War, received a different reception:

> Well, this is a small community here, so when you go to church, they all look at you, you know, like head to toe. Examine you, you know, to see if she's fit enough to belong in our church and things like that. . . . My husband belongs to this church. He went to church ever since he was young . . . so when I came, I thought everybody going to accept me and give me a nice wedding shower and gifts and all that. Nothing like that! . . . Just his sister and his mom and dad was nice to me. . . . I took a lot of criticism, and . . . people would call me, you know, nigger, Jap, Chinaman. And squaw. . . . They are not like that now. Not now, no. This is forty-three years ago. . . . It was real hard, because, you know, people come to my house and . . . we'd be eating, . . . having supper and they go around the table to see what kind of food you are serving. Well, you know, oh, yeah, she put a lot of fruit, vegetable, a lot of vegetable and rice and things like that, and fish. Everybody used to like potato and gravy and all that, but now everybody likes Oriental food. And people like to come to my house and eat my Oriental dishes now, and I have a good many friends now. It took many, many years for people to accept me. I used to cry a lot. A lot. The first five years is horrible.[35]

Women interviewed remembered their surprise about food as well as differences in everyday behaviors, dress, manners, and language. Odette Saylor had worked as a cook in France and also held strong feelings about American eating habits. "I was a cook. I loved to cook and I couldn't find everything. In those days, the only cheese you could find . . . it was all that yellow . . . processed cheese, yuck. . . . I didn't like corn, I didn't like peanut butter, I didn't like potato salad.

The first time I had potato salad . . . ah, I could have thrown up. . . . Sweet potato salad! Sweet tomato sauce!"[36]

In contrast, the dominant response to the availability of food was amazement. Doreen Richard recalled:

> We went and had a meal and I shall never forget that, because we had been on rations. And I hadn't had pork in so many years, and I had pork chops. . . . When it came, I had two pork chops. I couldn't believe it. I thought to myself, 'Well, I think that I am supposed to pass it to him and he will take his part.' . . . Then, a piece of pie. . . . Oh, my gosh. I thought that the Americans were the greediest people I had ever seen. Honestly, I'd walk around and see these people. They'd have half a pie and sometimes even ice cream on it. . . . Even after we were married when I would go shopping, it took me a long time before I could remember that I didn't have to ask, "May I have two loaves of bread?" Two, because I was so used to only being able to have one for so many years.[37]

Whereas the abundance came as a pleasant surprise, other cultural differences were less welcome. Janet Mohn, who moved from Rockhampton, Australia, to Kalispell, recalled, "When Bill [her husband] took me to a matinee or to a movie, I was so appalled to see these girls in their jeans and dirty saddle shoes and sweaters. I'd say, 'Are they going to the show like that?' He would say, 'You are in America now, love.'"[38]

Janet also remembered a difference in manners: "'Please' and 'thank you' just automatically came out of our mouths, and when somebody said, 'Pass the bread,' I got to the point where I didn't until they said 'please.'"[39]

Peggy Floerchinger also was surprised at some of the behavior she encountered. The English, she explained, are "very reserved, extremely reserved. . . . When I first came over here, I was invited to coffee, and they said, 'Well, I'm glad to have met you, you'll have to come to my house for coffee.' Well, I waited for the invitation . . . and it never came. . . . In England you didn't do that. . . . I was raised in a very strict family. . . . Consequently, I saw a lot of difference in children and the way they were raised. They were a little freer and they were extremely verbal, whereas I was not allowed to talk unless I was asked to speak . . . so I . . . raised my children pretty strict. And manners were extremely important to me."[40]

Other war brides also found Americans lax when it came to child-rearing. Joyce Barry, who came from Great Bloodworth to Kalispell, recalled, "I sort of went along with everything here, but I had my own ideas with raising children. The things that they couldn't touch and we could take them anywhere. They were good. Raising your kids with manners. And toilet training that I thought that they let go too long. I was careful about that."[41]

Odette Saylor recalled her sister-in-law's response when Odette "popped" her daughter "one on the butt":

Those people I met that had children, they raised their babies by what was then called "by the book"—no spanking. . . . One day I went with one of his sisters to town and I kind of hit my little girl. By that time, she was three years old and she had got lost in the store. I popped her one on the butt, and my sister [in-law] said, "Oh, you can't do that in public. You know you could be arrested." I said, "What! To give a tap to my child?" And she said, "Yeah, you can't do that here." . . . Well, of course, over there people spank their children. . . . They didn't beat them up. Everybody had a . . . wooden handle with several straps and lots of people spanked their kids when they were unruly. They'd slap them on the legs. . . . That was just a reminder.[42]

Publications tried to bridge the cultural gap—but without much success. The sheer number of war brides moving from Britain to the United States led the British *Good Housekeeping Magazine* to prepare *A Bride's Guide to the U.S.A.* in conjunction with the U.S. Office of War Information. Filled with advice about how to make the transition, the *Guide* encouraged women to "smile, use your British habit of thanking people for everything, ask questions, and you will make people feel that you want to be friendly." Other parts warned the reader about U.S. behaviors such as the use of first names and the informal style of making friends. Much of the *Guide* emphasized homemaking, noting, "In America practically every housewife does her own work.... Your main job, therefore, will be running the house." In the interviews, all the respondents talked about differences in language and manners and food, but housekeeping went unmentioned. Such emphasis was taken for granted, part of the generally accepted ideas about women in terms of wifehood, motherhood, and family building.[43]

One thing that eased the transition to American life for many of the women was the presence of other war brides. Elvia Stockton found a group of war brides from France in Billings, where she and her husband lived before moving back to his family's ranch in Grass Range, about seventy miles away. Joyce Vashro, alone for a large part of the time in Butte, took the initiative in creating a community. She would read about the arrival of women in the paper and call them. "These English girls were coming over at the time.... I met about ten of them altogether. When I'd see in the paper that so and so arrived from England, I'd call them up and say, 'I'm English, too,' and we'd get together for tea, or something, you know. I got to meet an awful lot of nice people. They saved my sanity—they really did."[44]

There were formal organizations concerned with the adjustment of war brides, such as the American Red Cross and the YWCA, but the most important organizations were war bride clubs.[45] In some communities, the YWCA or the Red Cross sponsored these clubs. However, most of the clubs were unaffiliated, organized when a war bride took the initiative, as Joyce Vashro did. In the absence of family support networks, membership in these clubs provided the opportunity to share some of their trials and tribulations as well as to laugh.

The Overseas Wives Club of Kalispell and Whitefish is illustrative.[46] Sheila Buck and Janet Mohn were two of the original members. The club, formed in 1951, grew from nine to twenty members by 1966. "We just took turns entertaining," Sheila Buck explained. "We went from one house to the other. We met once a month and we would exchange magazines, letters, and information. People were hearing from home. And then when we had visitors from overseas we would have an extra special party because somebody's mother came or some other family member came. We had a nice social evening. It was a night out for most of us."[47] As Joyce DeLong put it, the Overseas War Bride Club "was very important. You felt that you were with kinfolk when you were with someone from your own country."[48]

Neighbors could also take the place of kin, as Chub Tuss recalled of her first years in Lewistown. "The lady upstairs really took care of me . . . and she taught me. . . . She was like my mom." Church also provided a social network. Chub remembered, "Church members taught me how to play bridge and then I had a lot of friends. . . . Later on [I met people through] women's clubs."[49]

Similarly, when Muriel Morse's merchant marine husband Herb had to ship out the day after she came home from giving birth to her oldest son, neighbors provided social support. Muriel noted, "You are brought up very reserved in England. . . . You just didn't ask people. I just managed. . . . It happened that the lady in back of me . . . she saw me one day with Bruce [Morse's son]. She had her baby at the same time . . . same age and all. She came around. . . . We got to be friends then. In fact we kept in touch for quite a while until she passed away."[50]

Of course, where there was prejudice, as in Jung Van Dam's experience, there was no help. "See, I had to learn everything myself. Through TV . . . and I had to be so careful what I would say because, you know, in broken English, and maybe I would say something you don't understand what I mean, I might hurt your feelings. You know. Things like that."[51]

In spite of the difficulties, war brides learned to accommodate. Depending upon finances, there were transatlantic visits, although in some instances parting again was even more difficult than leaving the first time. Doreen Richard visited her parents in West Bromage before her children were born. Her first years of farm life had been extraordinarily difficult: the house she came to had no electricity and no running water, and the expectations were that she would cook for hired hands without help. She recalled, "I can remember I was due to come back [from England] and I shall never forget. . . . [Returning to Montana] was worse than when I had left home, because I knew what it would be like, [but] I [had] made a promise."[52]

Richard had a particularly difficult situation, not only because of the lack of amenities on the farm, but also because of her isolation. Where Richard worked hard on the farm, that work did not provide her with a social network outside the family. Other war brides, on the other hand, took jobs outside the home. Such paying work was useful, not only as a means to supplement the family's income, but as a way of meeting people other than one's immediate family. Work relationships also helped in an "Americanizing" process, a factor commonly ignored in the advice given to war brides. In fact, the British advice book, *A Bride's Guide to the U.S.A.*, reflecting a traditional view regarding women's work, suggested that taking a job would not be useful. "You may wish to take a job so as to increase your family income. If so, you will not be considered queer, nor will people look down on you. But do not waste your time. . . . Since your husband's prospects of promotion may be improved by an attractive home, you may add more to the family budget by homemaking than by working for pay, unless you can get a really good job at a good salary."[53]

World War II, however, changed some of the generally accepted ideas, both for American-born women and war brides. All of the respondents, for example, eventually entered the labor market. Of course, all the respondents had prior work experience either associated with the war effort or as part of a family effort. As adult women in the United States, a return to work was, for the most part, an economic necessity. In the case of the Goffs, of Great Falls, Elizabeth took a job to help earn money to buy a house, a fact her husband noted proudly in the interview.[54]

Elfriede Johnsen, who went to work after her divorce, described her various jobs with pride. "I worked in a grocery store as a meat wrapper for several years. I worked as a waitress. I worked in a diner as a cook, dishwasher, waitress. . . . I worked at a motel and I worked at the hospital in housekeeping for seventeen years. And I had actually never worked in Germany before."[55]

Peggy Floerchinger and Sheila Buck returned to school for further education. Both had been in college before the war interrupted their studies. Peggy recalled one of the precipitating events in her return to school:

My mother called me and she couldn't get hold of me and [when she did] she said, "Where have you been?" . . . I said, "Well I was out on the tractor!" She literally came unglued over the phone and she said, "I didn't raise you to be a tractor driver." . . . I didn't do it very often. . . . I think that was one of the reasons that through the years I decided to do something . . . to make me feel that I wasn't something to be used out in the field. . . . I applied for the job at the library. Through the years I went through a lot of different workshops and became a certified librarian. That fulfilled that emptiness that I had. . . . I didn't like farming. I make a joke of it now. I say, "Well, when I return in the next life, if a farmer comes towards me and asks me for a date, I['m] going to run like you-know-what . . . in the opposite direction."[56]

Peggy's dislike of farming was not a rejection of her choice to marry the farmer around whom she built her adult life. However, like all of the women interviewed, her embrace of her new life in America was not without contradictory feelings.

The interviews ended with the question, "Would you do it again?" and most of the women had a hard time answering. They mostly answered "yes," but the "yes" was infused with hesitancy.[57] The women weighed pluses and minuses connected to the loss of leaving family behind against the fact that they had made new lives—their children were here and they loved their husbands and life in Montana. In addition, their memories of their past struggles had inevitably faded over time.

Doreen Richard, who faced one of the most extreme transitions—to a farm without electricity or running water—at first answered "no," she would not do it again. However, as she considered the question, she added, "The strange thing is that I love America and I think this is a wonderful country. And of course my children are all here. I would not like to go back to England to live. . . . For many years I would have [returned to England] but not now because things have changed."[58]

For some, there were mixed feelings about national identity. Peggy Floerchinger's response illuminates the dilemma: "I took my

Most of the women answered "yes" when asked, "Would you do it again?" They loved their husbands and their children, and life in Montana. Time had faded past troubles. Here, Elsie Persicke in her Whitefish home shows her wedding photograph and English keepsakes. SEENA B. KOHL, COURTESY OF THE AUTHOR.

citizenship out very early because ... this is where I was going to live. ... I have always kept them [my children] aware of English heritage. ... I want to be in England ... and I love the United States. ... I wrote a story one time about ... my trip over here and what I did and how I felt and at the end of it I said simply, 'Losing one's country is like losing a child.' You never lose the love that you had for that child. I still have my love for the country I was born in, but I also have a love for this country."[59]

Chub Tuss, who also got her U.S. citizenship after four years, said, "I'm glad I came to Montana. ... Deep down, I'm still British. I'm so proud of being British for some reason. I don't know why but it's still home. ... I've got my little wall there [filled with cups and pictures of the royal family]. I don't push it because I don't want people to think

Both the specific circumstances of the war and the choice to marry and leave family behind shaped war brides' experiences. And just as they exercised personal choice in deciding to marry, most war brides found happiness in their new homes. Chub and Frank Tuss (center) wed on August 15, 1945. Afterward they heard church bells ringing—celebrating not their marriage but VJ Day, victory over Japan and the end of the war. COURTESY EVELYN "CHUB" TUSS.

I'm being disrespectful. Look what I've got from being an American . . . my lovely kids, my grandkids, and so I'm blessed. I've had a good life. I love Montana. I love the U.S."[60]

Elvia Stockton perhaps phrased this dual identity most clearly, distinguishing between being an American and being a Montanan: "I would say if somebody asked me if I feel very much like an American . . . well, I would say no, I feel like a Montanan. I don't know how to explain it, but that's the way I feel. I really love Montana and the people."[61]

Autobiography, as Eric Hobsbawm writes, should demonstrate the interconnections between a person's life and the larger social context in which they find themselves. The time and place offer "a shifting but always limited set of choices from which lives are made." People "do not make [choices] just as they please, they do not make [them] under circumstances chosen by themselves, but under circumstances directly encountered, given and transmitted from the past."[62]

Certainly, the narratives of these twenty Montana women show the intertwining of personal choice and the circumstances in which these remarkable individuals found themselves. Coming of age in the 1930s and 1940s, these women were shaped by the traditional view that marriage, children, and family should define a woman's life. All of the Montana respondents shared these expectations for their own lives in the face of an almost complete absence of local eligible men. They also shared ideas about love and romance and a youthful exuberance, which fed upon the presence of new attractive men who expanded the potential marriage pool and who brought excitement into a setting of privation. And so they fell in love with foreign soldiers and chose to marry.

The consequences of deciding to marry American GIs were varied, but all of the women had to deal with homesickness, loneliness, and the difficulties of adapting to life in a foreign land. They encountered Montana's wide-open spaces, limited population, and cultural differences. They also faced all of the ordinary challenges newlyweds confront in learning how to live with one another. And they met these challenges without the support of their natal family or long-term friends. Yet these women exhibited high levels of resilience that helped them survive their transition to life in Montana.[63] Perhaps their early experiences with privation, death, and living with uncertainty had, perversely, provided them with the resiliency to lead successful lives despite difficult circumstances.

This essay originally appeared in *Montana, The Magazine of Western History,* Autumn 2006.

Seena B. Kohl is Professor Emeritus of Anthropology at Webster University in St. Louis, Missouri. She is the coauthor of Settling the Canadian-American West, 1890-1915: Pioneer Adaptation and Community Building *(1995) and* Working Together: Women and Family in Southwestern Saskatchewan *(1976), as well as several articles, including "'Well I have Lived in Montana Almost a Week and Like It Fine': Letters from the Davis Homestead, 1910-1926," published in* Montana, The Magazine of Western History *51 (Autumn 2001).*

NOTES

1   Joyce DeLong, interview by Seena Kohl, Somers, Montana, Oral History (hereafter OH) 2046, Montana Historical Society Research Center, Helena (hereafter MHS). No one knows how many women came to the United States as recipients of Public Law 271, also known as the War Brides Act. However, estimates range to 70,000, the largest percentage of whom were British and from middle- and working-class backgrounds. The act waived previous visa requirements and provisions of immigration law.

2   Ibid.

3   Evelyn "Chub" Tuss, interview by Seena Kohl, Lewistown, Montana, July 17, 2001, OH 1940, MHS.

4   Ruth Batchen, interview by Seena Kohl, Billings, Montana, July 10, 2002, OH 2039, MHS.

5   Elvia Stockton, interview by Seena Kohl, Grass Range, Montana, July 17, 2001, OH 1941, MHS.

6   Doreen Richard, interview by Seena Kohl, Great Falls, Montana, June 26, 2002, OH 2033, MHS.

7   Jenel Virden, *Good-bye, Piccadilly: British War Brides in America* (Urbana, Ill., 1996), pp. 23-28.

8   Norman Longmate, *The G.I.'s: The Americans in Britain, 1942–1945* (London, 1975), pp. 101, 107

9   Marie Houtz, interview by Seena Kohl, Great Falls, Montana, June 25, 2002, OH 2030, MHS.

10 Longmate, *The G.I.'s*, 21–23; Juliet Gardiner, *Over Here: the GIs in Wartime Britain* (London, 1992), pp. 131-132.

11 Irene Owen, interview by Seena Kohl, Geraldine, Montana, July 9, 2002, OH 2041, MHS.

12 Beatrice "Pete" Berrenger, interview by Seena Kohl, Billings, Montana, July 8, 2002, OH 2040, MHS

13 Margaret "Peggy" Floerchinger, interview by Seena Kohl, Conrad, Montana, July 29, 2001, OH 1942, MHS.

14 Longmate, *The G.I.'s*, pp. 100-109; Elsie Persicke, interview by Seena Kohl, Whitefish, Montana, July 9, 2002, OH 2034, MHS.

15 DeLong interview.

16 Norma Duff, interview by Seena Kohl, Whitefish, Montana, September 8, 2002, OH 2043, MHS. In addition to Roy Duff, husbands Bill Barry, Richard Goff, and Herbert Morse participated. Marilyn Wade, daughter of Pete Berrenger, and Lynne Duff, daughter-in-law of the Duffs, also participated in the interviews.

17 Ibid.

18 Vera Cracknell Long, *From Britain with Love: World War II Pilgrim Brides Sail to America* (New Market, Va., 1999), pp. 21-22, lists the regulations for marriage.

19 Houtz interview.

20 DeLong interview.

21 Elizabeth Goff, interview by Seena Kohl, Great Falls, Montana, June 25, 2002, OH 2031, MHS.

22 Houtz interview.

23 Tuss interview.

24 Stockton interview.

25 Elfriede Johnsen, interview by Seena Kohl, Great Falls, Montana, July 16, 2002, OH 2038, MHS.

26 Tuss interview.

27 Doreen Richard, interview by Seena Kohl, Great Falls, Montana, June 26, 2002, OH 2033, MHS. In 1950, Great Falls's population was estimated at 43,000. Loma's population was 193 in 1940.

28 Floerchinger interview.

29 Johnsen interview. Jenel Virden notes that, based upon her survey of 105 war brides and 67 husbands, 88 percent first lived with their in-laws, 7 percent with other relatives, and 5 percent in boarding houses. Virden, *Good-bye, Piccadilly,* p. 165.

30 Floerchinger interview.

31 Tuss interview.

32 Joyce Vashro, interview by Seena Kohl, Helena, Montana, June 24, 2002, OH 2029, MHS.

33 *Great Falls (Mont.) Tribune,* April 5, 1946.

34 Johnsen interview.

35 Jung Van Dam, interview by Seena Kohl, Conrad, Montana, June 27, 2002, OH 2032, MHS.

36 Odette Saylor, interview by Seena Kohl, Billings, Montana, July 27, 2001, OH 1943, MHS.

37 Richard interview.

38 Janet Mohn, interview by Seena Kohl, Kalispell, Montana, September 11, 2002, OH 2045, MHS.

39 Mohn interview.

40 Floerchinger interview.

41 Joyce Barry, interview by Seena Kohl, Kalispell, Montana, September 2, 2002, OH 2042, MHS.

42 Saylor interview.

43 British *Good Housekeeping Magazine* and the U.S. Office of War Information, *A Bride's Guide to the U.S.A.* (n.p., n.d.), pp. 2, 7.

44 Vashro interview.

45 Jenel Virden notes that although there were church and state groups that developed programs to aid war brides in their transition to the United States, most women in her survey did not join them, but started independent clubs. Virden, *Good-bye, Piccadilly,* p. 106.

46 Dale J. Burk, "Many Lands Represented in Unique Club," *Kalispell (Mont.) Daily Inter Lake,* January 23, 1966.

47 Sheila Buck, interview by Seena Kohl, Kalispell, Montana, September 10, 2002, OH 2044, MHS.

48 DeLong interview.

49 Tuss interview.

50 Muriel Morse, interview by Seena Kohl, Kalispell, Montana, September 9, 2002, OH 2047 MHS.

51 Van Dam interview.

52 Richard interview.

53 British *Good Housekeeping Magazine* and the U.S. Office of War Information, *A Bride's Guide to the U.S.A.,* p. 9.

54 Goff interview.

55 Johnsen interview.

56 Floerchinger interview.

57 Similarly, Virden, *Good-bye, Piccadilly,* pp. 138-139, reports that 87 percent of British war brides do not regret marrying an American GI. As she noted, "Importantly the process of immigration, for British war brides, was tied irrevocably to their marital status. To decide not to immigrate would mean to decide not to marry their husbands."

58 Richard interview.

59 Floerchinger interview.

60 Tuss interview.

61 Stockton interview.

62 Eric Hobsbawm, *Interesting Times: A Twentieth-Century Life* (New York, 2002), p. xiii.

63 Within the past decade there has been an emerging focus within the field of psychology on resilience among survivors of traumas such as war, sexual abuse, battering, and other adversities. See, for example, Maureen Davey, Dawn Goettle, and Lynda Henley Walters, "Resilience Processes in Adolescents: Personality Profiles, Self-Worth, and Coping," *Journal of Adolescent Research,* 18 (2003), pp. 347-362; and Richard Ferraro, "Psychological Resilience in Older Adults following the 1997 Flood," *Clinical Gerontologist,* 26 (2003), pp. 139-183.

Breaking Racial Barriers:
'Everyone's Welcome' at the Ozark Club
Great Falls, Montana's African American Nightclub

— Ken Robison

Not all ethnic groups in Montana have been made up of recent immigrants to America. The Montana Métis would certainly not fit into that description. Nor would most African Americans. Indeed, the ancestors of most of today's African Americans came to America, albeit against their will, long before the ancestors of most of today's Euro-Americans ever arrived on these shores. The black experience in Montana, like that of the rest of the nation, is also one of long standing.

As was true for many other Americans in the years following the Civil War, large numbers of black Americans began moving westward for a variety of reasons. Some were sent by the U.S. Army, such as those enlisted in the all-black Ninth and Tenth Cavalry Regiments (the famed "buffalo soldiers") and the all-black Twenty-fourth and Twenty-fifth Infantry Regiments. The Twenty-fifth Infantry, in fact, was garrisoned for a time in Montana, where it performed many valuable services. Thousands of other blacks joined the developing cattle industry in the West. Few people today realize that roughly one-third of all the cowboys working in the post–Civil War era were either black or Mexican. The transcontinental railroads, which employed African Americans in select positions, added further to the black presence in the West.

Many black residents in the American West eventually settled in growing urban centers, including the Montana cities of Helena, Butte, and Great Falls. Within these communities, African Americans established businesses, created various social and civic organizations, and, in the case of both Butte and Helena, began their own black newspapers. As vibrant as these black communities were, living in Montana was not without its drawbacks. Although they suffered far less physical violence that those blacks remaining in the South during the Jim Crow era, African Americans in Montana were still forced to endure both social and legal discrimination, especially during the first half of the twentieth century. It was within this historical context that a nightclub known as the Ozark Club arose in Great Falls. That club, and the people who managed it, are the focal point of the following essay by historian Ken Robison. For almost three decades, the Ozark Club helped to break down racial barriers and provided an exhilarating form of music that could lift the human spirit and put a joyful smile on the listener's face.

Young Leo Phillip LaMar brought his hopes and dreams to Montana late in 1920. Born in Chicago in 1902, the son of an African-American mother and a Chinese father, Leo had been abandoned by both his parents and run away from home at age thirteen. He began a boxing career in Chicago when he was about fifteen years old, fighting as "Kid Leo." At five feet seven inches and 130 pounds, with a light-brown complexion, Leo LaMar was a handsome young man, a fact often remarked on in newspaper stories about his boxing career. In his late teens, LaMar hired on with the Great Northern Railway and traveled around the country as a Pullman porter, but it was in Great Falls that LaMar's drive and energy enabled him to transform a small "colored" social club into a renowned nightclub, where young and old, blacks and whites gathered to play and listen to jazz. LaMar's Ozark Club broke racial barriers and anchored nightlife on the Southside of Great Falls for almost three decades.[1]

The Great Falls that Leo LaMar encountered when he stepped

off the train at the Great Northern depot was bursting with energy. Fueled by growth during World War I and the homestead boom, the town had nearly doubled in population over the previous decade to 24,000, making it the second largest in Montana. Great Falls was principally an industrial city, with three Montana Power Company hydroelectric power stations on the Missouri River, a never-failing water supply, large coal deposits nearby, and gas and oil fields to the north, all contributing to economic development. The refining of copper and zinc and manufacturing of copper wire drew large numbers of workers to Great Falls, many of them immigrants, and the city's largest employers were the Anaconda Copper Mining Company refineries and the extensive repair shops of the Great Northern Railway.[2]

Great Falls' black residents lived on the lower Southside, a dense and ethnically mixed working-class neighborhood extending from First to Tenth Avenue South and from Second through Twelfth Street South. Black residents worked for the Great Northern and Milwaukee railroads and downtown service industries. They lived in black hotels, railroad porters' quarters, and modest family homes, and they worshipped at the black churches. Unofficial though pervasive segregation and discrimination placed many constraints on African Americans. For example, blacks were barred from restaurants and nightclubs except those few operated by blacks on the Southside. Nor could they join labor unions, and thus they were excluded from the best-paying jobs in the refineries and repair yards.[3]

The original social hub of the African-American community was the Union Bethel African Methodist Episcopal (AME) Church at 916 Fifth Avenue South, organized by the first black residents of Great Falls in 1890. From 1891, when the AME Church opened, through good times and bad, the church served as the cultural, social, political, and religious heart of the black community. The women of Union Bethel were the church's "soul" through their loyalty, hard work, and dedication. Great Falls' second black congregation, Immanuel Baptist, organized in 1920, and by early 1922 members had dedicated a new church at the eastern edge of the Southside neighborhood, at the corner of Twelfth Street and Fifth Avenue South. That year, the AME Church visited every black family to complete a survey of the

Originally a "colored" bar, the Ozark Club in the 1940s became a place where "everyone's welcome" and an institution in Great Falls and beyond. Leo LaMar (in white hat and coat) surveys his domain, while Bruce Brown tends bar and an unidentified customer nurses a shot. COURTESY THE LAMAR FAMILY.

community. It showed that thirty-nine percent (71 of the 183 respondents) preferred the AME Church, and eleven percent were affiliated with the new Baptist Church. There were six Roman Catholic respondents, two Episcopalians, and one Christian Scientist. Fifty-three percent had no church affiliation.[4]

The Southside's other social hubs were the "colored" social clubs—the Lime Kiln, Maple Leaf, Porters' Quarters, Rainbow Colored, Manhattan, and the most successful, the Ozark Club. These clubs provided entertainment and, in some cases, rooms, and were centers for black nightlife. From the early 1890s on, they opened and closed, changed locations, and frequently drew police raids to suppress fights or craps and other gambling games. The original Ozark Club was a nightclub operating at 119 Second Avenue South. When it incorporated as the Ozark Colored Club in June 1909, it counted 147 members, with only blacks eligible for membership. William Williams, a railroad porter, served as president. By 1916, the Ozark had moved to the second floor of the original fire station, a building owned by the city of Great Falls and within a half block of the police station. This club featured a bar and game room, and membership grew to more than 200, with white men occasionally visiting as guests of club members.[5]

The enactment of the National Prohibition Act on January 16, 1920, made the manufacture, transportation, and sale of alcoholic beverages illegal in the United States, though, ironically, it was not illegal to drink alcohol. The Ozark Club continued operations, serving soft drinks on the surface and alcohol under the table. It offered gambling on the side, and it became the informal boxing training center until the club closed in about 1922.[6]

In 1920, the federal census recorded 209 black residents of Great Falls. Of the 85 people who responded to the AME Church's 1922 survey about employment questions, most worked in low-paying service industry jobs. The survey showed just five college graduates and two graduates of musical conservatories. Without access to higher-paying union jobs and with just a handful of professionals in the black community, upward mobility was limited and generational prospects relatively bleak.[7]

In this milieu, Leo LaMar's opportunities were better than most. He arrived in Great Falls with a railroad job and boxing talent, and his timing was right. In 1919, the Montana legislature made boxing legal for the first time since defeat of the Kiley boxing law in 1914, with the provision that a portion of proceeds from matches go "for the benefit of soldiers, sailors and marines." Butte, Helena, Great Falls, and other Montana cities organized the boxing commissions required by law by January 1921, with Great Falls and Butte emerging as the state's leading boxing centers. Great Falls was home to standout boxers Pete Bross, Al Rossberg, Joe Simonich, and "Kid Leo" LaMar—and it would bring heavyweight champion Jack Dempsey to town for six weeks of training in 1923 before his championship fight in Shelby, Montana, on July 4.[8]

By January 1921, Kid Leo was training regularly at the Ozark Club with other black boxers. On January 26, the *Great Falls Tribune* made note of Leo LaMar for the first time, reporting on a scheduled match between "Two dusky scrappers from Chicago": "Rough" Reed, a World War I veteran, and "Kid Leo," who "has proved himself able to deliver the goods in Chicago and Minneapolis." In the first boxing card arranged by the new American Legion Athletic Association, LaMar fought as a lightweight in a six-round preliminary before a packed house of 1,500 at the Grand Opera House on February 14, 1921. His opponent was more experienced, yet Kid Leo defeated the heavier Reed in two rounds. Sportswriters reported that Kid Leo "took the 'Rough' out of 'Rough' Reed," calling LaMar "one of the cleverest youngsters who ever appeared here." Kid Leo was making a name for himself.[9]

"Kid Leo, the Yellow Hammer," fought his second bout on the American Legion card June 20 against Billy Smith, billed as the "Darktown Terror." Smith was known as a fancy boxer, and as the *Great Falls Leader* boxing reporter wrote, "A great many of the colored boxers in the city do not care to step into the ring with Billy." Outweighing his opponent by more than a dozen pounds, Smith fouled Leo with a low blow in the first round. A doctor examined Leo, but he was cleared to go on. As the four-round fight continued, Smith kept swinging for a knockout while Kid Leo hammered away until Smith was "groggy and distressed." The fight was declared a draw. The *Leader* declared Leo "far the more clever boxer, and made a showing against the larger man like a truck load of pork chops."[10]

Great Falls flourished as a major fight center during the next five years, regularly drawing crowds of well over a thousand to the Grand Opera House. Kid Leo served as sparring partner and fought occasional matches, often against heavier boxers and always with favorable press coverage. During 1921–1922, he was undefeated, winning three bouts and drawing two. His next known fight did not come until 1925, with two bouts against Young Trotchie, a Métis from Havre who had a ten-pound weight advantage. When Leo drew the first fight and lost the second against the talented Trotchie, he ended his boxing career. However, LaMar's reputation stayed with him over the years.

The Union Bethel African Methodist Episcopal Church was the center of the Great Falls black community. The second of two buildings, this 1917 brick veneer edifice replaced the original one-story frame church built in 1891.
COURTESY KEN ROBISON.

Two decades later, in 1945, when heavyweight champion Joe Louis visited military bases in Great Falls, the *Tribune* paid tribute to Kid Leo with a photo and a caption saying, "Remember Him? Boxing talk revives memories of Kid Leo whose speedy fists won him many fights here in the past."[11]

Leo LaMar balanced boxing with his job as dining-car waiter, but his attention was diverted from both when he met sixteen-year-old Garneil Winburn. The two married on October 23, 1923. Garneil's father, Roy Winburn, was a World War I veteran wounded in a German gas attack. Her mother, Mollie, was the daughter of Edward and Elizabeth Simms, Great Falls' first black residents and longtime leaders of the black community. The new Mrs. Leo LaMar carried on the tradition of Simms family involvement in the Union Bethel AME Church, helping with social activities, including frequent fund-raising dinners. She and her mother were active in the Dunbar Art and Study Club, formed by women of the Union Bethel in 1917. Over the next several decades, the Dunbar Club led the Great Falls black community in charitable and literary deeds and in promoting civil rights. It represented the city in the statewide Federation of Negro Women's Clubs.[12]

The LaMars lived in the Simms-Winburn family home at 519 Sixth Avenue South, and Leo LaMar joined his wife in church activities, including the 1924 Christmas pageant, "The Nativity of Christ," in which Garneil was cast as Mary and Leo as Joseph. In the years that followed, they had four children: Aline Cleo, known as Sugar, born October 26, 1924; Leo Phillip Jr., or Brother, born July 21, 1927; Mollie, born March 21, 1932; and Bernice, or Bunny, born September 19, 1934. Garneil LaMar raised her children in the AME Church, and in 1933 when the church organized a special choir under a director brought from Los Angeles, Garneil and the two oldest children were among the fifty-five choir members.[13]

Nineteen thirty-three was the year that Leo LaMar, trading on his dining-car experience, opened his own business. By 1933, the nation was ready to scrap Prohibition and have a legal drink. On December 5, Montana became "wet," and on that day LaMar opened a "colored" members-only club. The new Ozark Club operated from a small house at 413½ Fourth Alley South, between Third and Fourth Streets. Two days later, LaMar and Roger Berry, his bartender, were arrested for serving "intoxicating liquor" to a fifteen-year-old boy. District court judge H. H. Ewing ruled that "Leo Lamars [sic] had no connection with the offense charged," and his case was dismissed, although Berry was later fined. The acquittal marked a trend that continued for the rest of LaMar's life—Kid Leo had a special status in Great Falls.[14]

In his early years as a club owner, Leo LaMar continued to work for the Great Northern, and during his absence, John F. "Frenchy" Christian managed the new club; Ben Winburn, Garneil LaMar's brother, bartended; and Earl L. Thornton provided musical entertainment. Just six months after opening, the Ozark became the scene of the first murder in Great Falls in over two years when entertainer Earl Thornton shot Richard Chivers, a New Deal Civil Works Administration worker, over the latter's charge that the Ozark was being mismanaged. Thornton was convicted and sentenced to thirty years in prison.[15]

Despite the end of Prohibition, homemade moonshine kept flowing in Great Falls as bar owners sought to avoid paying federal excise taxes. In December 1934, Frenchy Christian and Ben Winburn were charged with serving moonshine liquor at the Ozark Club, then located in a larger, two-story building at 312½ Fifth Alley South, though these charges eventually were dismissed. The next year, the Ozark Club moved again, to 914 Second Street South. That April, the club

Union Bethel AME Church hosted the fifteenth annual convention of the Montana Federation of Negro Women's Clubs July 29 and 30, 1936. Garneil LaMar participated despite being pregnant with her fifth child. Tragically, a week later, she and her baby died in childbirth, leaving her husband, son Leo Jr., and daughters Cleo, Mollie, and Bernice.
TITTER STUDIO, COURTESY MONTANA HISTORICAL SOCIETY, HELENA, PAC 2002-36-5.

was raided, and Leo LaMar was charged with obstructing a federal agent; the case was one of the first under a statute that laid down rules regarding federal officers entering a place where tax-paid goods were dispensed. LaMar demanded a preliminary hearing, and U.S. Commissioner of Revenue O. B. Kotz dismissed the charge. Later in 1935, the Ozark Club moved to its final location at 116–118 Third Street South on the upper floor of a wood-frame building, above the popular Alabama Chicken Shack Restaurant.[16]

While Leo was balancing his time between the Great Northern and managing the nightclub, his wife and her mother, Mollie Winburn, continued to be leaders in the AME Church. In July 1936, the Montana Federation of Negro Women's Clubs held its fifteenth annual convention in Great Falls. Garneil LaMar and other members of the

Dunbar Art and Study Club served as hostesses; Garneil was an active participant despite being pregnant with her fifth child. The Montana Federation elected her to state office as historian. Tragically, one week later, on August 4, Garneil LaMar, just twenty-eight years old, died with her baby in childbirth, leaving her husband, son, and three daughters. Sugar LaMar, then thirteen years old, remembers her mother as "sweet. . . . Everybody loved her."[17]

The lives of the LaMars and the Ozark Club changed dramatically with Garneil's death. Mollie Winburn took over the challenge of raising the small children while Leo LaMar continued his circuit on the Great Northern, working from Great Falls to Havre, back to Great Falls, then to Butte over a ten-day period. During his time in Butte, he frequented the Silver City Club, which had been operated by Frank A. Yamer since 1917. While other "colored" nightclubs came and went, the Silver City Club was a permanent fixture of the city. It was one of the "swingingest" and most violent places in Butte. Leo LaMar became friends with Yamer, and in a police gambling raid on the club in May 1937, both were arrested and released on sixty dollars bail. At the Silver City Club, Leo also met Frank's wife, Grace, and her younger sister Charlene Beatrice Jeffers. Bea, as she was known, had been born in September 14, 1902, in Knoxville, Iowa, where she later graduated from high school and completed two years of college before coming to Butte. There, Bea attended Butte Business College while living with the Yamers. Leo LaMar married Bea Jeffers at the Silver Bow County Courthouse in Butte on August 24, 1937, and she soon became an active partner in the Ozark operation.[18]

Another change in the LaMars' lives occurred in the late 1930s when Leo began to suffer medical problems. After the doctors in Great Falls found no answers, he spent a month at the Mayo Clinic in Rochester, Minnesota, where doctors discovered he had diabetes. Leo decided to end his service with the Great Northern to devote full attention to the thriving Ozark Club. Thereafter, police raids and violence at the club lessened as LaMar imposed greater discipline on his employees and patrons and built closer ties with the city's leaders.[19]

The outbreak of World War II in 1941 brought thousands of workers to Great Falls. Soldiers arrived to operate two new U.S. Army air bases: Gore Field Air Base, where the Seventh Ferrying Group was stationed at the militarized civilian airport at Gore Hill, and the newly constructed Great Falls Army Air Base, informally known as East Base, home of the Second Bomber Group. These major commands also required large numbers of civilian workers. The population of Great Falls exploded from 30,000 in 1940 to an estimated 45,500 in 1944. Wartime Great Falls was bursting with workers seeking housing and entertainment.[20]

The war was also a catalyst for change in the Great Falls black community. By early 1943, several hundred black soldiers had arrived at the bases. They wanted fun in their off-duty hours, but they were not welcome at Great Falls restaurants, nightclubs, or even the new downtown United Service Organizations (USO) Club. Black servicemen joined the Union Bethel and Immanuel Baptist churches, and the local black community hastily organized a small black USO Club. However, it was at the Ozark Club that the soldiers found fun, music, and dancing.[21]

Early in the war, LaMar had quietly and successfully broadened the club's patron base to an interracial crowd under the motto "Everyone's welcome." The club incorporated as a nonprofit, the Ozark Club, Inc., on September 6, 1944, officially ending its status as a "colored" club. It was formed "to establish, maintain and manage a club for mutual improvement and the promotion of social intercourse and companionship among its members . . . and to assist in any matters pertaining to the welfare and advancement of the members for the attainment of the highest order of American citizenship." Leo and Beatrice LaMar, club employees Marguerite Elliott and John F. Christian, and local black businessmen Phil Chadwell and Walter Cummings served as directors.[22]

The Ozark Club's strategy for success rested on an exceptional package anchored by a talented house band. The key element of the band was a tenor sax man, Robert Mabane Jr., who had come up through Kansas City early in the bebop jazz era. Bebop, or bop, developed as a revolt against the restrictions on creative freedom typical of big bands during the swing era. Bebop began in the late 1930s in Kansas City and St. Louis and featured longer and more complex solos—a bop musician

With the outbreak of World War II and the influx of soldier and civilian workers to Great Falls, the Ozark Club became an entertainment sensation open to a multiracial crowd. Tenor sax man Bob Mabane, who had played with the nationally acclaimed Jay McShann Band in Kansas City, anchored the Ozark Boys, the club's house band. Mabane's presence meant that the club attracted some of the country's best jazz musicians. With Mabane are Chuck Reed on piano and Dick Brown on drums. COURTESY LAMAR FAMILY.

might never play a piece the same way twice. Young Bob Mabane, from Memphis, Tennessee, joined the Jay McShann Band in 1940 just as "Hootie" McShann was achieving national fame with his bebop Kansas City sound. Mabane played tenor sax side by side with the young musical genius Charlie "Bird" Parker on the alto sax until 1942 when Parker left the band. Mabane himself enjoyed success as a soloist, playing "an eclectic tenor saxophone style, sounding a bit like Hershel Evans on slow numbers and blues and Lester Young on riff numbers." He continued until the band was disbanded two years later.[23]

Bob Mabane arrived in Great Falls in 1948, after spending time in Denver, to assume leadership of the Ozark Club house band, the Ozark Boys, consisting of former leader Chuck Reed on piano, Dick Brown on drums, and himself leading on tenor sax. Thereafter, the

Ozark Club achieved fame for featuring jazz musicians, black and white, from all over the nation. It was known for being the only place in Montana where one could hear a live jazz band six nights a week. Mabane formed a close friendship with Leo and Bea LaMar, and in 1950 he married Modena Jeffers, a niece of Bea's from Iowa. The LaMars opened the Ozark Café, featuring ribs and fried chicken, on the street level below the club, and Modena Mabane was named manager.[24]

For the next decade, the Ozark Boys took the stage every night except Sunday with piano, drums, and tenor sax—playing their theme song "Jumpin' with Symphony Sid" and moving on to jazz classics like "Body and Soul" as well as new tunes. The band played without sheet music and with plenty of verve and a search for style. An observer in 1960 wrote:

> The musicians may be wildly happy; but more often they are tense and serious while they play. On an old-timer like *Sweet Georgia Brown,* the sax player's eyes are tightly shut while his instrument wails and sobs; the drummer's eyes are large and serious; the drum beats come like explosions, like staccato bursts of gunfire; the piano player hunches over his keyboard, mouthing words while his foot taps and his fingers ramble over the bass keys. With smooth co-ordination, the solo jumps from one player to another. Smooth yet spontaneous: this is real art, and it has been years in the building.[25]

In addition to the Ozark Band, Ozark Club entertainment included vocalists, exotic dancers, and comedians. The club became a major stop on the northern "Chitlin Circuit," a string of performance venues safe and acceptable for African-American entertainers that extended from the Fox Theatre in Detroit through Chicago, Minneapolis, and Great Falls to the West Coast. Some of these entertainers would later achieve fame. Top musicians Oscar Dennard, Stan Turrentine, Ellsworth Brown, Pops Teasely, and many others played with the band. Creed Jackson, master of tap, who at age ninety explained his life of tap dancing by saying, "Just pick your feet up and start," performed at the

Traveling musicians, singers, exotic dancers, and other performers took the stage at the Ozark nightly. Many would later achieve national fame, including musicians Oscar Dennard, Stan Turrentine, Ellsworth Brown, and comedian Redd Foxx. Torch singers such as Vivian Dandridge, shown here, also performed at the Ozark. COURTESY LAMAR FAMILY.

club. Young Redd Foxx practiced his early raunchy comedy routines. Torch singers such as Vivian Dandridge and Myra Taylor lit up the cold Montana nights. Female impersonator Mario Costello was billed as "The World's Most Glamorous Boy." Infamous striptease artist Miss Wiggles, "the Wiggleinest woman in the West," brought down the house with her contortions while dancing upside down on a chair and stripping to pasties and a G-string.[26]

A night at the Ozark was an exciting experience. Nestled on the edge of the railroad district, it was surrounded by seedy bars, cafés, hotels, and houses of ill repute.[27] Visitors, after walking several blocks past parked Hudsons and Studebakers, opened the door to the club and climbed the long, narrow, and poorly lit stairwell to the second floor, where Marguerite Elliott or one of Leo's men looked them over.

A waiter named Major Murdock, wearing a white coat and black bowtie, checked the identities of the young (even though he could not read or write). Once inside, patrons were seated at small round tables on either side of the dance floor, facing the bandstand. Sipping drinks under the watchful eye of bartender Harvey Clayborn Jr., better known as Woogie, patrons got the feeling that everything was very orderly. If they were there to look and listen, they weren't bothered because the staff didn't push drinks and left people pretty much alone, remembered James Todd Jr.[28] In the dim and smoky room, Leo held court, a fixture at the bar. At 9:00 P.M., the O-Club Combo, with Bob Mabane playing a full tenor sax tone, warmed up the crowd with smooth jazz, playing songs like "Perdido" and "Harlem Nocturne." Partners—married couples, servicemen with local girls, and blacks with whites—hit the dance floor. Show time came at 10:30. Perhaps the music would shift to bump and grind, or maybe a beautiful torch singer would take over, with Mabane's band serving up accompaniment of Kansas City swing. Two more shows followed over the next three hours. At two o'clock came sign-off time for the band, and the late-night crowd tromped down the long stairs and out into the dark evening.[29]

Over the years, readers of the *Great Falls Tribune* followed the club's activities through Saturday morning advertisements that offered clever commentaries on the times, focusing on such topics as the Space Age, the Cold War, and UFOs. The O-Club ad used just before the 1954 election read:

FLASH! REPUBLICANS and DEMOCRATS AGREE! In a bulletin released from both Democrat and Republican National Headquarters both parties agreed—Anita is their candidate for the best entertainment! See and Hear Anita Dare at the Ozark Club Tonight.

When a new singer, Candy, arrived, the ad cajoled readers with seductive copy:

Here's Candy A tantalizing bundle of sweet vocal charm!

M-m-m . . . Candy . . . for those who like it sweet! PLUS—Ted
. . . the man with the golden voice! A top notch M. C. DANCE
every nite to the real live . . . lilting melodies of the O-Club
COMBO! Where everyone's welcome . . . all the time![30]

Two blocks north, on Central Avenue, everyone was not welcome
at the clubs and restaurants. Great Falls had several prominent nightclubs—the 3-D, the Terrace Room at the Park Hotel, the Horizon
Club, and the Jockey Club—on Central Avenue and across the
Missouri River in Black Eagle. These clubs offered top-quality music,
featuring occasional traveling black musical acts, but they were not
open to black patrons. Nor did local black musicians perform. The
strong musicians' union in Great Falls did not allow any non-union
musician to perform, and blacks were not allowed to join the union.
Any given Sunday, however, several clubs featured evening jam sessions where musicians, black and white, went to have fun on their day
off. Bob Mabane played at these jam sessions on occasion, and local
musicians often reciprocated by attending Ozark Club jam sessions.[31]

Black celebrities, sports figures, and traveling bands also knew that
in Great Falls they were welcome only at the Ozark. When Sergeant
Joe Louis toured the air bases in 1945, he was "wined and dined" by
military leaders during the daytime, but he spent his evenings at the
Ozark Club. Pop Gates, Goose Tatum, and the Harlem Globetrotters
spent their off-court hours at the Ozark during their annual visits to
Great Falls. Teenager June Elliott, whose mother, Marguerite Elliott,
prepared snacks at the club, remembers vividly the night Leo LaMar
called the chief of police at home to gain permission for Lionel
Hampton and his big band, who were arriving in Great Falls very late,
to spend all night playing at the Ozark with the doors locked and the
music continuing until morning light.[32]

Jazz musicians came to the Ozark for jam sessions on Sunday afternoons. One young musician was Big Sandy farmhand Jack Mahood.
Just back from World War II service, Mahood packed his bag, grabbed
his alto sax, and weekly hopped on the "Galloping Goose" train to
Great Falls. Sunday afternoon he'd be on the bandstand with his sax
jamming alongside Bob Mabane and the Ozark Boys. Sixteen-year-

When boxing champion Joe Louis toured Great Falls army air bases in 1945, the town
"wined and dined" him during the daytime, but the sergeant spent his evenings at the
Ozark Club. Here, he posed (center) with Leo and Bea LaMar in the club.
COURTESY LAMAR FAMILY.

old John Huber, after playing with his own Great Falls High School
jazz quartet on Saturday night, headed for the Ozark with his trumpet
on Sunday. According to Huber, Mabane taught him to play Duke
Ellington blues songs like "Things Ain't What They Used to Be," expanded his understanding of how to integrate chords to jazz improvi-
sation, and "kind of mentored me to listen for the blues changes from
the piano player, and to get the feel of that type of jazz."[33]

Within the black community, Leo LaMar vied for leadership
through civic activities and with the support of his growing workforce at the club. LaMar became president of the Great Falls National
Association for the Advancement of Colored People (NAACP) in the
mid-1940s, and Sugar LaMar joined her father in NAACP activities
by serving as secretary. The Ozark Club was a co-sponsor with the
NAACP of the "colored" Boy Scout Troop 21. Leo LaMar served as
troop chairman, while Frenchy Christian was scoutmaster. Despite
the good work by Leo LaMar, there was tension between Union
Bethel Church and the Ozark Club during the 1940s and 1950s. June
Elliott and Ruth Parker, who grew up on the Southside, remembered

the split. Ruth Parker said her parents, stalwarts in Union Bethel, gave her a firm admonition: "Do not go to the Ozark Club."[34]

The Ozark Club did indeed have a shady side. A key element in Leo and Bea LaMar's business was gambling. The small back room at the Ozark Club had a pool table that was frequently used for games of chance. These games included craps and a Greek dice game called barboote. During World War II, Montana and the city of Great Falls legalized limited slot-machine gambling. In 1945, the Ozark Club legally operated two five-cent and one ten-cent slot machines, paying a small percentage to the city. By the late 1940s, Montana law prohibited slot machines, but illegal gambling and card games went on at the Ozark, quietly conducted and care-

Along with its licit fare, the Ozark Club also offered illegal entertainment. Dice and card games went on in the club's back room, and the upper floor of the nearby LaMar Hotel housed Bea LaMar's brothel. COURTESY LAMAR FAMILY.

fully controlled by Leo and generally tolerated by city police. On rare occasions, Ozark gambling became visible to the public. In July 1956, Roy A. "Boss" Harrison lost about $5,000 in a gambling game to Leo LaMar, and the *Tribune* covered the court case. The court ordered Harrison to pay $100 a month until the debt was paid, a verdict that underscores LaMar's position in the community.[35]

Bea LaMar operated another element of the Ozark Club's offerings. In 1948, the LaMars bought the Thompson Hotel at 304½ First Avenue South, just half a block and around the corner from the club. On the ground level was Brown's Furniture Company. By a separate entrance, stairs led up to the renamed LaMar Hotel, which became the residence for the LaMar family, with quarters for members of the Ozark staff and band and for traveling entertainers. The LaMar suite included a living room decorated with O. C. Seltzer paintings, bedrooms, a kitchen, and a playroom for Brother's daughter Charlene. The rest of the LaMar Hotel was given over to Bea's house of prostitution.[36]

The LaMars' business operated smoothly through the mid-1950s, but by 1957 dark clouds were forming. That year, news stories broke, revealing sordid details of prostitution operations at the Doyle Apartments (the renamed LaMar Hotel). In testimony at the trial of her husband, Glenn E. Totterdell, for shooting Richard Brown, Helen Totterdell, a white LaMar employee, testified that she worked as a prostitute for Bea LaMar at the Doyle Apartments. She revealed that the cost of her services ranged from $7.50 to $25.00, that three other girls worked at the apartments, and that the entire second floor of the building was used for prostitution. As a result of the testimony and subsequent police investigation, abatement proceedings to shut down the Doyle Apartments began. In a separate action, Bea LaMar was charged with keeping a house of prostitution and "with being a dissolute person who lives on the earnings of women of bad report." Leo LaMar was charged with residing in a house of ill fame. Over the next eighteen months, furious legal battles were fought over the state abatement action, twice involving the Montana Supreme Court and with lawyers of the stature of Wellington D. Rankin defending the LaMars. In the end, the Doyle Apartments remained open, and the LaMars emerged unscathed except in reputation.[37]

The death of Brother LaMar's second wife, Patricia, from a rifle gunshot wound to her abdomen brought more notoriety to the family in 1959. The couple had had a stormy relationship, twice divorcing and reconciling, and the county coroner quickly ruled Patricia LaMar's death a suicide without conducting an inquest. Two years later, in June 1961, Brother, together with four young friends, died in an early morning car-truck crash. It was a devastating blow to Leo Sr. and his son's many friends. One year later, Leo LaMar Sr. died from a heart attack on June 20, 1962.[38]

Leo LaMar's death marked the end of an era and, coincidentally, the end of the Ozark Club. The club's demise came three weeks later when a spectacular late-night fire forced the evacuation of about fifty staff and patrons as the Ozark Club burned to the ground.[39]

In 1962, Great Falls was not the same place it had been when Leo LaMar arrived in 1920. Decade after decade, black civic organizations such as the NAACP and particularly the Dunbar Club, led by Union Bethel Church women such as Emma Riley Smith and her daughter Alma Smith Jacobs, had fought for civil rights in Montana. In 1945, for example, Dunbar Club members wrote letters supporting civil rights legislation to President Harry Truman and Montana congressmen and joined the mayor, unions, and the NAACP in opposing discrimination against young black figure skaters by a Southern-born instructor at the Great Falls Skating Club. In 1948, they successfully protested a local theater's refusal to sell tickets to blacks. In 1950, after the integration of U.S. armed forces, Dunbar Club members served on an interracial committee to open access to local establishments for black airmen stationed at Malmstrom Air Force Base. Alma Smith Jacobs personally broke racial barriers when she was selected to serve as catalog librarian at the Great Falls Public Library in 1946 and then was appointed director of the library in 1954.[40]

By 1960, the black community in Great Falls had grown significantly for the first time in four decades, with 311 residents in the city and another 206 blacks stationed at Malmstrom. Blacks could rent or buy houses throughout the city. Unions finally began to open membership. Churches increasingly welcomed black members. No longer were African Americans turned away from restaurants and nightclubs. Great Falls also began to acknowledge and celebrate black role models, including country music superstar Charlie Pride, a resident in the 1960s. The Great Falls minor league baseball team, with its Brooklyn and Los Angeles Dodgers affiliation, brought such future stars as John Roseboro and Eddie Reed to the city. Alma Smith Jacobs was Great Falls' Woman of the Year in 1957, and Emma Smith was named Great Falls Mother of the Year in 1967. Black students served as class officers at Great Falls High School. In 1974, Geraldine Travis was elected to House District 43, becoming Montana's first, and to date only, African-American legislator.[41]

Although change was never easy and never quickly attained, Leo LaMar and his Ozark Club, where "Everyone's welcome," played an important part in transforming the Great Falls community.

Insight into the Ozark Club's story survived for posterity through a fortuitous meeting with retired Big Sandy farmer, musician, and art

collector Jack Mahood, then eighty-six years of age. In 2005 interviews by musician Phil Aaberg and the author, Mahood reminisced
about the early days of jazz in Great Falls, including the Ozark Club,
where as a young alto sax player he had jammed with Bob Mabane
and the band on Sunday afternoons. During the first interview session, Jack talked about the racial climate in Great Falls in 1950. When
he and his wife, Dora, took Bob and Modena Mabane out to dinner, for example, they had a single choice: they could enter the dining
room at the Park Hotel by a rear entrance and sit in a back booth.
During the conversation, Mahood casually mentioned that he had
Recordio disks recorded at the Ozark in about 1950. Jack brought his
disks to the next session, and the Ozark Club came alive as the sound
of "Sweet Georgia Brown," "Lady Be Good," and other jazz classics
filled the room. Phil Aaberg captured the moment: "Jack put the first
disk on and dropped the needle. It was 'Royal Roost,' a tune named
after a nightclub made famous by a Charlie Parker record. Honestly,
the hair on the back of my neck stood straight up."[42]

With Jack Mahood's recordings in hand, Phil Aaberg and the
author worked with The History Museum to bring the Ozark Club
back to life. The *Great Falls Tribune* published an extensive article
about the Ozark Club and Leo LaMar and invited comments from
readers. Stories poured in from across the country, from Alaska to
Washington, D.C. Leo LaMar's daughters, Sugar and Bunny LaMar,
who had not been back to Great Falls since their father's funeral, flew
in from Los Angeles, bringing dozens of photographs. The wife and
family of Ozark piano man Chuck Reed visited from Portland.[43]

On the memorable night of June 7, 2007, forty-five years after its
spectacular demise, the Ozark Club came back to life with "A Night at
the Ozark" celebration at The History Museum, featuring live jazz and
a packed house of over 300. An exhibit filled two rooms with photographs, handbills, and memorabilia—including the jukebox and Jack
Mahood's alto sax. From a stage re-created to look like the Ozark's,
museum director Chris Morris welcomed the crowd by shouting out,
"How many of you came to the original Ozark Club?" At least one in
four hands in the crowd shot up. Before the all-star cast of Montana
jazz musicians played, the crowd heard two of the original Ozark disks

The LaMar sisters, Bunny (left) and Sugar, enjoy The History Museum's first "Night at the Ozark" in June 2007. KEN ROBISON, COURTESY THE AUTHOR.

and a short history of the club; then John Huber, a teenage Ozark jammer of the 1950s, played several songs with Phil Aaberg and his band. Throughout the evening, stories and reminiscenses flowed. Leo LaMar's vision of a club where "Everyone's welcome," nurtured at a time in Great Falls when not everyone was welcome at most places, came alive as the Ozark flame reignited.[44]

Since the first gala, there have been seven "Nights at the Ozark" that have brought nationally prominent jazz musicians to The History Museum; the most recent was held September 20, 2014, with Kelly Roberti, Alan Fauque, Brad Edwards, and Ann Tappan. The Ozark Club stage and a small display of Ozark material are still on display at The History Museum. The Ozark Club has its own multimedia website, maintained by the *Great Falls Tribune* at www.greatfallstribune. com/multimedia/ozark.

This essay originally appeared in *Montana, The Magazine of Western History,* Summer 2012.

Ken Robison is historian at the Overholser Historical Research Center in Fort Benton, Montana, and at the Great Falls/Cascade County Historic Preservation Commission. He is the author of Fort Benton *(2009);* Cascade County and Great Falls *(2011);* Life and Death on the Upper Missouri: The Frontier Sketches of Johnny Healy *(2013);* Montana Territory and the Civil War: A Frontier Forged on the Battlefield *(2013); and Confederates in Montana Territory: In the Shadow of Price's Army (2014). Robison retired from the U.S. Navy after a career in naval intelligence. The Montana Historical Society honored him in 2010 with its "Montana Heritage Keeper" award.*

NOTES

1   Sugar LaMar, phone interview by author, May 9, 2007. For their assistance, I thank Bob Harris, Frank and Mary Ghee, Lt. Col. Bob Payne, Rev. Mercedes Tudy-Hamilton, June Elliott, Robert Lindsey, Joel Marshall, Kathy Reed, Ruth Parker, Wade Parker, Dorothy Novotny Parker, Chris Morris, Karen Ogden, Judy Ellinghausen, Roy Harrison, James Gilbert Todd Jr., Linda Short, Katherine Reed, Pam Sibley, Barbara Behan, Patty Dean, Jack and Dora Mahood, John Huber, Janet Thomson, Neil Hebertson, Philip Aaberg, and especially the daughters of Leo LaMar, Sugar and Bunny LaMar. Leo's original name was Lamars—this was changed in the late 1930s to LaMar, which is used in this article.

2   R. L. Polk & Co.'s *Great Falls and Cascade County Directory,* 1919, 1921 (hereafter Great Falls Directory [year]), copies in Montana Room, Great Falls Public Library, Great Falls, Montana; *Fourteenth Census of the United States, 1920: Population of the United States* (Washington, D.C., 1921); Works Progress Administration, *Great Falls Yesterday: Comprising a Collection of Bibliographies and Reminiscences of Early Settlers* (n.p., 1939), pp. v-xv; William J. Furdell and Elizabeth Lane Furdell, *Great Falls: A Pictorial History* (Norfolk, Va., n.d.), 116; Richard B. Roeder, "A Settlement on the Plains: Paris Gibson and the Building of Great Falls," *Montana, The Magazine of Western History* (hereafter Montana), 42 (Autumn 1992), pp. 4-19.

3   Ken Robison, *Cascade County and Great Falls* (Charleston, S.C., 2011), pp. 42-43; Barbara Behan and Ken Robison, "National Register of Historic Places Nomination Form, Union Bethel African Methodist Episcopal Church," May 15, 2003 (hereafter "Union Bethel National Register nomination"), copy in the Montana State Historic Preservation Office, Helena. Discrimination in Great Falls was not limited to African Americans. From its beginning, Great Falls imposed a policy of total exclusion of Chinese, and not until George B. Wong arrived in 1938 did Great Falls have its first Chinese resident. Great Falls did have Native American residents, but they often lived in marginal conditions in camps on the outskirts, on the west bank of the Missouri and later Wire Mill Road, Mount Royal, and Hill 57. See *Great Falls Tribune* (hereafter *Tribune*), Sept. 12, 1943; *Great Falls Leader* (hereafter *Leader*), Oct. 3, 1958; Christopher William Merritt, "'The Coming Man from Canton': Chinese Experience in Montana, 1862–1943" (PhD diss., University of Montana, 2010), p. 178. Unless otherwise noted, all newspapers cited were published in Montana.

4   "Union Bethel National Register nomination"; *Leader*, Sept. 24, Oct. 5, 1920, Aug. 25, 1921, Mar. 2, 1922. According to the U.S. census, by 1920 the largest black population centers of Montana—Butte (214 black residents), Great Falls (209), Helena (220), and Missoula (92)—were home to 48 percent of the state's black population. The U.S. censuses 1920–1950 show that while the black population dropped from 1,658 in 1920 to 1,256 ten years later, it then stabilized over the next two decades.

5   *Tribune*, June 30, 1909; *Leader*, June 16, 1910; *Tribune*, Sept. 15, 1916.

6   *Leader*, June 2, July 8, Nov. 10, 1921. Montana's own Prohibition Act took effect Dec. 31, 1918.

7   The professions listed in the results of the Union Bethel survey, published in the Sept. 24, 1920, *Leader*, included laborer, thirty-four; porter, ten; janitor, eight; rancher, five; chef, four; barber, two; mechanic, two; chauffeur, two; trucking and teaming, two; waiter, two; railroad clerk, two; maid, two; clerk, one; physician, one; lawyer, one; railroad fireman, one; and tailor, one.

8   Lester H. Loble, "The History of the Montana Veterans and Pioneers Memorial Building," Montana, 1 (Jan. 1951), 15; *Leader*, Dec. 13, 1920, Jan. 7, 1921; Jason Kelly, *Shelby's Folly: Jack Dempsey, Doc Kearns, and the Shakedown of a Montana Boom Town* (Lincoln, Nebr., 2010), pp. 100-102.

9   *Tribune*, Jan. 26, Feb. 13, 1921; *Leader*, Feb. 13, 14, 15, 1921. The *Tribune* reported LaMar's Chicago record as nine wins, one draw, and five losses in three years of fighting.

10 *Leader*, June 20, 21, 1921; *Tribune*, June 21, 1921.

11 *Leader*, Sept. 10, 1921, Feb. 25, May 3, 1922, Mar. 30, May 4, 1925; *Tribune*, Apr. 17, 1945. "Young Trotchie" was John Trotchie, grandson of Charles Trottier, an ally of Louis Riel. Jackie Trotchie, e-mail to author, May 26, 2012.

12 "Cascade County Marriage Book," no. 11749, county record in the collection of Great Falls Genealogy Society (hereafter GFGS); *History and Roster Cascade County Soldiers and Sailors, 1919* (Great Falls, Mont., n.d.); *Tribune*, Dec. 1, 1917, Aug. 5, 1922.

13 *Tribune*, Jan. 7, 1924, July 3, 1933; Sugar LaMar interview, May 2007.

14 *Sanborn Fire Insurance Map 1929, Great Falls, Mont.*, copy in The History Museum (hereafter THM); *Tribune*, Dec. 6, 7, 8, 1933.

15 *Tribune*, Dec. 5, 6, 1933; "Cascade County Register of Prisoners Confined in the County Jail," vol. 7, p. 61, county record in the collection of GFGS; *Tribune*, May 18, 19, 1934.

16 *Tribune*, Dec. 8, 9, 1934; *Leader*, Apr. 18, 26, 1935; *Great Falls Directory*, 1935, 1936; *Leader*, Oct. 30, 1935.

17 *Tribune*, Jul. 26, 31, Aug. 6, 1936; "Report of Clarinda Lowery to Montana State Federation of Negro Women's Clubs held in Great Falls 30–31 Jul at Union Bethel A. M. E. Church," folder 3, box 1, Montana Federation of Colored Women's Clubs Records, 1921–1978, Manuscript Collection 281 (hereafter MC 281), Montana Historical Society Research Center (hereafter MHS); Sugar LaMar interview, May 2007; *Leader*, Aug. 4, 6, 1936.

18 Walter Duncan, Perdita Duncan, Elmo Fortune, and William Fenter, interviews by Laurie Mercier, Butte, Montana, Mar. 24, 1983, Oral History Collection 483, MHS; *Butte City Directory* (Butte., Mont., 1917); Sugar LaMar interview, May 2007; *Helena Daily Independent*, May 2, 1937; "Silver Bow County Marriage Record," Sept. 14, 1937, Butte–Silver Bow County Courthouse, Butte, Montana.

19 Sugar LaMar, phone interview by author, Mar. 31, 2012.

20 U.S. Census, 1940; *Great Falls Directory*, 1940, 1945; Jane Willits Stuwe, *Air Transport Command Army Air Forces East Base, 1940–1946* (n.p., 1974).

21 *Leader*, Apr. 14, July 22, Sept. 16, 1943; Sugar LaMar, phone interview by author, Apr. 10, 2012.

22 *Leader*, Sept. 1, 1944.

23 "All That Jazz: The 'Bop Era," http://library.thinkquest.org/18602/history/bop/bopstart.html (accessed May 2012); "Jay McShann," http://en.wikipedia.org/wiki/Jay_McShann (accessed May 2012); Ross Russell, *Jazz Style in Kansas City and the Southwest* (Berkeley, Calif., 1973), pp. 187-195.

24 LaMar interview, May 2007; LaMar interview, Mar. 2012; Kay Reed, interview by author, Great Falls, Montana, June 8, 2007, recordings in the author's possession.

25 "The Ozark Club," *Modern Montana*, 2 (Winter 1962), pp. 2-8.

26 Creed Jackson oral history, 1976, copy in THM; "The Ozark Club," pp. 2-8. Names of performers are from an "Ozark Club Hall of Fame Performers" list compiled by the author from the weekly *Tribune* ads and interviews with people who worked at or attended the club.

27 James Gilbert Todd Jr., interview by Ken Robison and Judy Ellinghausen, Great Falls, Montana, July 9, 2010, copy in THM (hereafter Todd interview, July 2010).

28 Todd interview, July 2010; John Huber, interview by author, Great Falls, Montana, June 7, 2007, recording in the author's possession (hereafter Huber interview, June 2007); John Huber, interview by James Todd Jr., Missoula, Montana, Spring 2007, copy in THM (hereafter Huber interview, Spring 2007).

29 Huber interview, Spring 2007; *Tribune*, Dec. 15, 1956; "Ozark Club Entertainment Log."

30 *Tribune*, Oct. 30, 1954, June 2, Sept. 8, 1956.

31 Todd interview, July 2010; Huber interview, June 2007; Huber interview, Spring 2007.

32 LaMar interview, May 2007; *Leader*, Apr. 21, 1945; *Tribune*, Apr. 12, 17, 1945; June Elliott, interview by author, Great Falls, Montana, Apr. 12, 2007, recording in the author's possession.

33 Todd interview, July 2010; Huber interview, June 2007; Jack Mahood, four interviews by Ken Robison and Philip Aaberg, Great Falls, Montana, Apr.–May 2005, recordings in the author's possession. The "Galloping Goose," a one-car Great Northern passenger train, ran from Havre to Great Falls during the 1950s.

34 LaMar interview, May 2007; *Tribune*, Feb. 10, Apr. 22, 1946; *Leader*, June 20, 1962; June Elliott and Ruth Parker, interview by author, Great Falls, Montana, Sept. 2, 2011, recording in the author's possession.

35 Mahood interview; Todd interview, July 2010; *Leader*, Feb. 4, 1944; *Tribune*, July 16, 26, 1956, July 1, 1950.

36 *Great Falls Directory*, 1949; LaMar interview, Apr. 2012.

37 *Leader*, July 27, 31, Oct. 15, 16, 1957; *Tribune*, Aug. 1, 1957; *Leader*, Jan. 26, Feb. 4, 5, 11, 14, 18, July 9, 1958.

38   Leo's funeral service was held at T. F. O'Connor Company, followed by Mass at Our Lady of Lourdes Church. (Bea LaMar had never been active in the Union Bethel Church, and by the 1950s she had converted to Catholicism.) Bea shipped her husband's body to her hometown, Knoxville, Iowa, for burial. LaMar interview, Apr. 2012.

39   *Tribune*, Oct. 18, 25, 1959; *Leader*, June 26, 1961, June 20, July 12, 1962. The Ozark Club fire started in the adjoining Geiger Repair Shop and spread quickly to the Ozark. The city's fire department ruled the fire accidental, but rumors persist to this day that the fire was intentionally set. There was no police investigation. According to articles in the Aug. 21 and 23, 1962, *Leader*, the IRS presented Bea LaMar with an excise tax bill for the Ozark Club, Inc., for more than $100,000 in July 1962. Bea stayed on in Great Falls for several years, running the Doyle Apartments (by then renamed the Vista Apartments) with the help of longtime friend Major Murdock. About 1966, Bea LaMar moved to Livingston and in 1974 to Billings, where she worked as a home nurse and was active in the St. Bernard's Catholic Church. On August 14, 1989, LaMar passed away in Billings. *Billings Gazette*, Aug. 21, 1989.

40   *Tribune*, Apr. 6, 1945; "Dunbar Art and Study Club Annual Report," 1945, 1946, 1948, folder 12, box 1, MC 281, MHS; "An Inter-Racial Committee Report by the Cascade County Community Council," ibid.; *Leader*, Jan. 13, 1954. While serving as Great Falls Public Library director from 1954 to 1973, Alma Smith Jacobs became a leader in the Montana Library Association, the Northwest Library Association, and the National Library Association. In 1973, she was named Montana state librarian.

41   *Great Falls High School Roundup* (Great Falls, Mont., 1955); *Leader*, Sept. 9, 1958; *Tribune*, June 10, 1966, Mar. 12, 1967; *Great Falls Pennant*, Nov. 9, 1974.

42   Mahood interview. Made of aluminum and coated with acetate, Recordio disks were made one disk at a time on a portable machine brought by Recordio Company representatives into nightclubs across the country. Later, they used a tape recorder and cut multiple disks at the venues.

43   *Tribune*, Feb. 25, 2007.

44   Ibid., June 29, 2007.

Further Reading

This bibliographical essay is not meant to be exhaustive. Instead, I have attempted to identify the most significant books—and in some cases, a handful of articles—that are especially relevant to the topics covered in this volume. Readers are also encouraged to examine the notes attached to the various essays contained in **Montana: A Cultural Medley.**

A good starting point for discovering the diversity and importance of ethnic history within the American experience is Stephan Thernstrom, ed., *Harvard Encyclopedia of American Ethnic Groups* (Cambridge, MA: Harvard University Press, 1980). It should be augmented by Elliott Robert Barkan, ed., *Immigrants in American History: Arrival, Adaptation, and Integration,* 4 vols. (Santa Barbara, CA: ABC-CLIO, 2013). An impressive collection of primary-source materials, which also includes several interpretive essays, is Ronald H. Bayor, ed., *The Columbia Documentary History of Race and Ethnicity in America* (New York: Columbia University Press, 2004). See also Mae M. Ngai and Jon Gjerde, eds., *Major Problems in American Immigration History,* 2nd ed. (Stamford, CT: Wadsworth Cengage Learning, 2011).

Valuable one-volume surveys of the field of ethnic history include Leonard Dinnerstein, Roger L. Nichols, and David M. Reimers, *Natives and Strangers: A History of Ethnic Americans,* 5th ed. (New York: Oxford University Press, 2009); Ronald Takaki, *A Different Mirror: A History of Multicultural America,* rev. ed. (New York: Little, Brown and Company, 2008); James S. Olson and Heather Olson Beal, *The Ethnic Dimension in American History,* 4th ed. (Malden, MA: Wiley-Blackwell, 2010); and Roger Daniels, *Coming to America: A History of Immigration and Ethnicity in American Life,* 2nd ed. (New York: Perennial, 2002). Another book by Roger Daniels that provides a slightly different focus is *Guarding the Golden Door: American*

Immigration Policy and Immigrants since 1882 (New York: Hill and Wang, 2004).

The number of books focusing on the history of ethnic groups in the American West is massive, but the best single guide on the subject is Gordon Morris Bakken and Alexandra Kindell, eds., *Encyclopedia of Immigration and Migration in the American West*, 2 vols. (Thousand Oaks, CA: Page Publications, 2006). Valuable case studies are found in Frederick Luebke, ed., *European Immigrants in the American West: Community Histories* (Albuquerque: University of New Mexico Press, 1998). A thought-provoking book written from a very different perspective is *Outside America: Race, Ethnicity, and the Role of the American West in National Belonging* (Lebanon, NH: University Press of New England, 2005). An award-winning volume that details the often tragic clash of cultural views in the West is Elliott West, *The Contested Plains: Indians, Goldseekers, and the Rush to Colorado* (Lawrence: University Press of Kansas, 1998).

A good overview of the history of the fur trade may be found in David J. Wishart, *The Fur Trade and the American West* (Lincoln: University of Nebraska Press, 1979). For the role of Scottish highlanders in the transnational fur trade, a must-read is James Hunter, *A Dance Called America: The Scottish Highlands, the United States and Canada* (Edinburgh: Mainstream Publishing Company, 1994). For more on Angus McDonald and his family, see the same author's *Scottish Highlanders, Indian Peoples: Thirty Generations of a Montana Family* (Helena: Montana Historical Society Press, 1996). An excellent brief biography of the famed Scottish explorer, Alexander Mackenzie, is Barry Gough's *First Across the Continent: Sir Alexander Mackenzie* (Norman: University of Oklahoma Press, 1997). The single most important work on the Lewis and Clark expedition, other than the journals themselves, remains James P. Ronda, *Lewis and Clark among the Indians* (Lincoln: University of Nebraska Press, 1984).

Any study of the Métis experience in Montana must begin with Martha Harroun Foster's remarkable book, *We Know Who We Are: Métis Identity in a Montana Community* (Norman: University of Oklahoma Press, 2006). See also Bill Thackeray, ed., *The Métis Centennial Celebration Publication* (Lewistown, MT: Métis

Centennial Celebration Committee, 1979). To place the story of the Montana Métis within a broader context, readers should consider Jacqueline Peterson and Jennifer S. H. Brown, eds., *The New Peoples: Being and Becoming Métis in North America* (Lincoln: University of Nebraska Press, 1985); Gerhard J. Ens, *Homeland to Hinterland: The Changing Worlds of the Red River Métis in the Nineteenth Century* (Toronto: University of Toronto Press, 1996); and Lucy Eldersveld Murphy, *A Gathering of Rivers: Indians, Métis, and Mining in the Western Great Lakes, 1737-1832* (Lincoln: University of Nebraska Press, 2000). Joseph Kinsey Howard's dramatic account, *Strange Empire: A Narrative of the Northwest,* reprint ed. (St. Paul: Minnesota Historical Society Press, 1994), is still worth reading. An early scholarly account of the Métis in Montana is Verne Dusenberry, "Waiting for a Day that Never Comes: The Disposed Métis of Montana," in *Montana, The Magazine of Western History* 8 (April 1958), pp. 26-39.

Solid general histories of the Chinese in America include Shih-shan Henry Tsai, *The Chinese Experience in America* (Bloomington: Indiana University Press, 1986); Roger Daniels, *Asian America: Chinese and Japanese in the United States since 1850* (Seattle: University of Washington Press, 1988); and Iris Chang, *The Chinese in America: A Narrative History.* An important case study set in Montana's neighboring state of Idaho is Liping Zhu, *A Chinaman's Chance: The Chinese on the Rocky Mountain Mining Frontier* (Boulder: University Press of Colorado, 1997). An impressive study that demonstrates how immigrants often have to negotiate lives between two worlds is Madeline Y. Hsu, *Dreaming of Gold, Dreaming of Home: Transnationalism and Migration Between the United States and South China, 1882-1943* (Stanford: Stanford University Press, 2000).

The most important book to date that deals with the Chinese story in Montana is Rose Hum Lee, *The Growth and Decline of Chinese Communities in the Rocky Mountain Region* (New York: Arno Press, 1978). The account is essentially a case study of Rose Hum Lee's hometown, Butte, Montana. The volume is a reprint of Lee's 1947 doctoral dissertation in sociology completed at the University of Chicago. Recent articles that shed new light on the Chinese experience in Montana include Carrie Schneider, "The Montana Traveler: Remembering

Butte's Chinatown," in *Montana, The Magazine of Western History* 54 (Summer 2004), pp. 67-69; Laura F. Arata, "Beyond the 'Mongolian Muddle': Reconsidering Virginia City, Montana's China War of 1881," in *Montana, The Magazine of Western History* 62 (Spring 2012), pp. 23-35, 90-93; Mark Johnson, "Innovations in Education: The Montana Historical Society's Reach Extends Nationally and Internationally," in *Montana, The Magazine of Western History* 62 (Spring 2012), pp. 65-76; Hal Waldrup, "The Serendipitous Preservation of Butte's Mai Wah Noodle Parlor and the Wah Chong Tai Company," in *Montana, The Magazine of Western History* 62 (Autumn 2012), pp. 70-72; and Mark Johnson, "Becoming Chinese in Montana: The Chinese Empire Reform Association and National Identity among Montana's Chinese Communities," *Montana, The Magazine of Western History,* 64 (Winter 2014), pp. 58-71, 95-96. A moving, first-person account of more recent Chinese-American history is found in Flora Wong, with Tom Decker, *Long Way Home: Journeys of a Chinese Montanan* (Helena, MT: Sweetgrass Books, 2011).

On the Jewish experience, a good starting point is Moses Rischin and John Livingston, eds., *Jews of the American West* (Detroit: Wayne State University Press, 1993). The essay by Delores J. Morrow contained in this volume should be augmented by two other articles on the Jewish experience in Montana: Robert E. Levinson, "Julius Basinski: Jewish Merchant in Montana," in *Montana, The Magazine of Western History* 22 (Winter 1972), pp. 60-68; and Patricia Dean, "The Jewish Community in Helena," in *Montana Historian* 7 (May 1977), pp. 48-55. Although book-length, scholarly studies of the Jewish experience in Montana have yet to be written, historians might turn to monographs focusing on other Western states for inspiration. These should include William Toll, *The Making of an Ethnic Middle Class: Portland Jewry over Four Generations* (Albany: State University of New York Press, 1982); Floyd S. Fierman, *Guts and Ruts: The Jewish Pioneer on the Trail in the American Southwest* (New York: Ktav, 1985); Robert Goldberg, *Back to the Soil: The Jewish Farmers of Clarion, Utah, and Their World* (Salt Lake City: University of Utah Press, 1986); and Kenneth L. Kann, *Comrades and Chicken Ranchers: The Story of a California Jewish Community* (Ithaca: Cornell University Press, 1993).

To understand the Irish experience in Montana, David M. Emmons's awarding-winning volume, *The Butte Irish: Class and Ethnicity in an American Mining Town, 1875-1925* (Urbana: University of Illinois Press, 1989), is a must. Readers may wish to follow up *The Butte Irish* with Emmons's latest impressive study, *Beyond the American Pale: The Irish in the West, 1845-1910* (Norman: University of Oklahoma Press, 2010). There are many books that cover the history of Butte, but two are essential: Michael P. Malone, *The Battle for Butte: Mining and Politics on the Northern Frontier, 1864-1906* (Seattle: University of Washington Press, 1981); and Mary Murphy, *Mining Cultures: Men, Women, and Leisure in Butte, 1914-1941* (Urbana: University of Illinois Press, 1997). A solid biography of one of the most controversial figures in early Montana history is Paul R. Wylie, *The Irish General: Thomas Francis Meagher* (Norman: University of Oklahoma Press, 2007). A valuable article that uses extensive interviews to examine the history of Irish women in the community of Anaconda is Laurie K. Mercier, "'We Are Women Irish': Gender, Class, Religious, and Ethnic Identity in Anaconda, Montana," in *Montana, The Magazine of Western History* 44 (Winter 1994), pp. 28-41.

For a detailed and sophisticated analysis of the Dutch community in the Gallatin Valley, readers should turn to Rob Kroes, *The Persistence of Ethnicity: Dutch Calvinist Pioneers in Amsterdam, Montana* (Urbana: University of Illinois Press, 1992). An older work that provides solid information on Dutch immigration is Henry S. Lucas, *Netherlanders in America: Dutch Immigration to the United States and Canada, 1789-1950* (Ann Arbor: University of Michigan Press, 1955). A more recent study that examines the Dutch experience through a new lens is Suzanne M. Sinke, *Dutch Immigrant Women in the United States, 1880-1920* (Urbana: University of Illinois Press, 2002).

A solid introduction to the history of Finnish migration is A. William Hoglund, *Finnish Immigration in America, 1880-1920* (Madison: University of Wisconsin Press, 1960). Part of the Montana story is told in Leona Lampi, *At the Foot of the Beartooth Mountains: A History of the Finnish Community of Red Lodge, Montana* (Coeur d'Alene, ID: Bookage Press, 1998). An excellent new study of Finnish settlements in central Montana is Dena L. Sanford, "'Hewing Community out of Wilderness': Korpivaara and Kuhmoniemi Settlements in the Early Twentieth Century," in *Montana, The Magazine of Western History* 63 (Winter 2013), pp. 28-50, 93-95. On the community of Red Lodge, see Bonnie Christensen, *Red Lodge and the Mythic West: Coal Miners to Cowboys* (Lawrence: University Press of Kansas, 2002). To understand why some Finns, and many other industrial workers in Montana, would be drawn to socialism in the early twentieth century, readers should turn to Jeffrey A. Johnson, *"They Are All Red Out Here": Socialist Politics in the Pacific Northwest, 1895-1925* (Norman: University of Oklahoma Press, 2008); and Jerry W. Calvert, *The Gibraltar: Socialism and Labor in Butte, Montana, 1895-1920* (Helena: Montana Historical Society Press, 1988).

Anna Zellick wrote several important articles on the history of Slavic groups in Montana, including "The Men from Bribir: They Carved Their Hopes in Stone and Helped Build a Montana City," in *Montana, The Magazine of Western History* 28 (Winter 1978), pp. 44-55; and "'We All Intermingled': The Childhood Memories of South Slavic Immigrants in Red Lodge and Bearcreek, Montana, 1904-1943," in *Montana, The Magazine of Western History* 44 (Summer 1994), pp. 34-45. Background material on Croatians, Slovenians, and others is available in George J. Prpic, *South Slav Immigration in America* (Boston: Twayne Publishers, 1978). See also Adam S. Eterovich, *Croatians from Dalmatia and Montenegrin Serbs in the West and South, 1800-1900* (San Francisco: R & E Research Associates, 1971).

Scandinavians comprised some of the largest groups of people coming to Montana in the late nineteenth and early twentieth centuries. For the Danish migration to America, see Kristian Hvidt, *Flight to America: The Social Background of 300,000 Danish Emigrants* (New York: Academic Press, 1975); George R. Nielson, *The Danish Americans* (Boston: Twayne Publishers, 1981); and Frederick Hale, ed., *Danes in North America* (Seattle: University of Washington Press, 1984). While specific case studies have yet to be written on the Swedish and Norwegian experiences in Montana, recent publications focusing on the West may help show the way. The most important book on Swedish ethnic history is Jennifer Eastman Attebery,

Up in the Rocky Mountains: Writing the Swedish Immigrant Experience (Minneapolis: University of Minnesota Press, 2007), which uses some materials from Montana to tell its story. On Norwegian ethnic history, see Betty A. Bergland and Lori Ann Lahlum, eds., *Norwegian American Women: Migration, Communities, and Identities* (St. Paul: Minnesota Historical Society Press, 2011). See also Lori Ann Lahlum, "Mina Westbye: Norwegian Immigrant, North Dakota Homesteader, Studio Photographer, 'New Woman,'" in *Montana, The Magazine of Western History* 50 (Winter 2010), pp. 3-15, 91-93.

There is an extensive amount of literature on Mexican-American history, but little of it to date has focused on Montana. Valuable works that focus on the national story include Lawrence A. Cardoso, *Mexican Emigration to the U.S., 1897-1931* (Tucson: University of Arizona Press, 1980); Mark Reisler, *By the Sweat of Their Brow: Mexican Immigrant Labor in the U.S., 1900-1940* (Westport, CT: Greenwood Press, 1976); and David G. Gutierrewz, *Walls and Mirrors: Mexican Americans, Mexican Immigrants, and the Politics of Ethnicity* (Berkeley: University of California Press, 1995). Studies with a more regional focus include Erasmo Gamboa, *Mexican Labor & World War II: Braceros in the Pacific Northwest, 1942-1947* (Austin: University of Texas Press, 1990); Richard W. Slatta, "Chicanos in the Pacific Northwest," in *Pacific Northwest Quarterly* 70 (October 1979), pp. 155-162. An especially valuable piece is Steve Devitt, "We Montanans: The Billings Hispanic Community," in *Montana Magazine* (September 1987), pp. 6-13.

For a solid overview of the Japanese experience in the United States, see Roger Daniels, *Asian America,* mentioned earlier in this essay. Still useful is Robert A. Wilson and Bill Hosokawa, *A History of the Japanese in the United States* (New York: William Morrow and Company, 1980). On the issue of relocation and internment during World War II, see Roger Daniels, *Concentration Camps: North America Japanese in the United States and Canada During World War* II (Malabar, FL: Robert E. Krieger Publishing Company, 1981); and Peter Irons, *Justice at War: The Story of the Japanese American Internment Cases* (New York: Oxford University Press, 1983). For studies having a regional flavor, see Louis Fiset and Gail M. Nomura, eds., *Nikkei in the Pacific Northwest: Japanese Americans and Japanese Canadians in the Twentieth Century* (Seattle: University of Washington Press, 2005); Eric Walz, *Nikkei in the Interior West: Japanese Immigration and Community Building, 1882-1945* (Tucson: University of Arizona Press, 2012). On the 442nd Regimental Combat Team, see Masayo Umezawa Duus, *Unlikely Liberators: The Men of the 100th and 442nd* (Honolulu: University of Hawaii Press, 1987). On Montana, see Kevin C. McCann, "Montana's Treatment of Japanese Americans during World War II," in *Montana Vistas: Selected Historical Essays,* ed. Robert R. Swartout, Jr. (Lanham, MD: University Press of America, 1981); and George Oiye, *Footsteps in My Rearview Mirror* (Longwood, FL: Xulon Press, 2003).

Until recently, not much scholarly work had been done on the topic of war brides, perhaps because they do not fit easily into a particular ethnic category. An excellent place to begin, because of the breadth of the coverage, is with Susan Zeiger, *Entangling Alliances: Foreign War Brides and American Soldiers in the Twentieth Century* (New York: New York University Press, 2010). An excellent brief account of the 70,000 British war brides coming to the United States is found in Jenel Virden, *Good-Bye, Piccadilly: British War Brides in America* (Urbana: University of Illinois Press, 1996). See also Elfriedo B. Shukert and Barbara S. Scibetta, *War Brides of World War II* (Novato, CA: Presidio, 1988). The experience of war brides who settled in Canada is told in Melynda Jarratt, *War Brides: The Stories of Women Who Left Everything Behind to Follow the Men They Loved* (Toronto: Dundurn Press, 2009). Of course, not all war brides were from Europe, nor were they always part of the Second World War. For example, see Miki Ward Campbell, Katie Kaori Hayashi, and Shizuko Suenaga, *Japanese War Brides in America: An Oral History* (Santa Barbara, CA: Praeger, 2010); and Ji-Yeon Yuh, *Beyond the Shadow of Camptown: Korean Military Brides in America* (New York: New York University Press, 2004).

There is a growing body of literature available on the African-American experience in the West. Valuable introductions to the field are Quintard Taylor, *In Search of the Racial Frontier: African Americans in the American West, 1528-1990* (New York: W.W.

Norton & Company, 1998); and Douglas Flamming, *African Americans in the West* (Santa Barbara, CA: ABC-CLIO, 2009). The stories of nineteenth-century military experience are covered in two authoritative monographs: William H. Leckie and Shirley A. Leckie, *The Buffalo Soldiers: A Narrative of the Black Cavalry in the West*, rev. ed. (Norman: University of Oklahoma Press, 2007); and Arlen L. Fowler, *The Black Infantry in the West, 1869-1891* (Westport, CT: Greenwood Publishing Corporation, 1971). For a story that has an important Montana connection, see Kay Moore, *The Great Bicycle Experiment: The Army's Historic Black Bicycle Corps, 1896-97* (Missoula: Mountain Press Publishing Company, 2012). For a biography of an early black pioneer in Montana, see James A. Franks, *Mary Fields* (Santa Cruz, CA: Wild Goose Press, 2000). Elements of the twentieth-century story are told in Rex C. Myers, "Montana's Negro Newspapers, 1894-1911," *Montana Journalism Review* 16 (1973), pp. 17-22; William L. Lang, "The Nearly Forgotten Blacks of Last Chance Gulch, 1900-1912," in *Pacific Northwest Quarterly* 70 (April 1979), pp. 50-56; and Daniel J. Whyte, "The Black Community of Butte, Montana: Growth and Decline from 1890 to 1950" (Senior Honors Thesis, Carroll College, 1985).

Index

benevolent and fraternal organizations,
131, 225, 232–233
Berger family, 60–62, *61*, 64–65, 70,
75–76, *75*, 78, *79*
Billings (MT): Mexican American
restaurants in, 291–292; Mexican
Americans residing in, 275–277,
283–284, 286–288, 290–291,
293–294; racial tensions in, 276; as
sugar beet industry center, 273–277,
273; war brides in, 334, 339
Billings Sugar Company, 273–274
Bishop, John F., 254–255
Blackfeet Indians, 29, 60, 78
Blum, Charles, 125, 127
Board of Domestic Missions of the
Presbyterian Church in America, 180
boycotts, 111, *112*
Bozeman (MT), 134, 180, 308, 310
bracero program, 281
Breen, James, 304–305
Breen, Walter, 159
Briceno, Sal, 275–276, 279, 282–283,
291–292, 295
Bride's Guide to the U.S.A., 338–339, 341
Broadus (MT), 336
Brown, Richard "Dick," 361, *361*, 368
Brown v. Board of Education, 15
Broze family, 228–230, 241
Bruyères (France), 311–312
Buck, Sheila, 339–341
buffalo, 55–60, 63–64, 69, 84
"buffalo soldiers," 350
buffalo trade: as Métis livelihood, 55–60,
67, 81; on Milk River, 63–64;
pemmican, 56, 58, 62–63, 65, 81;
robes, 55–56, 58, 60; tariff laws, 67;
transportation of goods, 58–60, 63;
westward movement, 62–63
Bureau of Mines, 149–150
Butte (MT): African Americans in,
351, 359; boycott against Chinese
merchants in, 111, *112*; Chinese
Americans in, 100, 105, 107–109,
111, 112; as ethnically mixed
community, 147, 253; Finnish

Americans in, 219; Irish Americans
in, 150–152, 166–167; labor issues in,
8–9, *165*; as mining center, 146–147,
148, 149, 167–168; nationalism in,
8–9; racism in, 113; war brides in,
335, 339; working conditions in, 147,
149–151
Butte, Anaconda and Pacific Railway, 243
Butte Miners' Union, 152, 156, 162,
164–165, *165*, 168

C

California, 12, 94, 98, 106, 109, 122,
127–129, 135, 272
Camp Three, 227, 229, 233, *234*, 235, 242
Canada: Danes in, 252; fur traders in,
26; Métis, connection with, 55–57,
67–72, 74, 83, 85–86; as refuge
for Indians, 48–49; as source of
immigrants to Montana, 2
Cantu family, 278–279, 282, 284–285,
288–289, 291
capitalism: dichotomy with Catholic
Church, 160–162; Finnish attitudes
toward, 200–201, 207, 216
Carranza family, 281–282
Carroll Trail, 57, 74
carts, Red River, 59–60, *59*, 70, 76, 78
Castro, Liz, 289, 292
Catholic Church: African Americans
in, 353; Irish Americans in, 152,
159, 161–162; Métis in, 84; Mexican
Americans in, 288–289; Slovenian
and Croatian immigrants in, 226, 242;
social principles of, 161
census information: Chinese American,
98, 100, 105, 107; Danish American,
249, 251t, 253–257, 256t, 257t,
261–264, 263t; general immigration,
1–4, 11, 204; Indian, 41; Japanese
American, 303; Métis, 61, 81, 83–84;
Mexican American, 297–298
Central Pacific Railroad, 101
Charboneau family, 82
Chicago, Milwaukee, St. Paul & Pacific
Railway, 224, 226, 228, 243, 352

unions. *See* labor unions
United Mine Workers of America,
212–215, 213, 232–233
United Service Organizations (USO)
Club, 360
United States: Armed Forces, 70,
301–303, *302–303*, 308, 311–316,
312, 314–315, 329, 331, 350,
359–360; Bureau of Mines, 149–150;
laws, 9–11, 14–15; Office of War
Information, 338–339; Supreme
Court, 15
Utah and Northern Railroad, 146

V

Van Dam, Jung, 336, 340
Van den Hoek (Reverend), 184
Van Dijken family, 181, 183
Vashro family, 334, 335, 339
Victor (Flathead/Salish chief), 46
Virginia City (MT), 108, 254, 258m
Volstead Act, 237

W

war brides, 321–349; community
involvement of, 322, 339–340;
discrimination against, 336;
education, 341; emigration, attitudes
toward, 331–332, 342–343; employ-
ment, 341–342; in-laws of, 333–335;
personal adjustments by, 323–324,
333–338; religion, 340; resilience
of, 345
War of 1812, 41–42
Wells family, 62, 82, *83*
West Gallatin Irrigation Company,
179–180
Western Federation of Miners, 212
White Bird (Nez Percé chief), 48–50
"Whose Country Is This?" (Coolidge), 11
Wilkie family, 61, 75–76
William, King of Great Britain, 35–36
Winburn family, 356–359
Winnipeg (MB), 29, 58
Women's Auxiliary Air Force (Great
Britain), 324

Women's Land Army (Great Britain), 324
Wood Mountain, 63, 64
Woodrow, Wilson, 166
Workmen's compensation, 164; 166
World War I: agricultural prices and,
187; effect on European emigration,
4; effect on immigration, 7–10, 217,
219–220; Finland during, 199; Finnish
Americans and, 199–200, 215–216;
labor unions' decline from, 8; mail
disruption by, 199, 215; Marttunen's
ideas about, 207, 212, 219; nationalism
during, 201, 204, 215, 225
World War II: food scarcity during, 321,
324–325, 327; immigration issues and,
15; as impetus for international
marriages, 321–324; Japanese
Americans and, 13–14, 300–302,
308–315; labor force changes caused
by, 281; Mexican Americans and,
272, 281, 283; social changes caused
by, 326; women's roles changed by,
324, 341
Wormser, A., 180–181, 184

Y

Yakima Indians, 44–45
Yamer family, 359
Yellowstone Growers' Association, 280
Yellowstone National Park, 228
Yellowstone Sugar Beet Oral History
Project, 297–298
Yellowstone Valley (MT), 271–273
YMCA, 239
Yugoslav history, 225–226
Yugoslavian immigrants, 334
YWCA, 322, 339

Z

Zickovich family, 230, 245
Zupan family, *234*, 235–236, *235*, 240
Zupan Store, *234, 235, 235*

About the Editor

Robert R. Swartout, Jr., is Professor Emeritus of History, Carroll College, Helena, Montana, where he taught both United States and East Asian history from 1978 to 2014. Professor Swartout was born in Portland, Oregon. He received both his bachelor's and his master's degrees from Portland State University and his doctorate from Washington State University.

Dr. Swartout served as a U.S. Peace Corps volunteer in Korea from 1970 through 1972, and was a Fulbright Senior Scholar in Korea from 1986 to 1987 and again from 1994 to 1995. He has been a visiting professor on numerous occasions in Korea, teaching at Korea University, Yonsei University, Ewha Women's University, and Hankuk University of Foreign Studies. From 1998 to 2008, he served as an Honorary Consul in Helena for the Republic of Korea.

He was corecipient of the first Burlington Northern Outstanding Teacher Award at Carroll College in 1985. He received Carroll's Outstanding Teacher Award for Research in 1997, the Distinguished Scholar Award in 2009, and the Outstanding Teaching Award in 2013. He has served as a member of the Original Governor's Mansion Restoration Board in Montana and was a member of the Board of Editors for *Montana, The Magazine of Western History* from 1997 through 2013. In 2006, he received the Outstanding Educator's Award from the Montana Historical Society Board of Trustees. In early 2013, he was awarded the Governor's Humanities Award by the state of Montana and Humanities Montana.